Terror and Democracy in Wes

In 1970, the Red Army Faction declared war on West Germany. The militants failed to bring down the state, but, this book argues, the decade-long debate they inspired helped shape a new era. After 1945, West Germans answered long-standing doubts about democracy's viability and fears of authoritarian state power with a "militant democracy" empowered against its enemies and a popular commitment to antifascist resistance. In the 1970s, these postwar solutions brought Germans into open conflict, fighting to protect democracy from both terrorism and state overreaction. Drawing on diverse sources, Karrin Hanshew shows how Germans, faced with a state of emergency and haunted by their own history, managed to learn from the past and defuse this adversarial dynamic. This negotiation of terror helped them to accept the Federal Republic of Germany as a stable, reformable polity and to reconceive of democracy's defense as part of everyday politics.

Karrin Hanshew is an assistant professor of history at Michigan State University.

Terror and Democracy in West Germany

KARRIN HANSHEW
Michigan State University

CAMBRIDGE
UNIVERSITY PRESS

32 Avenue of the Americas, New York NY 10013-2473, USA

Cambridge University Press is part of the University of Cambridge.

It furthers the University's mission by disseminating knowledge in the pursuit of education, learning and research at the highest international levels of excellence.

www.cambridge.org
Information on this title: www.cambridge.org/9781107429451

First published 2012
First paperback edition 2014

A catalogue record for this publication is available from the British Library

Library of Congress Cataloguing in Publication data
Hanshew, Karrin, 1975–
Terror and democracy in West Germany / Karrin Hanshew.
p. cm.
Includes bibliographical references and index.
ISBN 978-1-107-01737-5
1. Rote Armee Fraktion – History. 2. Terrorism – Germany (West) – History. 3. Germany (West) – Politics and government – 1945–1990. 4. Democracy – Germany (West) – History. I. Title.
HV6433.G3R68 2012
363.3250943′09045–dc23 2012006483

ISBN 978-1-107-01737-5 Hardback
ISBN 978-1-107-42945-1 Paperback

Contents

Acknowledgments		*page* vii
List of Abbreviations		ix
	Introduction	1
	Prologue	18
1	Democracy Made Militant: The Federal Republic of Germany	34
2	Disobedient Germans: Resistance and the Extraparliamentary Left	68
3	"Mister Computer" and the Search for Internal Security	110
4	The Security State, New Social Movements, and the Duty to Resist	152
5	The German Autumn, 1977	192
6	Civility, German Identity, and the End of the Postwar	236
Select Bibliography		263
Index		277

Acknowledgments

With the publication of this book I am grateful to repay, in some small way, those whose faith and goodwill helped to bring it about. Of the many I would thank, it seems fitting to start with Bob Nichols, Dolores Peters, and Eric Weitz, who first opened up to me the idea of pursuing history as a profession and in many ways set the standard for scholarship and teaching I seek to achieve today. I owe a tremendous debt to Michael Geyer, Andreas Glaeser, Leora Auslander, John Boyer, and Ron Suny, as well as to the larger community of scholars, friends, and colleagues I came to live and work with at the University of Chicago. I can honestly say that I moved to Chicago for the minds, but stayed for the people. Living in Berlin, I met many brilliant young historians, several of whom – despite or because of life's many dramas – I am happy to call friends as well as colleagues. I thank the German Studies Association for facilitating our annual reunions. More recently, I am lucky to have started life as an assistant professor with a fabulous cohort of junior faculty and in a department that believes rigorous scholarship does not preclude humaneness. I extend particular thanks to Leslie Moch and Lewis Siegelbaum for their guidance, critical feedback, and cherished friendship. It is less important that we solve the world's problems than that we continue to try – and doing so over a good bottle of wine doesn't hurt.

Over the years I have presented portions of this work at conferences and workshops on both sides of the Atlantic where I benefited from the comments and challenges offered by Jeremy Varon, Dagmar Herzog, Belinda Davis, Detlef Siegfried, Axel Schildt, Philipp Gassert, Jacco Pekelder, Jeremi Suri, Paul Steege, Larry Frohman, Ken Ledford, Frank Biess, Jonathan Sperber, and countless others. Thanks as well to K. D. Wolff, Oskar Negt, Daniel Cohn-Bendit, and especially Konrad Schacht for being willing interview partners. I owe a particular debt of gratitude to Wolfgang Kraushaar for taking time to meet with a rather green graduate student who – ten years ago – had no idea what she had gotten herself into by taking up the question of violence in 1970s West Germany. My sincere thanks, too, to Konrad Jarausch for pushing me early on to grapple with the entire "left space" that lies at the heart of this book. And the book would not be as it is today were it not for all my anonymous readers, most particularly the two who read the initial manuscript in its entirety and with such care. Their comments and suggestions undoubtedly sharpened the argument and – by pushing me to go that extra distance – improved the overall quality of the book. Whatever foibles, flaws, and faux pas remain are most certainly mine.

The financial generosity of several institutions made my research possible and granted me invaluable time to write. I thank the Social Science Research Council – Berlin Program for German and European Studies, the United States Institute of Peace, and Michigan State University for their generous – and vital – support of this project. I am similarly beholden to the archivists and scholars who helped me make my way through personal papers, new and sometimes unordered archival collections, and closely guarded government documents. My particular thanks to Christoph Stamm of the Friedrich-Ebert-Stiftung; Reinhard Schwarz at Hamburg's Institute for Social History; Kerstin Schenke at the Koblenz Bundesarchiv; and Mieke Ijzermans, Axel Diederich, and Eef Vermeij, who introduced me to the treasures held by the International Institute for Social History in Amsterdam. And my heartfelt thanks to Cambridge University Press, first for taking on my manuscript and, then, for helping transform it into the present book. I am especially grateful to Eric Crahan and Abigail Zorbaugh, my navigators through the unfamiliar world of publishing.

Finally, I am humbled to acknowledge the love and support of my parents, Terry and Jill; my grandparents, Dale, Melba, Harold, and Lois; and my brother, Ken, as well as his wife, Gosia, and their two lovely girls. In many ways this is a book about foundations and I am aware of how lucky I am never to have doubted the stability of mine. This includes the friendship of several dear and persistent individuals, whom I may neglect to call and rarely find time to visit but always cherish. There is only one person, however, who truly knows the intellectual and emotional journey that is this book. Though there are not books enough to express my gratitude or my love, I dedicate this one to Sean, for believing in me and making me a better person and scholar as a result.

Abbreviations

APO	Extraparliamentary Opposition
AStA	Student Government
BBU	Federal Association of Citizens' Initiatives for Environmental Protection
BfV	Federal Office for the Protection of the Constitution
BGS	Federal Border Guard
BKA	Federal Criminal Office
BMI	Federal Ministry of Interior
BMJ	Federal Ministry of Justice
BND	Federal Intelligence Agency
BPB	Federal Office for Political Education
BUU	Lower Elbe Environmental Protection Citizens' Initiative
CDU	Christian Democratic Union
CSU	Christian Social Union
FBI	U.S. Federal Bureau of Investigation
FDP	Liberal Democratic Party
FRG	Federal Republic of Germany
GDR	German Democratic Republic
GG	Basic Law
IRA	Irish Republican Army
KBW	West German Communist League
KPD	German Communist Party
MfS	East German Ministry for State Security
NATO	North Atlantic Treaty Organization
PFLP	Popular Front for the Liberation of Palestine
RAF	Red Army Faction
RC	Republican Club
RZ	Red Cells

SA	Nazi Stormtroopers
SDS	German Socialist Student League
SED	East German Socialist Unity Party
SHB	Social Democratic Student Association
SPD	Social Democratic Party

Introduction

> History teaches that grave threats to liberty often come in times of urgency, when constitutional rights seem too extravagant to endure.
>
> Justice Thurgood Marshall (1989)[1]

On September 6, 1977, the front page of every West German daily bore news of the latest attack by members of the Red Army Faction (RAF). Captured in stark black-and-white images were scenes from Cologne the night before: two Mercedes Benz stopped short by a third, their doors flung open; three bodies, hastily covered where they had fallen, with a fourth hidden inside one of the cars; a baby carriage, abandoned after serving its purpose as decoy and roadblock. Missing from the picture was the owner of the two ambushed vehicles, Hanns-Martin Schleyer, a prominent industrialist and president of the West German Employers' Federation. After initial confusion concerning the nature of the crime, Schleyer's kidnapping was confirmed by local authorities and dragnet operations were launched in a desperate attempt to apprehend the white Volkswagen bus seen fleeing the scene a half hour before. As the news hit the wire, police forces across the Federal Republic of Germany (FRG) went on high alert and federal officials descended upon the Rhenish city to assess the situation. From his office in Bonn, Chancellor Helmut Schmidt released a nationally televised statement four hours after the attack to calm growing fears and to ask that all West Germans support the state in its ongoing struggle against terrorism. By the time Schmidt concluded his talk, the white Volkswagen had been found with nothing more than a ransom note – left by the RAF – to connect the vehicle to Schleyer and his kidnappers. Though police officers continued to comb the area, federal authorities resigned themselves to the fact that they could do little but wait for the RAF's demands and the next chapter in the burgeoning terrorist crisis.

[1] U.S. Supreme Court Justice Marshall, dissenting opinion in *Skinner versus Railway Labor Executives' Association*, 489 *United States Reports* 602, 635 (1989).

The kidnapping of Hanns-Martin Schleyer and the brutal murder of his chauffer and three police escorts launched a manhunt that lasted six weeks and initiated a chain of events that placed the FRG in an undeclared state of emergency. Rather than negotiate with the RAF, West German authorities used various stalling tactics in hopes of buying police the necessary time to gather clues and find Schleyer. As Bonn officials waited for security experts – or luck – to provide them with information on the industrialist's whereabouts, West Germans voiced growing fear and anger over the situation in the FRG. The successful attack on Schleyer, who weeks earlier had been identified as a possible target, made the limits of crime prevention and the fragility of personal protection painfully clear. As the fourth and most violent strike that year, it also heightened existing fears that law and order had been lost to the streets, with the events in Cologne alternately compared to the gangster violence of Al Capone's Chicago and the political terror that paralyzed Germany's first democracy, the Weimar Republic, shortly before the Nazis came to power in 1933.[2] How was it, a popular news magazine asked in astonishment, that a band of "violent anarchists" had grown strong enough to declare war on the West German state?[3] More pressing was the question of how to make it stop. Politicians and newspaper editors cried that Germans had had "enough!" and demanded an end to the "drama," "nightmare," and "mad joke" that had begun more than seven years earlier.[4]

Formed in 1970, the Red Army Faction understood itself as part of a larger liberation movement intent on furthering the goals of third world anti-imperialist fighters and the transnational student rebellion of the 1960s. In answer to Latin American revolutionary Che Guevara's call to make "two, three, many Vietnams," the RAF and other West German "urban guerrilla" groups such as the 2nd of June Movement and Red Cells (RZ) attacked the military and economic symbols of American imperialism. These groups also considered the FRG (and West German society more generally) a legitimate target, both as a direct client state of the United States and as a polity that had failed to purge itself of the remaining vestiges of German fascism. Above all, the groups' illegal acts aimed to communicate the vulnerability of the current state and thereby make West Germans conscious of the potential for radical change. Their repeated defiance of the law would, the RAF argued, undermine Germans' traditional "habit of obedience" and, at the same time, force the state to reveal openly

[2] See, e.g., "Schwarze Stunde," *Frankfurter Allgemeine Zeitung*, September 6, 1977, 1 (hereafter, *FAZ*); Hans-Herbert Gaebel, "Das kostbarste Geschenk," *Frankfurter Rundschau*, September 9, 1977, 3 (hereafter, *FR*); Harry Pross, "Fahndung in der Geschichte: Der politische Mord bedroht nicht den Staat, sondern die Republik," *Die Zeit*, October 14, 1977, 4. Also: "Im Wortlaut: Brandt erinnert an Weimar," *FR*, September 7, 1977, 4.

[3] "Killer-Krieg gegen den Staat," *Der Spiegel* 38 (September 12, 1977), cover; "Stark genug, den Krieg zu erklären?" ibid., 17–21.

[4] "Schwarze Stunde;" "Fall Schleyer: 'Die Dramatik muß raus,'" *Der Spiegel* 39 (September 19, 1977), 21.

its fascism.[5] Violence, in this context, was understood as a simultaneous act of self-emancipation and self-defense – the latter understood as progressive counterviolence (*Gegengewalt*) legitimated and even necessitated by the initial violence of the state. By attacking the FRG, the militant groups sought nothing less than to liberate West Germans from a state and society that did not live up to its professed democratic ideals.

Following an initial rash of bank robberies and deadly skirmishes with police, the RAF launched a "May Offensive" in 1972, bombing U.S. military bases in Frankfurt and Heidelberg, the Springer Press headquarters in Hamburg, the Munich and Augsburg police headquarters, and a federal judge's car in Karlsruhe. They killed four soldiers and injured dozens of bystanders and Springer employees. The arrest and imprisonment of founding members Ulrike Meinhof, Gudrun Ensslin, and Andreas Baader shortly thereafter moved the war to the prisons, where they and their allies launched repeated hunger strikes and an international campaign accusing the FRG of torturing political prisoners. On the outside, the RAF's original political aspirations fell by the wayside in remaining members' single-minded pursuit to free their imprisoned leaders. From 1974 onward, succeeding generations joined the 2nd of June Movement and the RZ in carrying out a string of actions designed to pressure the state. Aside from one spectacular victory in 1975, in which the West German government not only released several imprisoned militants but provided them with money and air transportation out of the FRG, the groups met with little success. Bungled kidnappings became assassinations and two large-scale hostage takings – of the West German embassy in Stockholm in 1975 and the 1976 Entebbe hijacking carried out with members of a militant Palestinian faction – caused the deaths of hostages, police officers, and terrorists alike. In 1977, the RAF initiated a new wave of violence in response to the death of Meinhof on May 9, 1976, and the sentencing of Baader, Ensslin, and Jan Carl Raspe – the remaining RAF leaders – to life in prison on April 28, 1977. The assassination of Attorney General Siegfried Buback in May and Dresdner Bank president Jürgen Ponto at the end of July ensured that, when news of Schleyer's kidnapping hit the newspapers in early September, West Germans' nerves were already stretched taut.

[5] For a primary source collection on the RAF, see *Rote Armee Fraktion: Texts und Materialien zur Geschichte der RAF* (Berlin: ID-Verlag, 1997). Among the growing literature on the RAF and left-wing terrorism in the FRG, see Tobias Wunschik, *Baader-Meinhofs Kinder: Die zweite Generation der RAF* (Opladen: Westdeutscher Verlag, 1997); Jeremy Varon, *Bringing the War Home: The Weather Underground, the Red Army Faction, and Revolutionary Violence in the Sixties and Seventies* (Berkeley: University of California Press, 2004); Wolfgang Kraushaar, ed., *Die RAF und der linke Terrorismus*, 2 vols. (Hamburg: Hamburger Ed., 2006); Klaus Weinhauer, Jörg Requate, and Heinz-Gerhard Haupt, eds., *Terrorismus in der Bundesrepublik: Medien, Staat und Subkulturen in den 1970er Jahren* (Frankfurt: Campus, 2006); Willi Winkler and Bernd Klöckener, *Die Geschichte der RAF* (Berlin: Rowohlt, 2007). The *Baader-Meinhof Komplex* remains a favorite since it was first published in 1985. The latest English-language edition: Stefan Aust, *Baader-Meinhof: The Inside Story of the R.A.F.*, trans. Anthea Bell (Oxford: Oxford University Press, 2009).

To be certain, the violence unleashed by the RAF was shocking to a society where murders were not common and which had systematically stigmatized radicalism of any sort since 1945. And average West German citizens like Sonja Siemsen, who lived in fear for her and her daughter's safety since coincidence placed her at the 1972 bombing of the IG-Farben building in Frankfurt, felt genuinely terrorized by the RAF.[6] But the FRG is a superlative example of how physical acts of violence are dramatically exacerbated in their effects by the doubts, fears, and hidden insecurities to which they give free rein. From the very beginning, terrorism was seen as a litmus test for German democracy, where the responses of the state and populace were taken as evidence of the lessons West Germans had or had not learned from the past. At best, this was a dubiously subjective exercise carried out by West Germans and a watchful international community. At worst, it encouraged the population to interpret the situation in zero-sum terms with the fate of the FRG hanging in the balance. To these already high stakes was added the question of the RAF's relationship to the student movement that preceded it. Those eager to roll back the developments of the 1960s claimed a direct connection between terrorism and activism, arguing that the former was the logical conclusion of the latter's amoral and destructive tendencies. This argument gained traction with the help of widespread anticommunism, which not only painted the world in terms of East and West but reified a left–right political framework that, as Belinda Davis rightly notes, can obscure as much as it explains about the content and practices of postwar popular politics.[7] In response, former activists and self-identifying leftists underscored the student movement's emancipatory and humane goals in contrast to the violent path pursued by the RAF and, more important, to the system of violence originating with the state. Proving they could give as good as they got, "'68ers" also argued that the systemic exploitation and repressive violence of capitalism were, in fact, at fault, having first victimized the RAF's members and then inspired them to rebellion. These opening shots guaranteed that the question of terrorism became a crucial battleground in the fight to define the legacy of the 1960s.

Rather than encourage consensus, then, each new attack furthered a debate over terrorism and counterterrorism to which even convicted or suspected terrorists contributed. Conservatives, still smarting from the 1969 electoral defeat that placed the postwar Social Democratic Party (SPD) at the head of government for the first time, accused the new government of downplaying the threat posed by left-wing extremism and inadequately defending the "free democratic order." The explanation they offered for this lack of action? The SPD's socialist sympathies and its traditional skepticism toward the German state. Presenting themselves as Germany's natural leaders, members of the Christian

[6] Letter from Sonja Siemsen to Helmut Schmidt, Frankfurt, September 22, 1977, Bundesarchiv (Koblenz) Bundesministerium des Innern: 83808.

[7] Belinda Davis, "What's Left? Popular Political Participation in Postwar Europe," *American Historical Review* 113 (April 2008): 363–90.

Democratic Union (CDU) proposed their own counterterrorism program predicated on swift and punitive state action. On the other end of the spectrum, West Germany's highly diverse extraparliamentary left perceived the SPD-led counterterrorism efforts as exceeding the bounds of acceptable state force and as exemplary of a larger assault on leftist politics. Citing illegal police raids, the flouting of civil liberties, and the alleged torture of convicted terrorists as evidence, members of the extraparliamentary left accused the government of slowly dismantling – rather than protecting – democracy in its attempts to combat terrorism. Not surprisingly, the governing Social Democrats – along with their junior coalition partners, the Liberal Democrats (FDP) – repudiated both assessments. They presented themselves as bastions of calm and reason in contrast to the "reactionary" and overwrought responses coming from their right and left. Behind closed doors, however, Social Democrats proved torn between the two poles – seeing danger in too light as well as too heavy a hand on the part of the state.

There can be little doubt that memories of the Third Reich weighed heavily on West German efforts to combat terrorism, working to escalate fears and raise the emotional register of debate. No matter who levied an accusation against whom, each carried barbed references to past failures and the moral responsibility of every German to avoid their repetition. Because fascism retained a powerful hold on political imaginations, West Germans struggled to distinguish real from imagined conditions in the FRG. On the one hand, the violence of the RAF evoked the specter of Weimar Germany and the dangers of a too permissive state. On the other, shrill calls for law and order awoke fears of Germany's inability to break free from its fascist past. These anxieties split unevenly along generational lines, with members of the older generation often moving with alarm to avert a repetition of Weimar while their children railed loudly against perceived continuities with National Socialism. The entwining dialogues revealed a population besieged as much by its own past as by terrorism and crystallized the extent to which the confrontation with terrorism in the 1970s was necessarily a confrontation with the Nazi past.

Because the battle cries of the 1960s and the ghosts of the Third Reich loomed large in the minds and rhetoric of West Germans confronting 1970s terrorism, the process of *Vergangenheitsbewältigung*, or "coming to terms with the past," frames most historical discussions of the period.[8] But wrapped in the potent allusions to Weimar and the Third Reich was an older German debate, a debate over democracy and its ability to successfully confront a state

[8] Among them, e.g., Norbert Elias, *The Germans: Power Struggles and the Development of Habitus in the Nineteenth and Twentieth Centuries* (New York: Columbia University Press, 1996), 229–97; Hans-Jürgen Wirth, ed., *Hitlers Enkel oder Kinder der Demokratie? Die 68er, die RAF und die Fischer-Debatte* (Giessen: Psychosozial, 2001); Gerd Koenen, *Das rote Jahrzehnt: Unsere kleine deutsche Kulturrevolution, 1967–1977* (Cologne: Kiepenheuer & Witsch, 2001); Varon, *Bringing the War Home*; Wolfgang Kraushaar, *Die Bombe im Jüdischen Gemeindehaus* (Hamburg: Hamburger Ed., 2005); idem, Karin Wieland, and Jan Philipp Reemtsma, *Rudi Dutschke, Andreas Baader und die RAF* (Hamburg: Hamburger Ed., 2005).

of emergency, to which West Germans' experience of terrorism contributed. If there was one image in the six weeks of the so-called German Autumn that competed for emotional resonance with the Cologne murder scene, it was that of a besieged state – government buildings walled in by sandbags and patrolled by SWAT teams.[9] For some, it illustrated the German state in crisis: battered down and seemingly helpless in the face of a handful of terrorists. For others, it revealed what they suspected had been there all along: the face of authoritarian or fascist power. Viewed alongside the heavily circulated mug shots of suspected terrorists, this image, with its two divergent interpretations, captures the competing fears that defined West Germans' experience of terrorism. The violent anarchy of a state too weak to defend itself or a police state at war with its own population – these, West Germans feared, were the high stakes in *Die Zeit*'s tagline, "State behind barbed wire?"[10]

In the postwar period, Weimar and National Socialism – as well as the besieged state – operated as reference points for the anarchy and authoritarianism Germans had long suspected was the inevitable result of a democratic state under siege. Since the early nineteenth century, the conviction that democracy was both inherently weak and particularly ill-suited for the German lands had promoted these fears and guaranteed that the issue of democracy's defense resurfaced time and again as Germans attempted to address the problem. Some did so – to powerful effect – by rejecting democracy altogether, while others planned less successfully for the extraordinary mobilization of the state or its citizens – or both – as a solution in times of crisis. Though the end of the Third Reich and Allied occupation certainly silenced those who might use democracy's need for defense as an argument against it, the supposed rupture of 1945 did not otherwise change the terms of the debate. The viability of German democracy remained the million-dollar question while the solutions – the rejection of political passivity in favor of militant (*wehrhafte*) democracy and a commitment to popular resistance (*Widerstand*) to antidemocratic forces – built off previous conclusions regarding the legitimate means for democracy's defense.

If the debate retained its basic contours, the stakes did not. The Reichstag's self-dissolution by way of the 1933 Enabling Act and the German people's complacency under the Third Reich confirmed fears regarding democracy's inherent weaknesses and, worse, fed suspicions that neither the state nor the population would act reliably as its safeguards. This conundrum assured that democratic stability would remain a topic of postwar discussion, with Weimar and Nazism serving as both a lesson and a threat. Before 1945, German imaginings of democracy's demise had, at worst, envisioned the return of monarchical

[9] See, e.g., "Der Staat geht in Stellung," *Der Spiegel* 39 (September 19, 1977), cover; Klaus Dreher, "Wenn das Schweigen regiert," *Süddeutsche Zeitung*, September 28, 1977, 3 (hereafter, *SZ*); "Präsidentenaufstritt 1977," *SZ*, October 7, 1977, 1; "Bonn: Stadt in Angst," *Quick* 40 (September 22, 1977), 14–15.

[10] "Staat hinter Stacheldraht?" *Die Zeit*, September 30, 1977, 3.

rule or defeat by outside forces. As of 1945, democracy's collapse was associated with Germany's total moral and physical devastation. Desperate to avoid such a fate, Germans made militant democracy and popular resistance central pillars of postwar political culture. This encouraged avid policing – of the population by the government, of the population by the population, and of the government by the population – and an antifascist vigilance ill-suited to the compromise and political tolerance commonly associated with civil society.[11] This dynamic escalated dramatically in the 1970s, when terrorism – and the reactions to it – provoked a range of social actors to turn the very tools for democracy's defense on each other as German fought German out of a common desire to protect democracy.

The civil war atmosphere that gripped the FRG at the height of the terrorist crisis dominates Germans' collective memory of the events and regularly resurfaces in new debates and political scandals, to say nothing of films and art installations. Sabine von Dirke sees this – and what she describes as an identity-shaking uncertainty about whether the constitutional state was preserved or suspended during the German Autumn – as evidence that West German terrorism qualifies as a collective historical trauma.[12] Others emphasize the media's role in creating a sense of existential crisis, arguing that terrorism was more spectacular than it was traumatic.[13] To be sure, the importance of the media is difficult to exaggerate, for modern terrorism is nothing if not a media event. But whether such representations or traumatic recollections sufficiently illuminate the importance of the German Autumn and the experience of terrorism more generally in German history seems less certain. Moreover, unless one dismisses the substance of Germans' fears, still missing is a convincing explanation for how West Germans evolved from a population at war with itself to the relatively civil society of the 1980s.[14] This book suggests that the explanation for terrorism's significance and for the changed political climate of the 1980s can be found in the successful containment of terrorism at the end of

[11] On the concept, see Jean L. Cohen and Andrew Arato, *Civil Society and Political Theory* (Cambridge: MIT Press, 1992). For exemplary scholarship that interrogates both the historically constructed nature of civil society and the ever-changing definitions of civility, see John Keane, *Civil Society: Old Images, New Visions* (Stanford: Stanford University Press, 1998) as well as Sven Reichardt, "Civility, Violence and Civil Society," in *Civil Society: Berlin Perspectives*, ed. John Keane (Providence: Berghahn, 2006), 139–67.

[12] Sabine von Dirke, "The RAF as Trauma and Pop Icon in Literature since the 1980s," in *Baader-Meinhof Returns: History and Cultural Memory of German Left-Wing Terrorism*, eds. Gerrit-Jan Berendse and Ingo Cornils (Amsterdam: Rodopi, 2008), 105–23.

[13] E.g., Hanno Balz, "Gesellschaftsformierungen: Die öffentliche Debatte über die RAF in den 70er Jahren," in *Der "Deutsche Herbst" und die RAF in Politik, Medien und Kunst: Nationale und internationale Perspektiven*, ed. Nicole Colin (Bielefeld: transcript, 2008), 170–84.

[14] For examples of historical analyses that evoke the move from crisis to relative stability without any explanation, see A. D. Moses, "The State and the Student Movement in West Germany, 1967–1977," in *Student Protest: The Sixties and After*, ed. Gerard J. Degroot (London: Longman, 1998); Belinda Davis, "Activism from Starbuck to Starbucks, or Terror: What's in a Name?" *Radical History Review* 85 (Winter 2003): 37–57.

the 1970s and the different conclusions regarding the state of German democracy that this involved. At stake, then, are questions of political culture, defined here simply as the values, expectations, and implicit rules that express and shape collective political intentions and actions. "Resistance" and "militant democracy" were not inert legal concepts but rather political symbols expressive of the basic assumptions that guided West Germans' political activity after 1945. They served to limit and legitimate certain courses of action even as they remained conceptually promiscuous – open to multiple interpretations and affected by the various actors who laid claim to them through their own actions. This study reconstructs the German debate over democracy's viability and defense in order to reveal continuities and shifts in political culture that have otherwise been obscured.

Like many recent histories of postwar Germany, this one challenges traditional notions of 1945 as a sharp caesura separating postwar Germans from their prewar political imaginings. Unlike other works, it shows how, in this instance, the 1960s were also less a point of rupture and more a crucial moment in which key conceptions of resistance and militant democracy were reaffirmed. Most important, an approach that focuses on outcomes as well as the debates that precede them – practice as well as discourse – demonstrates how, at the height of the terrorist crisis, West Germans of widely varying stripes revised long-standing assumptions about the state of democracy in Germany and acted to combat terrorism (and counterterrorism) accordingly. The RAF self-destructed, but the challenge of the terror it perpetrated became the impetus for West Germans to draw new conclusions regarding the legitimate use of state and popular violence within the FRG.

Viewing the German Autumn as a transformative event will strike some as a surprising claim for two reasons. First, in the long term historians have moved away from a focus on the event in favor of histories that emphasize underlying structural processes. And second, of those moments that *do* stand out in popular and scholarly histories of postwar Germany, 1977 is not generally among them. To understand the German Autumn as I treat it here – as an historical juncture that transformed key elements of West German political culture – requires one to take seriously different actors' fears and anxieties, regardless if they seem unwarranted or if some fears seem more justified than others. For it is precisely this experience of widespread insecurity that generated an atmosphere in which resistance and militant democracy, the categories of legitimate violence, were opened up to creative interrogation and rearticulation for a specific period of time. As a transformative event, the German Autumn contributed to the breakdown and reconfiguration of commitments and social networks that had defined politics since 1945.[15] Though the consequences of this were many, one of the most direct was the successful integration

[15] For a conceptualization of "the event" along these lines, see William H. Sewell, Jr., "Historical Events as Transformations of Structures: Inventing Revolution at the Bastille," *Theory and Society* 25 (1996): 843–81.

of a large, disaffected activist population that had, since the end of the 1960s, been a source of social tension and civil strife. By forcing a reconsideration of the limits of legitimate state and civil action, West Germany's terrorist crisis helped to usher in the relatively stable civil society that still defines Germany today, whose conflicts, even when acrimonious, are fought on fundamentally changed ground.

A significant number of citizens experienced the German Autumn of 1977 as anything but a triumph of democracy; still, the events gave key actors unprecedented clarity concerning the nature of West Germany's actually existing liberal order and the avenues open to its defense – and its critique. Extraparliamentary leftists did not join the RAF in mass armed revolt, the Social Democrats did not crumble under pressure or suspend the constitution, and no coup was staged by the right. Confronting a state of emergency and plagued by the specters of their history, Germans managed to learn from the past and even to use those lessons to defuse the adversarial dynamic driving their postwar political culture. This negotiation of terror not only facilitated a resolution to the immediate crisis but also freed West Germans to accept the Federal Republic as defined neither by its weaknesses nor its totalitarian past and thus to view democracy's defense as a matter of normal, rather than extra-ordinary, politics.

This shift in Germans' political sensibilities did not occur overnight and was not the product of terrorism alone. West Germans' confrontation with terrorism was a culmination of years of public debate as well as broader developments in state and society. It is also true that neither terrorism nor the responses it provoked can be understood without their international context.[16] Indeed, the 1970s saw an explosion of violence not only in the FRG but around the globe, with nearly every Western industrialized nation feeling itself the potential target of terrorism and struggling to counter this threat. Though terrorism was anything but a new phenomenon, it took a turn in the late 1960s marked by transnational networks, well-educated perpetrators, and the effective use of technology and mass media. The 1972 Lod airport massacre in Tel Aviv is an oft-cited example.[17] During the massacre, carried out by members of the Japanese Red Army on behalf of the Popular Front for the Liberation of Palestine, the militants used Czech assault rifles obtained over Italy and turned them on an internationally mixed group of civilians that included sixteen

[16] The literature on terrorism is immense. Among the long-term comparative studies, see Walter Lacquer, *A History of Terrorism*, 3rd ed. (New Brunswick: Transaction, 2001); Martha Crenshaw, *Terrorism in Context* (University Park: University of Pennsylvania Press, 1995); Isaac Cronin, *Confronting Fear: A History of Terrorism* (New York: Thunder's Mouth, 2002); Randall D. Law, *Terrorism: A History* (Cambridge: Polity, 2009); and Michael Burleigh's polemical *Blood and Rage: A Cultural History of Terrorism* (New York: HarperCollins, 2009).

[17] However frequently Lod finds its way into general English-language narratives of international terrorism, it is seldom examined in detail. For a rare account, see Yoshihiro Kuriyama, "Terrorism at Tel Aviv Airport and a 'New Left' Group in Japan," *Asian Survey* 13 (March 1973): 336–46.

Puerto Rican religious pilgrims. Though the RAF operated largely on West German soil, it too fit this new profile: Its members trained in Fatah camps, received weapons via an international network, and could disappear into the larger population thanks to their middle-class backgrounds and the ease with which they obtained fake identity papers and new license plates. And, just as television revolutionized the way the Western world experienced war – bringing scenes of death and destruction from Vietnam into American and European living rooms – it also provided self-styled revolutionaries with an international audience. To court that audience's political sympathy, terrorists insisted that their demands be televised, circumvented government control by releasing statements directly to newspapers eager to sell more copy, and, when interest in their cause waned, they made more headlines by striking again.[18] In this way, the "propaganda of the deed," a strategy first deployed by nineteenth-century anarchists, reached new heights in the 1970s as each terrorist attack became a ready-made media spectacle.[19]

The strategies Western democracies employed in response tell us as much about the late twentieth-century security state as about the unprecedented challenge presented by the new international terrorism. In particular, counterterrorism offers a keen lens onto two significant trends: the ascendancy of technocratic methods of control and growing international cooperation in matters of domestic security. While the majority of Western states defined terrorism as a violent crime to be pursued within existing legal frameworks, they did not employ the same old crime-fighting tactics.[20] The 1970s saw the rise of a more technologically and strategically savvy police force as terrorism and other "new" crimes gave governments an excuse to push through modernizing programs they had conceived a decade before. Computers, with the power to store and cross-reference limitless amounts of data, revolutionized intelligence gathering and drove forward dreams of the well-managed society. Meanwhile, terrorism joined crimes such as drug trafficking, gun proliferation, and computer hacking, as well as novel dangers such as environmental catastrophe, in making a mockery of state boundaries and security solutions tied exclusively

[18] For the argument that terrorism is "primarily a communicative strategy," see Peter Waldmann, *Terrorismus: Provokation der Macht* (Munich: Gerling, 1998). On the relationship between the media and international terrorism, see, among others: Alex P. Schmid and Janny de Graaf, *Violence as Communication: Insurgent Terrorism and the Western News Media* (London: Sage Publications, 1982); Steven Livingston, *The Terrorism Spectacle* (Boulder: Westview, 1993); Gabriel Weimann and Conrad Winn, *The Theater of Terror: Mass Media and International Terrorism* (New York: Longman, 1994); and Brigette Lebens Nacos, *Mass-Mediated Terrorism: The Central Role of the Media in Terrorism and Counter-Terrorism* (New York: Rowman & Littlefield, 2002).

[19] For the nineteenth-century variant, see Claudia Verhoeven, *The Odd Man Karakozov: Imperial Russia, Modernity, and the Birth of Terrorism* (Ithaca: Cornell University Press, 2007). On hijacking as the fullest expression of this phenomenon: Annette Vowinckel, *Flugzeugentführungen: Eine Kulturgeschichte* (Göttingen: Wallstein, 2011).

[20] Peter Chalk, *Western European Terrorism and Counter-Terrorism: The Evolving Dynamic* (New York: St. Martin's, 1996), 97.

to them. Thus, at the same time that states' capacities to know and intervene in the lives of their populations blossomed, heads of government and security experts confronted the limits of their own domestic policies and charted the unfamiliar waters of supranational cooperation. Indeed, the need to look beyond the nation-state to combat terrorism prompted one prominent U.S. political scientist to suggest that terrorism raised the question of "whether the state as we know it is becoming obsolete."[21] That citizens, too, were actively seeking security outside of the nation-state at this time – mobilizing transnational networks and watchdog organizations in an attempt to check abuses of government power – made this question all the more apt.

Of course, the problems raised by terrorism both then and now far exceed the matter of its mere containment. For, unlike other forms of government, democracy has a particularly difficult task when it comes to its own defense. Because the rule of law and protection of civil liberties are integral to democratic understandings of security, not all means are acceptable. A government's desire for swift, effective action in order to maintain control and not appear weak – either to its assailants or to members of its own population – cannot sacrifice the rule of law or individual rights without risking a loss of legitimacy. As Aharon Barak, a justice of the Israeli Supreme Court, put it, at times a democratic state finds it has no choice but to fight with one hand tied behind its back.[22] This holds all the more true in cases where undemocratic acts by the state will only support the claims made by terrorists against it.

These problems are well known, yet the idea of one-handed defense has never found much favor with heads of state, threatened populations, or constitutional scholars. Why? Because postwar West Germans were far from alone in judging those powers of state ordinarily granted a democracy as too hampered by legal norms and parliamentary procedures to successfully defend against external attacks or internal enemies. For centuries, democratic rule has been regarded as a privilege of peace – inappropriate to times of crisis when speed and unity are deemed crucial to survival.[23] For this reason, democratic states have long been outfitted with more or less explicit mechanisms for suspending constitutional constraints with the idea that once the threat passes, life and liberty will resume as before. In his 1948 study of crisis governments, Clinton Rossiter in fact argued that modern democracies have repeatedly survived crisis (war, rebellion, and economic upheaval) by instituting a constitutional dictatorship – a temporary empowerment of the executive at the expense of the

21 David E. Apter, "Notes on the Underground: Left Violence and the National State," *Daedalus* 108 (Fall 1979): 170.

22 Aharon Barak, "Forward: A Judge on Judging: The Role of a Supreme Court in a Democracy," *Harvard Law Review* 116 (2002): 148.

23 Written in the early sixteenth century, Machiavelli's reflections on the Roman republic and dictatorship remain among the most famous on the subject: Niccolò Machiavelli, *The Discourses* (London: Penguin, 2003). For a more recent examination, see Peter Baehr and Melvin Richter, eds., *Dictatorship in History and Theory: Bonapartism, Caesarism, and Totalitarianism* (Washington, DC: German Historical Institute and Cambridge University Press, 2004).

citizenry in order for the threat to be eliminated and, then, democratic order restored.[24] Though he was aware of the potential for this sort of temporary stewardship to slip into a permanent dictatorship – like postwar Germans, he had the example of Hitler before him – Rossiter nonetheless argued that dictatorship was truly democracy's best defense.

In many ways, Rossiter's position is a typically American one. Perhaps because Americans have never suffered the reign of kings, they are relatively unafraid of strong executives and confident of their democratic institutions. Criticism of the George W. Bush administration for its wiretapping, torture, and frequent obstruction of congressional oversight in the "war on terror" following September 11, 2001 – as well as the Obama administration's contradictory attempts to reckon with their legacy – demonstrate, however, that Americans are not immune to the dangers and debates surrounding wartime dictatorship. Indeed, the controversy over counterterrorism strategies has provoked a reexamination of executive privilege rarely seen in the United States.[25] There are, of course, other methods of empowering a democratic state, though none free of problems or critics. The British, historically concerned with protecting parliamentary authority, established a model for confronting national crises via temporary legislation. Civil liberties might be suspended and the state might intervene in society in unprecedented ways, but only at the sufferance of parliament. The USA PATRIOT Act of 2001, reauthorized repeatedly since, is a recent American example of this sort of defensive action. Just like temporary dictatorship, however, stop-gap legislation can threaten democracy by permanently altering the constitutional order through its repeated suspension or reinterpretation of fundamental legal norms. For this reason, a majority of democratic states have chosen a third option: to constitutionally regulate states of emergency.[26] The working assumption here is that acknowledging a time of crisis with something akin to a separate, emergency constitution protects the normal democratic order from both intentional and unintentional encroachment.[27] The fact that these same states have routinely opted to pass

[24] Clinton Rossiter, *Constitutional Dictatorship: Crisis Government in the Modern Democracies* (New Brunswick: Transaction, 2002).

[25] See esp. the exchange between Sanford Levinson, "Constitutional Norms in a State of Permanent Emergency," *Georgia Law Review* 40 (2006): 699–751 and Mark Tushnet, "Meditations on Carl Schmitt," *Georgia Law Review* 40 (2006): 877–88 as well as between Bruce Ackerman, "The Emergency Constitution," *Yale Law Journal* 113 (2004): 1029–91 and Laurence H. Tribe and Patrick O. Gudridge, "The Anti-Emergency Constitution," *Yale Law Journal* 113 (2004): 1801–70. Also, Jonathan Mahler, *The Challenge: Hamdan v. Rumsfeld and the Fight over Presidential Power* (New York: Farrar, Straus, and Giroux, 2008).

[26] For an early discussion of the 1996 Anti-Terrorism Act and the 2001 Patriot Act and their influence on free liberal society: David Cole and James X. Dempsey, *Terrorism and the Constitution: Sacrificing Civil Liberties in the Name of National Security* (New York: New Press, 2002).

[27] David Dyzenhaus, "The Permanence of the Temporary: Can Emergency Powers be Normalized?" in *The Security of Freedom: Essays on Canada's Anti-Terrorism Bill*, eds. Patrick Macklem, Kent Roach, and Ronald J. Daniels (Toronto: University of Toronto Press, 2001), 21–37. For a general discussion favoring the constitutional regulation of emergency, see John Ferejohn and

new legislation rather than declare a state of emergency suggests, however, that a suspension of constitutional norms – even if it is constitutionally regulated – is perceived as too destabilizing (for the state) or too alarming (to its citizens).

All three models for democracy's defense open the door to what might be called a two-handed fistfight, on the crucial assumption that the executive, legislature, or constitution would guard against irreparable damage to the state's founding principles. Implicit in each is a leap of faith – a belief that democracy can and will withstand the damage inflicted by friends and foes alike. This faith, however, is precisely what Germans historically have lacked and what West Germans still did not possess in the 1970s, though their constitution provided for the extraordinary mobilization of both state and society in times of crisis. As A. Dirk Moses has recently shown, the collapse of Germany's first liberal democracy in 1933 and the failure of the new republic to make a sharp break with Nazism after 1945 encouraged many Germans to view the FRG with deep pessimism and deprived the young state of a basic consensus regarding the legitimacy of its liberal institutions.[28] The 1970s clearly demonstrate how skepticism over the viability of democracy "after Hitler" dovetailed with longer-standing perceptions of representative government as inherently weak to create a situation in which the need to protect democracy became a crisis all its own.[29] Without confidence in democracy's resiliency, its defense remained a constant source of anxiety and state and society remained fundamentally "undersecure."[30]

Sheer exhaustion is one common explanation for the relative quiet following the "German Autumn," in which after a decade or more of constant conflict West Germans chose security. Moses himself argues that democratic legitimation came with the passing of generations and thus the stigma of National Socialism in the twenty-first century. Each in its own way is too passive to explain the emergence of basic confidence in German liberal democracy. The terrorist crisis is often portrayed, from the left, as having pushed West Germany for a time off a cliff into dictatorship.[31] From the right and center, where the majority of security experts sit, counterterrorism appears as

Pasquale Pasquino, "The Law of the Exception: A Typology of Emergency Powers," *I.CON* 2 (2004): 210–39.

[28] The absence of such a basic consensus is taken as a given in recent works on the postwar period and the 1960s in particular. Dirk Moses's work on postwar intellectuals offers one of the first explanations as to *why* this was so. A. Dirk Moses, *German Intellectuals and the Nazi Past* (Cambridge: Cambridge University Press, 2007).

[29] Konrad H. Jarausch, *After Hitler: Recivilizing Germans, 1945–1995* (New York: Oxford University Press, 2006).

[30] Mariano Grondona, "Reconciling Internal Security and Human Rights," *International Security* 3 (Summer 1978): 3–16. In his discussion of Latin American cases, Grondona uses the term "undersecure" in order to capture a more structural and long-term state than "insecure" implies. An undersecure state theoretically favors human rights but internal security is most often a practical priority.

[31] E.g., Sebastian Cobler, *Die Gefahr geht von den Menschen aus: Der vorverlegte Schutz* (Berlin: Rotbuch, 1976); Klaus Hartung, ed., *Der Blinde Fleck: Die Linke, die RAF und der Staat*

an unproblematically legitimate response to dangerous antidemocratic extremism.[32] Both perspectives miss the actual leap of faith from all sides that the aftermath of the terrorist crisis inspired. The fact that the republic survived the assaults of both terrorism and counterterrorism was crucial to revising assumptions – at home and abroad – about democracy's viability in Germany. Only then did those who had stood skeptically awaiting the FRG to prove itself – as either fascist or too weak – put aside such expectations and agree to move forward on the assumption that West Germany was a secure and reformable liberal democracy. The realignment of left politics that occurred at the end of the decade – with the SPD's shedding of both right-wing and left-wing supporters, the advent of the Greens, and the integration of the extraparliamentary left – as well as the resurgence of a conservative project to reclaim a usable national identity in the 1980s are indicators of the depth of the transformation in West German political culture, one that survived long after the confrontation with terrorism had passed.

The argument that follows is about Germans' efforts to defend democracy, with militant democracy and popular resistance as two preferred but hotly contested answers for legitimate political action in the postwar period. The language West Germans reached for as they worked out their position on democracy's defense was often that of *Gewalt*, whose range of meanings encompasses violence and coercion but also power and authority. This is why I do not provide the reader with an operative definition of violence. Rather, I defer to my actors' words – as they referred to the state's military force, the authority of political institutions, the systemic violence of capitalist society, or physical harm done to bodies or property – in an effort to reconstruct this wide-ranging debate. While it is true that violence was a constant presence, what different actors meant by "violence" varied widely and changed over time. Indeed, the proper definition of violence was in many ways *the* point of contention – and misunderstanding – in fights over militant democracy and resistance, one that carried over to politically charged characterizations of the RAF (and even antinuclear activists) as either terrorists or freedom fighters. To privilege "guerrilla" or "violent extremist" in discussing the RAF is thus to take sides in the historical debate. I have tried to ensure that I am rendering my actors' judgments rather than my own by using the term or terms of the time most appropriate to a given context.[33] When necessary, I have fallen back on "militant" as a relatively neutral

(Frankfurt: Neue Kritik, 1987); Helmut Janssen and Michael Schubert, *Staatssicherheit: Die Bekämpfung des politischen Feindes im Innern* (Bielefeld: AJZ, 1990).

[32] E.g., Hans Josef Horchem, *Die verlorene Revolution: Terrorismus in Deutschland* (Herford: Busse Seewald, 1988); Konrad Low, ed., *Terror und Extremismus in Deutschland: Ursachen, Erscheinungsformen, Wege zur Überwindung* (Berlin: Duncker & Humboldt, 1994); Uwe Backes and Eckhard Jesse, *Politischer Extremismus in der Bundesrepublik Deutschland*, 4th ed. (Bonn: Bundeszentrale für politische Bildung, 1996).

[33] In a chapter devoted to "Defining Terrorism," Bruce Hoffmann discusses our inability to reach a consensus, with one result being that the decision to call someone a "terrorist" remains

(and adjectivally modifiable) designation. I approach references to repression in a similar fashion. In this instance, however, policy makers as well as critics spoke of the state's "repressive" measures, since for supporters of militant democracy the use of repression was not only legitimate but freed from negative connotation. For this reason, then, I do not shy away from using the term either. The political and social phenomenon of "terrorism," as I understand it here, is in many ways the sum of these two parts. It includes acts of political violence and the responses to them, and it involves not only violent militants and state actors but an entire society.

My attention to their language reflects an effort to empathically reconstruct the historical actors' values in the vein of what sociologist Max Weber called an "ideal type." It is through this approach that the book can show the distinctive features of several different positions, what it meant when each position was held consistently, and under what conditions those positions changed. Tradeoffs are involved, of course. In order to underscore the different approaches West Germans took to defend democracy (itself a highly contested concept), I have necessarily simplified the range of values and experiences among individual actors. My goal has not been to manufacture an illusory consensus or to excuse still contested choices but rather to reconstruct and to understand.[34] That antifascist vigilance outlived the actual threat of fascism and that the "free democratic order" was never fundamentally at risk seems clear to many today. Determining the accuracy of West Germans' stated fears, however, is far less important to this study than demonstrating their influence on people's judgments and actions. Indeed, it argues West Germans' very inability to correctly assess conditions in the FRG was not a product of hysteria – a word frequently used to describe the German Autumn – but rather of immanently understandable uncertainties about democracy's viability. Establishing what these were and how they were eventually resolved is the purpose of this book. Though it focuses predominately on the left – as the parliamentary party in power during the 1970s and the most challenging extraparliamentary force – the conservatives are not absent. For conservatives' ability to quiet their own fears of liberal democracy's weakness was also essential to realizing a stable political order.

The tensions that run between the state power and civil liberties and define key conditions for democratic security also run through this book, as it tacks back and forth between government and citizenry as well as between fears of anarchy and repression. Chapters 1 and 2 establish the twin concepts of militant democracy and resistance as postwar solutions to securing democracy in

"unavoidably subjective." Whether he would characterize my approach as a "slavish devotion to terminological neutrality" or reserves such judgments for the contemporary media is unclear. See, Bruce Hoffmann, *Inside Terrorism* (New York: Columbia University Press, 1998), 13–44, esp. 30–3 and 37.

34 The corollary, as Weber pointed out, is that "to understand is not to excuse." For an illuminating discussion of Weber's interpretive sociology and its political valences, see Peter Breiner, *Max Weber and Democratic Politics* (Ithaca: Cornell University Press, 1996).

Germany. Precisely because mainstream conservatives largely came to define the concept of militant democracy, Chapter 1 takes care to reconstruct alternative visions, particularly the one favored by Social Democrats in the drafting of the constitution. It demonstrates how protest over rearmament in the 1950s and the 1968 Emergency Laws rehashed initial disagreements over non-neutral state intervention and increasingly did so outside of parliament. Chapter 2 covers roughly the same twenty-year period but examines the population at large as the object of postwar efforts to create resistance-capable Germans and the agent of actual protest. Although the SPD attempted to restrict democratic opposition to parliament and legal institutions at the end of the 1950s, the chapter argues that it was an ongoing commitment to antifascist resistance that provided a diffuse and institutionally isolated extraparliamentary left with its cohesion and, in the 1970s, West German terrorists with their sympathizers.

Chapter 3 begins with the ascendency of the SPD to government in 1969 and Social Democrats' efforts to supplement conservative concepts of militant democracy with their own. The government's attempts to simultaneously undermine terrorism and guard against the state's potential abuse of power – through the modernization of police power, political education, strict legal regulations, and, not least, international cooperation – received heavy criticism from conservatives for being too "soft" and from members of their own party and the extraparliamentary left for endangering civil liberties. All questioned what was being lost and won in the government's search for "internal security." Chapter 4 pursues this question by examining both left solidarity with the RAF and the actions taken by citizens convinced of the state's undemocratic behavior. Protesters mobilized international opinion against their own government and formed new networks and alliances – reminding us that counterterrorism was only one of several fields on which West Germans contested the state's intervention, and that protest and resistance were not the exclusive property of the left. As confrontations between police and protesters escalated, however, violence threatened to fracture the coalition of diverse citizens' initiative groups. Here, where the extraparliamentary politics of a self-conscious left overlapped with those of the ecological and feminist movements, a sustained debate on popular resistance and *its* necessary limits began to unfold.

Chapters 5 and 6 serve as culmination and finale. Chapter 5 focuses on the months leading up to Schleyer's kidnapping in September 1977 and the ensuing crisis. It shows that the extraparliamentary left's consensus on resistance had begun to crumble by the spring of 1977 and, along with it, its previous sense of cohesion. Also, it demonstrates that despite disagreements within the SPD over the legitimate use of state force, the government's decision to arm the state in ways it had previously avoided heralded the party's new understanding of state power as successfully democratized and thus no longer an authoritarian threat. Chapter 6, then, examines the aftermath of the German Autumn in order to present the lasting changes wrought to West German political culture by the experience of terrorism. It argues, on the one hand, that the political impotence and disillusionment experienced by extraparliamentary leftists created a desire to reengage the mainstream political public and, correspondingly, an unprecedented appreciation of nonviolent politics. On the other hand, the chapter contends that the fight against terrorism acted as a mobilizing force for a newly revamped conservatism. The German Autumn not only settled old doubts about democracy, but helped conservatives reclaim national pride and traditional values as an antidote to the moral vacuum revealed by that decade's violence. Together, these three contemporaneous developments contributed not merely to the conservative bent of the 1980s but to a new agreement on the polity's democratic viability.

Prologue

> Some say ... the democratic state simply does not suit Germany. It contradicts the German character! Democratic institutions are "Western" ... They would be a strange people, these Germans, if they alone were incapable of keeping step with the political developments of all civilized humanity.
>
> Hugo Preuß (1925)[1]

If all liberal democracies wrestle with the tensions between national security and civil liberties, Germans have a long history of turning the question of how to reconcile the two into a source of public conflict. While this book examines the particularly torturous debate that took place after 1945 – when all of Europe struggled to overcome the legacies of fascism within the narrow confines of the Cold War – it cannot ignore the conflicts and negotiated answers that came before. It cannot do so largely because postwar Germans could not. Doubts over democracy's viability in theory and in Germany in particular were long-standing and West Germans repeatedly looked to past answers in fear as well as in hope of finding a new way forward.

Much as the absence of a nation-state did little to staunch imaginings of a united Germany before 1871, the absence of democracy did not discourage people living in the German lands from debating its pros and cons before the Weimar Republic was founded in 1919. Civil servants and scholars of law and politics, whose opinions informed the interworkings of nineteenth-century state bureaucracies, generally agreed that Germans' vulnerable position between Russia and France made liberal democracy an inappropriate form of government. A state surrounded by powerful and hostile neighbors, it was imagined, could ill afford slow parliamentary procedure; its very survival required a strong executive able to move swiftly and decisively in the event

[1] Hugo Preuß, "Die Bedeutung der demokratischen Republik für den sozialen Gedanken," reprinted in *Weimar: Jurisprudence of Crisis*, eds. Arthur J. Jacobson and Bernhard Schlink (Berkeley: University of California Press, 2000), 116–27; here, 117.

of war, occupation, or internal revolt.[2] Many a German historian supported this line of thinking, arguing that it was no accident that democratic political culture had taken hold in England and not in the German lands.[3] As they told it, representative government was just one of the many luxuries geopolitics afforded an island nation. Nor was this a position confined to grizzled old monarchists and conservative ministers. Even as German liberals clamored for a constitution and political representation, the majority of them shared the perception that democracy and state security made difficult, if not impossible, bedfellows.[4] They betrayed their own reservations regarding the weaknesses of democracy in arguing for a constitutional, hereditary monarchy over a republic and helped set the terms for what would become a distinctly German argument, namely that a constitutional monarch was preferable precisely because he could become the guarantor of civil society in exceptional circumstances. In times of crisis, liberals too counted on the executive to suspend parliamentary procedures and thereby save representative government from its own inability to effectively defend state security.

The collapse of Germany's first democratic government in 1933 has been the subject of scholarly inquiry almost since the moment it happened, with the months and days leading up to the Nazis' capture of power inspiring searches for wrong turns and the roads not taken as well as a careful reconstruction of historically contingent events.[5] Though it enjoyed years of economic and diplomatic stability as well as a flowering of artistic genius, the history of the Weimar Republic has been read first and foremost as one of crisis – economic, political, and cultural.[6] While German democracy was not

[2] Not until the First World War decisively demonstrated the democracies' (military) strength over old monarchical regimes was this argument for German exceptionalism significantly revised. Brendan Simms, *The Impact of Napoleon: Prussian High Politics, Foreign Policy and the Crisis of the Executive, 1797–1806* (Cambridge: Cambridge University Press, 1997), esp. 5f; 315–25.

[3] The "Land der Mitte" or "Primat der Außenpolitik" argument is present in the works of Otto Hintze, Hermann Oncken, and Gerhard Ritter, who were among the historians to distinguish between "insular" and "continental" state forms. Ibid., 9–11.

[4] For an overview of the debates internal to German liberalism, see Dieter Langewiesche, *Liberalism in Germany* (Princeton: Princeton University Press, 2000), esp. 1–55.

[5] I borrow "capture" from Richard Bessel, who convincingly argues that "seizure" is too active a description for how the Nazis came to power acknowledges that power was not merely gifted them either. See Richard Bessel, "The Nazi Capture of Power," *Journal of Contemporary History* 39 (April 2004): 169–88. Also, Hermann Beck, *The Fateful Alliance: German Conservatives and Nazis in 1933: The Machtergreifung in a New Light* (New York: Berghahn, 2008). Among the many tomes dedicated to Weimar's last days, the seminal works remain Karl Dietrich Bracher, *Die Auflösung der Weimarer Republik* (Stuttgart: Ring, 1955) and Hans Mommsen, *The Rise and Fall of Weimar Democracy*, trans. Elborg Forster and Larry Eugene Jones (Chapel Hill: University of North Carolina Press, 1989). For a more recent account: Dirk Blasius, *Weimars Ende: Bürgerkrieg und Politik, 1930–1933* (Göttingen: Vandenhoeck & Ruprecht, 2005).

[6] The subtitle of Detlev Peukert's influential work *The Weimar Republic: A Crisis of Classical Modernity*, trans. Richard Deveson (New York: Hill & Wang, 1993) neatly captures a generation's

without its defenders and even succeeded in winning over a number of pragmatic democrats – those who supported the new government out of a sense of political realism if not actual democratic conviction – the upheaval caused by war and economic devastation made the Republic an all too easy target for the fears and frustrations felt by most interwar Germans.[7] Even in the realm of constitutional theory, legal theorists intent on making a case for democracy found themselves on the defensive – repeatedly confronted with the old arguments that democracy was antinational, "Western" and thus un-German, or synonymous with weak state power.[8] In their efforts to counter antidemocratic positions and address the political crises that wracked the Weimar Republic, leading jurists such as Hugo Preuß, Gerhard Anschütz, and Hans Kelsen investigated the preconditions for democratic government. And each of them came to the inescapable conclusion that democracy relied on the population's active support. While the victory of France, Britain, and the United States in the First World War had proven modern democracy's strength over the old authoritarian regimes in matters of war and external defense, nothing, they observed, could save a democracy from internal collapse if it lacked loyal citizens and effective leaders. As Gerhard Anschütz argued in 1922, "A good constitution can guarantee that the choice of [leaders] is carried out correctly ... but every choice requires material, people among whom to choose ... in the end, it requires an entire people that thinks and feels politically. These are conditions that no constitution can create...."[9] If previously geopolitics seemed the biggest impediment to democracy, the emphasis was now on domestic prerequisites. And by 1930, there was mounting evidence to suggest that these were sadly lacking in Germany.

During the Weimar Republic's final year, the sense that the country teetered on the brink of civil war became particularly acute. Political violence spiked dramatically during the "hot" summer months of 1932, with few cities or towns in Germany left untouched by the street brawls and incidents of violence that rose right alongside the Nazi movement. Nor was the countryside spared, as Nazi stormtroopers (SA) clashed with the paramilitaries formed by their opponents – the republican *Reichsbanner*, the Iron Front (founded in 1931 by the SPD and trade unions), the Communist Red Front (banned in 1929 but, like the SA, still active), and its successor, the Anti-Fascist Fighting League (founded

thinking on Weimar. This interpretation is currently undergoing revision by a younger generation of historians. See, e.g., Moritz Föllmer and Rüdiger Graf, eds., *Die "Krise" der Weimarer Republik: Zur Kritik eines Deutungsmusters* (Frankfurt: Campus, 2005).

7 The literature on the Weimar Republic is expansive, to say the least. For an introduction to the politics, culture, and complex social fabric out of which Germany's first democracy struggled to make a go of it, see Eric D. Weitz, *Weimar Democracy: Promise and Tragedy* (Princeton: Princeton University Press, 2007).

8 A reproduction of texts that capture the scope of this debate can be found in: Jacobson and Schlink, *Jurisprudence of Crisis*.

9 Gerhard Anschütz, "Three Guiding Principles of the Weimar Constitution," reprinted in Jacobson and Schlink, *Jurisprudence of Crisis*, 132–50; here, 149.

in late 1930).[10] As Richard Bessel describes it, by 1933 political violence was a "ubiquitous feature of the German political landscape," driven by the SA as they mobilized and transported thousands of men to various locations throughout Germany, picking fights in working-class areas and rallying supporters in parades and demonstrations.[11] Well-publicized cases of violence magnified reactions to smaller incidents and contributed to Germans' shared experience of cumulative terror. Though one might argue that the climate of violence was more symptomatic of the regime to come than life in the Republic, it became intimately associated with Weimar in the memories of postwar Germans.

The immediate reason for the summer wave of violence was the government's rescission of the ban previously placed on the SA, followed by the fiercely contested Reichstag elections at the end of July.[12] The ten days leading up to the elections saw the worst fighting, with twenty-four people killed and 284 seriously injured in political confrontations in Prussia alone.[13] Rather than taper off after the election as one might expect, the violence continued. In an "outburst of Nazi terrorism," the SA – disappointed by the party's failure to win an absolute majority – engaged in premeditated acts of arson, bombings, and assassination attempts.[14] After having lifted the SA ban, Chancellor Franz von Papen was now forced to regain control of the streets. On August 9, his government issued two emergency decrees against political terrorism that not only extended a ban on all political rallies until the end of the month but also made political murders punishable by death. Acknowledging the unique nature of the crimes, special courts presided over cases that fell under the purview of the new laws. On the one hand, the new antiterrorism legislation was highly effective in stopping the terror campaign. However eager they were to confront Social Democratic and Communist paramilitaries, Nazis shied away from direct conflict with the state.[15] On the other hand, the decrees were a political disaster. The first case to come before the special courts was the brutal, premeditated murder of Communist sympathizer Konrad Pietzuch by thirteen local Nazis in the small Silesian village of Potempa.[16] Overnight, those who

[10] Richard Bessel, *Political Violence and the Rise of Nazism: The Storm Troopers in Eastern Germany, 1925–1934* (New Haven: Yale University Press, 1984), 76–7.

[11] Ibid., 83.

[12] The ban of April 13, 1932 was the result of intense pressure from state ministers of interior, who threatened to take independent action if Defense Minister Groener did not act. Groener matched the ban on the SA with a ban on communist and other "atheist organizations" so as to avoid accusations of left favoritism. Mommsen, *Rise and Fall of Weimar*, 418–21.

[13] Bessel, "Nazi Capture of Power," 180.

[14] The shift away from more spontaneous street fighting to what Bessel describes as "planned acts of terrorism" occurred in response to Chancellor von Papen's political truce that temporarily prohibited all political rallies. Bessel, *Political Violence*, 89–92. For a brief discussion of the July elections, see Mommsen, *Rise and Fall of Weimar*, 455–9.

[15] Bessel, *Political Violence*, 75–96.

[16] For the most detailed English-language account of the murder, trial, and surrounding events, see Richard Bessel, "The Potempa Murder," *Central European History* 10 (September 1977): 241–54.

had praised the decree (assuming – not without justification – that conservative courts would use it primarily against the left) turned to publicly condemning it. At the trial, the Nazis pled self-defense – specifically the right to defend oneself against communist terror – and proved themselves more than willing to continue that struggle in skirmishes inside and outside of the courtroom. When five of nine defendants were sentenced to death on August 22, Adolf Hitler deftly used the situation to consolidate control over his impatient and unruly movement. In a widely publicized telegram, Hitler declared his unwavering loyalty to the convicted terrorists and immediately made restoring their freedom a point of Nazi honor.[17]

It took only two weeks for von Papen's government to give in to Nazi pressure and commute the sentences to life imprisonment. According to Erich Eyck, a Berlin municipal politician and later historian of Weimar, it was an unprecedented moment that assured the killers would soon see freedom: "Never before had a German government bowed so openly to political terror."[18] For Eyck and countless others, von Papen's decision was a particularly bitter pill to swallow, given that von Papen issued the ruling not as chancellor but in his new capacity as the minister president of Prussia, whose duly elected government he had dismissed in July on the paper-thin pretense of restoring peace and public order.[19] A violent battle between parading Nazis and Communist snipers in Hamburg a few days earlier provided the excuse, while a decree from President von Hindenburg provided the emergency powers authorizing the federal takeover of the country's largest and most politically significant state.[20] It was a coup designed to dismantle the SPD-led coalition that ruled Prussia – remembered as the last "bulwark of the Republic" – and close out Social Democrats from politics completely. Convinced of the blatantly unconstitutional nature of the federal government's intervention, SPD leaders – Otto Braun and Carl Severing, president and interior minister of the ousted government, along with members of the party's executive committee – contemplated armed resistance only to rule it out. In their memoirs, both men argued that they had no choice; with Prussian police forces already under federal control and the army as well as Nazi volunteers armed against the SPD and its sympathizers, an organized revolt would only have ended in civil war, bloody defeat, and, perhaps worst of all, a moral victory for the NSDAP.[21] In his own account, Eyck conceded

[17] Bessel, "Nazi Capture of Power," 181.

[18] Erich Eyck, *A History of the Weimar Republic*, trans. Harlan P. Hanson and Roberg G. L. Waite (Cambridge: Harvard University Press, 1963), 421.

[19] Von Papen publicly justified the takeover by citing the Prussian government's failure to take action against the "Communist terrorist groups" whom he blamed for recent disturbances. On the coup generally, see Mommsen, *Rise and Fall of Weimar*, 444–53. For a detailed discussion of the accusations leveled by von Papen's government, see Dietrich Orlow, *Weimar Prussia, 1925–1933: The Illusion of Strength* (Pittsburg: University of Pittsburg Press, 1991), 225–33.

[20] Prussia was by far the largest state in both population and geographic size, making up 61 percent and 62.5 percent of Germany's total numbers respectively. Beck, *Fateful Alliance*, 107n67.

[21] Otto Braun, *Von Weimar zu Hitler* (New York: Europa, 1940), 409; Carl Severing, *Mein Lebensweg*, vol. 2, *Im auf und ab der Republik* (Cologne: Greven, 1950), 347, 352. Historians'

that Social Democrats had good reasons not to "meet von Papen's force with forces of their own" but nonetheless called their failure to resist "a blot on their names." For "whoever surrenders without a struggle forfeits the sympathy of contemporary and later opinion."[22] Written from London nearly two decades after Eyck and his family escaped Hitler's Germany, Eyck's opinion was seconded by many – if not in 1932, then in retrospect with the merciless clarity of hindsight.[23]

If they chose not to call on the masses, members of the Prussian government did not simply step aside either. Instead, they demonstrated their commitment to the existing legal order by challenging the presidential decree's validity in open court. Because the decree rested on the emergency powers granted the president under Article 48 of the Weimar constitution, the case automatically went before the State Court (*Staatsgerichtshof*) created to resolve constitutional disputes between federal and state governments.[24] By the time the court announced its decision at the end of October, there was little to be salvaged; Prussia's administration had been purged of Social Democrats and their sympathizers and the federal government now asserted an exclusive monopoly on legitimate violence. The court upheld the emergency decree, confirming that the president was constitutionally entitled to seize control of the Prussian state and asserting that the Prussian government had failed to prove that he had overstepped these discretionary powers.[25] Moreover, even if their allegations of a conspiracy between the federal government and the Nazis to depose the Prussian government were correct, they had failed to establish that the decree's primary aim was not, in fact, to restore public order. Despite these rulings, Prussian authorities had reason to be pleased. For the court also clearly rejected von Papen's own justifications, namely his highly publicized claim that the Prussian ministers had been disloyal to the Reich – collaborating with the Communists to bring disorder – and limited the president's emergency powers

accounts of the powers arrayed against the SPD and Prussia government vary but most also concede the near impossibility of executing a general strike under conditions of mass unemployment.

[22] Eyck, *A History*, 414, 417. Eyck essentially criticized SPD leaders for being naïve and outdated in their desire for domestic and international peace: "to them, a statesman who caused bloodshed was guilty of the worst political crime. They can scarcely be censured for this conviction. Yet it certainly cannot be denied that this same civilized point of view made them easy prey for enemies on both the right and the left." Ibid., 416–17.

[23] Offering the most in-depth examination of Social Democrats' contradictory reactions to the July 20 coup, Donna Harsch voices a regret and critique common to many, arguing that even if hopeless in terms of political strategy, the act of armed resistance would have proved an invaluable – perhaps even history-changing – inspiration. Donna Harsch, *German Social Democracy and the Rise of Nazism* (Chapel Hill: University of North Carolina Press, 1993), 190–202.

[24] For an accessible discussion of Weimar constitutional theory and its political consequences, see Peter C. Caldwell, *Popular Sovereignty and the Crisis of German Constitutional Law: The Theory and Practice of Weimar Constitutionalism* (Durham: Duke University Press, 1997).

[25] On the legal positions presented in the case: David Dyzenhaus, *Legality and Legitimacy: Carl Schmitt, Hans Kelsen, and Hermann Heller in Weimar* (Oxford: Oxford University Press, 1997).

by insisting that they too were bound by the constitution's federalist principles. This last ensured that some shadow of the former Prussian government remained in place and that Prussia would not become the model for an authoritarian restructuring of the German state.[26]

The court's decision has been described as a grand failure – a missed opportunity to halt the dissolution of the Republic.[27] Like the previous decision against armed resistance, however, it is doubtful that a different verdict would have altered the course of history given the proto-fascist climate that had already begun to take hold.[28] To be sure, the State Court made Hitler's work easier by laying down the legal framework that he later used to destroy the constitutional system.[29] But in the present context, the constitutional review of the coup is notable for other reasons too. For, even if it was less memorable than the violence and political intrigue surrounding Weimar's last days, the discussion of democracy's defense that took place in response to the federal government's intervention set fundamental challenges to liberal democracy. With Germany's most important constitutional theorists either in the courtroom or commenting from outside, what started as a legal argument became, as one scholar puts it, "a battle of legal philosophies."[30] The logic supporting the court's ruling declared Carl Schmitt the official winner. But it was democracy's implosion six months later that truly elevated this already prominent scholar in the annals of political and intellectual history, not only as the Nazis' most famous legal advisor – or the "Crown Jurist of the Third Reich," as he was called – but also as the man who astutely pinpointed the vulnerability of liberal democracy in modern pluralist societies.[31]

In his argument before the court as well as in his published work, Carl Schmitt repeatedly returned to what he perceived to be parliamentary democracy's inherently contradictory character. In moments of national crisis, no one would disagree that identifying the threat is a vital first step to reestablishing state security. Schmitt, however, argued that only the executive, as the true sovereign, was capable of and called to such a task; parliament was too entrenched

[26] Caldwell, *Crisis of German Constitutional Law*, 165–8; Dyzenhaus, *Legality and Legitimacy*, 31–6; Mommsen, *Rise and Fall of Weimar*, 452.

[27] E.g., Bracher, *Auflösung*, 556–63.

[28] Martin Broszat, *Hitler and the Collapse of Weimar Germany* (Oxford: Berg, 1987), 121.

[29] For this discussion: Caldwell, *Crisis of German Constitutional Law*, 174–5.

[30] David Dyzenhaus, "Legal Theory in the Collapse of Weimar: Contemporary Lessons?" *American Political Science Review* 91 (March 1997): 122.

[31] Carl Schmitt has experienced a renaissance and even rehabilitation of sorts, first in the mid-1990s when a new wave of translations familiarized English speakers with his greater body of work, and then again after September 11, 2001 placed the subject of democracy's defense back on many people's radar screens. For a review of newer literature, see Peter C. Caldwell, "Controversies over Carl Schmitt: A Review of Recent Literature," *Journal of Modern History* 77 (June 2005): 357–87. On Schmitt's far-reaching influence in Germany and farther afield, see Jans Werner Müller, *A Dangerous Mind: Carl Schmitt in Post-War European Thought* (New Haven: Yale University Press, 2003). Giorgio Agamben's *State of Exception*, trans. Kevin Attell (Chicago: Chicago University Press, 2005) makes clear the post-September 11 issues and debate.

in party interests and too hamstrung by its liberal commitment to neutrality and pluralism. In various tracts, Schmitt attacked legal positivism, the notion dominant among liberal thinkers such as his counterpart Hans Kelsen that, like a science, the essence of law can be found within laws themselves. Blind to the subjective aspects of law and justice, which entwined their practice with political interests and political power, liberal positivism presumed that the formal law-making process is neutral and therefore intervention in favor of one set of values over another is not only unnecessary but undemocratic in its violation of free, pluralist debate.[32] All of this Schmitt dismissed as the worst kind of delusion – for him, conflict was the very stuff of politics and its denial was liberalism's Achilles heel. Parliaments, he asserted, did not represent the people but rather the interests of their political parties; legislation was thus not the neutral product of mutually mediated truths but, at best, the tempered opinion of the ruling party or parties. When it came to protecting the state from those eager to exploit vulnerabilities in the system, Schmitt argued that only the president was equipped to handle the situation because only he stood above the conflict. Only he could legitimately distinguish legal from illegal parties, and it was this ability to determine friend from foe that ultimately defined sovereignty for Schmitt.[33] Far from neutral, the president was the "guardian" of the polity. He expressed the common will and guaranteed its supremacy (with all necessary bias) against the special interests that perpetually threatened to divide the German people and their state.[34]

What, then, did Schmitt concretely propose before the court as a solution? In a 1921 work entitled *Dictatorship*, Schmitt distinguished what he referred to as a "commissarial dictatorship" that temporarily suspends the constitution in order to protect its concrete existence from a sovereign dictatorship aiming to destroy existing institutions and replace them with an entirely new political order.[35] To no one's surprise, in August 1932, he therefore argued that the best way to protect the core of the Weimar constitution was to declare a state of exception and thereby legitimate the temporary suspension of those

[32] Hans Kelsen is widely considered the most important scholar of legal positivism in the twentieth century. Both Caldwell and Dyzenhaus's longer work provide excellent analyses of his work and contribution to Weimar jurisprudence.

[33] In the court case, for example, Schmitt argued that the decision by the SPD government to suppress the Nazis was illegal as they could not legitimately determine friend from foe on behalf of the larger polity. As parties involved in the struggle for parliamentary power, the ministers acted according to who was *their* friend and enemy. Dyzenhaus, *Legality and Legitimacy*, 33.

[34] Schmitt works out this position in a number of works during the Weimar period: Carl Schmitt, *The Concept of the Political*, trans. George Schwab (Chicago: University of Chicago Press, 1996); idem, *The Crisis of Parliamentary Democracy*, trans. Ellen Kennedy (Cambridge: MIT, 1994); idem, *Dictatorship* (Cambridge: Polity, 2012); idem, *Der Hüter der Verfassung* (Berlin: Duncker & Humblot, 1996). For an insightful treatment, see John P. McCormick, "The Dilemmas of Dictatorship: Carl Schmitt and Constitutional Emergency Powers," in *Law as Politics: Carl Schmitt's Critique of Liberalism*, ed. David Dyzenhaus (Durham: Duke University Press, 1998), 217–51.

[35] Carl Schmitt, *Dictatorship* (Cambridge: Polity, 2012).

constitutional provisions that inhibited the swift restoration of public order. It was, his opponents quickly pointed out, a supra-legal course of action that allowed the executive to go wholly unchecked, outside the bounds of the regular rule of law. In his commentary on the case, Hans Kelsen explicitly attacked this attempt by Schmitt to expand presidential power. He accused him of dressing up naked politics in a cloak of legality and for glorifying Article 48 to such an extent that parliamentary democracy itself could be regarded as a threat to public security.[36] Kelsen was every bit the brilliant constitutional theorist. But his own thinking on the court's decision seemed only to prove Schmitt correct, at least as far liberalism's suicidal tendencies were concerned.

Kelsen had long defended the court's right to review executive action, understanding it as simply the most effective way to ensure governments remained subject to the law. This did not, however, prevent him from openly criticizing what he saw as the court's "fundamentally and irreparably contradictory" decision in this case. In his assessment, the court's review of von Papen's actions vacillated between positions that granted the president unfettered powers of discretion and those that sought to limit that very discretion. Rather than blame the judges, however, Kelsen located the source of the problem in the constitution itself. He argued that the flawed ruling was the result of technical deficiencies, specifically the constitution's failure to provide effective checks for its own preservation. In the case of Article 48, the Reichstag had never gotten around to codifying the exact nature of legitimate state intervention (as Article 48, Paragraph 5 prescribed), and the court was thus left without a general norm dictating the limits of presidential power. Until this deficit was addressed, Kelsen stated, the proper use of emergency powers would remain a matter of interpretation, and in this he understood the presidential decree to be preferable to the court's read of Article 48. This was so, he argued, for no other reason than that the former was internally consistent. What mattered to a man of legal science was not whether the court ruled to uphold or invalidate the decree but rather that the order it issued be clear and constitutive – in this sense, there was no room in Kelsen's legal or political theory for the qualitative difference between the legal order of parliamentary democracy and that of a dictatorship.[37] This was, of course, precisely the neutrality for which Schmitt condemned positivist thinkers, and it lay at the heart of the problem democracy's defenders would struggle to overcome as they searched for solutions to the weaknesses Schmitt had diagnosed.

In a short essay devoted to the subject of democracy's defense, Hans Kelsen himself confronted the tension between legal neutrality and a pluralist society – what he summed up as democracy's "tragic fate" to support both its friends and its enemies.[38] For his part, he placed his hopes completely in the

[36] Dyzenhaus, "Legal Theory," 127.

[37] My discussion of Kelsen draws heavily from Dyzenhaus, *Legality and Legitimacy*, 102–60.

[38] Hans Kelsen, "Verteidigung der Demokratie," reprinted in *Demokratie und Sozialismus: Ausgewählte Aufsätze*, ed. Norbert Leser (Vienna: Wiener Volksbuchhandlung, 1967), 60–8. First published 1932.

self-governing population. If the time came when a democracy no longer had the support of its own citizens – as increasingly seemed the case in Germany – there was little to be done. The enforcement of democracy against majority opinion was a simple contradiction in terms for Kelsen, as any such act was, by definition, undemocratic. A state such as the Weimar Republic could not be defended from "the people," who were its own sovereign body. Standing on the precipice of National Socialist dictatorship when he wrote the piece, what possible avenues did Kelsen see open to democracy's defense? What guidance did he offer democrats at that late hour? With a note of bittersweet resolve, the jurist maintained his position that a democrat had no other recourse than to "remain true to his flag, even when the ship is sinking ... taking with him, into the depths, merely the hope that the ideal of freedom is indestructible and that the deeper it has sunk, the more passionately it will be restored."[39]

Many found Kelsen's odd combination of fatalism and optimism regarding democracy's defense far from satisfactory. But a fully developed counterposition that addressed the problems raised by both Schmitt and Kelsen came late, after the collapse of Germany's first republic, and from outside Germany, in the works of exiles Karl Loewenstein and Karl Mannheim. Writing independently at a time when fascism was at its height and the fate of liberal democracy very much in doubt, Loewenstein and Mannheim sought the source of democracy's existential crisis in order to save it. From their respective refuges in the United States and Great Britain, both men formulated a distinct solution to liberal democracy's defense based on their particular understanding of the threats to it posed by fascism and communism, which they grouped together as "totalitarian" movements. Loewenstein called upon democracies to fight fire with fire by equipping their states with powers normally associated with undemocratic government. Security was not to be found in the strict adherence to democratic principles once the state was under siege, he insisted, but rather in effectively undermining its enemies so as to return – as quickly as possible – to institutionalized, peacetime norms. Mannheim, too, believed that the only course of action was to beat fascism and communism at their own game. For him, however, this meant a program of social engineering through values education and state planning that would restore democracy as a force of inspiration and consensus. However different their visions, both men used the phrase "militant democracy" to refer to the form of democratic government whose time they believed had come – one capable of recognizing the challenges presented to it by mass politics and technological innovation and, subsequently, capable of fighting for its continued survival.[40] This new, militant democracy was not

[39] Ibid., 68.

[40] Thomas Mann is also sometimes referenced in relation to the concept. In 1937 he opined that the future German constitution must be one "of freedom tempered by authority, a manly regime which will withstand the temptations of the spirit to cast doubt on its earthly rights, and will know how to defend itself against fraud which uses freedom only to destroy it." See Thomas Mann, *War and Democracy* (Los Angeles: Adcraft, 1940) as well as Harry Pross, "On Thomas Mann's Political Career," *Journal of Contemporary History* 2 (April 1967): 65–80.

intended by either theorist to be a temporary solution to the challenges of fascism but rather a permanent improvement over what both Loewenstein and Mannheim saw as the outmoded liberal democracy of the previous century.

As early as 1931, jurist and political scientist Karl Loewenstein voiced the opinion that a democratic state had a duty to defend itself and that the usual means accorded it were insufficient.[41] Forced to flee Nazi Germany in 1934 and resettle in New England, Loewenstein's thinking on democracy's defense radicalized along with global events.[42] Indeed, by 1937 the optimism Loewenstein once possessed about democracy's progress had evaporated along with most of Europe's fledgling democracies. He saw the continent pitched in battle, with democracy on one side and "autocracy" – which he understood as synonymous with a politics and government of emotional manipulation – on the other.[43] What was incredible to Loewenstein was that democracy might lose the fight due to the sheer passivity brought on by the sort of "naïve romanticism" expressed by Kelsen and what he referred to as the "tolerant confidence" that truth and history were on democracy's side. Weimar's collapse was, in his assessment, the result of a "democratic fundamentalism and legalistic blindness" that allowed democracy's enemies the freedom to destroy it.[44] In Italy and Germany, "democracy was doomed to failure ... because it was pacifist instead of militant."[45] As Loewenstein understood it, the challenge fascism presented to democracy was less ideological than tactical. It was a political technique designed to gain and maintain power by capitalizing on the fact that liberal democracy had no way of deflecting antidemocratic politics dressed "in the garb of legality, propaganda, and military symbolism."[46] This was its strength but, as Loewenstein was keen to underscore, also its weakness, for fascism and the "politics of emotionalism" it practiced depended upon the uninhibited circulation of its propaganda. If democracy was going to win the war against fascism, it had to overcome "constitutional scruples" and the notion that any kind of encroachment on "democratic fundamentals" automatically endangered democracy:

> If democracy believes in the superiority of its absolute values over the opportunistic platitudes of fascism, it must live up to the demands of the hour, and every possible effort must be made to rescue it, even at the risk and cost of violating fundamental principles.[47]

[41] Loewenstein stated this in reference to internal sabotage in a discussion over electoral reform. Vereinigung der deutschen Staatsrechtslehrer, *Verhandlungen der Tagung der Deutschen Staatsrechtslehrer zu Halle am 28. und 29. Oktober 1931* (Berlin: Walter de Gruyter, 1932), 192–3.

[42] For a rare glimpse into the man behind the concept, see Markus Lang, *Karl Loewenstein: Transatlantischer Denker der Politik* (Stuttgart: Franz Steiner, 2007).

[43] Karl Loewenstein, "Autocracy versus Democracy," *American Political Science Review* 29 (1935): 571–93, 755–84.

[44] Karl Loewenstein, "Militant Democracy and Fundamental Rights, I and II," *American Political Science Review* 31 (1937): 417–32 and 638–58. Here, 423–4.

[45] Loewenstein, "Autocracy vs. Democracy," 580.

[46] Loewenstein, "Militant Democracy," 426.

[47] Ibid., 431–2.

Fascism's exploitation of civil liberties and the rule of law laid bare the truly intolerable nature of democratic tolerance.

Loewenstein's rhetoric and logic undoubtedly evoked conditions of war. If, in developing its own technique for maintaining power, democracy "learns from its ruthless enemy and applies a modicum of the coercion that autocracy will not hesitate to apply against democracy," it could hardly be blamed.[48] To his mind, the basic principles of liberal democracy were designed for times of peace, not crisis; every democracy made concessions – whether explicit or not – in order to maintain a functioning government in a state of siege. Indeed, the First World War provided him with ready examples of democratic governments that had, in a time of crisis, copied their autocratic enemies' concentration of powers and suspension of fundamental rights and done so without destroying constitutional government in the long run. In the current fight against fascism, Loewenstein advocated legislative and judicial measures that would deny extremists the public platform they so desperately required for success. In addition to strengthening existing criminal codes, Loewenstein called for legislation that directly targeted subversive groups' legal status, their propaganda apparatuses, and their paramilitary forces. Such legislative acts included banning subversive parties as well as the commission or incitement of political violence (via armed groups, propaganda against specific groups or individuals, and "hooliganism"), the suspension of civil liberties (freedom of speech, press, and political representation when used for antidemocratic ends), a heightened control of all civil servants, and the creation of a political police force responsible for monitoring subversive activities.[49] Loewenstein did not deny the repressive and ultimately undemocratic nature of these measures, and what he described came close to Schmitt's "commissarial dictatorship." The crucial difference was that in Loewenstein's scenario, emergency powers were legislated by parliament, thus maintaining their democratic character. He was convinced that if democracy was not to be undermined by the rabble-rousing emotionalism of self-appointed leaders, it had to be revised to meet the new conditions of mass society and the technological age. The good old days of nineteenth-century liberal politics were over but those who sought to control the emotionalism of the masses could, in Loewenstein's words, "be made, by constitutional processes, ultimately and irrevocably responsible to the people."[50]

Loewenstein was the first to admit, however, that even the most perfectly conceived statutes were worthless if not accompanied by the state's will to survive – the same will to unity and action that won wars. In this, Loewenstein's essay was just as much a response to the antidemocratic treatises of Carl Schmitt

48 Loewenstein, "Autocracy vs. Democracy," 593.

49 Loewenstein assembled his list from what seemed the successful measures adopted by various democratic governments in Europe over the course of the 1930s. See esp. "Militant Democracy," 638–58.

50 A running theme throughout the two-part essay, this argument appears most succinctly in Loewenstein's conclusion. Ibid., 657–8.

as it was to legal theorists like Kelsen. Though Loewenstein would later, as a leading advisor to American occupation forces, push for Schmitt's prosecution as a war criminal, there is little doubt that he took Schmitt's critique of liberalism seriously as a diagnosis of the problems and weaknesses besetting democracy in the twentieth century.[51] Militant democracy was Loewenstein's proposed antidote not only to contain the fascist threat but for the ailments liberal democracy suffered more generally. Critical of liberalism's "suicidal lethargy" but not of liberalism per se, Loewenstein ultimately took a typically liberal position against political extremism and the organized detours into mass mysticism (the breeding ground of autocracy) that, to his mind, characterized interwar European and modern politics as a whole. Loewenstein did not envision extensive state intervention – this would have been as incompatible with liberalism, and thus his particular conception of democracy, as political extremism. Instead, he promoted a focused strategy aimed at securing the social conditions for democracy. His definition of democratic militancy also extended to include the international realm, with the argument that democracies must approach their troubled neighbors with the same will to unity and action that they showed enemies at home. This included, if necessary, waging war against antidemocratic states.[52] After 1945, Loewenstein turned away from the active defense of liberalism to its propagation, concentrating on the political tutelage of new or at-risk allies of the Western bloc in the Cold War era. But his attack on the "dogma of internal self-determination" proved that he insisted as adamantly as ever that liberal democracy should not fall victim to outdated concepts and blind confidence. Calling for the same political intolerance he had advocated when democracy was struggling to survive, Loewenstein flatly rejected the principle of nonintervention – specifically the notion that, after such a hard-won victory in an unprecedentedly destructive war, any country might be allowed to choose a nondemocratic government. Once again, in the struggle for a peaceful world order, neutral respect for others' self-determination was not an option; if the democratic nations were not to end up in a third world war, they had to actively promote democracy's global proliferation.[53] Of course, in an era when democracy's definition was not simply contested but everyone called themselves democratic, Loewenstein gave few pointers on how democratic states were to identify friend from foe – other than his own implicit assumption that friends, democrats, and liberals were all of a kind.

[51] In his memoirs, Loewenstein opined that if Schmitt's critique of liberalism had been taken seriously it would have saved the Weimar Republic. On Loewenstein's postwar engagement with Schmitt, see Lang, *Transatlantischer Denker*, 249–52.

[52] Though he had earlier referenced the need for a "democratic International," it was not until after war broke out in Europe and Loewenstein sought to convince Americans of their need to enter it that his vision of militant democracy called for intervention abroad. Karl Loewenstein and Lawrence Packard, *America's Eleventh Hour* (Easthampton, MA: Easthampton News Co., 1940).

[53] Karl Loewenstein, *Political Reconstruction* (New York: Macmillan, 1946).

As a lecturer and later professor of education in Great Britain, sociologist Karl Mannheim also sought the answer to democracy's defense in the conditions that led to fascism's swift rise among the democracies of Europe.[54] However, the conclusions he reached suggested a much more expansive line of attack was needed if democracy was to regain its footing. Like Loewenstein, Mannheim blamed the current crisis on liberalism mistaking neutrality for tolerance and its subsequent failure to privilege – and thus defend – its own set of beliefs and objectives over those of others. By perverting the meaning of democratic tolerance (as well as that of scientific objectivity), liberal democracy had essentially taught its citizens *not* to stand up for what they believed but rather to avoid controversial subjects, heated debate, and thus critical learning in a general "neutralization" of thought and attitude.[55] Mannheim poured a good deal of vitriol on liberalism's pedagogical shortcomings because his developing interest in education was intimately tied to his conviction that democracy had to wage a war against fascism. In striking contrast to Loewenstein, he understood this war to be primarily "a war of ideas" – winnable only by proving democracy the better doctrine. Democracy teetered on the brink of collapse precisely because its citizens – particularly its youth – had no idea what they believed in and could therefore offer little "mental resistance" to the new totalitarian campaigns against it.[56] Militant democracy, as Mannheim envisioned it, aimed to rectify this situation and thereby ensure democracy's survival.

Mannheim strove to save the abstract concept of democracy and refashion it into a new form of democratic government that was more powerful and more actively committed to the concept of human freedom. The success of fascism and communism clarified for him the reactive nature of "laissez-faire democracy." It struggled only to maintain the status quo and was therefore slow to adapt to new situations within society or even constructively to discuss the changes required to address them. Mannheim's prescription was quite straightforward. If democracy was to survive, it had to be alive; it had once again to be a vibrant doctrine possessing "true and timely ideas" that "appealed to the imagination of [the] younger generation," not least by remaining open to the kind of change Mannheim associated with youth.[57] The first step toward a militant and dynamic democracy thus began with developing the "courage to agree" on the "right procedure of social change and those basic virtues and values … which are the basis of the peaceful functioning of a social order."[58] Described as a cooperative effort, this new consensus was to lay the foundation

[54] In this section I draw primarily from the second edition of Mannheim's *Diagnosis of Our Time: Wartime Essays of a Sociologist* (London: K. Paul, Trench, Trubner, 1943). On the evolution of Mannheim's critique of liberalism and ideas on democratic planning, see Colin Loader, *The Intellectual Development of Karl Mannheim: Culture, Politics, and Planning* (Cambridge: Cambridge University Press, 1985).

[55] Mannheim, *Diagnosis of Our Time*, esp. 7, 67–70.

[56] Ibid., 73.

[57] Ibid., 61.

[58] Ibid., 7.

for democratic security simply by exchanging neutrality for principled clarity and silence for active discussion. The second condition was no less critical than the first. Mannheim was adamant that suppressing the discussion of vital issues – a strategy often employed by embattled democracies – would not protect the basic consensus that every democratic government needed in order to function. These, after all, were the defensive tactics of a weak democracy that only crippled the constructive powers of the population, led to political stasis, and recruited friends for the enemies of democracy.[59] Democratic consensus could only be achieved by the open and constant engagement of ideas, for the only insurance against militancy tipping over into repression or reverting back into lethargy was revision and reform. Yet Mannheim stated in no uncertain terms that the last decades had confirmed "that the citizen ... has a perfect right to hate and to exclude those who wish to misuse the methods of freedom for abolishing freedom."[60] How was one to distinguish between the sort of constructive criticism that was crucial for democracy's revitalization and the sort of anticonsensual behavior that could legitimately be excluded? Here, the means were decisive. For, according to Mannheim:

> [T]he essential thing about true democracy is that differences in opinion do not kill solidarity as long as there is fundamental agreement on the method of agreement, i.e. that the peaceful settlement of differences is better than one by violence. Democracy is essentially a method of social change, the institutionalization of the belief that adjustment to changing reality and the reconciliation of diverse interests can be brought about by conciliatory means, with the help of discussion, bargaining and integral consensus.[61]

Social conflict did not need to be eradicated to keep democracy safe, but it had to adhere to the nonviolent procedures institutionalized in parliamentary democracy.

Without a doubt Mannheim's approach to democracy's defense betrayed a pedagogue's emphasis on the importance of the means for the successful realization of the end and was nothing if not holistic. While he rejected the repressive techniques of dictatorship, he also argued for the comprehensive coordination of social processes and the deliberate cultivation of a society's values.[62] Mannheim had little doubt that the furthering of democratic consent relied on overcoming the social injustices perpetuated by unregulated capitalism as well as actively fostering citizens' democratic thinking. He thus regarded social planning and education as essential components of a militant democracy. For years, Mannheim had fought against identifying planned with totalitarian societies, arguing that a planned society could, in fact, be democratically controlled.[63] As representatives of the popular will, parliament could hold planners

[59] Ibid., 68.

[60] Ibid., 49.

[61] Ibid., 69.

[62] Ibid., 46.

[63] Mannheim developed this argument most extensively in *Man and Society in an Age of Reconstruction: Studies in Modern Social Structure* (New York: Harcourt, Brace, and World, 1940).

accountable to those whose lives they planned. And the pedagogical cultivation of democratic personalities – secure, open to change, tolerant of others, with an awareness of the world and their responsibilities to it – would eventually pay off in new generations of citizens capable of mentally resisting antidemocratic propaganda and democratic planners trained to intelligently conceive of a total scheme of action accepted by all.[64] It was not planning that threatened democratic freedom, in Mannheim's opinion, but rather the failure to acknowledge and take control of the state's growing and increasingly centralized administrative functions. Indeed, a government that coupled modern regulatory techniques with new education strategies on the basis of a new consensus on basic values would have the power to match legal with social equality, balance individual against community interests, and foster democratic consciousness – and thereby promote democracy's health and defense.[65] Militant democracy was nothing less than a "third way" – *the* alternative to the old crisis-ridden liberal democracies and the new dictatorships of Hitler and Stalin that promised to save democracy from the former and economic planning from the latter. Direction, or "co-ordination," was Mannheim's answer to keeping democracy alive and on the offensive.

Mannheim's critique of liberalism and faith in productive conflict may have made him appear radical compared to Loewenstein, but at the end of the day both men shared a similar confidence in legislation and democratic institutions. Indeed, it was precisely this that freed one man to embrace undemocratic measures and the other to reject them for coordinated planning. After 1945, of course, the sort of social engineering and political policing advocated by Mannheim and Loewenstein, respectively, resonated uncomfortably with the policies of the Nazi regime. But the idea of militant democracy was far from dead. On the one hand, the sense that democracy could not simply pick up where it had left off in the interwar period was widespread. On the other hand, the Red Army's presence in Eastern Europe coupled by the swiftly cooling friendship between Stalin and the Western Allies convinced many liberal and socialist anticommunists that democracy desperately needed defending. Perhaps then it is of little surprise that in West Germany, where memories of Weimar's collapse vied with fears of Soviet aggression, the concept of militant democracy was eagerly pursued in both its variations.

[64] Mannheim, *Diagnosis of Our Time*, 31–53; 102.

[65] Ibid., 1–11; 100–30; 144–6.

1

Democracy Made Militant

The Federal Republic of Germany

> [T]he mechanism of democracy is the Trojan horse by which the enemy enters the city.
>
> Karl Loewenstein (1937)[1]

Many have described West German reconstruction as a search for economic stability driven by memories of destitution and severe material shortages as well as a general rejection of politics after fascism.[2] Crucial as the experience of scarcity was to Germans' stark desire for security, neither their postwar political endeavors nor their sense of well-being can be summed up as a single-minded pursuit of material wealth. For the first time in history, Germans' fate was understood to depend on democracy's success. Diverse political loyalties and Germans' particular experiences of National Socialism guaranteed that their visions for postwar democracy varied greatly, but all understood it to be the solution to the moral, material, and political crisis besetting postfascist Germany. Germans from various walks of life thus took seriously the political and social reconstruction before them. If they had questioned democracy's viability before 1933, however, recent events seemed only to confirm their fears regarding the weaknesses of representative government. Democratic stability thus remained a source of anxiety for postwar Germans while the radically heightened stakes – political and moral catastrophe – expanded the scope of what might legitimately be done to protect democracy.

1 Karl Loewenstein, "Militant Democracy and Fundamental Rights, Part I." *The American Political Science Review* 31 (June 1937): 424.

2 See, e.g., Hartmut Kaelble, ed., *Der Boom 1948–1973: Gesellschaftliche und wirtschaftliche Folgen in der Bundesrepublik Deutschland und in Europa* (Opladen: Westdeutscher, 1992); Michael Wildt, *Am Beginn der "Konsumgesellschaft": Mangelerfahrung, Lebenshaltung, Wohlstandshoffnung in Westdeutschland in den fünfziger Jahren* (Hamburg: Ergebnisse Verlag, 1994); Lutz Niethammer, "'Normalization' in the West: Traces of Memory Leading Back into the 1950s," in *The Miracle Years: A Cultural History of West Germany, 1949–1968*, ed. Hannah Schissler (Princeton: Princeton University Press, 2001), 237–65.

Intent as they were to avoid the mistakes of the past, it is hardly surprising that the Weimar Republic loomed large in the debates on democracy's future. Its tragic demise crystallized German fears regarding the fate of democratic government at the same time it offered a guide for what not to do the second time around.[3] Of course, it was the occupying powers who ultimately established the conditions for German discussions. As the Allies turned from fighting fascism to fighting one another, "democracy" became part of the Cold War's semantic arsenal, with its definition sharply limited to the dictates of Anglo-American liberalism and Soviet communism. Germans in both the western and eastern zones had little choice but to conform to the swiftly changing climate. In the west it was agreed that a new kind of political order was called for in Germany, one that openly proclaimed a bias toward democracy and defended it and its values from those who sought their destruction. This commitment to a "militant democracy" had significant consequences for postwar political culture. Almost overnight, democracy's defense went from a point of academic debate to a cornerstone of West Germany's liberal order, evident in the constitutional designation of the state as a *wehrhafte Demokratie* – literally, a democracy well-fortified to defend itself – and in the vigorous contemporary endorsement of citizens' moral obligation to resist tyranny and antidemocratic forces wherever they appeared.

Conscious of Germany's weaknesses – not only in regards to democratic traditions but also as a state deprived of national sovereignty and the active support of its citizenry – the constitutional framers steadfastly pursued a course intent on avoiding a state of emergency both now and in the future. By doing their best to circumscribe the possibilities for war, economic crisis, or internal revolt, they hoped to circumvent any actual test of German democracy – the strength of its institutions or its political culture. This shared goal did not eliminate genuine differences in the participants' worldviews, however, and whenever discussion touched on the necessary conditions for political security, these differences threatened to prove irreconcilable. The subject was divisive not least because it ran up against differing visions of democratic governance and legitimate state power. Two distinct strains of thinking on what it meant for a democratic state to be militant ultimately emerged in the debate. One resembled Karl Loewenstein's vision in its preference for negative (in the non-normative sense) measures commonly associated with strong, even authoritarian states. In this scenario, executive power and the use of coercive force were understood as an exceptional and temporary response to an equally exceptional, temporary situation. The other scenario approached state and society more holistically, echoing Karl Mannheim's faith that efforts in social engineering might positively (again, in the non-normative sense) create and then maintain the conditions necessary for democracy. As the largest of the postwar political parties

[3] For an overview: Sebastion Ullrich, *Der Weimar-Komplex: Das Scheitern der ersten deutschen Demokratie und die politische Kultur der frühen Bundesrepublik, 1945–1959* (Göttingen: Wallstein, 2009).

and frequently at odds with one another, the newly formed Christian Union (CDU/CSU) and the reconstituted Social Democratic Party came to roughly represent these two different conceptions of militant democracy and to fight for their preferred definition's codification in the new West German constitution, or Basic Law.

By the end of the 1960s, the CDU/CSU was the undisputed victor of the debate in as far as militant democracy was (and is now) understood exclusively in terms of its conservative variant. But, as this chapter will demonstrate, the exact parameters of a fortified democracy were not established by the ratification of the Basic Law in May 1949 and Social Democrats did not abandon their original conception of what constituted legitimate state intervention. This ensured that the debate over executive privilege, armed force (police and military), and emergency legislation did not end in 1949 but continued on, among political and intellectual elites and, as time passed, among growing numbers of West Germans concerned that their first chancellor, Konrad Adenauer, did not have democracy's best interests at heart. His pursuit of rearmament and emergency laws would undoubtedly fortify the West German state but, many asked, at what cost? This question kept the subject of democratic militancy on the table and open for debate until the end of the 1960s.

FORTIFYING DEMOCRACY IN THE BASIC LAW

When the Allied powers occupied Germany in 1945, they found that the Germans had not waited for them – or the end of the Third Reich – to begin discussing what form the future German state should take. Exiles in New York City and Moscow, members of resistance groups, and even prisoners in Buchenwald had sketched proposals for a future German constitution in anticipation of Hitler's fall.[4] These, as well as the hundreds of constitutional drafts drawn up at the war's end, formed the basis for discussions carried out in the journals, political circles, and social networks that sprouted up in the first years of occupation – discussions calling for everything from the radical social and economic restructuring of Germany, to a United States of Germany that placed decisive power with the Länder, to a mere updating of the Weimar constitution.[5] Though one should not exaggerate the average German's interest in this early constitutional debate – when many struggled simply to survive – the sheer number of proposals sent by private citizens to the American military

[4] Wolfgang Benz, "Konzeptionen für die Nachkriegsdemokratie: Pläne und Überlegungen im Widerstand, im Exil und in der Besatzungszeit," in *Deutschland nach Hitler: Zukunftspläne im Exil und aus der Besatzungszeit, 1939–49*, eds. Thomas Koebner, Gert Sautermeister, and Sigrid Schneider-Grube (Opladen: Westdeutscher, 1987), 201–13.

[5] Not all of them envisioned a democratic, let alone a liberal democratic, state. A representative sample has been republished in Wolfgang Benz, ed., *Bewegt von der Hoffnung aller Deutschen: Zur Geschichte des Grundgesetzes. Entwürfe und Diskussionen 1941–1949* (Munich: Deutscher Taschenbuch, 1979).

government or directly to General Clay suggests that what form the future German state would take was more than an elite preoccupation.[6]

The pressure to fulfill the basic needs of a war-ravaged population, coupled with initial uncertainty over Germany's fate as a nation, meant that reconstruction began at the local and regional levels. Not until the summer of 1948, after a U.S.-initiated currency reform and the subsequent Soviet blockade of Berlin, was the plan to create a separate western German state implemented and the process of drafting a federal constitution set in motion. On July 1, the Western Allies officially presented the minister presidents of the existing Länder with the "Frankfurt Documents" outlining their guidelines for a West German state.[7] Document I specifically addressed the constitution and preempted German discussion by dictating that the new state must take the form of a parliamentary democracy structured along federalist lines with an "adequate central authority." A third document took up the future relationship between the German government and the Allied authorities. Among other things it stipulated that in the case of a political or military emergency, the Western Allies retained the right to seize control of the German state until order had once again been restored.[8]

Under these strictures and ongoing supervision by the occupying powers, Germans in the three western zones set about drafting a constitution. A convention dominated by legal experts gathered to hammer out fundamental issues at a Bavarian villa in Herrenchiemsee, closely followed by a larger Parliamentary Council ultimately responsible for presenting the Allies with an acceptable draft.[9] Both bodies confirmed the strong presence of political parties in West German reconstruction. In addition to the reestablishment of the Communist (KPD) and Social Democratic parties, liberals of progressive and nationalist persuasions came together in the new Liberal Democratic Party, while the wide range of Christian and conservative impulses that existed before and after the war were corralled in the Christian Democratic Union and Christian Social Union (CSU). A number of small (and generally short-lived) parties also attended the proceedings, though they, like the KPD and the FDP, were dramatically outnumbered by the SPD and CDU/CSU delegates. With the exception of the KPD, who continued to fight the creation of a western German state, the different parties proved willing to compromise and adhere

[6] Edmund Spevack, *Allied Control and German Freedom* (Piscataway, NJ: Transaction, 2001), 262.

[7] *Der Parlamentarische Rat 1948–1949: Akten und Protokolle*, ed. Volker Wagner, vol. 1, *Vorgeschichte* (Boppard am Rhein: Harald Boldt, 1975), 17–21 (hereafter, *Parl. Rat* 1).

[8] The Frankfurt Documents reprinted in *Der Parlamentarische Rat 1948–1949: Akten und Protokolle*, ed. Peter Bucher, vol. 2, *Der Verfassungskonvent auf Herrenchiemsee* (Boppard am Rhein: Harald Boldt, 1981), 30–5 (hereafter, *Parl. Rat* 2).

[9] For a concise history of the Parliamentary Council, see Michael F. Feldkamp, *Der Parlamentarische Rat, 1948–1949* (Göttingen: Vandenhoeck & Ruprecht, 1998). For the history and debates of the Constitutional Convention at Herrenchiemsee before the Council convened, see *Parl. Rat* 2, esp. VII–CXXVIII.

to Allied expectations in order to achieve the measure of self-government that even a provisional constitution promised. Because of this, the Parliamentary Council is remembered both positively and negatively for its moderate politics. Those who hoped for radical change undoubtedly experienced it as a missed opportunity, which neither charted a third way between "Western" liberalism and "Eastern" state socialism nor broke thoroughly with the logics and institutions of Germany's past. Regardless, the Constitutional Convention and Parliamentary Council offered an important forum for postwar political debate, one furthered by commentary from critical publicists, constitutional scholars, and their reading publics.

For, along with whatever other baggage the new constitution can be accused of retaining, it also held on to Germans' pessimism regarding democracy's viability. Indeed, the conviction that democracy did not stand a chance if left to its own devices was a strong source of consensus as well as a guiding principle in the drafting of the new constitution. Even if the delegations did not define democracy the same way, they were each determined to create a state capable of functioning in times of crisis as well as peace. They agreed that this time around, German democracy would reject all claims of neutrality and be equipped with the tools to defend itself against harm. Widespread agreement on the need to fortify democracy against future disaster, however, immediately ran up against diverging perceptions of where the greatest danger to democracy lay and who or what was its best safeguard. These were far from small differences of opinion but reflected each party's particular understanding of democracy, the preconditions necessary to its success, and, correspondingly, what form the new German state should take. The Basic Law as a whole, then, and not merely the articles devoted to its explicit defense, must be viewed as part of the founders' attempts to realize a militant democracy.

The debate over whether the future state's form should be a confederation of states (*Staatenbund*), a federal state (*Bundesstaat*), or a decentralized unitary state (*Einheitsstaat*) is a case in point. The question of federalism brought out strong disagreements over where the greatest threat to democratic freedom lay – at the federal or Land level. Though the Frankfurt Documents established that the western German state was to be federalist in form, little consensus existed over how power was to be distributed between the federal and state levels and what constituted an "adequate central authority." The proposed answers to these questions roughly divided the council in two, with the SPD, Communists, and left-leaning members of the FDP blaming democracy's previous failure on an excess of federalism, and the conservative parties arguing that only strong Länder could protect freedom in the new state. Both sides betrayed a concern with the experiences of Weimar and National Socialism and argued that their preferred state formation held the key to overcoming the political conflict attendant on the deep social fissures of modern industrial society. Though the paths they pursued to achieve it varied dramatically, the constitution's framers agreed that social cohesion – that which had eluded Germany's earlier nation builders – was essential to the new republic's fortification.

The diverse group of Christians that came together under the banner of the CDU/CSU tended to share the conviction that democracy could not exist without federalism. Though they differed greatly over the degree of sovereignty to be granted the member states, with southern Germans generally (and the CSU in particular) supporting a confederation of states over northerners' vision of a more unitary state, all argued that federalism made for a healthy, vital democracy of the sort the Weimar Republic had lacked. At the most basic level, German federalists refuted that "democracy from above" was, in fact, democratic and insisted that individual states maintain significant independence and an organized voice in national politics.[10] Germans' recent experience with centralized power provided ready evidence of centralization's perils; when sparring over federal and state jurisdiction, federalists repeatedly reached for the examples of National Socialism and of Soviet communism to argue that centralism paved the way to dictatorship. In his capacity as the official speaker for the CDU/CSU, Adolf Süsterhenn described the task of creating a constitution as "a spiritual decision [*geistige Entscheidung*]," with the goal to reflect the nation's character, cultural structure, and social fabric.[11] Defining federalism as the opposite of the "totalitarian centralized compulsory systems" in which "personal freedom and human dignity have neither ethical nor political value," Süsterhenn did not doubt that the spirit of Germany was a federalist one. In debate, the lawyer Otto Küster built off this by explicitly linking the rise of Nazism to the extremism of national government. In his opinion, stability against crisis was the number one reason to have a federalist system, for only the Länder could provide the necessary local safeguards against a distanced national politics prone to "fevers" and party struggles.[12] Others looked to the Länder to break what they described as the undemocratic and stifling power monopoly exercised by party machines at the national level.[13] Here, and elsewhere, conservatives unmistakably voiced their distrust of mass democracy. Federalism, as Süsterhenn had it, was "a vote for freedom" and "against oppression in individual or parliamentary form."[14]

[10] See, e.g., Friedrich Glum, "Bemerkungen zum organisatorischen Teil einer künftigen deutschen Verfassung," *Süddeutsche Juristen Zeitung* 3 (March 1948): 113–18. Glum, the Bavarian government's constitutional expert, may have been most explicit but this point underscored the federalist position as a whole.

[11] *Der Parlamentarische Rat 1948–1949: Akten und Protokolle*, ed. Wolfram Werner, vol. 9, *Plenum* (Munich: Harald Boldt, 1996), 54 (hereafter, *Parl. Rat* 9).

[12] Küster cited Länder governments' campaign against the introduction of Reich commissioners to the Reichsrat as evidence of their independence and organized resistance in 1933. *Parl. Rat* 2, 131. See also Otto Küster, "Föderative Probleme einer deutschen Verfassung," *Süddeutsche Juristen Zeitung* 3 (March 1948): 118–31.

[13] Friedrich Glum best articulated this desire to end parties' monopoly on national politics. He not only advocated for a second legislative house – a Länder parliament, or Bundesrat – but he proposed it be the sole representative organ. He was, needless to say, for a radical federalist state formation. See Glum, "Bemerkungen," 116–17.

[14] *Parl. Rat* 9, 54.

Federalists' conviction that democracy was best served in a political structure where power originated with the Länder did not, however, rely solely on negative definitions of centralized power. Many arguments in favor of federalism started with the assumption that self-government was a natural right of individuals, families, congregations, and communities of widely varying size. To protect this right, members of the CDU/CSU argued for a federalist solution in which decisions were made at the lowest level of authority possible. The essence of this subsidiarity principle – long a cornerstone of Catholic social doctrine – was captured by one delegate's insistence that "what the family can achieve [on its own] should be ... the responsibility of the family." Only that which it – or the Länder – could not effectively accomplish should pass to a more centralized authority.[15] So conceived, federalism was a structuring of power based not only on the tenet that power tends toward abuse but, just as importantly, on the recognition of the rights and duties that evolved organically from immediate relations among persons – for which the family was assumed to constitute the "natural" model.

Federalism promised more than the protection of basic rights, however. Its proponents argued it held the key to overcoming political apathy and social conflict by directly involving more people in decision-making processes which, in turn, would reestablish the importance of individual and communal experience in national politics. Central to this was a deep appreciation for associational life, what Süsterhenn described as the wealth of independent organizations connecting individuals to the nation-state as well as to one another. A federalist system, he argued, would (re)personalize politics and ensure a pluralist society in which individual personalities were allowed to develop freely according to their customs and beliefs.[16] Eugon Kogon, a left-wing Catholic who indirectly contributed to the proceedings as a publicist and as a member of the influential Ellwanger Circle, agreed. In Kogon's words, federalism was essential to realizing a democracy that approximated "a lively organism, not a schema" and a freedom that was "the fruit not of constraining, but rather stabilizing, bonds as suggested by nature and by the tasks at hand."[17] Süsterhenn insisted that the "manifoldly subdivided organism" was *the* guardian of rights and general well-being; Kogon understood it to offer an alternative to the liberal individualism and communism tearing Europe – and Germany – apart. In the end, the two men had distinctly different visions for society, and Kogon parted company with the CDU when it became clear that his vision was not widely shared by its members.[18] But both understood local or state-level self-government as the first step to securing a democratic culture.

[15] Johannes Brockmann in ibid., 145.

[16] Süsterhenn in ibid., 58, 55.

[17] Eugon Kogon, "Demokratie und Föderalismus," *Frankfurter Hefte* 1 (September 1946): 66–78.

[18] On the history of the Hessian CDU's left-wing founders, including Kogon, and the rapid eclipse of this direction within the party, see Joachim Rotberg, *Zwischen Linkskatholizismus und bürgerlicher Sammlung: Die Anfänge der CDU in Frankfurt am Main 1945–1946* (Frankfurt: Knecht, 1999).

Where the federalists saw plurality and vibrant politics, the Social Democrats saw backwater provincialism, regional separatism, and a politics strangled by traditional elites. And with conservatives favoring federalism at least in part as a check on the national assembly, Social Democrats had one more reason to oppose granting the Länder significant powers. Indeed, the SPD's legal experts were perhaps nowhere more eloquent than when they described the perils of federalism and their belief that democracy and peace could only be achieved by a central government's guiding hand. The party's constitutional expert, Walter Menzel, and rising star Carlo Schmid both railed against the competing provincial interests of the Länder that, in their minds, too often impeded the effective functioning of the national government and thus progress itself. Each associated particularist politics, social and economic disparity, political irresponsibility, and popular apathy with federalism and in this way understood the Länder to be the main obstacle to a prosperous democratic society. Schmid equated strong federalism with a politically doomed state stymied in archaic milieu mentalities and the bourgeois "Biedermeierei" of the previous century.[19] Concern for the common good routinely lost out to individual and group self-interest. Following this logic, a loosening of individual Länder loyalties would encourage a more other-regarding, national politics – the necessary first step toward what men such as Menzel and Schmid understood to be an international and thus future- and peace-orientated politics.[20] To overcome provincialism and place democracy on sure footing, therefore, the SPD sought to arm the state so that essential powers, even when executed at the local or regional level, originated with the federal government. As Schmid proclaimed at the outset of the Parliamentary Council, the SPD's motto was "construction from below but planning from above!"[21]

The importance of this decentralized centrism to Social Democrats' vision of militant democracy was articulated by Hermann Brill, a former Reichstag deputy, who asserted that relying on resistance or action of any sort in the moment of crisis was woefully shortsighted: "Should the dam break again, as we experienced it [in 1933], the flood will not be held back by any artificial institutions."[22] Social Democrats maintained that prevention – via state-directed planning and finely crafted legislation – was necessary to build and protect democracy in Germany. Indeed, a kind of legal perfectionism characterized the SPD's efforts not merely to contain abuses of power and reactionary tendencies within the constitutional-legal order, but to eliminate both by using that framework itself to reshape state and society. For this reason, for

[19] Carlo Schmid, "Gliederung und Einheit: Die verfassungspolitischen Richtlinien der SPD," *Die Gegenwart* 3 (August 20, 1948): 15–17; idem, "Rückblick auf die Verhandlungen," *Die Wandlung* 4 (July 1949): 652–69. Also, Petra Weber, *Carlo Schmid: 1896–1979: Eine Biographie* (Munich: Beck, 1996), 286ff.

[20] Walter Menzel, "Zur deutschen Verfassung," *Die Zeit*, April 17, 1947; Schmid, "Gliederung und Einheit;" idem, "Rückblick auf die Verhandlungen."

[21] *Parl. Rat* 9, Zweite Sitzung des Plenums, September 8, 1948, 44.

[22] *Parl. Rat* 2, 132–3.

example, the SPD insisted on federal priority over the Länder in fiscal matters. Not trusting affluent regions and districts to give to the less fortunate or the Länder governments to act in anyone's interests but their own, Social Democrats understood a centralized economy to be the only solution to the social and economic disparity that plagued Germany, especially given wartime devastation and the demands of reconstruction. Granting power to the federal government over finances aimed at the equalization of wealth – a long-standing Social Democratic demand that would democratize prosperity and avoid the disharmony and popular unrest that characterized modern German history. Similarly, the SPD deemed a unified legal code crucial for the realization and maintenance of democracy. To the minds of Social Democrats, a unified legal system leveled the political playing field and gave all German citizens a common language of governance as well as an understanding of the rights accorded them by the new state. Together with economic equality, it would safeguard democracy from below by ensuring that democracy was alive and meaningful for those who lived under it.

The democratizing power that the SPD attributed to the federal government also explained its members' position on federal police power. No one, not even Social Democrats, wanted a centralized police force due to its strong association with the Nazi state, which first took police power from the hands of local authorities. Members of the Parliamentary Council agreed that a federal police and a federal criminal police were potential instruments of state terror and inconsistent with democratic rule.[23] Social Democrats, however, considered police force particularly prone to abuse at the local level, where, according to them, police chiefs often resembled "little führers."[24] They insisted that the federal government could – and should – curtail these tendencies and that equipping the new state with a modicum of police power now, at its founding, would prevent having to do so later, under extralegal (thus uncontrolled and potentially undemocratic) circumstances. In that spirit, the SPD proposed a federal police agency (*Bundespolizeiwesen*) that would, on the one hand, collect and disseminate intelligence information, and on the other, regulate all West German police officers' employment, payment, promotion, and uniforms.[25] The former was seen as vital for fighting national and international crime, not only by Social Democrats but by CDU leaders as well.[26] The latter aimed to curb Länder independence – and to eliminate little führers all together – by intervening at the local level. Individual officers (it was imagined) would learn

[23] *Der Parlamentarische Rat 1948–1949: Akten und Protokolle*, ed. Wolfram Werner, vol. 3, *Ausschuß für Zuständigkeitsabgrenzung* (Boppard am Rhein: Harald Boldt, 1986), 222n54a (hereafter, *Parl. Rat* 3).

[24] Fritz Hoch in ibid., 157–8.

[25] Walter Menzel in *Parl. Rat* 3, 174–80, 208–14, and 217n47a.

[26] Christian Democrats rejected the proposed reform program but welcomed a federal agency that could coordinate efforts to protect the constitution and the "internal political situation" from communism. See Rainer Salzmann, ed., *Die CDU/CSU im Parlamentarischen Rat: Sitzungsprotokolle der Unionsfraktion* (Stuttgart: Klett-Cotta, 1981), 77 and 550.

the democratic principles legislated at the federal level and these principles would then infuse their behavior and, eventually, their attitude toward their work.[27] In this way, Social Democrats understood the federal regulation of police power to not only check against its abuse, but also to lay the groundwork for a future police force that had internalized the democratic administration of power.

Though the SPD proposal was stonewalled by the CSU, which insisted that police were part of local culture and therefore off limits to federal intervention, it is worth noting on two counts.[28] The envisioned police force vividly captured Social Democratic convictions that central state power was potentially progressive and thus not an inherent threat to human freedom. And the party's plan was directly connected to its refusal to grant the state extraordinary powers in an emergency. For Social Democrats the point was this: If the state was properly outfitted and its fundamental legal constitution sound, no provision for exceptions would be necessary. In a perfected legal order, democracy would already be militant. Having failed to achieve significant police reform in 1949, it was no accident that the SPD made it a top priority when they gained control of government in 1969.

ARMING DEMOCRACY

If delegates remained divided over the question of federalism, they were nonetheless unanimous that the preservation of the state required legally equipping it with tools for democracy's affirmative defense. Those present at Herrenchiemsee and Bonn roundly rejected what Hans Nawiasky called the "principle of democracy as suicide."[29] And nothing demonstrated this consensus more than the ban on undemocratic parties. In contrast to the Weimar Republic, the framers of West Germany's Basic Law bound political parties to the constitution. Any party which, "by reason of their aims or the behavior of their adherents," sought "to undermine or abolish the free democratic basic order" was declared unconstitutional.[30] The degree of unanimity on the need to empower the state in this way was striking, with the Parliamentary Council endorsing the ban – first proposed at Herrenchiemsee – without debate.[31] A similar consensus existed for the prohibition on associations "directed against the constitutional order" and the assertion that any right used to "combat the free democratic basic order" was subject to forfeiture.[32] Such provisions were justified not because the state was understood to have primacy over the individual (as had previously been the case) but because any attempt to destroy

[27] *Parl. Rat* 3, 211.
[28] For CSU opposition, see ibid., 184–7, 199–200, and esp. 410–11.
[29] *Parl. Rat* 2, 229.
[30] Federal Republic of Germany Basic Law, art. 21, sec. 2.
[31] Feldkamp, *Der Parlamentarische Rat*, 70.
[32] Basic Law, art. 9, sec. 2 and art. 18.

the state was seen to violate the will of the people – and could therefore legitimately be prevented as antidemocratic. Any qualms about potential abuses were laid to rest by making implementation subject to judicial review by the Federal Constitutional Court. After weighing evidence on a case-by-case basis, the high court alone would decide whether punitive action on the part of the state was indeed warranted.

Agreement over democracy's explicit defense did not, however, extend to the constitutional regulation of national crises. While both positive and negative conceptions of militant democracy prescribed intolerance toward forces that opposed the system, they diverged dramatically over what means the state could legitimately utilize to shore up or restore the normal democratic order. How to prevent emergency legislation from being wielded indiscriminately; who or what actually determined the state of emergency; and, once determined, what measures were permissible – these were the three questions confronting those who sought to draft a successful emergency law. The need to guard against the possible abuse of the law was asserted repeatedly throughout the deliberations, with the crisis years 1923–4 and 1930–3 acting as stark reminders of how Article 48 had hypertrophied executive and eviscerated legislative authority. Early proposals attempted to solve the problem by laying out preconditions for the law's mobilization – restricting its use to cases where public security and order were in "imminent danger."[33] While this phrase was retained in later drafts, many members of the committee preferred a more precise safeguard. As the SPD's Walter Menzel pointed out, a similar prerequisite in the Weimar constitution had done little to prevent Article 48's repeated misuse.[34] He thus proposed using a "purely external, technical circumstance" to establish the need for emergency action: the impossibility of parliament to assemble. According to this schema, only when "higher powers" prevented the "sovereign organ of the people" from functioning was it appropriate or necessary to declare a state of emergency.[35] Despite expressed misgivings, Menzel's solution to the problem of misuse became an accepted precondition.[36] As such, it was the jumping off point for discussing who should be granted the power to declare a state of emergency and what powers would be granted to whom as a result. Delegates' inability to agree on these questions betrayed fundamental differences in how the parties approached government generally and militant democracy specifically. And this debate was the first – if largely forgotten – chapter in the history of the fiercely protested 1968 Emergency Laws.

33 Version of Article 111 in the report put forth by the Constitutional Convention, *Parl. Rat* 2, 604.

34 *Der Parlamentarische Rat 1948–1949: Akten und Protokolle*, ed. Wolfram Werner, vol. 13, *Ausschuß für Organisation des Bundes/Ausschuß für Verfassungsgerichtigkeit und Rechtspflege* (Munich: Harald Boldt, 2002), 592 (hereafter, *Parl. Rat* 13).

35 Ibid., 592–3. Earlier in the same session, Menzel offered his own version of Article 100. See 579–81.

36 *Der Parlamentarische Rat 1948–1949*, ed. Michael Hollmann, vol. 7, *Entwürfe zum Grundgesetz* (Boppard am Rhein: Harald Boldt, 1995), 167–9.

The three most significant points of contention regarding the regulation of emergency situations were the empowerment of the executive, curtailment of civil liberties, and dissolution of parliament. Postwar conservatives continued to view the executive as the indisputable head of state and, as such, the state's natural guardian. For them, the president's particular importance lay overwhelmingly in his esteemed "personality," what could be described as his ability to represent the German people as a whole (rather than a particular political party, social milieu, or organized interest) and give a human form to the new German state.[37] Only a president could provide the population with a positive figure for identification – someone other than the policeman, judge, and taxman – and, at the same time, act as a neutral force between the government and parliament.[38] Liberals conceived of the executive quite differently, preferring a U.S. model where the president held full executive power and, correspondingly, full political responsibility – and was thus immersed in the daily workings and conflicts of government rather than serving as a *pouvoir neutre*.[39] But postwar conservatives and liberals held the same basic conviction: that parliamentary authority alone was not viable – a strong executive was needed to safeguard democracy from paralysis-inducing parliamentary politics. Without a clear authority figure acting for the good of the whole, nothing would hold a mass society together or protect the polity from outside forces.[40] Important in times of calm, the president was absolutely critical in times of crisis. For this reason both parties called for an emergency law that gave the federal president significant discretion, allowing for the kind of executive independence they deemed crucial to the timely return of law and order.

If Social Democrats viewed the state as an essentially neutral tool that could be used for either good or evil, depending on its wielder, they were far less sanguine when it came to executive power.[41] Party delegates flatly rejected the idea that an executive could ever remain neutral or above politics; as their position on police power demonstrated, they perceived the executive – big and small – as all but synonymous with uncontrolled and thus undemocratic power. In times of crisis, not only did the potential for abuse rise exponentially but, the SPD argued, the mere existence of a president threatened democracy by evoking an alternative to parliamentary rule.[42] For Social Democrats, the

[37] Attention to psychological or emotional considerations was common among conservatives, who frequently portrayed themselves as fighting party machines and/or functionaries. See, e.g., Paul de Chapeaurouge in *Parl. Rat* 13, 329–30.

[38] For conceptions of the president as a *pouvoir neutre*, see the arguments of Wilhelm Heile and Paul de Chapeaurouge as well as Robert Lehr, in ibid., 119, 319, and 325–30.

[39] "Antrag Max Becker und Thomas Dehler zur Einführung eines Präsidialsystems," in ibid., 1024–40.

[40] On the tradition of an idealized strong leader, see Richard Evan Frankel, *Bismarck's Shadow: The Cult of Leadership and the Transformation of the German Right, 1898–1945* (New York: Berg, 2005).

[41] On the parties' differing conceptions of the state: Manfred Opp de Hipt, *Denkbilder in der Politik: Der Staat in der Sprache von CDU und SPD* (Opladen: Westdeutscher, 1987).

[42] Among the most dismissive: Hermann Brill in *Parl. Rat* 2, 293n46.

state's logical guarantor was instead parliament, as both the indivisible site of sovereignty and the very embodiment of democracy. Where the CDU/CSU and FDP saw chaos and conflict, the SPD saw an institution that controlled for extremism and – unlike the executive – for its own abuse of power by providing a forum in which competing interests could be civilly negotiated and all decisions subordinated to the rule of law. The SPD therefore insisted that even at the height of crisis the executive should act in consultation with parliamentary leaders and be confined to either standard procedures or a precisely regulated code of emergency action. In this scenario, the rules and regulations of parliamentary government might be truncated by law but they could not be suspended and were thus not dependent on the good graces of the president or chancellor.

Tied to the issue of executive empowerment was the politically fraught question of who officially declared a state of emergency. For even those who disagreed vehemently with Carl Schmitt were unable to deny the force of his dictum that "sovereign is he who decides on the state of exception."[43] According to Elisabeth Selbert (SPD), one of the four "mothers" of the Basic Law, the task of determining whether a threat to public order and safety existed "could not be left to a single person" but was rather "a holy right of the [popularly elected] Bundestag."[44] Her fellow Social Democrats more or less agreed. Party members suggested that the president of the Bundestag was in the best position to determine whether parliament was unable to fulfill its duties; moreover, by requiring agreement from the president of the Bundesrat – the legislative body ultimately created to represent the Länder – they could avoid both a one-man decision and the exclusion of the Länder from the process.[45] The SPD thus formally proposed that the executive might initiate emergency proceedings but the declaration itself required the agreement of the chambers' two presidents.[46] In contrast, members of the CDU/CSU and FDP favored the federal president for the task of declaring a state of emergency. Opposition to granting the presidents of the two legislative houses decisive emergency powers ultimately reiterated the reasons why both conservatives and liberals called for the federal president's more general empowerment: emergency situations required the swift and decisive actions of a national leader.[47]

Whom one granted the right to declare a state of emergency was naturally influenced by what such a declaration meant. Emergencies caused by the Bundestag's inability to assemble were treated differently from those brought

[43] Carl Schmitt, *Political Theology: Four Chapters on the Theory of Sovereignty*, trans. George Schwab (Cambridge: MIT, 1986), 5.

[44] *Parl. Rat* 13, 583.

[45] Ibid., 588, 591.

[46] Ibid., 577.

[47] That this remained a majority opinion is evident in the parties' internal discussions. See, for example, the meeting protocols from November 4 and November 24 reprinted in Salzmann, *CDU/CSU im Parlamentarischen Rat*, 136, 172.

about by a legislative impasse.[48] In the first instance, the state's ability to legally suspend individual freedoms such as speech and assembly was proposed as critical to the reestablishment of order. Those who advocated the measure did not do so lightly. The protection of civil liberties was of tremendous importance to the Basic Law's framers, intent as they were to distance the new state from the crimes of Nazism.[49] To illustrate the new state's decisive break with the past, for example, the Basic Law posited "human dignity" as the fundamental ground of all rights and liberties and all state authority, which was duty bound to "respect and protect" it.[50] In stark contrast to the Weimar constitution, which understood rights as legally granted to citizens by the state, the West German constitution conceived of them as "natural" or God-given – existing outside of the state yet commanding the state's protection.[51] The Basic Law's "eternity clause" went even further by making it impossible for these "basic rights" and other fundamentals of the constitutional order to be amended out of existence, as they had been under the Weimar Republic.[52]

That said, the obligation of the state to respect human dignity and individual liberties was always predicated upon the citizen's obligation to respect the existing constitutional order. As evidenced by the ban on undemocratic parties and codified in Article 18, the drafters of the Basic Law insisted that citizens' disregard for that obligation could legitimately lead to the forfeiture of their rights. The state's guardianship was roundly qualified by the assertion that individual freedoms were not ensured in order for them to endanger or destroy democracy. Repeating the fundamental tenet of militant democracy, namely that the democratic state need not tolerate those intent on its destruction, the legal experts gathered at the Herrenchiemsee Convention were nearly unanimous on the need to legislate for the emergency suspension of certain rights – in particular, the freedoms of speech, press, assembly, and association. This was no longer the case when the Parliamentary Council took up the matter a few months later, however. The Council's more political (versus the Convention's academic) bent may be one explanation for the sudden change of heart, as could the strong influence of Carlo Schmid as acting leader of the SPD and chair of the Council's executive committee. At Herrenchiemsee Schmid made clear his opposition to emergency legislation, arguing that it promoted false

48 This was a partial concession made by members of the organization committee to the demands of the editorial board – partial because it did not also treat states of exception as requested.

49 For an eloquent summation of civil liberties' importance in the wake of National Socialism, see Georg August Zinn (SPD) in *Der Parlamentarische Rat 1948–1949: Akten und Protokolle*, eds. Eberhard Pikart and Wolfram Werner, vol. 5, *Ausschuß für Grundsatzfragen* (Boppard am Rhein: Harald Boldt, 1993), 34 (hereafter, *Parl. Rat* 5). At the time, Zinn was serving as Hesse's minister of justice.

50 Basic Law, art. 1.

51 Lange explains the unanimity on the inviolable nature of civil liberties as the result of overlap between Christian understandings of natural rights and secular humanist conceptions of mankind. Erhard H. M. Lange, *Die Würde des Menschen ist untastbar* (Heidelberg: Decker & Müller, 1993), 118–19.

52 Basic Law, art. 79, sec. 3.

hope and political immaturity by encouraging legislators to turn over power and trust in the "*deus ex machina* of some article penned to order emergencies" rather than confront the situation with the tools at hand.[53] For whatever reason, Social Democrats now unanimously rejected the suspension of individual rights as antithetical to democracy. "Having a democracy entails a state that can govern without such tactics," Rudolf Katz told his fellow council members. "The less we make it possible to suspend civil rights, so much the better for civil rights."[54] Against the undemocratic curtailment of civil liberties, Schmid, too, continued to espouse the position that when it came to a genuine crisis the threat would have to be confronted using the state's given powers. He suggested that if normal police forces were not enough to control the situation, it was simply too late for state intervention.[55] Visible in both men's statements was Mannheim's assertion that emergency repression was used by weak democracies, not by militant ones, as well as the conviction that the time to act was before a crisis arose, not after.

Members of the CDU/CSU and FDP ultimately agreed with the inadvisability of suspending the freedom of the press and that no measure would be effective if the state acted too late.[56] But whereas Social Democrats mobilized the latter argument against granting the state extraordinary powers, conservatives and liberals made the case for more expansive action. Regular police measures were deemed simply insufficient to stop a "state-endangering avalanche once it was rolling."[57] Like Karl Loewenstein, the CDU/CSU and FDP remained adamant that democracy under siege should not hang by its peacetime principles and argued that the suspension of civil liberties was a weapon the state could not be denied. Gustav Zimmermann (CDU) explained that if emergency measures were to have any chance of restoring order then they had to "get at and eliminate the roots of evil" wherever manifest.[58] He considered temporarily suspending the right to free speech, assembly, and association important to achieving that goal, while memories of Weimar street violence convinced others that in extreme circumstances such measures were the only way to avoid bloodshed.[59] Sensitive to the problem of repression, Hermann von Mangoldt (CDU) took pains to emphasize the measures' productive or liberalizing effects. Using the example of free speech, he argued that its suspension in times of crisis served democracy in two ways: negatively, by limiting the communication among and thus mobilization of antidemocratic forces, but also positively, by allowing for a plurality of voices when only the loudest – organized interests

[53] *Parl. Rat* 2, 422–3. Also: Schmid, "Gliederung und Einheit," 389.

[54] *Parl. Rat* 13, 578 and 615.

[55] *Parl. Rat* 5, 190.

[56] See, for example, the statements made by Gustav Zimmermann and the conclusions reached by Jakob Kaiser (CDU) that prompted him to vote against the proposed Art. 111. *Parl. Rat* 5, 191–2.

[57] Ibid., 191.

[58] Ibid.

[59] *Parl. Rat* 13, 579.

and extremists – might otherwise be heard.[60] In that sense, such measures were themselves prodemocratic as well as critical for neutralizing antidemocratic discourse.

Ultimately, Mangoldt was one of many who argued that the rights or needs of the majority justified the suppression of individual or minority rights, with Social Democrats demonstrating strong sympathies for this line of reasoning as well. But the shift in the SPD's position between the Convention and the Council demonstrated that its delegates were of two minds. In debates over emergency legislation, SPD delegates returned time and again to the experience of Nazism and, finally, determined the persecution of minorities an unacceptable risk. After initial attempts at compromise, the SPD blocked the legislation's inclusion in the final draft of the Basic Law. Later rulings by the Constitutional Court would, however, prove the centrality of majority rights to the fortification of West German democracy. Precedent-setting cases in the early 1950s repeatedly favored the common or "general good" over the rights of individuals deemed a danger to it.[61]

If Social Democrats rejected enabling the state to suspend civil liberties, then what was their proposed alternative to democracy's defense? SPD delegates had clearly established their perception that democracy's first line of defense was the well-formed and fully utilized regular powers of the state. Should those fail, however, they offered up the citizenry as the best and last remaining means of saving democracy. Rather than answer crisis with repressive "authority" – in this case, by suppressing political speech and courting Gestapo-style state terror – Social Democrats called instead for "political clarification."[62] The Parliamentary Council's youngest member, Rudolf Heiland, described this as an exciting process of politicization: "We have a singular ... opportunity to educate the public in the genuine formation of political opinion."[63] Rudolf Katz seconded this position. Much more practical than the curtailment of civil liberties, he stated, would be to "instill active consciousness of these freedoms in the minds of all Germans so that no government could take them away."[64] At the end of the day, the SPD's official position held that if a threat could not be contained by ordinary state forces, democracy's only hope for survival was its citizenry. Here, the memory of the 1920 Kapp Putsch, in which German workers successfully answered Social Democratic President Friedrich Ebert's call to put down an attack on the Republic with a general strike, played a critical role

[60] *Parl. Rat* 5, 190.

[61] Most famously, the Lüth decision upholding the Hamburg boycott of Veit Harlan's film, *Immortal Lover*, established the courts' position on the balance of interests. See David P. Currie, *The Constitution of the Federal Republic of Germany* (Chicago: University of Chicago Press, 1994), 177–9.

[62] Schmid explicitly accused the CDU/CSU of opening up the doors to state terror. *Parl. Rat* 5, 186–8.

[63] *Parl. Rat* 13, 847–8.

[64] Ibid., 577–8.

in Social Democrats' imaginations.[65] It served as a model for the successful cooperation of popular and official politics in defending democracy.

The SPD's preference for the population over emergency state action struck most members of the CDU/CSU as naïve and thoroughly out of touch with both the political history and current realities of Germany. According to Gerhard Kroll, 1933 had proven that "Germans would not fight for democracy or freedom" and he predicted that "disasters will occur for another hundred years or more before you can count on the [German] population."[66] Contrary to what their fellow council members may have thought, Social Democrats suffered few delusions regarding the political proclivities of postwar Germans. If anything, memories of their own persecution and the failure of Germans to resist the Nazi dictatorship left them more inclined to judge the average German negatively and assume that Nazi sympathies still ran rampant. They did not, in other words, deny that it would be a long time before democracy was safe in Germany. Social Democrats were adamant, however, that a republic was only as secure as its citizens were democratic. For this reason, they argued for the importance of political education and pushed for solutions that would train German citizens in the civic art of democracy. Though these measures resonated with the party elites' historically paternalist relationship to the working class, the SPD's postwar pedagogy marked a novel strategy, one that aimed to help control crisis situations and make future ones less likely. Social Democrats' position on emergency legislation expressed not only the conviction that the Basic Law had to assume a future, democratic citizenry – or risk institutionalizing undemocratic structures – but also that it could act as a primer for postwar Germans' political education.

Social Democrats approached legislative emergencies in a similar fashion. If government was unable to pass important legislation because it lacked a parliamentary majority or the Bundestag was unable to remove a "minority chancellor" because internal divisions made a "constructive vote of no confidence" (which required electing a new chancellor) impossible, political paralysis would ensue. Both the imagined emergency and its possible resolutions pit executive against parliamentary power – and divided conservatives and liberals on one hand from Social Democrats on the other. Members of the CDU/CSU viewed such a situation as a crisis not of parliament but rather of government; it was the executive that was rendered powerless and, therefore, *it* that needed protecting.[67] For this reason, the party faction understood the federal president's right to dissolve the Bundestag as an essential component of emergency legislation.[68] The Christian Union made clear to its members and its peers that it rejected a reinstatement of Article 48's dictatorial potentials. Still, its leaders

[65] Schmid repeatedly drew on the example of the Kapp Putsch to argue against emergency legislation. See *Parl. Rat* 2, 423.

[66] *Parl. Rat* 5, 189.

[67] *Parl. Rat* 13, 864–5.

[68] See Salzmann, *CDU/CSU im Parlamentarischen Rat*, esp. 172.

believed that dissolving parliament would remove the most immediate impediment to government. Members of the FDP agreed with this assessment and argued that even the mere possibility of dissolution was a powerful tool to encourage compromise among Bundestag members. Just as they had at every other step of the debate, the FDP and CDU/CSU perceived executive action as the quickest and most assured route to regaining order and stability.

Unsurprising, given the political and symbolic importance Social Democrats ascribed to parliament, the SPD opposed its dissolution. Most critical, in Social Democrats' eyes, was the risk such measures ran of delegitimating parliament and thus representative government itself. Social Democrats therefore proposed that the constitution should focus on mandating "educational work" among legislators, rather than open doors by which they might flee responsibility. Specifically, the SPD argued that parties needed to be weaned off prioritizing electoral popularity and party antagonisms and instead taught accountability and a willingness to cooperate and form coalitions.[69] Though hardly a flattering portrayal, it did not stem from a lack of faith in parliament or political parties – as might be said of liberals and conservatives – but rather from the conviction that Germans, including their elected representatives, were politically immature. The SPD thus proposed a solution that kept parliamentarians at the negotiating table and learning on the job. In the event government-sponsored legislation failed to secure a majority, it would go before parliament a second time; failure to reach a compromise solution again would not kill the bill but rather send it on to the Bundesrat, which then had the power to make it law.[70] Criticized as overly complicated by members of the CDU/CSU and FDP, this proposed process promised to accomplish no less than five things at once. In addition to encouraging parliament to govern, it gave the government an alternative path to push through critical laws, but limited that right to a case-by-case basis and, in turn, prevented any lasting transfer of legislative powers. The crowning achievement was how the process avoided the character of an emergency order altogether, requiring neither a declaration of emergency nor direct executive interference. This did more than protect legislative rights and banish specters of Article 48; it enabled the SPD to demote legislative crises from emergency legislation (proposed Article 111) to a failure of parliamentary procedure under the regulations established for a vote of constructive no confidence (proposed Article 90b).[71] In the final draft, this shining example of SPD legal gymnastics became the controversial Article 81.

The drafters of the Basic Law were, in fact, masters of compromise. But the different factions were unable or unwilling to reach an agreement when it came

[69] Rudolf Katz in *Parl. Rat* 13, 849; Elisabeth Selbert in ibid., 849–50.

[70] Walter Menzel introduced the proposal to the organization committee on December 1 to much debate. See *Parl. Rat* 13, 845–57, partic. 850ff.

[71] Rudolf Katz argued the more appropriate place to treat the legislative crisis in question was as a supplement to Art. 90a, which treated parliamentary paralysis brought on by a minority chancellor. This, then, fully removed the legislation (originally proposed by Menzel as Art. 111a) out from under emergency auspices. Ibid., 856–7.

to emergency legislation. Objections were raised by the CDU/CSU that SPD demands for greater clarity and precision in the regulation of legislative emergencies tied the hands of the executive to an indefensible extent.[72] Indeed, when confronted with Article 81, Christian Democratic leader and Parliamentary Council chair Konrad Adenauer declared it "irreconcilable with a healthy democracy."[73] Rather than regulate legislative emergencies in such a fashion, the CDU/CSU as well as members of the FDP opted not to regulate them at all – a decision that would at least grant the executive room to maneuver. With the parties divided over this, the curtailment of civil liberties, and executive privilege, emergency legislation reached an impasse. The drafted Article 111 was not eliminated from the Basic Law until the very last minute, however, indicating the reluctance with which the Parliamentary Council abandoned the widespread conviction that a German democratic state would need at least special procedures if not extralegal powers in order to weather future states of emergency.

REACTIONS TO THE BASIC LAW AND MILITANT DEMOCRACY

On the occasion of the constitution's ratification, publicist Walter Dirks observed that "it belongs to the nature of compromises that [the Basic Law] made no one entirely happy."[74] This was to put it mildly. Tensions over cultural matters and fiscal jurisdiction had seriously strained party relations so that twelve of the sixty-five council members voted against the Basic Law.[75] In contrast to the flaring tempers expressed by politicians, the average West German paid little attention when the constitution was introduced to the public. Only twenty-one percent of Germans polled in March 1949 stated an interest in the future constitution; the remainder acknowledged moderate (thirty-three percent) to complete (forty percent) indifference.[76] Those who *were* interested were highly critical of the proceedings and their end result: the Federal Republic of Germany. Observers from different political camps criticized the secrecy in which the Parliamentary Council worked, construing the lack of popular participation and openness in drafting the Basic Law as indicative of its fundamental illegitimacy. Conservative as well as left-leaning critics viewed the constitution as a product of occupation and found common cause in opposing the dominant role allotted to the political parties in first drafting the constitution and then acting as its self-appointed protectors. Most significant for those concerned that Germans "get it right" this time around, commentators from across the political spectrum agreed that the Basic Law's

[72] Robert Lehr in *Parl. Rat* 13, 585.

[73] Salzmann, *CDU/CSU im Parlamentarischen Rat*, 247.

[74] Walter Dirks, "Bundesrepublik Deutschland," *Frankfurter Hefte* 4 (June 1949): 457.

[75] The dissenting votes were issued by the KPD, Center, DP, and the majority of voting CSU members.

[76] Elisabeth Noelle and Erich Peter Neumann, eds., *The Germans: Public Opinion Polls, 1947–1966* (Bonn: Allensbach-Institut, 1967), 227.

studied avoidance of any and all potential upheaval did not ensure a viable political order. Conservative jurists joined left-liberal publicists in arguing that a fortification of democracy based on fear left democracy open to ruin, while others attacked Article 81 (defining legislative crisis as a procedural problem) and the normalizing tactics it engendered. Together, these early critiques of militant democracy laid the groundwork for a recurring postwar debate over the terms and means of democracy's defense. They would return most notably in the conflict over rearmament in the 1950s, the Emergency Laws of the 1960s, and, finally, the counterterrorism program of the 1970s.

Among those standing critically on the sidelines was a group of conservative thinkers whose main source of commonality was their intellectual debt to Carl Schmitt.[77] With the new German state bereft of both sovereignty and political unity, the FRG seemed to them a mechanistic entity that lacked real legitimacy. The Basic Law's studious attempt to avoid a state of emergency was taken as symptomatic of the state's coldly administrative nature – the fact that it was constituted as an agglomeration of laws and institutions rather than by the act of a sovereign people or monarch. In an essay written shortly after the Basic Law's ratification, jurist Werner Weber threw out the discomforting thesis that the FRG was neither well-fortified nor authentically democratic.[78] Unlike the Weimar Republic, which Weber described as a "true constitutional creation" born of popular uprising as the "existential decision" of the German people, he stated that the Federal Republic lacked fundamental legitimacy because Germans – occupied and divided by foreign powers – were not in the position to make any genuine (meaning self-constituting) decisions.[79] In this, Weber judged the Parliamentary Council's disinterest in public opinion, the public's disinterest in the Parliamentary Council, and the last-minute decision against a national referendum on the Basic Law as wholly consistent with political reality – and all the more deserving of criticism.[80]

The two trespasses for which Werner Weber could not forgive the Basic Law were its significantly weakened executive and refusal to acknowledge a state of exception. As Weber saw things, both left the state vulnerable and without the means to defend itself. His critique undoubtedly betrayed a characteristic aversion to parliamentary democracy, targeting the primacy of the Bundestag, the privileging of political parties, and its identification of the judiciary – not,

77 Ernst Forsthoff is frequently cited as the leader of the school's postwar wing. Other important members include Werner Weber, Armin Mohler, and Reinhart Koselleck. On conservative thought in the early postwar as well as Schmitt's strong influence: Jan-Werner Müller, *Dangerous Mind: Carl Schmitt in Post-War European Thought* (New Haven: Yale University Press, 2003) and Dirk van Laak, *Gespräche in der Sicherheit des Schweigens: Carl Schmitt in der Geistesgeschichte der frühen Bundesrepublik* (Berlin: Akademie, 1993).

78 Werner Weber, *Weimarer Verfassung und Bonner Grundgesetz* (Göttingen: Fleischer, 1949).

79 Ibid., 7–8. Forsthoff similarly argued that the Weimar Republic was more of a "state" than the FRG. See Ernst Forsthoff, *Der Staat der Industriegesellschaft: Dargestellt am Beispiel der Bundesrepublik Deutschlands* (Munich: Beck, 1971), 61.

80 Weber, *Weimarer Verfassung*, 9–10.

as Schmitt had it, the president – as constitutional guardian.[81] This very aversion was part and parcel of the extreme importance Weber (like his mentor) placed on the exception rather than the rule in determining a state's strength and merit. It was not so much democracy that troubled Weber as it was the Basic Law's attempt to rule out instability and crisis – the very stuff of politics – and to thereby avoid the problem of state power and the executive all together. Weber argued that the framers' determination to locate and cut out the roots of previous political disaster had produced a constitution that was not only oriented to past actions but also politically weak, clouded by complex regulations, and closed to its own population. Fear of the past, of state power, and of the people structured the entire constitution and, as a result, left it dangerously ill-equipped to face the future.[82] His antipathy to the Weimar Republic had earned him a flourishing career under National Socialism, yet Weber praised the Weimar constitution and its drafters. With Article 48, they proved that they were everything members of the Parliamentary Council were not, namely impartial jurists with the political savvy to anticipate the need to suspend normal politics and the boldness to entrust the restoration of order to the president. If this last was a risk "in which blessing and danger meet," Weber denied that the nature of political life offered any alternatives. The Parliamentary Council could reject Article 48 and the concentration of powers, strictly regulate the few exceptional situations it did allow for, and grant decisive power to the constitutional courts, but none of this could prevent future political upheaval.[83] And this, in a nutshell, was Weber's fear. Deprived of authority and the means to act, the new Germany would meet its next enemy and be found wanting. It was an intolerable position for students of Schmitt and, time would show, many members of the conservative mainstream.

Leftists tended to see the problem as too much rather than too little self-protective power. Parallel to Weber, left-liberal journalist Dolf Sternberger understood the new constitution and the fortification of democracy to have been guided primarily by fear – of the weaknesses inherent to democracy, of claims made on the individual, and of repeating the past.[84] Indeed, he described a German population so obsessed with avoiding the mistakes of Weimar (tantamount, in his words, to a "public sickness") that it forgot to consider what actually went into making a good constitution.[85] The inherent problem with this negative orientation was, according to Sternberger, that the means by which the Basic Law sought to safeguard democracy were correspondingly negative. Fear had turned the constitution's framers into unwilling repressors. The Parliamentary Council's decision to set hurdles to parties' entry into

[81] Carl Schmitt, *Hüter der Verfassung* (Tübingen: Mohr, 1931).
[82] Weber, *Weimarer Verfassung*, 15–28.
[83] Ibid., 22.
[84] Dolf Sternberger, "Demokratie der Furcht oder Demokratie der Courage?" *Wandlung* 4, no. 1 (1949): 5–13.
[85] Ibid., 8.

parliament, institute a proportional rather than majority voting system, and privilege the large, bureaucratic parties that might deliver was not based on the needs of democratic politics, he insisted, but rather on fear of political conflict and government instability. Sternberger was convinced that in this form, militant democracy would whittle away free expression, open parliamentary debate, and governmental responsibility – in other words, all that distinguished parliamentary rule from a tyranny of the majority.[86]

Sternberger was interested in exposing the dangers specific to democracy's fortification not in order to condemn the project (as a later generation would do) but rather to save it. Indeed, three years earlier he had himself trumpeted the cry "no freedom for the enemies of freedom!"[87] By dissecting the fear-driven actions of the Parliamentary Council and his fellow (West) Germans, Sternberger hoped to reveal that the only chance for security lay in what he called the "positive use of freedom," a defense of democracy built on courage.[88] Currently, he argued, Germans lacked the courage to trust themselves and so they attacked any sign of weakness and sought refuge in numbers. They believed that the legitimacy of the Basic Law depended upon the support of both the SPD and CDU/CSU (rather than simply a majority of delegates), that only a united front would "keep the wolves outside" at bay. All this was smoke and mirrors in Sternberger's assessment, who argued that such fear-driven calls for consensus actually hid a fear of majority rule antithetical to both democracy and its defense.[89] Similar to Mannheim a decade before, Sternberger concluded that negative, repressive measures would kill, not protect, German democracy. He thus called on Germans to retrace their steps and to start over, but this time with trust. Rather than suppress political pluralism, the constitution had to have the courage to guarantee it; rather than press for grand coalitions, it had to recognize the right of changing majorities to govern and the corresponding minorities' right to stand in loyal opposition; rather than granting Germans freedom *from*, it should grant them freedom *to*. Militant democracy was far from a doomed concept, in Sternberger's opinion, but it had to start from the standpoint of freedom or it would lose its way. Should West Germans continue on their present course, the scenario the publicist imagined for his readers was a government driven to terrorize its own population in desperate attempts to reanimate what was, in essence, a dead constitution.[90] As we will see, the image of state terror entailed in Sternberger's critique of overzealous militant democracy did not fade with the passage of time but instead gained popular resonance each time the West German state was further armed.

By far the most specialized point of debate was that over Article 81, which effectively relegated legislative crises to a matter of parliamentary procedure.

86 Ibid., 5–9.

87 Dolf Sternbrger, "Herrschaft der Freiheit," *Wandlung* 1, no. 7 (1946): 567.

88 Sternberger, "Demokratie der Furcht," 9.

89 He accused FDP leader Theodor Heuss of deliberately circumventing majority rule. Ibid., 10–11.

90 Ibid., 12.

A discussion dominated by jurists, it explicitly took up the question of where the greater danger lay: in the constitutional provision for emergency situations or their normification. As Article 81 was more or less a product of Social Democrats' efforts to realize the latter, its most vocal critics were those convinced of the inherent danger in normifying the exceptional and leaving it – and all other aspects of the constitution – open to judicial interpretation. Speaking before a professional gathering of West German constitutional jurists, one of the association's youngest members, Hans Schneider, stated that only the sharp demarcation of emergency legislation from the normal constitutional order could ensure it was not affected by future crises and new legislation.[91] Anyone aware of legislation such as the recent U.S.A. PATRIOT Act or Great Britain's various Prevention of Terrorism Acts can appreciate that one need not fundamentally alter the constitution (prohibited by the Basic Law itself) to radically reshape the legal order and the workings of state. According to Schneider, however, this was even more true in the FRG given the Basic Law's decision to make the judicial branch the guardian of the constitution. Here the young jurist echoed more established state theorists who loudly argued that the failure to draw a line between the exceptional and the normal also threatened the line between the executive and the judiciary. This was a complaint oft heard coming from the right.[92] But its Schmittian line of reasoning was also found among progressive thinkers like Social Democrat and future Constitutional Court judge Ernst-Wolfgang Böckenförde, who were also troubled by the lack of distinctions between the normal and the exceptional. As Böckenförde explained it, militant democracy in its present form promoted a "totalitarianism of the constitution" by treating the Basic Law rather than the people as sovereign and establishing a hierarchy or "empire" of values that it then foisted on the population as "natural" or universal.[93] An actually subjective frame was thus rendered permanent, with only itself as a referent. By endowing the judiciary with decisive power and not distinguishing normal laws from extraordinary measures, the drafters of the constitution blurred the line between politics and justice. And this, in Böckenförde's opinion, opened the door to far more

[91] Vereinigung der Deutschen Staatsrechtslehrer, *Kabinettsfrage und Gesetzgebungsnotstand nach dem Grundgesetz; Tragweite der Generalklausel im Art. 19 Abs. 4. des Bonner Grundgesetzes: Berichte* (Berlin: DeGruyter, 1950), 32–5.

[92] Forsthoff argued that the only institutional authority that existed in the FRG was the "authority of German justice," that is, the German courts. See Ernst Forsthoff, *Rechtsstaat im Wandel: Verfassungsrechtliche Abhandlungen, 1950–1964* (Stuttgart: Kohlhammer, 1964), 109. Werner Weber argued that militant democracy's reliance on a judge's ruling meant West Germans faced the "judicial state" Carl Schmitt had warned of in the late 1920s, which ignored the limits to normal legal devices. Weber, *Weimarer Verfassung*, esp. 28.

[93] Ernst-Wolfgang Böckenförde, "Entstehung und Wandel des Rechtsstaatsbegriffs" and "Zur Kritik der Wertebegründung des Rechts," in *Recht, Staat, Freiheit: Studien zur Rechtsphilosophie, Staatstheorie, und Verfassungsgeschichte* (Frankfurt: Suhrkamp, 1991), 143–69 and 67–91, respectively. On democracy's inability to guarantee its own preconditions: idem, "Die Entstehung des Staates als Vorgang der Säkularisation," in *Staat, Gesellschaft, Freiheit: Studien zur Staatstheorie und zum Verfassungsrecht* (Frankfurt: Suhrkamp, 1976), 42–64.

illiberal acts than would the recognition of emergency powers.[94] The absence of emergency legislation was simply unacceptable to anyone convinced that emergency situations could not be wished away, rendered unexceptional, or effectively dealt with by anyone other than the executive.

MILITANT OR MILITARIST? REARMAMENT AND THE EMERGENCY LAWS

The Christian Union's strong showing in the first West German elections and, in particular, the election of Konrad Adenauer as the country's first chancellor ensured that the arguments for equipping the state with stronger tools of defense did not go unrecognized. In his fourteen years as chancellor, Adenauer's famously autocratic style left little doubt as to his preference for a strong executive.[95] He energetically used the powers granted to him in order to turn the Chancellor's Office into a comprehensive instrument for governmental coordination and to effectively secure the chancellorship from the unwelcome interference of either the Bundesrat or the opposition in parliament.[96] In addition, Adenauer's decision to pursue a "policy of strength" in both foreign and domestic realms demonstrated a conviction that restoring those powers traditionally associated with a strong and fully sovereign state was vital to the FRG's stability and well-being.

Here, the boundaries of militant democracy – as a domestic versus foreign policy – blurred. Securing democracy internally was often mentioned in the same breath as defending the Federal Republic from the encroaching East. This was not only because, in the 1950s, anticommunism was ipso facto democratic militancy. Finance Minister Ludwig Erhard's "social market" economy aimed to make the FRG economically stable and prosperous, with the expected benefit that this would undercut the lure an East German alternative might hold for citizens. Overwhelmingly successful in the first instance, Erhard was likewise successful in the second. The "economic miracle" of the 1950s steered public discourse away from politics toward a language of economics that in many

[94] In discussing the need to acknowledge states of exception, Böckenförde did not argue for emergency powers' regulation but, much like Loewenstein and postwar conservatives, recognition of their potentially undemocratic nature. Crucially, he goes on to advocate that, having recognized this fact, the exercise of emergency powers should be subject to review by a board or committee designed for that very purpose. Ernst-Wolfgang Böckenförde, "Der verdrängte Ausnahmezustand: Zum Handeln der Staatsgewalt in außergewöhnlichen Lagen," *Neue Juristische Wochenschrift* 38 (1978): 1881–90.

[95] Adenauer has inspired numerous studies over the years. See the two-volume classic, Hans-Peter Schwarz, *Konrad Adenauer: A German Politician and Statesman in a Period of War, Revolution, and Reconstruction* (New York: Berghahn, 1995). Also, Anselm Doering-Manteuffel and Hans-Peter Schwarz, *Adenauer und die deutsche Geschichte* (Bonn: Bouvier, 2001).

[96] Hans Mommsen, "The Origins of Chancellor Democracy and the Transformation of the German Democratic Paradigm," *German Politics and Society* 25 (2007): 7–18. Further: Hans-Peter Schwarz, *Konrad Adenauers Regierungsstil* (Bonn: Bouvier, 1991); Anselm Doering-Manteuffel, "Strukturmerkmale der Kanzlerdemokratie," *Der Staat* 30 (1991): 1–18.

ways vaccinated West Germans against Soviet communism.[97] Adenauer, meanwhile, worked to reestablish Germany's strong diplomatic position by ensuring the FRG's contribution to a Western European security bloc. Even before its foundation, the Christian Democratic leader had concluded that this was the key to making West Germany an equal and sovereign power capable of commanding the respect of its peers and, by implication, its enemies – wherever they might be.[98] A neutral or unarmed Germany was, to his mind, as antithetical to this goal as was denying the nation a clear and decisive leader in times of either peace or national crisis. From the moment Adenauer became chancellor, therefore, military defense and emergency powers were back on the table as legitimate means of ensuring the new republic's survival.

Not even the most talented of clairvoyants could have predicted that only a decade after their unconditional surrender to the Allies in 1945, West Germans would once again field an army and be welcomed into the North Atlantic Treaty Organization (NATO).[99] The controversy surrounding this development and the decade-long debate over emergency laws that followed close on its heels differed little in content from the initial postwar skirmishes. Both the CDU/CSU and the FDP – who made up the ruling coalition – used their position in government to revise restraints on state power they had never supported while Social Democrats fought to maintain them by opposing rearmament and various emergency measures. Unlike the earlier constitutional debates, however, these mobilized a broad political public. Where few West Germans had concerned themselves with the Basic Law, many held strong opinions about remilitarization and, in the 1960s, the state's need for emergency laws. The SPD did not take a pacifist stance on military power, and it eventually agreed to a package of emergency-related legislation. But its refusal to diverge from its own conception of militant democracy and accept the need for extraordinary means of defense significantly influenced the policies' final form. In the early years of the Federal Republic it also made the SPD the parliamentary conduit of a popular opposition (discussed in the next chapter).

[97] On this endeavor, see James C. Van Hook, *Rebuilding Germany: The Creation of the Social Market Economy, 1945–1957* (Cambridge: Cambridge University Press, 2004) and Mark E. Spicka, *Selling the Economic Miracle: Economic Reconstruction and Politics in West Germany, 1949–1957* (New York: Berghahn, 2007).

[98] On Adenauer and rearmament: David Clay Large, *Germans to the Front: West German Rearmament in the Adenauer Era* (Chapel Hill: University of North Carolina Press, 1996) and Wolfgang Krüger, *Adenauer und die Wiederbewaffnung* (Bonn: Bouvier, 2000). Complicating Adenauer's image as a straightforwardly pro-West politician is Ronald J. Granieri's *The Ambivalent Alliance: Konrad Adenauer, the CDU/CSU, and the West, 1949–1966* (New York: Berghahn, 2002).

[99] For a history of West Germany's rearmament proper, see Large, *Germans to the Front*. Also Dieter Krieger, *Das Amt Blank: Die schwierige Gründung des Bundesministeriums für Verteidigung* (Freiburg: Rombach, 1993). In the longer-term context: Ute Frevert, *A Nation in Barracks: Modern Germany, Military Conscription and Civil Society*, trans., Andrew Boreham (Oxford: Berg, 2004).

Rabidly anticommunist, the party's leaders and defense experts did not oppose military power per se.[100] Social Democrats on the whole were in fact convinced of the need for self-defense against the Soviet threat. The sticking point between them on the one hand and liberals and conservatives on the other was the SPD's long-standing antimilitarism. Social Democrats understood the German military to have played handmaiden to a series of authoritarian regimes and were convinced that it would only continue to breed antidemocratic attitudes unless dramatically overhauled.[101] In this, their antimilitarist position resembled their position on police force and the state generally. For the SPD, the silver lining to Europe's recent devastation was that it provided an unprecedented opportunity to reorient defense away from the nation-state and to cripple traditional militarism once and for all. In 1952 and then again in 1954, the SPD therefore offered an alternative military defense plan that would subordinate German personnel and defense agendas to an international framework – specifically the United Nations – while simultaneously pursuing a strong "economic and social offensive." In this context, members of the SPD happily reminded those who would listen that even in the West political and social equality had yet to be fully realized.[102] If Mannheim had urged social and economic reform on a world threatened by fascism, Social Democrats now insisted that improving freedom and economic well-being would strengthen democracy at home and give people elsewhere the courage to stand up to communism.

When rearmament ceased to be a question and discussion turned to the concrete task of creating a new German army, Social Democrats sought to check the threat of armed force and executive power in the same manner as they had before. SPD concern for the undemocratic or politically immature German soldier was abundantly evident. While the FDP – known for its disproportionate share of nationalists and Nazi elements – immediately established itself as the defender of army tradition, the SPD sought to root out those very symbols and rituals of Germany's military past.[103] Its goal was to create a wholly

[100] For a summary of the party's motives and reasons for opposing remilitarization at the time of the parliamentary debates, see Christoph Butterwege and Heinz-Gerd Hofschen, *Sozialdemokratie, Krieg und Friede: Die Stellung der SPD zur Friedensfrage von den Anfängen bis zur Gegenwart. Eine kommentierte Dokumentation* (Heilbronn: Distel, 1984), 234–5. Also Gordon D. Drummond, *The German Social Democrats in Opposition: The Case Against Rearmament* (Norman: University of Oklahoma Press, 1982).

[101] For background on Social Democratic antimilitarism, see Nicholas Stargardt, *The German Idea of Militarism: Radical and Socialist Critics, 1866–1914* (Cambridge: Cambridge University Press, 1994).

[102] "Aktionsprogramm der SPD, beschlossen auf dem Dortmunder Parteitag am 28. September 1952, erweitert auf dem Westberliner Parteitag am 24. Juli 1954," in *Jahrbuch der Sozialdemokratischen Partei Deutschlands 1954/55* (Bonn: Vorstand der SPD, 1956), 285–317.

[103] Gerard Braunthal, "The Free Democratic Party in West German Politics," *The Western Political Quarterly* 13 (June 1960): 332–48, here 341. On the debate: Alaric Searle, *Wehrmacht Generals, West German Society, and the Debate on Rearmament, 1949–1959* (Westport, CT: Praeger,

different military ethos where a soldier did not prize the traditional values of honor, obedience, and fatherland above the universal values of civil liberties and international law. Social Democrats rejected the central tenet of militaries everywhere by arguing that democracy did, in fact, have a place within military institutions. Toward this end, the party successfully advocated for the new soldier's right to unionize.[104] In a near perfect reenactment of the constitutional debate over executive power, the SPD also fought for parliamentary control over supreme military command. The party countered FDP and CDU/CSU proposals to concentrate power in the hands of either the federal president or the chancellor with a proposal for a "parliament's army," in which the Defense Ministry would not only hold the reins in war, just as it did in times of peace, but also be directly responsible to parliament rather than the chancellor.[105] In this instance, however, the two major parties managed a compromise. In exchange for a parliamentary defense ombudsman (*Wehrbeauftragter*) and a Bundestag security committee with full investigative powers, the SPD gave up its demands for direct parliamentary control – and removed the last major obstacle to the West German Bundeswehr.[106]

Of course, the existence of armed forces acknowledged the possibility of war and the need to establish how it – or any other national crisis warranting their mobilization – would be declared. Thus, in addition to more immediate fears of war and militarism, an army raised unsettled questions regarding states of exception. Successfully amending the Basic Law to provide for the Bundeswehr and external emergencies closed one debate, in other words, only to reopen another. It again underscored the connections – and easy slippage – between militant democracy as a domestic and a foreign policy. This was particularly true given that new amendments such as that allowing for the Bundeswehr's use in domestic disturbances were effectively meaningless. They could not go into effect until the Basic Law was further amended to include emergency legislation.[107]

With only a handful of years separating the Social Democrats' last-minute veto of emergency legislation and the subject's political resurrection, the actors essentially picked up where they had left off. Adenauer's single-minded pursuit

2003) and Donald Abenheim, *Reforging the Iron Cross: The Search for Tradition in the West German Armed Forces* (Princeton: Princeton University Press, 1988).

[104] Large, *Germans to the Front*, 195. For an official history of Germany's military union, the German Armed Forces Association, see Rüdiger Andel, *50 Jahre Bundeswehrverband* (Dortmund: Lensing, 2007).

[105] Large, *Germans to the Front*, 194.

[106] The CDU/CSU won military control for the chancellor in times of war, partially offset by granting the Bundestag the power to declare a "state of defense" necessitating the army's mobilization. In situations where parliament was unable to assemble, that power passed to the federal president – contingent upon the chancellor's support and consultation with the Bundestag and Bundesrat presidents. Gerard Braunthal, "Emergency Legislation in the Federal Republic of Germany," in *Festschrift für Karl Loewenstein*, ed. Henry Steele Commager (Tübingen: Mohr, 1971), 71–86; Large, *Germans to the Front*, 248–50.

[107] Braunthal, "Emergency Legislation," 75.

of German sovereignty matched a persistent preoccupation with state authority within conservative and liberal circles. Right-wing intellectuals and journalists like Ernst Forsthoff and Winfried Martini, for instance, produced one work after another with such ominous titles as *The End of All Security* (1954), *Constitutional Problems of the Social State* (1954), "The Political Problem of Authority" (1956), and *Freedom Pending Recall: The Life Expectancy of the Federal Republic* (1960).[108] Each one discussed the dismal conditions of the modern state and whether the FRG was, as its founders intended, crisis resistant. Neither Forsthoff nor Martini answered in the affirmative. Both were convinced that by the mid-1950s the West German state had been deprived of all possible authority, first by the occupation powers, then by the drafters of the Basic Law, and, most recently, by the growth of the social welfare state. It was argued that by erasing the few remaining lines between state and society, the welfare state in particular opened government to the whims and self-interest of political parties, social groups, and prominent individuals at the same time it made Germans physically and psychologically weak by encouraging dependency and risk aversion.[109] For these conservatives, the FRG's chances of survival looked very grim indeed. Without the political authority to positively or negatively affect its fate, the state could only be tossed about on the waves of international and domestic developments. The ultimate paradox, according to Forsthoff, was that at the very same time that decisive rule (*Herrschaft*) had become impossible in the FRG, no state in history had ever needed it more to face impending crises. This was true not only because of the FRG's particular geopolitical position but also, he opined, because the modern social and redistributive state risked unrest every time it failed to protect citizens from a dip in the economy.[110]

Given this pessimistic read and the heavy emphasis on state authority, it is no surprise that the Basic Law's failure to acknowledge a possible state of exception and the need for authoritative power at such times was a sore point to which right-wing jurists like Forsthoff and Werner Weber as well as journalists like Martini returned time and again with increasing urgency. More mainstream conservatives did not have to subscribe to these men's exact logic for it to resonate with their conviction that a national crisis could not be

[108] Winfried Martini, *Das Ende aller Sicherheit: Eine Kritik des Westens* (Stuttgart: DVA, 1954); idem, *Freiheit auf Abruf: Die Lebenserwartung der Bundesrepublik* (Cologne: Kiepenheuer & Witsch, 1960); Ernst Forsthoff, *Verfassungsprobleme des Sozialstaates* (Münster: Aschendorff, 1954); idem, "Das politische Problem der Authorität," *Horizonte* 1 (1956): 1–12.

[109] This argument was most fully developed by Forsthoff who rejected the social state in any form. For an enlightening foray into Forsthoff's state theories, see Peter Caldwell, "Ernst Forsthoff and the Legacy of Racial Conservative State Theory in the Federal Republic of Germany," *History of Political Thought* 15 (Winter 1994): 615–41, esp. 631–6. Also Jan-Werner Müller, "From National Identity to National Interest: The Rise (and Fall) of Germany's New Right," in *German Ideologies since 1945: Studies in the Political Thought and Culture of the Bonn Republic*, ed. idem (New York: Palgrave, 2003), 185–205.

[110] Ernst Forsthoff, "Problem der Autorität," *Rechtsstaat im Wandel: Verfassungsrechtliche Abhandlungen, 1954–1973*, 2nd ed. (Munich: Beck, 1976), 14–24, esp. 21–2.

contained unless the effectiveness and authority of the executive was secured.[111] With everything from the Korean War to the 1953 workers' uprising in East Germany reminding them of their dependency on the Allies for protection from internal and external threats, this was not an abstract concern. It was not until 1954 and the Paris Treaties, however, that Adenauer's government got the excuse it needed to pitch a constitutional amendment for emergency legislation. The Treaties ended West Germany's occupied status but continued to deny the FRG full sovereignty by retaining the Allies' right to intervene on German territory. This would not change until the Allies, concerned for the safety of their own troops and military bases, were fully satisfied that a West German government could restore security and order in the event of an attack or internal unrest.[112]

Overnight, obtaining authority over domestic emergencies became part of Adenauer's campaign for national sovereignty. Conservatives argued that it alone would demonstrate that West Germans had a plan for managing crises and thereby free them, once and for all, from Allied control. As with rearmament, however, the Christian-Liberal government quickly discovered that many West Germans were perfectly happy to leave security matters in the hands of the Western powers. But whereas Western military interests and the panic triggered by the Korean War made rearmament a diplomatic as much as a domestic affair – propelled along by priorities and passions external to the FRG – emergency legislation was left for West Germans to fight out on their own.[113] And fight they did – for thirteen consecutive years, over what remains one of the most notorious pieces of legislation in postwar German history. There were certainly other major controversies involving the balance between liberty and security. For instance, the "Spiegel Affair," discussed further in Chapter 2, pitted press freedom against national security and was critical for encouraging Adenauer to finally retire in 1963. But no other dispute spanned two decades or served as a lightening rod for extraparliamentary opposition.

The debate over the 1968 Emergency Laws is well covered in the literature, particularly as it contributed to the student and protest movements of the late

[111] This was the reason for emergency legislation (rather than, say, the security of democratic freedom) most frequently articulated when it was first proposed by Adenauer's government in 1954/55. Michael Schneider, *Demokratie in Gefahr? Der Konflikt um die Notstandsgesetze: Sozialdemokratie, Gewerkschaften und intellektueller Protest, 1958–1968* (Bonn: Neue Gesellschaft, 1986), 38.

[112] Article 5, Sections 1b and 2 of the general treaty stated that the Allies could use military force on German territory "without the consent of the Federal Republic" in cases of perceived emergency. See "Convention on Relations Between the Three Powers and the Federal Republic of Germany, May 26, 1952, As Amended by Schedule I of the Protocol on Termination of the Occupation Regime in Germany, Signed at Paris, October 23, 1954," reprinted in *Documents on Germany, 1944–1970* (Washington, DC: U.S. Government Printing Office, 1971), 248–53.

[113] For the Korean War's importance to German rearmament, see Large, *Germans to the Front*, 62–8. On the Allies' influence: Hubert Zimmermann, *Money and Security: Troops, Monetary Policy and West Germany's Relations with the United States and Britain, 1950–1971* (Washington, DC: German Historical Institute and Cambridge University Press, 2002).

1960s.[114] There is, however, little if any appreciation for this debate as a continuation of the postwar discussion on militant democracy. For this reason, many have interpreted the parties' decision to support or oppose the Emergency Laws as one of sheer political opportunism.[115] Though the FDP has not been spared this critique, its brunt has been borne by the SPD. After initially taking a firm stance against the proposed emergency legislation and defeating each new version of the bill put forth by government, the SPD changed its position in late 1965.[116] The party not only switched sides on the matter of emergency legislation but moved from opposition to government when it entered into a Grand Coalition with the CDU/CSU one year later. That the passage of the Emergency Laws was the price Social Democratic leaders agreed to pay to get into government is clear. But the corresponding assertion that the parties' earlier claims amounted to no more than thirteen years of opportunistic window dressing is unconvincing in light of long-standing debates on the broader question of militant democracy. The Social Democrats – like conservatives – can be seen to have remained more loyal than not to the concept they first staked out in the immediate postwar years.

Carlo Schmid was one of the first figures to make a public statement when the matter of emergency legislation resurfaced. On June 30, 1955, not long after the Paris Treaties went into effect, he admitted to radio listeners that he could see no way around emergency laws. Ever the pragmatist, Schmid declared it preferable "that we Germans decide what happens in times of crisis, rather than have the occupation powers do it for us."[117] He then went on to enumerate the seven criteria that any future legislation would have to meet in order to win SPD approval, a list that placed precise limits on the state's empowerment and ultimately defined Social Democrats' official position for the next decade.[118] Because this short catalog bore such a striking resemblance to the

114 For the history of the 1960s debate over emergency laws, see Schneider, *Demokratie in Gefahr?* Also Maren Krohn, *Die gesellschaftlichen Auseinandersetzungen um die Notstandsgesetze* (Cologne: Pahl-Rugenstein, 1981) and Boris Spernol, *Notstand der Demokratie: Der Protest gegen die Notstandsgesetze und die Frage der NS-Vergangenheit* (Essen: Klartext, 2008). Works which also treat the Emergency Laws at length, include Karl A. Otto, *Vom Ostermarsch zu APO: Geschichte der außerparlamentarischen Opposition in der Bundesrepublik, 1960–1970* (Frankfurt: Campus, 1977) and Nick Thomas, *Protest Movements in 1960s West Germany: A Social History of Dissent and Democracy* (Oxford: Berg, 2003).

115 See, e.g., Braunthal, "Emergency Legislation," 77–8.

116 The last time the SPD voted as a block against the emergency laws in June 1965, the numbers split 238 versus 167, with all but two of the dissenting votes coming from the SPD. *Verhandlungen des Deutschen Bundestages: Stenographische Berichte* (hereafter, *Verhandlungen*), IV. Bundestag, 192. Sitzung (June 24, 1965), 9737.

117 Hessischer Rundfunk interview of Carlo Schmid reprinted in Friedrich Schäfer, *Die Notstandsgesetze: Vorsorge für den Menschen und den demokratischen Rechtsstaat* (Cologne: Westdeutscher, 1966), 23–4. Here, 23.

118 1) The Bundestag had the sole right to declare an emergency situation. 2) Under no circumstances could either the government or the federal president hold the power of emergency decree. 3) The military was subordinate to civil governance at all levels. 4–5) Parliament retained

party's earlier position on emergency legislation, the Christian-Liberal government could not abide it. But neither could its members alone obtain the two-thirds majority required of the Bundestag for a constitutional amendment.[119] Compromise was thus necessary but by no means inevitable, for liberal and conservative leaders were no less wedded to executive power than they were before. Had there been any doubts on this score, Interior Minister Gerhard Schröder (CDU) put them to rest when introducing the government's bill for emergency laws in September 1960. Before the Bundestag, Schröder explained that "the hour of exception is the hour of the executive." At that moment, "things must be dealt with," and the continued adherence "to the whole prescriptive work" that defined parliamentary democracy was simply not possible.[120] Just as this explanation – and the corresponding conception of militant democracy – had failed to move Social Democrats during the Parliamentary Council's deliberations, Schröder's speech did not sway them to pass the proposed bill ten years later.

For five years the SPD continued to oppose the proposals put forth by the government, even when, by the early 1960s, the majority of Social Democrats had come to share Schmid's position that some sort of legislation was necessary. Here, pressure from the trade unions was a critical factor, opposed as they were to any law that could be used to undermine workers' right to strike. In the end, a new generation of party leaders –Willy Brandt, Helmut Schmidt, and Herbert Wehner among them – determined the SPD's course. Reformers all, Brandt was the undisputed charmer and fresh face of the party whose outspokenness against both Soviet repression and polarized East–West relations won him admirers and critics alike. In 1962, two years before Brandt was appointed chairman of the party, he was already engaged in negotiations with conservatives over a possible coalition in which emergency legislation played a central role. The SPD's visible willingness to cooperate on this score was widely criticized by rank-and-file Social Democrats as well as sympathetic leftist commentators. Left-liberal intellectuals like Jürgen Habermas and Jürgen Seifert, historian Karl Dietrich Bracher, and even future interior minister Werner Maihofer joined leaders of the trade union federation and numerous student organizations to publicly debate the legitimacy of the Emergency Laws and the apparent lack of opposition from within the Bundestag.[121] SPD leaders were

control of every emergency measure ordered and had the right to rescind them at any time. 6) Each emergency situation required its own law stating the specific measures allowed in that particular case. 7) Emergency legislation could in no way be used to disable or limit officially organized labor strikes. Schäfer, *Die Notstandsgesetz*, 23. Also, Krohn, *Auseinandersetzungen um die Notstandsgesetze*, 29.

[119] A simple majority, however, gave Adenauer's government the power to push through one emergency-related law after another between the years 1956 and 1965. See Braunthal, "Emergency Legislation," 76–7.

[120] *Verhandlungen*, III. Bundestag, 124. Sitzung (September 28, 1960), 7177. For the official position of the CDU/CSU, see Ernst Benda, *Die Notstandsverfassung* (Munich: Olzog, 1966).

[121] See the special edition of *neue kritik* entitled *Demokratie vor dem Notstand: Protokoll des Bonner Kongresses gegen die Notstandsgesetze am 30. Mai 1965* (Frankfurt: neue kritik,

not deaf to criticism and sought to overcome strong disagreements within their party and in dialogue with union representatives. But at the end of the day, they ultimately spurned these forums of extraparliamentary opposition. When an opportunity finally presented itself for the SPD to enter government with the CDU/CSU in 1966, the party leadership opted to compromise.[122] Rather unexpectedly, it was the Liberal Democrats – propelled by their own crop of young reformers, most notably Hans-Dietrich Genscher – who rescinded their support for the proposed Emergency Laws at the last minute and came to voice the interests of a swelling protest movement. Now the (lone) source of parliamentary opposition, the FDP remembered its ideological roots and argued that the proposed legislation threatened individual civil liberties and was thus incompatible with democratic security.[123]

Despite mass protest, conservatives realized their long-sought goal of emergency legislation on May 30, 1968 – thanks to the votes of the SPD.[124] To be fair, however, the SPD did more than sign off on a CDU/CSU project. Over the course of debate and negotiations, Social Democrats rejected proposals by the Christian Union that transferred power to the executive, insisting on the inviolable role of parliament and the Constitutional Court even at the height of crisis. More specifically, they refused government the right to declare a national emergency and made provisions for a crisis parliament – a "joint committee" (*Gemeinsamer Ausschuß*) made up of the legislature's appointed representatives – to act for the Bundestag in the event it could not assemble or proved ineffective.[125] Social Democrats also successfully limited the extent and degree to which the state legitimately could use armed force. In seeking to preserve workers' rights, for example, the SPD placed explicit restrictions on police intervention in strike situations.[126] In addition, it guarded against the possibility of armed forces being used against the German population by insisting on the strict delineation of internal police forces (*Schutz-* and *Kriminalpolizei*) from forces such as the Federal Border Guard (*Bundesgrenzschutz*, or BGS) intended to protect the state from

1965) and Hans Heinz Holz, "Notstand der Demokratie – Ergebnisse und Perspektiven des Frankfurter Kongresses," *Blätter* 2 (1966): 976–82. A bit further on the right: Karl Jaspers, *Wohin treibt die Bundesrepublik? Tatsachen, Gefahren, Chance* (Munich: R. Piper, 1966).

122 Schneider, *Demokratie in Gefahr*, 103; 105f. For the SPD's elaborated position, see Schäfer, *Die Notstandsgesetze*.

123 Schneider, *Demokratie in Gefahr*, 213–16. Though written in 1960 and therefore before the renewed debate on emergency legislation, Braunthal's article on the FDP remains one of the best treatments of that party's internal divisions and even radically opposed impulses. Braunthal, "The Free Democratic Party."

124 Fifty-three SPD deputies, one member of the CDU, and all but one FDP representative voted against the bill.

125 In addition to establishing a check on the executive, the provision (Article 53a GG) complied with a Europe-wide push to standardize and coordinate crisis administrations. An emergency parliament along these lines was first proposed by the SPD in the Parliamentary Council. See *Parl. Rat* 13, 845–72; 984–92.

126 Schneider, *Demokratie in Gefahr*, 43–6.

external dangers.[127] Demonstrating continued disagreement with conservatives over the suspension of basic rights, Social Democrats also significantly reduced the number of civil liberties the state could curtail and insisted that the new legislation strictly demarcate the length of time it could do so.[128]

The final condition for Social Democratic support of the 1968 Emergency Laws was a piece of supplementary legislation amending the Basic Law to also include resistance among the rights guaranteed every German citizen. A *Widerstandsrecht* similar to that of the Land constitutions of Hesse and Bremen was called for in 1948 by Social Democrats and Liberals seeking to include one in the federal constitution as well.[129] With many of their own party colleagues disputing the need or, more accurately, the point of legally recognizing the right to resist the motion was soundly defeated. Apprehension over the impending emergency legislation, however, resurrected the idea among Social Democrats in the mid-1960s and eventually tipped the scales in its favor.[130] In the earlier debate, those who favored the bill argued that placing resistance among Germans' constitutional rights would raise political awareness and inspire bravery. Now, supporters understood the right to directly counter the threat posed by the proposed emergency laws. After various false starts, the party majority finally threw its full weight behind a 1968 bill to include not only a right but every German's "duty and right to resistance against a threat [*Bedrohung*] to the free and democratic order" in the Basic Law.[131] While the proposed measure did little to ease others' opposition to the emergency legislation, it eased the minds of many Social Democrats. This was because they understood the SPD to have matched a constitutional provision for the empowerment of the state with a similar provision for the empowerment of its population.

That many conservatives also perceived this to be the case was clear in the Christian Union's initial rejection of a *Widerstandsrecht*. Leading members of the CDU/CSU expressed their opinion that granting citizens the right to resistance defeated the very purpose of the Emergency Laws.[132] Frustrated by the

[127] Ibid., 232. They accomplished this largely by legislating distinctions between national catastrophe and cases of internal emergencies of defense and of unrest. Moreover, each category carried its own, strict definition of legitimate state force. In the case of a catastrophe, for example, both German troops and border guards were acceptable under the condition that they did not carry arms.

[128] The constitutional right to free correspondence and the freedom of assembly and association were made "emergency proof." Ibid., 199.

[129] For the debate in the Parliamentary Council, see *Parl. Rat* 2, 227fn116 and *Parl. Rat* 1, 5 Sitzung von 19.8.1948, 46f. A reprint of the Hessian model, which explicitly stated that resistance was "everyone's right and duty," can be found in *Parl. Rat* 5, 152n55.

[130] For a detailed discussion of the 1960s debate, see Christopher Böckenförde, "Die Kodifizierung des Widerstandsrecht im Grundgesetz," *Juristenzeitung* 25 (1970): 168–72.

[131] For the different proposals under consideration: Hans Matthöfer, "Widerstandsrecht ins Grundgesetz," *Frankfurter Rundschau*, January 12, 1968.

[132] The proposal was discussed on the main floor of the Bundestag on May 15 and 30, 1968. On the odd exercise of legalizing that which is inherently illegal, see David Clay Large, "Normifying

prospect of compromise and the political climate more generally, Ernst Lemmer confronted his colleagues on the Union's executive board with what seemed to him the bitter truth of the matter: "We are, because we live in a democracy, at a disadvantage. Democracy is weak.... Over [in the GDR] everything remains systematic, logical, disciplined, purpose-driven, while here there is ... the cloudy chaos of public opinion. Soviet observers must be greatly encouraged at the sight of our so-called public opinion."[133] Increasingly unnerved by the protest wave of the late 1960s, and with the Emergency Laws' successful passage hanging in the balance, the CDU/CSU ultimately felt it had no choice but to concede the *Widerstandsrecht*.[134] The parties' leaders did find a silver lining, however: The codification of resistance just might have the unanticipated benefit of letting them define it, and legitimate civil action more generally, in the FRG.[135]

the Unnormifiable: The Right to Resistance in West German Constitutional History," in *The Cornerstone of Democracy: The West German Grundgesetz, 1949–1989*, ed. Detlef Junker (Washington, DC: German Historical Institute, 1994): 83–95; here, 87.

133 Bundesvorstandssitzung, October 9, 1967, Archiv für Christlich-Demokratische Politik (Sankt Augustin) 07–001 – 16/5.

134 Basic Law, art. 20, sec. 4.

135 Large, "Normifying the Unnormifiable," 87–9.

2

Disobedient Germans

Resistance and the Extraparliamentary Left

> We must continually ... try to make connections between what is happening now and our past actions or inactions, see present events in light of the historic struggle against tyranny.
>
> Ernst Reuter (July 20, 1953)[1]

> Why do we not respond to the emergency exercises of the state authority machinery, why don't we respond with emergency exercises of our own?
>
> Rudi Dutschke (July 1967)[2]

The student movement looms large in popular memories of 1960s West Germany as well as in scholarly literature on the period. There are a number of reasons for this, some naturally better than others.[3] Most compellingly, student protest and the German Socialist Student League (SDS) that served as its mouthpiece makes tangible what might otherwise remain an amorphous "spirit" of the times; the movement's leaders and activists give body to the struggle for a more egalitarian society and, just as crucially, to the experience of that future society prefigured in the protest actions themselves.[4] But there are also a number of problems with using the student movement as a sort of

[1] Commemoration speech quoted in Peter Steinbach, "Widerstandsforschung im politischen Spannungsfeld," *Aus Politik und Zeitgeschichte* 28 (July 8, 1988): 4.

[2] Interview with *Der Spiegel* 29 (July 10, 1967), 30–3.

[3] The diagnosis of generational conflict encouraged a focus on youth revolt and the often uncritical acceptance of students' own self-understanding as the analytic framework. In addition, scholars used structures like the SDS and APO to distinguish the sustained protest of the 1960s from sporadic unrest as well as earlier organized forms. See, e.g., Karl-Werner Brand, Detlef Büsser, and Dieter Rucht, *Aufbruch in eine andere Gesellschaft: Neue soziale Bewegungen in der Bundesrepublik* (Frankfurt: Campus, 1983); Gerd Langguth, *Protestbewegung: Entstehung, Entwicklung, Renaissance* (Cologne: Wissenschaft & Politik, 1977); Gerhard Bauss, *Die Studentenbewegung der sechziger Jahre* (Cologne: Pahl-Rugenstein, 1983).

[4] See Wolfgang Kraushaar, "Autoritärer Staat und Antiautoritäre Bewegung," in *Frankfurter Schule und Studentenbewegung: Von der Flaschenpost zum Molotovcocktail, 1946 bis 1995*, ed. idem (Hamburg: Roger & Bernhard, 1998), 1: 15. For works that grasp the (self-)creative project

shorthand for the more general phenomenon of 1960s extraparliamentary politics. The overly sharp demarcation of generational conflict – between parents and children, between "old" and "new" left, or between youthful activists and an adult establishment – tends to reproduce a polarizing ethical and political narrative of liberating revolt against an oppressive system or, alternately, the illiberal destabilization of a flawed but functional order. It reduces the complexity of historical actors involved on both sides and is ultimately better suited to rehashing the debates of the time than to historicizing them.[5] Moreover, it shapes how we understand the 1970s, a decade commonly conceived as a coda to the 1960s. The collapse of both the SDS and the oppositional umbrella organization APO (*Außerparlamentarische Opposition*) at the end of the 1960s, followed by global stagflation and Americans' continued presence in Vietnam, encourages interpretations of the 1970s as a working out of held-over issues or, worse, as something of a wasteland for oppositional politics. In this often melancholic frame, the extraparliamentary left exists but has little beyond the shared memories, conflicts, and disillusionment of "1968" to give it form. One way to avoid these difficulties is to extend the temporal frame. Doing so demonstrates how student protesters both broke with the social and cultural codes of their parents and, by means of an extremely successful intergenerational transference of ideas, ultimately maintained long-standing convictions about the existing West German state that were central to postwar political culture.

Of course, the importance of resistance after 1945 was not immediately self-evident given Germans' relatively poor track record. During and immediately after the Third Reich, both German and non-German scholars argued that Germany had veered from the revolutionary examples set by France and Britain and had, instead, taken its own peculiar and very flawed path to becoming

at the center of protesters' experience, see, e.g., Belinda Davis, "A Whole World Opening Up: Transcultural Contact, Difference, and the Politicization of 'New Left' Activists," in *Changing the World, Changing Oneself: Political Protest and Collective Identities in West Germany and the U.S. in the 1960s and 1970s*, eds. idem, et al. (New York: Berghahn, 2010), 255–73; Gerd-Rainer Horn, *The Spirit of '68: Rebellion in Western Europe and North America, 1956–1976* (Oxford: Oxford University Press, 2007).

5 The early reductionism is recreated in newer scholarship. See, e.g., Kraushaar, *Frankfurter Schule* and Ingrid Gilcher-Holtey, *Die 1968 Bewegung: Deutschland, Westeuropa, USA* (Munich: Beck, 2001). Even Gerd-Rainer Horn's transnational study, against the thrust of his own analysis, confirms this narrow interpretation for the FRG as a signal case of his thesis that students dominated where the '68er movement was weakest. Contemporary anti-68ers also fixate on bipolar conflict, but reverse the good/bad signs: Gerd Koenen, *Das rote Jahrzehnt: Unsere kleine deutsche Kulturrevolution, 1967–1977* (Cologne: Kiepenheuer & Witsch, 2001); Gerd Langguth, *Mythos '68: Die Gewaltphilosophie von Rudi Dutschke. Ursachen und Folgen der Studentenbewegung* (Munich: Olzog, 2001); Götz Aly, *Unser Kampf 1968 – ein irritierter Blick zurück* (Frankfurt: Fischer, 2008). Exceptions are growing more common. See, e.g., Detlef Siegfried's masterful cultural history, *Time Is On My Side: Konsum und Politik in der westdeutschen Jugendkultur der 60er Jahre* (Göttingen: Wallstein, 2006) and Belinda Davis, who recognizes the need to escape conventional frameworks and the difficulty in doing so in current treatments of oppositional politics. Belinda Davis, "What's Left? Popular Political Participation in Postwar Europe," *American Historical Review* 113 (April 2008): 363–90.

a modern nation-state.[6] Nazism and the population's failure to overthrow it were understood as the culmination of this *Sonderweg* – the latest, most egregious, example of Germans' submissive relationship to power. Though there were certainly scholars who denied the specifically German roots of fascism – conservatives, for example, typically pointed a finger at the Europewide phenomena of mass politics, modernization, and secularization – the argument for Germany as an aberration from the West stuck.[7] And the theory's particular salience within the German left had significant consequences for the ways resistance was talked about – and pursued – in the postwar period. Left-leaning intellectuals and publicists explicitly connected the weakness of Germans' efforts at resistance to the nation's lack of democratic political culture. From there, it was but a short jump to understanding postwar democracy's success and the prevention of fascism's return to depend on their fellow nationals' acculturation to resistance.

Such thinking only exacerbated postwar Germans' already conflicted relationship to resistance when the term was associated inextricably with opposition to Nazism. Considered in the abstract, the value of such resistance was clear. Its contraposition to fascism placed resistance indisputably on the side of democracy and, for most postwar Germans, of Western Christian tradition. Indeed, in a country searching for democratic traditions upon which to rebuild state and society, resistance alone had the power to bestow democratic legitimacy. For this reason, political parties and individual Germans attempting to secure Allied favor were eager to tout their antifascist credentials. Conservatives emphasized the importance of Christian conviction to resistance, liberals their commitment to individualism and personal freedom, and the left its record of early organized opposition. This exercise of retroactively confirming anti-Nazi resistance was often indistinguishable from Germans' simultaneous efforts to combat what they took to be widespread accusations of collective guilt – the claim that every German was morally and politically culpable for the crimes committed under Nazism.[8] Toward this end, Germans of every political persuasion sought to document an "other Germany," one that had resisted cooptation by the Nazis by either actively opposing the regime, going into exile abroad,

6 See, e.g., William M. McGovern, *From Luther to Hitler: The History of Fascist-Nazi Political Philosophy* (Boston: Houghton Mifflin, 1941); Alexander Abusch, *Der Irrweg einer Nation* (Berlin: Aufbau, 1946); Fritz Helling, *Der Katastrophenweg der deutschen Geschichte* (Frankfurt: Klostermann, 1947).

7 Not to be debunked until the mid-1980s by David Blackbourn and Geoff Eley in *The Peculiarities of German History* (Oxford: Oxford University Press, 1984). For notable conservative interpretations, see Friedrich Meinecke, *Die deutsche Katastrophe: Betrachtungen und Erinnerungen* (Wiesbaden: Brockhaus, 1946); Gerhard Ritter, *Europa und die deutsche Frage: Betrachtungen über die geschichtliche Eigenart des deutschen Staatsdenkens* (Munich: Münchner Verlag, 1948); and Hans Windisch, *Führer und Verführte: Eine Analyse des deutschen Schicksals* (Seebruck am Chiemsee: Herring, 1946).

8 On Germans' exaggeration of the Allies' interest in pronouncing all Germans guilty, see Jeffrey K. Olick, *In the House of the Hangman: The Agonies of German Defeat, 1943–1949* (Chicago: University of Chicago Press, 2005).

or retreating from public life in "inner emigration." *This* was the Germany of intellectuals, philosophers, and musical geniuses and, according to the political expediencies of the 1940s and 1950s, the country to which the average German belonged.[9] The vast majority of Germans, of course, did not actively oppose the Nazi regime and few if any escaped collaboration. But just as a legacy of resistance provided postwar political leaders like Konrad Adenauer, Theodor Heuss, and Kurt Schumacher with the necessary credentials, that same legacy freed Germans to accept the role of democrat. In this way, resistance became a pillar of postwar political culture.

There were Germans, of course, for whom resistance played a more direct role in the constitution of their postwar identity. This was true of communists and socialists in the western and Soviet zones, who understood their anti-Nazi records to make them the only ones capable of leading Germany out of its moral abyss. No one captured or successfully communicated this sentiment better than Kurt Schumacher, the leader of the SPD from 1945 until his death in 1952. His antifascist credentials were unassailable; his ten years in various Nazi camps were written on his broken body and they embittered him to those who later sought to deny responsibility for their previous inaction.[10] Surely the conspicuous trumpeting of what so many West Germans *in practice* viewed ambiguously or with open distaste – namely resistance – was one factor in Social Democrats' narrow loss to Adenauer and the CDU in the first national election. The establishment of an "antifascist" communist regime in East Berlin did not help in this regard. Indeed, the fact that the GDR's Socialist Unity Party (SED) used anti-Nazi resistance to legitimate its rule made it increasingly difficult for those living in West Germany to lay claim to this same legacy. The SPD joined conservatives in equating German communism with Soviet totalitarianism but this did not save them – or left politics more generally – from being routinely implicated in the SED dictatorship next door.

Not that Schumacher or the SPD commanded the loyalties of the West German left. A wide range of positions and, especially among intellectuals, a lingering antipathy toward party politics meant that quite a few leftists were underwhelmed by the newest incarnation of German social democracy. In the end, what united these critical outsiders with the majority of Social Democrats in the 1950s was Adenauer's chancellorship and what they perceived as the "restoration" of the political and economic structures that had led to National Socialism in the first place. This, more than anything, kept antifascism alive and encouraged leftists' continued identification with a resistance defined in

[9] Most famously, Thomas Mann represented a small minority who argued against this assertion of a good versus bad Germany, insisting instead that Nazism was an intrinsic part – but not the entirety – of German culture and tradition. See, for instance, Erika and Klaus Mann's *The Other Germany* (New York: Modern Age, 1940), written while in exile. Also: Hermann Glaser, *The Rubble Years: The Cultural Roots of Postwar Germany* (New York: Paragon, 1986), 73–81, and Olick, *House of the Hangman*, 144–52.

[10] Among the many biographical treatments, see Willy Albrecht's *Kurt Schumacher: Ein Leben für den demokratischen Sozialismus* (Bonn: Neue Gesellschaft, 1985).

terms of opposition to the state.[11] For those convinced of the FRG's ongoing fascist potential and therefore the need for active vigilance from all democrats, resistance was the conceptual counterpart to militant democracy. It was their answer to democracy's defense, one that, like militant democracy, rejected passivity – this time on the part of the populace – and did not rule out the possible use of force. Unlike militant democracy, however, resistance was by definition oppositional. That meant that all measures taken under the rubric of this strategy were conceived as reactive, not proactive, in nature. This distinction became most relevant at the end of the 1950s, when the SPD relinquished its oppositional position in parliament and effectively amputated an extraparliamentary left it had previously represented. Rather than encourage political integration, the SPD's attempt to redefine both itself as a party and the scope of legitimate opposition encouraged a kind of negative alliance to take shape among diverse constituencies on the left, people who often had little more in common than their skepticism regarding West German democracy and an unchanged commitment to opposing fascism in all its forms and stages of development.

Conflict between the government and its population over rearmament in the 1950s and then Vietnam, the Grand Coalition, and the Emergency Laws in the 1960s helped to galvanize this alliance. Oppositional actions, even those deemed tactically wrongheaded, were interpreted, first, as attempts to counter the violence inherent in the system and, second, as evidence of Germans' newfound ability to resist. The extraparliamentary left's vigilant approach to democracy's defense encouraged interpretations of state force as authoritarian or quasi-fascist and entailed a deeply ambivalent view of violence. Given the centrality of solidarity to the project of resistance and, indeed, to the left's continued existence in conservative times, this was enough to hold the diverse coalition together. Even when they vehemently disagreed with those radicals who took up arms against the state in 1970, the vast majority of extraparliamentary actors were unwilling or unable to deny the fundamental premise upon which such militancy was predicated, namely the legitimacy of counterviolence as resistance.

THE PROBLEMS OF RESISTANCE

For all its importance to the new state's democratic legitimacy, resistance was a highly contentious subject, one that provoked controversy right up to the end of the twentieth century.[12] There were several reasons for this, the most obvious being that praising resistance raised the uncomfortable implication that the average German *should* have resisted. Feelings of guilt or defensiveness

[11] David Clay Large, "'A Beacon in the German Darkness': The Anti-Nazi Resistance Legacy in West German Politics," in *Resistance against the Third Reich, 1933–1990*, eds. Michael Geyer and John W. Boyer (Chicago: University of Chicago Press, 1992), 250.

[12] German reunification reopened the question of resistance, as Cold War exclusions and narratives quickly became outdated and/or less tenable. Bill Niven, *Facing the Nazi Past: United Germany and the Legacy of the Third Reich* (New York: Routledge, 2002), 77–94.

were complicated, however, by the fact that many Germans equated resistance with treason. The positive valuation of resistance simply did not fit with their own consciously held convictions. Much ambivalence and even open hostility toward anti-Nazi resistance had to do with its specific wartime context. Questioned about the appropriateness of opposing the Nazi state during war, thirty-four percent of West Germans polled in 1952 answered that the resisters should have waited until after the war (in addition to fifteen percent who stated that there should have been no resistance at all; only twenty percent valued the resisters positively).[13] The problem in postwar Germany was this: presenting resistance as the morally correct choice called into question the actions of those who had fought until the bitter end, not to mention the millions who died ostensibly for the good of the nation.[14] In short, the traditional values of obedience to authority and loyalty to one's country, coupled with Germans' experience of wartime sacrifice, greatly muddied the moral waters around German anti-Nazi resistance. Germans on the whole – and not just political elites – walked a fine line to both affirm the anti-Nazi resistance legacy and confirm the average soldier's honorable execution of his duty.[15]

The result was a very selective history of both anti-Nazi resistance and the *Wehrmacht*. The army was neatly cordoned off from Nazism and, as a result, the crimes perpetrated in Germany's name.[16] At the same time, Claus Schenk Graf von Stauffenberg entered the pantheon of FRG heroes, along with his co-conspirators, for the attempted assassination of Hitler on July 20, 1944. Despite the fact that many of the high-ranking army and state officials involved originally supported Hitler's regime and never ceased to disdain parliamentary democracy, Stauffenberg and the July 20 plot came to stand for resistance generally. While the GDR laid claim to antifascism by commemorating communist resistance groups like the so-called Red Orchestra, the FRG reiterated its anti-communist commitments by denouncing those same men and women as Soviet spies. And individual resisters like Georg Esler were written out of textbooks altogether because they were of no political or symbolic use to either of the two young states.[17]

[13] Elisabeth Noelle and Erich Peter Neumann, eds., *The Germans: Public Opinion Polls, 1947–1966* (Allensbach: Verlag für Demoskopie, 1967), 200.

[14] Michael Geyer has emphasized the degree to which German military honor and integrity was defended after the war. It was, he argues, a defense of the self – of one's personal integrity and life story – and not of Hitler as others have suggested. Michael Geyer, "Cold War Angst: The Case of West German Opposition to Rearmament and Nuclear Weapons," in *The Miracle Years: A Cultural History of West Germany, 1949–1968*, ed. Hannah Schissler (Princeton: Princeton University Press, 2001), 376–408; here, 383–4.

[15] The popularity of Carl Zuckmayer's famous 1947 play, *The Devil's General*, rested on its success at doing just this. Mariatte C. Denman, "Nostalgia for a Better Germany: Carl Zuckmayer's 'Des Teufels General,'" *The German Quarterly* 76 (Autumn 2003): 369–80.

[16] Omer Bartov, *Germany's War and the Holocaust: Disputed Histories* (Ithaca: Cornell University Press, 2001); Hannes Heer, *The Discursive Construction of History: Remembering the Wehrmacht's War of Annihilation* (New York: Palgrave, 2008).

[17] Niven, *Facing the Nazi Past*, 64–7, 69–72.

That Stauffenberg became the face of German resistance under the Third Reich incited understandable bitterness among leftists in the FRG. For, if anti-Nazi resistance provoked accusations of treason from some quarters in West Germany, it was central to the self-identity of those who had actively opposed the Nazi regime – and suffered greatly for it. Figures on the left were no more inclined than the average German to probe the messy realities of collaboration and resistance in the Third Reich, where the latter frequently depended on the former and elided easy categorizations of guilt and innocence.[18] With few exceptions, the postwar left approached resistance in familiar black-and-white terms – as a force for good in the historical struggle against oppression. New was their sense that Germans, having failed to revolt against the Nazis, were now duty bound to resist all future manifestations of fascism and state repression. In both cases, the main question resistance raised for the left was whether or not Germans could actually be made capable of it. This was, of course, no small question, for leftists of all stripes agreed that safeguarding freedom under the conditions of mass society required citizens who would defend civil liberties. In other words, if the newest German democracy was to be spared the fate of Weimar, Germans had to learn to be disobedient. Social Democratic efforts to use the constitution as a pedagogical tool were thus just one example of how leftists, seeking to fortify German democracy against potential abuses of state power, advocated for the political reeducation of Germans. Learning certainly entailed denazification, but this was conceived as part and parcel of a larger process, namely the fashioning of critical citizens able and willing to take active responsibility for their world.

The question of how to create resistance-capable Germans was pursued most thoroughly by those who took the question of German guilt and analyses of National Socialism as the jumping-off point for reforming society and politics. Discussions of democratic renewal abated somewhat in the 1950s, but in the years immediately after the war a broad spectrum of public intellectuals confronted the problems of Germany's past in an effort to secure its future. In particular, this group of "engaged democrats" sought to overcome what they (and other proponents of the *Sonderweg* theory) touted as the German bourgeoisie's historical failure to actualize their "free self-development" in the world as their revolutionary French and British counterparts had done.[19] They argued, for example, that only in the planning and preparing, the suffering and fighting, and – finally – in the winning of a revolution did one come to "nurture an understanding of what one wants."[20] The Germans' repeated failure to

[18] On resistance and the difficult truth of collaboration, see Michael Geyer, "Resistance as Ongoing Project: Visions of Order, Obligations to Strangers, and Struggles for Civil Society, 1933–1990," in Geyer and Boyer, *Resistance*, 325–50.

[19] Sean A. Forner, "Für eine demokratische Erneuerung Deutschlands: Kommunikationsprozesse und Deutungsmuster engagierter Demokraten nach 1945," *Geschichte und Gesellschaft* 33 (2007): 228–57.

[20] Walter Dirks, "Die Zweite Republik: Zum Ziel und zum Weg der deutschen Demokratie," *Frankfurter Hefte* 1 (April 1946): 12–24; here, 15.

revolt was, in short, interpreted as the root cause of their long-standing habit of subjecting themselves to external authority.

Referring to this particular German malady as one of corpse-like obedience, publicists such as Eugon Kogon and Walter Dirks sought to cure the population's condition through the cultivation of an active and resistance-capable citizenry.[21] In 1946 Dirks and Kogon founded the *Frankfurter Hefte*, a journal explicitly intended to draw reflective and engaged readers into making "distinctions and decisions." The men understood this process as the first step toward the development and courageous assertion of the reader's own opinion. "We repeat this because it is important: have the courage to say no and even more to say yes. With insight, we hope to nourish the strength of heart and spirit that such courage entails."[22] In declaring this its mission, the journal made clear that education to democracy would not take place passively but required the active participation of the reader. Democracy, participation, and education were each presented as vital to the realization of the other, and each as essential to the creation of personalities in the fullest sense of the word. By actively engaging its readers on matters of political culture, the *Frankfurter Hefte* sought nothing less than to approximate the learning process of a successful revolution. The hope for Dirks and Kogon, at least, was that this would both eliminate the need for an actual revolution (and the violence it implicitly entailed) and help mold a new German population, one jealous of its freedom and capable, if necessary, of resisting any state that lost its claim to democratic legitimacy.

This preoccupation with a particular German inability to rebel against state authority dovetailed with work undertaken by émigré sociologists, political scientists, and philosophers of the neo-Marxist "Frankfurt School" on the subject of authoritarianism more generally. On the one hand, the theoretical drive behind their analyses of Nazism – its social preconditioning and effects as well as its political structure – unhinged the postwar left's discussion on resistance from its immediate German referent. In this way it differed from that of Kogon and Dirks. On the other hand, the groups' different approaches intersected in the belief that resistance was a matter not merely for the past but for the present and future. Having successfully relocated their Institute for Social Research from Frankfurt to the United States by the late 1930s, critical theorists Max Horkheimer, Theodor W. Adorno, Friedrich Pollock, Herbert Marcuse, Erich Fromm, Franz Neumann, and Otto Kirchheimer turned their scholarly attention to the terror they had just escaped. In a desire to better understand the susceptibility of modern masses to psychic manipulation, the Institute launched an empirical social research program culminating in the

[21] References to Germans' *Kadavergehorsam* abound. See, e.g., Abusch, *Der Irrweg einer Nation*, esp. 187–9, 247–8.

[22] "An unsere Leser!" *Frankfurter Hefte* 1 (April 1946): 1–2; here, 2. In the same issue, Dirks goes on to describe how the goals embodied in the new state were not to be constructed from ideals but rather had to be developed from its realities in a process of distinctions and decisions (*Scheidung und Entscheidung*). Dirks, "Die Zweite Republik," 15–16.

five-part *Studies in Prejudice*, of which the Adorno-led research project on the "authoritarian personality" was the centerpiece.[23] After studying over two thousand white, native-born, non-Jewish, middle-class Americans, Adorno and his collaborators concluded that the authoritarian syndrome was predicated on ego weakness. Whether one's potential for authoritarian behavior was made manifest depended on the environment; outside forces of a suitable intensity and direction could activate and draw upon the repressed urges of these individuals.[24]

Character structure alone, however, could not explain the cement of fascism or reveal the possibilities for its overcoming; the Frankfurt School's analysis of the authoritarian personality was embedded in an analysis of the authoritarian state. Confronted by a set of deeply dispiriting developments – the conquest of Europe by Nazism, its (temporary) alliance with Stalinism, and their own experience of American consumer capitalism – Critical Theory took a pessimistic turn in the early 1940s. The Institute's core members, Horkheimer, Adorno, and Pollock, came to hold a monolithic view of the fate of the masses in advanced industrial societies across the globe, subjected to technocratic forms of domination at the hands of authoritarian states.[25] The latter had trumped the economic frictions of class society through political control by bureaucratic and managerial elites; they dominated their subjects through the unremitting application of terror and coercion or by more refined psychosocial means, in which fascist propaganda and consumerist gratification seemed to fuse into two sides of the same manipulated unfreedom. Under such auspices, these men came to theorize forms of domination that seemed to pervade modern society and to operate beyond conscious control, becoming far more insidious and insurmountable than traditional forms of political and economic repression.[26] In this way, they argued, the authoritarian state could be explained neither as uniquely German nor as an aberration from Western society. Instead, National Socialism was only the most extreme example of a general trend in mass societies under modern states. As Adorno put it some time later, even Auschwitz was "the expression of an extremely powerful societal tendency," namely that

[23] Thomas Wheatland, *The Frankfurt School in Exile* (Minneapolis: University of Minnesota Press, 2009), 219–57.

[24] Their findings are recorded in Theodor W. Adorno et al., *The Authoritarian Personality* (New York: Harper, 1950). On this project, see Martin Jay, *The Dialectical Imagination: A History of the Frankfurt School and the Institute of Social Research, 1923–1950* (Boston: Little, Brown, 1973), 219–52; Rolf Wiggershaus, *The Frankfurt School: Its History, Theories, and Political Significance*, trans. Michael Robertson (Cambridge: MIT Press, 1995), 408–52.

[25] Its two key expressions were essays of 1940 and 1942, respectively: Friedrich Pollock, "State Capitalism: Its Possibilities and Limitations," and Max Horkheimer, "The Authoritarian State," in *The Essential Frankfurt School Reader*, ed. Andrew Arato and Eike Gebhardt (New York: Continuum, 1982), 71–117.

[26] The classic statement is Horkheimer and Theodor W. Adorno, *Dialectic of Enlightenment: Philosophical Fragments*, trans. Edmund Jephcott (Stanford: Stanford University Press, 2002). On this and the above, see Jay, *Dialectical Imagination*, 152–8, 165–6, 212–18.

"barbarism itself is inscribed within the principle of civilization;" as such it was, indeed, repeatable.[27]

All told, the Institute's analysis of authoritarianism, one that applied to the advanced capitalist societies of the West but likened them to "totalitarian" systems elsewhere, was bleak. A ray of light was to be found, however, in a source not unlike that offered by Kogon and Dirks. While the degree of optimism varied significantly among these thinkers, they shared the belief that whatever chance for emancipation existed, existed in a method of critique as resistance. What was for Kogon and Dirks a practical attempt to cultivate educated readers corresponded to a theoretical method for the Frankfurt School. As social researchers, they approached the objects they investigated – capitalist social relations, bourgeois culture, consumer goods – in their sociohistorical context and interrogated them for their internal tensions, in particular for the ways these social products and practices failed to realize the ideals and values they themselves espoused. Horkheimer called this critical method "immanent;" its crucial move was to proceed from *within* the object in question, breaking through received truths to reveal alternate possibilities embedded in the world.[28] This was seen as one, very small means by which an individual might confront the existing order, uncover contradictions within it, and thus resist its aspirations to total domination. Adorno developed this perspective into what he called "non-identity thinking." What he had in mind operated within the space separating general concepts from their particular objects. While "identity thinking" subsumed the latter under the former, Adorno sought to preserve worldly objects in their concrete interconnections with one another, resisting both the violent dissolution of objects and the false erasure of tensions.[29] He asserted, moreover, that the latter sort of thinking represented a kind of opposition to authoritarian structures. Its cultivation in individuals would encourage habits of critical reflection, self-determination, and resolute "not joining in" (*nicht mitmachen*). The latter had been a watchword at the Institute since the 1930s and would be reformulated for a later audience as Marcuse's "Great Refusal."[30] Though theorists Horkheimer and Adorno traversed a different trajectory than publicists of Dirks and Kogon's persuasion, their goal and the means by which they sought to achieve it were parallel. Crucially, each group provided its audience with arguments for the importance of resistance to first building and then sustaining democracy in Germany.

27 Theodor W. Adorno, "Education after Auschwitz," in *Can One Live After Auschwitz? A Philosophical Reader*, ed. Rolf Tiedemann (Stanford: Stanford University Press, 2003), 19–33; here, 19–20.

28 For a summary, see David Held, *Introduction to Critical Theory: Horkheimer to Habermas* (Berkeley: University of California Press, 1980), 183–7.

29 Ibid., 212–18.

30 Jay, *Dialectical Imagination*, 111, 291, 321n122.

RESISTING RESTORATION: THE FRG IN THE 1950S

As the Cold War heated up, Allied interest in early efforts to reeducate Germans waned, and, with it, the best hope for large-scale denazification.[31] Reform lost out to the realities of a devastated infrastructure, scarce resources, and local intransigence, so that only the most egregious offenders were denied their previous positions as professors, judges, or the heads of industry. By the time the FRG celebrated its tenth anniversary, all hopes for dramatic economic restructuring or a united, neutral Germany were crushed and the Christian Union's 1957 campaign slogan, "no experiments!" captured the popular mood.[32] The average West German understood the lean years to be behind them and the credit Ludwig Erhard's social market won for this "economic miracle" lent legitimacy to Adenauer's government.[33] It was a period of political and economic stability unknown to the Weimar Republic – yet many still found reason for unease. In retrospect, Adenauer's decision to integrate former Nazis into West German society may have helped domesticate the conservative and revanchist right, but left observers at the time viewed the placement of former Nazis in prominent government and industry positions as evidence of the continuities between new and old regimes.[34]

Adding to their fears was the perception – shared by religious leaders and an increasingly marginalized segment of the CDU – that materialism ran rampant over all aspects of life in the FRG. If West Germans had been taught anything, it appeared, it was to associate freedom and happiness with consumption.[35] While Christian socialists feared for West Germans' souls, frustrated leftists feared the absence of a critical citizenry and understood the shiny happy consumer culture of the FRG to have depoliticized the average West German – including the left's traditional working-class base. It was not mere disappointment, then, that leftists struggled to confront in the postwar period. It was the conviction that, failing reform, West Germany retained a fascist potential. This point bears repeating. For those on the political left, the failure

[31] James F. Tent, *Mission on the Rhine: Reeducation and Denazification in American-Occupied Germany* (Chicago: University of Chicago Press, 1982); Brian Puaca, *Learning Democracy: Education Reform in West Germany, 1945–1965* (New York: Berghahn, 2009).

[32] Hans-Otto Kleinmann, *Geschichte der CDU, 1945–1982* (Stuttgart: DVA, 1993), 166.

[33] On winning West Germans over to the social market: Mark E. Spicka, *Selling the Economic Miracle: Reconstruction and Politics in West Germany, 1949–1957* (New York: Berghahn, 2007).

[34] Famously Hans Globke, who wrote the 1935 legal commentary on the Nuremberg Laws, was one of Adenauer's closest aides, particularly active in national security and anticommunist activities. See Norbert Frei, *Adenauer's Germany and the Nazi Past: The Politics of Amnesty and Integration* (New York: Columbia University Press, 2002).

[35] See the aptly titled essay by Arnold Sywottek, "From Starvation to Excess? Trends in the Consumer Society from the 1940s to the 1970s," in Schissler, *Miracle Years*, 341–58. On the tensions within this project, see, among others, Dorthee Wierling, "Mission to Happiness: The Cohort of 1949 and the Making of East and West Germans," in ibid., 110–25 and Erica Carter, *How German Is She? Postwar West German Reconstruction and the Consuming Woman* (Ann Arbor: University of Michigan Press, 1997).

to restructure and institute sweeping reforms in those first years after the war was not simply a missed opportunity at democratic socialism but, more fundamentally, a missed opportunity to eliminate the preconditions for fascism.

Conservative efforts to expand the purview of militant democracy – discussed in the last chapter – only worked to confirm suspicions of the state's authoritarian tendencies and to mobilize the left. Clashes over Adenauer's policy of strength were indeed testament to the fact that even though militant democracy and popular resistance shared a common goal – the defense of democracy – this did not mean they saw eye to eye on the source of greatest threat and the measures necessary to contain it. Social Democrats and extraparliamentary leftists did not pursue resistance in the form of blanket opposition to state power; for the vast majority, the state remained the preeminent potential agent of social progress. As anti-Nazi freedom fighters and socialists, members of the early postwar left resisted not the state per se, but the illegitimate use of state force. As the German language itself acknowledges, states govern by force. *Gewalt* can mean "violence" as well as "authority" or "force" and the word for the authority of the state and its organs – *Staatsgewalt* – makes explicit the state's presumed relationship to violence. What differentiated authoritarian from democratic forms of government for West German leftists, therefore, was not the use of force itself but rather democracy's observation of established boundaries on legitimate violence. Their early and still un-nuanced understanding of Nazism mirrored this same logic. The Nazi state was judged an extreme form of authoritarianism and criminal mainly in its unrestrained use of force on the populations under its control. To postwar leftists sensitive to the dangers of unchecked state power, the creation of a West German army, continued calls for emergency laws, and the mass death that both nuclear arms and NATO membership were seen to promise all resonated with the violence perpetrated by the Nazis.[36] This alone was enough to make them impermissible in their eyes and in those of numerous nonleftists as well.

The Christian Union won an absolute majority in the 1957 Bundestag elections and, with it, the power to arm the state as Adenauer chose.[37] Trounced three times running, Social Democratic leaders decided to change the game the SPD had played thus far. They did so by shedding the party's oppositional and working-class identity with the aim of becoming a "people's party" with far-reaching appeal. Independent and communist critics further to the left had long argued, of course, that the SPD's loyalty to parliamentary politics and liberal institutions was neither revolutionary nor socialist.[38] Still, the party had

36 Postwar Germans were uncannily familiar with total annihilation, emphasizing the threat of collective death above all else (such as radiation poisoning, cost, Christian morality, or even pacifist convictions) in their discussion of nuclear armament. See Michael Geyer, "Cold War Angst," in Schissler, *Miracle Years*, 397–8.

37 On how to make sense of West Germans' seemingly contrary behavior at the polls, see ibid.

38 Speaking for "socialists outside the parties," Walter Dirks described the SPD as the "social reform party of the small man." Walter Dirks, "Sozialisten ausserhalb der Parteien," *Das Sozialistische Jahrhundert* 3 (January/February 1949): 10.

heretofore maintained its Marxist framework and its explicit commitments to class struggle and to a socialist economy. These were the positions it officially abandoned in the 1959 party program issued at Bad Godesberg, which in many ways brought the SPD's official theory in line with its actual practice. The Godesberg Program did not renounce popular resistance like it did Marxism, but it did very explicitly close the door to a revolutionary strategy that both the injunction to resistance and Marxist politics had left open. The sort of popular, nonrevolutionary opposition the SPD envisioned was already visible in its efforts to coordinate extraparliamentary and parliamentary protest against the government's plan to acquire atomic weapons beginning in 1957.[39] The SPD-sponsored campaign to "Fight Nuclear Death" (*Kampf dem Atomtod*, KdA) evolved into a broad movement with committees at local and regional levels and a wide repertoire of actions intent on limiting state power in this crucial arena.[40] Party leaders supported this kind of popular opposition so long as it roughly mimicked the SPD's relationship with the trade unions, excluded communists, and could be used to influence parliamentary debate. Their dissolution of the KdA in 1958, despite participants' and extraparliamentary leaders' demonstrated desire to not only keep it going but expand its scope, made abundantly clear what the SPD did *not* want: a permanent and independent extraparliamentary movement. Reminiscent of Karl Mannheim's liberal democratic ideals, Social Democrats' new party program conveyed the belief that social conflict was fine and good – so long as it ultimately fed into the agreed upon parliamentary and constitutional channels.

Though Social Democratic leaders had never categorically rejected military power, as antipacifist as they were antimilitarist, it was also at Godesberg that the SPD formally committed itself to national defense.[41] This, in turn, paved the way for the party's retroactive acceptance of West Germans' membership in NATO. With a booming economy at home and a bleak example of communism next door, Social Democrats for all intents and purposes conceded the reigning political and economic order – and in so doing broke ranks with the postwar left. Those who stood at arm's length from the SPD took its changed course as yet another contraction of the space for public critique in the FRG. However critical they were of the party, extraparliamentary leftists had nonetheless understood it to represent the voice of opposition within existing institutions

[39] Hans Karl Rupp, *Außerparlamentarische Opposition in der Ära Adenauer: Der Kampf gegen der Atombewaffnung in den fünfziger Jahren* (Cologne: Paul-Rugenstein, 1970), 130; Andrei S. Markovits and Philip S. Gorski, *The German Left: Red, Green, and Beyond* (New York: Oxford University Press, 1993), 41–4.

[40] Rupp, *Außerparlamentarische Opposition*; Mark Cioc, *Pax Atomica: The Nuclear Defense Debate in West Germany during the Adenauer Era* (New York: Columbia University Press, 1988).

[41] SPD defense expert Fritz Erler explained their earlier position as a refusal to play the political puppet to either the United States or the Soviet Union but rather to say "yes" and "no" on a case-by-case basis. Fritz Erler, *Soll Deutschland rüsten? Die SPD zum Wehrbeitrag* (Bonn: Vorstand der SPD, 1952).

and had relied on it as such. Many within the party also believed that, as of Godesberg, the SPD ceased to be part of the left. Announcing their dissatisfaction with the newly minted people's party, these Social Democrats revoked their membership. By cutting ties, they sought to establish a voice of critique outside of the SPD, either by forming a new left party or, taking what they had learned from the KdA, by way of a permanent extraparliamentary opposition.

This was the constituency of West Germany's "homeless left" – those who had never committed themselves to an existing political party as well as those deprived of party affiliation by either the SPD's reorientation or the Constitutional Court's 1956 ban of the German Communist Party. In the years following Bad Godesberg, they coalesced into a loose, extraparliamentary alliance based on their shared, conscious opposition to the existing system. Convinced of the illegitimate oppressive force inherent within the reconstructed capitalist economy and monolithically conservative politics, these leftists held that democratic, antifascist vigilance was still every bit as necessary in the FRG's second decade as it was in its first. This "negative alliance" might not have manifested itself publicly and may even have dissolved entirely with the legitimacy time alone can give a state, had it not been for the SPD's decision to disown its affiliated student organization, the German Socialist Student League, in 1961.[42] The disputes that led to the split between the SPD and the SDS were bound up with the latter's critique of what it saw as the party's weak and conformist policies and what the parent organization found to be the students' intolerable anti-anticommunism (i.e., their Marxist sympathies).[43] Coming on the heels of the Godesberg Program, the SPD–SDS power struggle became a focal point for older leftists still committed to Marxism as well as for those interested in revitalizing a more revolutionary politics of the left. When the SPD renounced all connections to the SDS, therefore, the student organization became a forum and point of identification for leftists without a party-political home – whether they could remember their own school days or not.

The new course set by the SPD in 1959 placed resistance, specifically violent resistance, at the center of debates internal to the left for the first time in the postwar period. Within various left milieus, the legitimacy of both the existing state and forms of potential resistance hung partly on the question of violence, and felt allegiances to either the parliamentary SPD or a diffuse extraparliamentary coalition correlated strongly with diverging answers to this question. The extraparliamentary left was more than a coming together of

[42] In their book on the German left, Markovits and Gorski define the APO as a "loosely constituted negative alliance between an array of groups against a shared 'opponent.'" This approach is well-suited for thinking about the postwar extraparliamentary left as a whole. Markovits and Gorski, *Red, Green, and Beyond*, 47.

[43] Willy Albrecht, *Der Sozialistische Deutsche Studentenbund (SDS): Vom parteikonformen Studentenverband zum Repräsentanten der Neuen Linken* (Bonn: Dietz, 1994); Siegward Lönnendonker, Bernd Rabehl, and Jochen Staadt, *Die antiautoritäre Revolte: Der Sozialistische Deutsche Studentenbund nach der Trennung von der SPD, 1960–1967* (Wiesbaden: Westdeutscher, 2002).

political outsiders to oppose Adenauer's Germany. For underneath their sometimes tenuous solidarity lay a shared set of understandings that saw the state as the initiator of an ongoing dynamic of state and civil violence. If different ways of construing that violence developed and competed for dominance over the course of the 1960s and 1970s, extraparliamentary leftists nonetheless agreed that it originated with the state, often as the agency of oppression upholding the capitalist system. This basic view encouraged a perception of the political landscape as effectively divided between perpetrators and victims – between those who initiated violence in order to maintain the status quo and those who were the objects of that violence. In addition to providing a working map of the political terrain in which the state was *the* perpetrator against which all others were allied, this conception of originary state violence also entailed a reciprocal conception of legitimate civil violence. Any force used to oppose the initial violence perpetrated by the state was legitimated as purely defensive in character. Here, older conceptions of antifascist resistance fit easily with newer articulations of counterviolence (*Gegengewalt*) and were critical for bridging the generational divide. Resisting an oppressive state, or "the system," violence was deemed progressive.

Classical Marxist understandings of structural and revolutionary violence, anti-imperialist perspectives, as well as analyses of psychosocial coercions in advanced industrial society, helped members of the extraparliamentary left to conceive of themselves as allies in a struggle against the state.[44] Above all else, the actual maintenance and mobilization of this alliance relied heavily on leftists' commitment to the corresponding notion of resistance. It was this that proved the attractive force across generations, across political camps, and even across the demise of the SDS and APO. With National Socialism forming the backdrop of the West German political stage, moreover, the fascist state provided the privileged image for the otherwise nebulous forces of structural violence. This association radicalized the limits to which oppositional action could legitimately go and strengthened solidarities among the West German extraparliamentary left. Understood in terms of absolute evil, the possibility of fascism's repetition made these leftists unwilling or unable to exclude the possibility of violent resistance. Learning from the skepticism of older leftists regarding the state of democracy in the FRG, a new generation of Germans also embraced the commitment to resist authoritarian or fascist forces. Generational differences and disagreements on crucial matters of tactics, strategy, and theory among various groups led to substantive, often heated debate, but as we shall see, these developed within a frame set ultimately by the logic of the negative alliance.

[44] For a nuanced overview that highlights the linkage of new left ideas on violence to strategies of subversion, see Ingrid Gilcher-Holtey, "Transformation by Subversion? The New Left and the Question of Violence," in Davis et al., *Changing the World*, 155–69. Notably, the common denominator to all the strategies detailed there is the bipolar framework outlined here.

COUNTERVIOLENCE AS RESISTANCE: THE EXAMPLE OF ANTI-IMPERIALISM

This alliance remained inactive or dormant until its sympathies were aroused and the left mobilized by the apparent or potential abuse of state power. One of the clearest examples of this dynamic was imperialism, perhaps the only example of structural violence that could compete with the evils of the Nazi state in the postwar German imaginary. The West German left's interpretation of events in the decolonizing world was, of course, colored by its members' own identities as freedom fighters and by the conditions of postwar occupation. The presence of U.S. troops and the left's commitment to resistance encouraged feelings of solidarity (and identification) with the victims of colonial oppression. The liberation movements also provided hope to a broad spectrum of leftists who believed that traditional class struggle had become irretrievably stalled in Europe. They eagerly interpreted colonial revolt as both a fight for national liberation and the first step in the global overthrow of capitalist oppression. This dual significance made the decolonizing world an extremely powerful location for analyses of structural violence and the possibility of resistance. Here, where violence seemed most apparent and totalizing, the extraparliamentary left's consensus on counterviolence as legitimate resistance went uncontested. This was true for Social Democrats in the 1950s as well as for the older new leftists, younger old leftists, and, most famously, the antiauthoritarian protesters in the 1960s.

Already in the early 1950s, West German socialists were reading the revolutionary texts of Mao Zedong and Ho Chi Minh and testing the Western powers' patience with petitions on behalf of the world's colonized people. But it was not until the 1956 election of a center-left coalition in France, led by the socialist party (Section Française de l'Internationale Ouvrière, or SFIO), that they publicly mobilized to the side of the anticolonial movement.[45] The reason for their sudden action was nothing less than the perceived betrayal of socialism. After having pledged to end the two-year-old war between French forces and the National Liberation Front in Algeria, the SFIO instead initiated a new wave of fighting. Quickest to respond were members of the SDS (whose first president, it bears remembering, was future chancellor Helmut Schmidt). They vehemently argued that the Social Democrats had no choice but to renounce the French precisely because of German socialists' own experiences of oppression and opposition – specifically their history as both victims and resisters under the Nazi regime.[46] According to the logic of progressive struggle the young socialists followed, to do anything other than ally with the Algerians in this struggle would be to side with the forces of oppression.

Social Democrats at the 1958 party congress essentially agreed. Though party leaders were more concerned about domestic battles than they were

[45] Albrecht, *Der SDS*, 297–300.
[46] Ibid., 301–3.

about events in Algeria, they nonetheless put forth a resolution demanding French socialists end the war and formally recognize Algerians' right to self-determination.[47] Although an unprecedented breach of socialist solidarity, the resolution only drew the floor's criticism on one score: its rebuke of the "violent actions" taken by the Algerian rebels themselves.[48] Echoing the SDS's logic, the majority of those present insisted that one could not judge the victims by the same standards as the "murderers." Despite strenuous objections from the party's chairman, Erich Ollenhauer, the sentence was therefore stricken.[49] With this, a strong contingency of German socialists conveyed the belief that colonialism maintained a system of violence which its victims, in self-defense, were justified in destroying with violent means. By grafting the liberation movement onto a specifically German narrative of resistance and oppression under Nazism, moreover, they made SPD support for such actions internally obligatory. Ten years before students would fight for the decolonizing world in the name of antiauthoritarianism, West German socialists proved committed by a tradition of anti-Nazi resistance to fight imperialism around the globe.

After Bad Godesberg and the SPD–SDS split, this campaign largely shifted to the extraparliamentary realm, as the SPD (if not all of the party's members) strictly qualified its support for resistance movements in the decolonizing world. In fact, as an early and seemingly unambiguous example of morally legitimate counterviolence, the national liberation movements provided a source of cohesion for members of the "homeless left" at a moment of critical political flux. As the decade progressed, newly founded journals, demonstrations against the war in Vietnam, and informal reading groups circulated new and old anti-imperialist theories and the concept of structural violence that they presumed. In this capacity, the anti-imperialist movement marked a crucial moment in the formation and propagation of a self-consciously extraparliamentary left.

One prominent figure in the anticolonial discourse of the 1960s was Hans Magnus Enzensberger, publicist and founder of *Kursbuch*, a leading organ of the West German new left since its first publication in June 1965. Its pages confirmed the prominent place held by the decolonizing world in the political imaginary of the extraparliamentary left generally. An early issue, for example, ran articles on "Iran and its Benefactor" and the Sino–Soviet split as well as translations of Frantz Fanon and Fidel Castro, revealing the journal's strong engagement with conditions in the third world as well as with the theories of national liberation leaders.[50] In the same issue, Enzensberger's own essay on the relationship between industrialized and developing countries epitomized the way in which the oppositional left understood the colonial and neo-colonial

[47] SPD-Vorstand, *Protokoll: Der Verhandlungen des Parteitages der sozialdemokratischen Partei Deutschlands vom 18. Mai bis 23. Mai 1958 in Stuttgart* (Bonn: Neuer Vorwärts, 1958), 36–51.

[48] Ibid., 52–85.

[49] One hundred ninety-one voted against the sentence versus 160, with Ollenhauer defending the original wording due to the fractured nature of the Algerian liberation movement and the over-simplification that seeing only the positive sides entailed. Ibid., 80–5.

[50] See *Kursbuch* 2 (August) 1965.

situation.[51] The article led with the assertion that the world was divided not between East and West but rather between North and South – between the rich industrialized and the poor underdeveloped – and that Europe now sat on the "periphery" of international class struggle and thus world politics. The "epicenter" of the struggle between rich and poor now lay in southeast Asia, Africa, and Latin America, where a direct and indirect means of oppression maintained old and new relations of dependency.[52]

The notion of resistance became the vehicle for Enzensberger to align the history of class struggle in Europe with the contemporary anticolonial struggle. He concluded that, from the vantage point of the poor, the only answer to an extreme type of systemic violence was a similarly extreme form of resistance: armed rebellion. As he pointed out by drawing on spokesmen such as Frantz Fanon, some insisted that only violence could remedy that which was maintained by violence.[53] For his part, Enzensberger neither called for armed revolt nor did he condemn it. The heart of his argument, however, espoused the conviction that counterviolence was a natural, even inevitable response to structural violence. Inevitable, that is, if nothing changed. First and foremost, Enzensberger's article was intended as a wake-up call. The publicist gave readers a glimpse of the future – a new world war more encompassing than the last – in the hopes of convincing the citizens of the European periphery to stop passively observing events in the decolonizing world. He urged them to fight for a radical reworking of the relationship between North and South as if their lives depended on it. The clear implication of his reflections on Fanon's justification of violent revolt was that Enzensberger could not rule out the possible legitimacy of counterviolence by Europeans in the struggle to prevent global war by overthrowing capitalist oppression.

In 1965, American combat troops arrived in Vietnam and the first of nearly eight million tons of bombs were dropped on North Vietnam in the Operation Rolling Thunder aerial campaign. Even those who did not identify themselves as leftists or particularly political could easily conceive of the Vietnam War as a heinous mobilization of Western power against a local population's right to self-determination. For this very reason, students in the FRG joined their counterparts in the United States and other European nations in denouncing the war and the industrial-military complex driving it.[54] Protests against the war occurred on every university campus in West Germany, with Berlin's position as a stage for Cold War drama lending protest demonstrations in that city – and on the campus of the "Free" University – particular political potency. This was all the more true of those who went beyond demanding an end to the war to openly allying with the Vietcong, the enemy combatants of the U.S. military. One of the most frequently cited examples is the West Berlin *Plakataktion*

[51] Hans Magnus Enzensberger, "Europäische Peripherie," *Kursbuch* 2 (August) 1965: 154–73.
[52] Ibid., 171.
[53] Ibid., 165.
[54] On the movement's transnationality, see Horn, *Spirit of '68*; Gilcher-Holtey, *68er Bewegung*.

("poster action") carried out in early February 1966. Thousands of posters were hung throughout the city and the Free University campus, boldly declaring Chancellor Ludwig Erhard and the "Bonn parties" accessories to murder in Vietnam. The posters went on to assert that, in the face of global capitalism's armed strength, "only the taking up of arms" remained an option for the oppressed peoples of Asia, Africa, and Latin America. "For them the future is called: REVOLUTION.... How much longer will we allow murder to be committed in our names? Americans get out of Vietnam! INTERNATIONAL LIBERATION FRONT!"[55]

As intended, the *Plakataktion* outraged government officials by casting them on the side of tyranny and the Vietcong on the side of human freedom. Rather than inspire West Berlin students to find their own revolutionary praxis or to donate money to help arm the Vietcong, however, the posters provoked sharp criticism from within the SDS and a call to oust those involved from the organization. Despite the controversy, the action's fame rests on the growing importance of the "antiauthoritarians" who disseminated the posters, namely Rudi Dutschke, Bernd Rabehl, and Dieter Kunzelmann. Originally outsiders – Dutschke and Rabehl having escaped to West Berlin from the GDR and Kunzelmann coming from Munich – the former quickly came to dominate the SDS while the latter became a major player in West Berlin's counterculture.[56] In retrospect, too, the *Plakataktion* possessed the core elements later associated with the antiauthoritarian wing of the SDS, in particular its international, revolutionary framework and willingness to transgress convention to the point of entertaining violence in the name of self-defense and self-emancipation. Leftists' disagreement over the action can thus be seen to presage later strategy debates and an unbridgeable divide between the antiauthoritarians and those within the larger extraparliamentary movement whom they labeled "traditionalists." But just as anti-imperialism did not start with Vietnam, the call for solidarity – and the legitimation of violent resistance that such calls frequently entailed – was also never limited to the student movement's antiauthoritarian wing.

Around the time that *Kursbuch* first appeared, doctoral students in Marburg established a working group on the "sociology of development," whose project and positions they then outlined in the West Berlin journal *Das Argument*. Not a part of the antiauthoritarian movement and a generation younger than Hans Magnus Enzensberger, the Marburgers nonetheless shared the others' convictions regarding the origins of violence and legitimacy of counterviolence as resistance. Over the course of three articles, Frank Deppe, Kurt Steinhaus, and Rüdiger Griepenburg analyzed the historical background of "underdevelopment" and "national liberation," taking the example of Vietnam as an

[55] Tilman Fichter and Siegward Lönnendonker, *Macht und Ohnmacht der Studenten: Kleine Geschichte des SDS* (Hamburg: Rotbuch, 1998), 119.

[56] Though all once members of the Situationist-inspired group, Subversive Aktion, it was Kunzelmann who stayed close to these roots – one of the original members of Kommune I and, later, the militant Tupamaros West-Berlin. See Wolfgang Kraushaar, *Die Bombe im Jüdischen Gemeindehaus* (Hamburg: Hamburger Ed., 2005).

archetype for colonial revolt. The group pointed to the systematic constriction and exploitation of economies in the colonial and quasi-colonial world and concluded that class struggle between the bourgeoisie and the proletariat had been reproduced in the third world between Europeans and exploited local populations. Enzensberger hoped to avoid further violent revolt in the colonies by preemptively changing the existing global capitalist system; the Marburg students, in contrast, welcomed such escalation. More wedded to orthodox Marxism than the elder new leftist, they asserted that only revolution could bring about the needed change. To ensure the successful proliferation of colonial revolt, the Marburg students advocated fusing the revolutionary tactics of Europe and the third world. Deppe and Steinhaus agreed with Lenin on the need for a vanguard, trained revolutionaries who would politicize the masses and help them achieve the consciousness necessary to overthrow the status quo.[57] Introducing many, especially younger, West Germans to the guerrilla theories of Ernesto Che Guevara and Mao Zedong, they also made clear their conviction that the success of this vanguard and the revolution as a whole depended on the use of focused but unpredictable, violent action against the oppressors and close contact with the people. In their analysis of Vietnam, for example, Griepenburg and Steinhaus argued that the armed partisan struggle was the only possible means to transform the colonial situation.[58] Though they may not yet have read Fanon, the Marburg students clearly agreed that the remedy for violence of such a totalizing nature was (counter)violence.

In keeping with their hopes for worldwide socialist revolution, the Marburgers saw the national liberation fronts as only the beginning of a larger struggle for freedom. So comprehensive was the force used to maintain the imperialist system, and so great the disparity between its haves and have nots, that its overthrow was considered an historical necessity. For the Marburg students and their readers, Vietnam was *the* extreme case of structural violence and counterviolence. The Vietcong were pitted against the military and industrial might of an American-led imperialist system in the struggle for social and national emancipation. If the United States were defeated in Vietnam, it would be not only a resounding victory for freedom but also an inspiration for oppressed peoples elsewhere. This perception that the global future was being decided in Vietnam elevated West German solidarity with the Vietcong to an urgent necessity in the minds of the Marburg students. If they were vague on what that solidarity entailed, its goal was clear: not simply an end to war in Vietnam but the victory of the Vietcong over its oppressors. Their conception of counterviolence, in other words, was just as absolute as the structural forces

[57] Frank Deppe and Kurt Steinhaus, "Zur Vorgeschichte des 'underdevelopment' und der 'nationalen Befreiung,'" *Das Argument* 34 (1965): 17.

[58] Rüdiger Griepenburg and Kurt Steinhaus, "Zu einigen sozioökonomischen und militärischen Aspekten des Vietnamkonflikts," *Das Argument* 36 (1966), 45. The authors are credited with bringing the theories of Che Guevara to the FRG – by way of the GDR. Ingo Juchler, *Die Studentenbewegung in den Vereinigten Staaten und der Bundesrepublik Deutschland in den sechziger Jahren* (Berlin: Duncker & Humblot, 1996), 86.

they fought. Successful resistance in this instance meant the destruction of the source of violence, not a truce.

The *Plakataktion* in West Berlin is evidence enough that the Marburgers were not the only ones to equate the injunction to solidarity with a pro-Vietcong position. The acknowledged failure of that action, however, demonstrated that solidarity with the Vietnamese stopped short of facilitating any violence against human beings for the majority of SDS members and associates.[59] This is not to say that disagreement over what exactly solidarity entailed and over protesters' antimilitarist commitments meant a questioning of violent resistance's legitimacy in the colonized world or in the face of a potential resurgence of fascism. Increasingly, in fact, the conviction that violence was an often necessary if regrettable part of transforming structural injustice competed with the conception of counterviolence itself as an act of individual emancipation. Among other things, this reflected a growing urgency among extraparliamentary leftists to solve the problem originally posed by the left in the immediate postwar years, namely: how to make disobedient Germans?

*un*CIVIL DISOBEDIENCE: THE WEST GERMAN STRATEGY OF DIRECT ACTION

At the same time that the anticolonial discourse on resistance was gaining a wider audience, West Germans and, in particular, West German students were exposed to the civil rights and free speech movements sweeping the United States. Whereas anti-imperialism drew attention to oppression in Africa, Asia, and Latin America, America's domestic protest movements directed the extraparliamentary left's gaze toward questions of freedom back home. Even a quick survey of the 1960s shows that leftists were not particularly encouraged by what they found. In 1962, police seized *Der Spiegel*'s Hamburg office and arrested its editors for treason after the magazine published undisclosed information on the dismal state of West Germany's new army. Masterminded by Minister of Defense Franz-Josef Strauß, the "Spiegel Affair" was a blatant government attempt to suppress a critical press; the scandal that erupted openly questioned a militant democracy that privileged national security over a (temporary) loss of civil liberties. Though Adenauer's government was ultimately disappointed, the incident left a bitter taste in the mouths of many and set the tone for subsequent developments. Talk of emergency laws – and the increasing likelihood of their passage from 1965 on – mobilized a broad spectrum of citizens, not only within the extraparliamentary left but also among trade unionists and Social Democrats who perceived in the proposed legislation a

[59] Rudi Dutschke described its failure as evidence that Western sensibilities were such that no revolutionary terror directed at humans could be successful in the urban centers of Europe or America. See Rudi Dutschke, "Antisemitismus zum Antikommunismus," in *Rebellion der Studenten oder, Die neue Opposition: Eine Analyse*, idem, et al. (Reinbek: Rowohlt, 1968), 58–85.

direct threat to democracy.[60] Compounding these fears was SPD leaders' decision to pursue a course of reconciliation with conservatives, a decision that culminated in the creation of a Grand Coalition government in 1966. Though true that the SPD sat firmly in the center by this point, it was only by forming a government with the Christian Union that the party actually ceased to be in opposition for the first time in postwar history. It was a development that caused some to pronounce parliamentary democracy's complete demise.[61] That Kurt-Georg Kiesinger – a former, if repentant, Nazi official – was made chancellor of the new government did not help matters. Neither, of course, did international developments such as the Vietnam War, which not only cast doubt on American democracy but also the FRG as its protégé and stalwart ally.

Members of the West German student movement, especially those who had been exchange students in the United States, played a key role in the transfer of political ideas and practices across the Atlantic.[62] The circulation of ideas and actors among nation-states and across continents was fundamental to the protest movements of the 1960s – making it possible to view them as a transnational event in both content and form.[63] In the process, of course, some things got lost in translation. As with all cultural transfers, they were adapted (often unconsciously) to fit the cultural context at their destination. This can be seen in the West German appropriation of the American civil rights movement's early strategy of "direct action." This long-standing protest form gained new life in 1960 when four African American college students sat down at the "whites only" lunch counter at the Woolworth department store in Greensboro, North Carolina – and then refused to leave. The power of their action and those of numerous sit-ins to follow came from the stark juxtaposition of protesters' principled peaceful resistance and the violence they provoked from both onlookers and the state.[64] These were the images of civil disobedience that flashed across the country's television screens and moved public opinion. And this was the communicative protest form West Germans admired and adopted. An examination of the discourse on civil disobedience and its implementation

[60] See, e.g., *Demokratie vor dem Notstand: Protokoll des Bonner Kongresses gegen die Notstandsgesetze am 30. Mai 1965* (Frankfurt: neue kritik, 1965); Hans Heinz Holz, "Notstand der Demokratie – Ergebnisse und Perspektiven des Frankfurter Kongresses" *Blätter* 2 (1966): 976–82.

[61] This was the position of the Frankfurt SDS as summarized by Frank Wolff. Cited in Lönnendonker, *Die antiautoritäre Revolte*, 113–14.

[62] For a study of this transatlantic partnership, see Martin Klimke, *The Other Alliance: Student Protest in West Germany and the United States in the Global Sixties* (Princeton: Princeton University Press, 2010).

[63] See, among others, Horn, *Spirit of '68*; Gilcher-Holtey, *68er Bewegung*; and Davis et al., *Changing the World*.

[64] The Student Nonviolent Coordinating Committee (SNCC), founded amid the mobilizations the Greensboro sit-in helped spark, presented the philosophical and religious ideal of nonviolence as a founding principle, representative of its beliefs, goals, and chosen mode of action. See Clayborne Carson et al., eds., *The Eyes on the Prize: A Civil Rights Reader* (New York: Penguin, 1991).

in the strategy of "limited rule breaking" in the FRG, however, reveals a West German new left whose understanding of the state desensitized it to notions of nonviolence so integral to civil rights strategies across the Atlantic. This is not to say that the extraparliamentary left advocated the use of violence; in a sense, theirs was a sin of omission not commission. Gandhi and Martin Luther King, Jr., however much admired, were passed over for Marx and third world revolutionaries on the list of "must reads" circulating within the left milieu. Just as the first phase of the American civil rights movement reflected the Christian pacifism of its early leaders – a principled commitment to nonviolence that activists later questioned – West German protest exhibited the anti-Nazi, anti-authoritarian commitments of those who had survived or fled the Third Reich. Nonviolent or violent, resistance was the goal, one that distinguished their direct actions from the strategies they first sought to emulate.

In 1965, Michael Vester published an article introducing the West German SDS to the new protest forms of the U.S. civil rights and student movements.[65] Returning to the FRG after living in the United States, Vester hoped to use his experiences in the American SDS to jump start what he saw as a politically isolated and out of touch West German left.[66] In his opinion, the latter concentrated all its energies on national politics and abstract moral campaigns that did not concern average people in their everyday struggles. Scorning even the early peace movement's annual Easter March, Vester argued that West German leftists needed to adopt the direct action tactics used by protesters in the United States.[67] Direct actions, he claimed, effectively used people's concrete, commonplace concerns to open up new avenues of political mobilization. In contrast to the top-down action forms and paternalist politics traditionally favored by the organized left, direct action began local and small. Its power came not from numbers but from the fact that it was a voluntary act carried out by (and not on behalf of) the subjects themselves, on the very site of their oppression.[68] As

[65] Michael Vester, "Die Strategie der direkten Aktion," *neue kritik* 6 (1965): 12–20. It is worth underscoring that this translation of American civil disobedience occurred before the U.S. civil rights movement began to radicalize in 1966 and groups such as SDS and SNCC broke with their initial commitment to nonviolence. For a discussion of the American student movement that pays specific attention to these two distinct phases, see Todd Gitlin, "Das doppelte Selbstverständnis der amerikanischen Studentenbewegung," in *1968 – Vom Ereignis zum Mythos*, ed. Ingrid Gilcher-Holtey (Frankfurt: Suhrkamp, 2008), 75–84.

[66] Vester actively participated in events as they were unfolding early on in the United States. He was, for example, present at the 1962 drafting of the Port Huron Statement. For more on Vester and his emissarial role between the two SDSs, see Klimke, *Other Alliance*. Also, Michael Schmidtke, *Der Aufbruch der jungen Intelligenz: Die 68er in der Bundesrepublik und den USA* (Frankfurt: Campus, 2003), 194.

[67] Vester, "Strategie der direkten Aktion," 12–13. Though Vester associated the Easter March with old left demonstration tactics, it is frequently interpreted as a new left project and the start of extraparliamentary opposition. See the classic, Karl A. Otto, *Vom Ostermarsch zur APO: Geschichte der außerparlamentarischen Opposition in der Bundesrepublik, 1960–1970* (Frankfurt: Campus, 1977).

[68] Vester, "Strategie der direkten Aktion," 15.

Vester described it, direct action was an intrinsically emancipatory act, first enlightening the oppressed about their circumstances and then providing them with tools for confrontation and opposition.

The particular language Vester drew on in his discussion of direct action revealed his engagement in a specifically German analysis of the authoritarian state and citizenry that decreed the legitimacy of potentially violent resistance. His analysis explicitly addressed the role of nonviolence by way of Vester's claim that direct action "only made sense as passive resistance and only as such was it successful." His position on violence was tactical and very consciously so, since an earlier generation's failure to act had largely discredited passive resistance among postwar Germans. Vester thus reassured the reader that his rejection of violence did not stem from a Christian dictate to "love thy neighbor" but rather from nonviolence's "superior striking power." He excluded violent direct action not because violence was morally problematic but because it hit its opponent – the state – where it was strongest. To take up arms would be "cheap revolution," according to Vester, because the action would only "crumble in the face of a militarily and bureaucratically armed state force." Success relied on protesters confronting the state on the ground where it was weakest, and this, Vester explained, was in the arena of physical nonviolence.[69] Vester did not elaborate, but the theories of structural violence and the logic of *Staatsgewalt* he invoked made the point for him: Nonviolent action was something the state could not replicate. The state's inevitably violent efforts to contain even passive resistance revealed the coercion, injustice, and hypocrisy of the existing system to an ever broader audience. Under current conditions, it was the force of public opinion and not the fist that would bring change.[70] Missing was any sense of nonviolence as a principled position.[71]

Unsurprisingly, Michael Vester's translation of American protest forms necessarily built on a common sense about the FRG's authoritarian, potentially fascist state and society that was already current among the postwar left. For this reason, the protest form he advocated offered more than a way out of the political ghetto in which Vester imagined the West German left. It provided a practical implementation to the Frankfurt School's earlier call for the immanent theoretical critique of society.[72] Direct action *auf Deutsch* was a fusion of "theory and praxis, of immanence and transcendence, of democratic goals and the democratic path."[73] Like immanent critique, it confronted the authoritarian

[69] Ibid., 13–15.

[70] Vester's point of reference here was the 1963 March on Washington and its politically effective mass mobilization as a sort of culminating point for the civil rights movement. Ibid., 15.

[71] For a different read of Vester's translation of direct action, see Klimke, *Other Alliance*, 53–4, 58–9. He, like others, assumes Vester's principled stance against violence and thus the reconciliation of resistance and prefigurative politics.

[72] On Adorno's influence on Vester, see Wolfgang Kraushaar, *1968 als Mythos, Chiffre und Zäsur* (Hamburg: Hamburg Ed., 2000), 63.

[73] Vester, "Strategie der direkten Aktion," 19. He was even more explicit when discussing the power of the "sit-in" and "teach-in": "The suffix 'in' summarizes the origins of [direct action's]

character of capitalist and proto-fascist society from within, forcing it to expose its internal contradictions.[74] In an unrelenting attack on traditional leftist politics, Vester put the Critical Theory of dissident neo-Marxists into practice, demonstrating that he shared older leftists' preoccupation with creating a German society capable of resisting capitalism's authoritarian tendencies.

What one might call the "Germanization" of civil disobedience was explicitly theorized in the later works of Herbert Marcuse. Though Marcuse never returned to live in Germany after fleeing the country in 1933, he took an abiding interest in the West German student movement, having established links with the American SDS from his position as a professor at Brandeis University and the University of California, San Diego.[75] His analysis of advanced capitalist society and potentials for opposition to it combined thinking born of his generation's experience of National Socialism with the global postwar discourse of anti-imperialism. In a short essay entitled "Repressive Tolerance," Marcuse laid down a framework for the legitimate use of force that built off of a traditional Marxist belief in progressive violence as well as the examples of anticolonial struggle and the American civil rights movement he witnessed firsthand. The essay combined a radical critique of imperialism with an equally radical critique of advanced industrial society and refused to renounce *a priori* violence against "violence" – that is, the oppressive state – in the struggle for emancipation.[76] By explicitly bringing the two strands of anti-imperialist and antiauthoritarian discourse on resistance together, Marcuse shifted the focus on resistance away from its postwar emphasis on the specifically German incapability to revolt to a new, general reconceptualization of resistance as a natural right.

For Marcuse, the principle of nonviolence was yet another example of false consciousness working to keep the oppressed down. Nonviolence, according to him, was a necessity masked as a virtue, preached to and exacted from the weak. "Ethics" had no place in the matter: "To start applying them at the point where the oppressed rebel against the oppressors, the have-nots against the haves is serving the cause of actual violence by weakening the protest against

success: as passive resistance direct action is strictly immanent ... it positions itself at the heart of the system's internal contradictions in order to demonstrate the irrationality of its [the system's] so-called logic." Ibid., 17.

74 For an analysis of the reception of Critical Theory among the West German new left along similar lines, albeit one that focuses on Dutschke and Krahl (addressed later), see Ingrid Gilcher-Holtey, "Kritische Theorie und Neue Linke," in *1968: Vom Ereignis zum Gegenstand der Geschichtswissenschaft*, ed. idem (Göttingen: Vandenhoeck & Ruprecht, 1998), 168–87.

75 On Herbert Marcuse and the American new left: Wheatland, *Frankfurt School in Exile*, 296–334.

76 The essay, which first appeared in the collected work, *A Critique of Pure Tolerance*, eds. Robert P. Wolff, Barrington Moore, Jr., and Herbert Marcuse (Boston: Beacon, 1965), was translated into German at the same time as Frantz Fanon's *Wretched of the Earth* in what Rolf Wiggershaus terms a "literary symbol of what had begun to take place in West Germany among intellectuals and students." Wiggershaus, *The Frankfurt School*, 611–12.

it."[77] Marcuse's position represented not a departure but a reiteration of the conceptualization of violence long held by the German left, namely that violence originated at the top, while acts of violence from "below" necessarily had a defensive nature. As he put it, "law and order are always and everywhere the law and order which protect the established hierarchy; if those who suffer from it ... use violence, they do not start a new chain of violence but try to break an established one."[78] Whereas Enzensberger fell back on human nature, Marcuse argued that oppressed and overpowered minorities had a "'natural right' of resistance," a right he explicitly extended to the use of "extralegal means." He justified this in part by differentiating between the historical function of violence practiced by the oppressed versus the oppressors. Whereas political violence on the part of potentially subversive movements bore overwhelming witness to the progress of civilization – the English civil wars, the French Revolution, and the Chinese and Cuban revolutions being but a few, distinguished examples – Marcuse observed that there was no such relation to progress with respect to violence emanating from "above."[79] Invoking the juxtaposition of "progressive" to "reactionary" violence, he gave the former full legitimacy.

Crucial for the student movement and West German counterculture was Marcuse's analysis of social "outsiders" as the potential agents of radical change in advanced industrialist society – what became the students' theory of *Randgruppen*, or "marginal groups."[80] Marcuse believed that the conditions for revolution existed within the increasing gap between what the modern consumer society promised and what it actually delivered and the corresponding increase in the number of people who experienced that gap. In order to cultivate the potential for societal protest, he argued for the development of an organized radical left that would – like the vanguard of the Marburg students – awake the masses to their oppression as well as to the means of their liberation.[81] Amid the affluent societies of the postwar boom, revolution would not be led by workers but rather the underprivileged, those persons Marcuse conceived of as outside the established system, such as the outcast poor, the victims of racial oppression, and all those struggling to survive in the neo-colonial third world. He also acknowledged that there were some among the privileged, such as students and intellectuals, "whose consciousness and instincts break through or escape social control" and were therefore potential rebels as well.[82]

[77] Marcuse, "Repressive Tolerance," 103.

[78] Ibid., 116–17.

[79] Ibid., 107–8.

[80] Marcuse first introduced this notion in *One-Dimensional Man* (Boston: Beacon, 1964), 256. Though many West Germans were familiar with the longer work, it was not widely read until it, too, was translated into German four years later, in 1968. On the new left's self-emancipation in this regard, see Gilcher-Holtey, "Kritische Theorie und Neue Linke," in idem, *Ereignis zum Gegenstand*, 184–5.

[81] Herbert Marcuse, *Counterrevolution and Revolt* (Boston: Beacon, 1972), 124.

[82] Herbert Marcuse, *Five Lectures: Psychoanalysis, Politics, and Utopia*, trans. Jeremy J. Shapiro and Shierry M. Weber (Boston: Beacon Press, 1970), 84–94.

Here, then, was a German population not only capable of resistance but also endowed with the natural right to it.[83]

Determined to prove Marcuse correct, young (and no longer so young) people across the FRG embraced their revolutionary role and the conceptions of state and society it presumed. University campuses were the site and planning ground for a whole repertoire of direct actions, ranging from university sit-ins and teach-ins to creative and often playful demonstrations inspired by the Situationists and Provos in neighboring countries.[84] Just as one mass demonstration was winding down in West Berlin on December 10, 1966, for example, a group of roughly student-aged protesters held a smaller "Christmas happening" on Kurfürstendamm, West Berlin's major retail boulevard.[85] Amidst harried shoppers, the protesters sang songs while decorating a Christmas tree with the American flag, a papier-mâché head of U.S. president Lyndon B. Johnson, and a caricature of Walter Ulbricht, East Germany's head of state. According to those present, the protest action intended to dispel the peace-on-earth myth promulgated by stores and shoppers at Christmas time by reminding onlookers of the brutal war in Vietnam and Germany's less than peaceful position as a pawn in U.S.-Soviet hostilities. Toward this end, the protesters' final act was to set fire to the tree, burning its various decorations in effigy.

This "happening" and the mass demonstration preceding it made national news, though not because of its novel form or the use of arson. Rather, it was the swift and brutal force used to arrest protesters and disperse their supporters that triggered a public outcry. Eyewitnesses described police as beating and indiscriminately arresting defenseless demonstrators; both implicitly and explicitly, the officers were accused of having incited violence so as to justify their own violent tactics and an outright suppression of protest.[86] References to Nazism abounded and, in a rare reversal of roles, West Berlin officials found themselves compared to their East Berlin counterparts. Commentators suggested that bloody-headed protesters and police wielding rubber truncheons did not match the image of democratic – versus communist – Germany that the

[83] And Marcuse was very much speaking to German students here. He lectured to packed houses at the FU in Berlin in 1967, with the lectures reproduced in *Das Ende der Utopie*, ed. Hansmartin Kuhn and Horst Kurnitzky (Berlin: Maikowski, 1967), after having participated in the 1966 Frankfurt Vietnam Congress.

[84] Some have questioned whether West German sit-ins were a departure from the labor movement's traditional sit-down strikes. See, e.g., Kraushaar, *1968 als Mythos*, 63–5. For the best discussion of the International Situationists and, in particular, the Provos and their trans-European development, see Horn, *Spirit of '68*, 5–18, 38–42.

[85] A detailed account of the demonstration and "happening" can be found in Nick Thomas's *Protest Movements in 1960s West Germany: A Social History of Dissent and Democracy*, (Oxford: Berg, 2003), 78–82.

[86] For national coverage of the event, see, e.g., "Polizei verprügelt Demonstranten in Westberlin," *Frankfurter Rundschau*, December 11, 1966; "Berlins Polizei verstand den Spaß nicht," *Süddeutsche Zeitung*, December 19, 1966; Kai Hermann, "Die 'Rote Garde' von Berlin," *Die Zeit*, December 30, 1966.

Kurfürstendamm was routinely touted to symbolize.[87] As anticipated, it was the police response to the demonstration more than the demonstration itself that awoke the public to contradictions in the existing system.

This and similarly violent confrontations with police greatly influenced the course that civil disobedience took in the FRG. Where theory and the experiences of an older generation may otherwise have failed to convince younger leftists of the state's continued fascist or authoritarian potential, their own experience of violence at the hands of police served to confirm all they had been taught (and in a visceral way). It also suggested the effectiveness of direct action, or what West Germans most frequently referred to as limited rule breaking, for revealing the fascist tendencies of the state.[88] Speaking at an April 1967 sit-in, Peter Schneider located the origins of limited rule breaking in students' sense of political impotence. Protests carried out over legal avenues like petitions, open letters, and approved demonstrations had, in Schneider's experience, received no noticeable response. What *was* noticeable, he stated, was that as soon as you stepped on someone's lawn or refused to talk about Vietnam in the same quiet tones as one talked about the weather, you got people's attention. From there, the logic of limited rule breaking was clear:

> Then the idea came to us that we first had to destroy the lawns before we could destroy the lies about Vietnam; that we first had to change the [approved] march route before we could change something in the Emergency Laws.[89]

Schneider's frustration over rules that only served the rulers and the decision to confront such norms by crossing the boundary of the socially acceptable betrayed the students' indebtedness to Marcuse as well as the dual function of limited rule breaking. The West German strategy of civil disobedience aimed to undermine the habit of obedience associated with Germany's authoritarian past as much as it sought to resist the illegitimate use of state power. There were indeed student leaders eager to stress the limited and symbolic character of this overstepping of rules and laws, but without a consensus on this point, the exact boundaries were left vague. At a minimum, Schneider's statement expressly endorsed violence against property. The implicit rationale behind his position was also what gave the action form its provocative drive: Like other leftists, Schneider viewed his opponent as the unquestioned initiator of violence.

As an act of transgressing norms as well as the means of revealing the authoritarian structures that maintained them, disobedience easily became a goal in itself. Not only was limited rule breaking increasingly intended to

[87] Kai Hermann's commentary for *Die Zeit* was most explicit on this point.

[88] Reading through the speeches and literature of the 1960s, the direct translation of civil disobedience, *ziviler Ungehorsam*, rarely appears in either strategy discussions or more general references. Instead, the West German case is dominated by its own concept of *begrentzte Regelverletzung*.

[89] Peter Schneider, "Wir haben Fehler gemacht," in *Demonstrationen: Ein Berliner Modell*, ed. Bernard Larsson (Berlin: Voltaire, n.d.), 163.

provoke state violence, but defining the existing order as proto-fascist or authoritarian all but guaranteed that lingering attachments to civility would lose out to the growing urgency of resistance. That provocation could legitimately slip into violent action on the part of protesters was confirmed by Free University students following a demonstration outside the West Berlin Amerika Haus on February 5, 1966. In this instance, it was the actions of the protesters that generated much outraged commentary. Some 200 students broke from a mass antiwar demonstration nearby in order to take their protest, at least symbolically, to the Americans. Reaching the Amerika Haus – a stone and mortar affirmation of German–American friendship found in cities across the FRG – they lowered its flag to half mast, and, at the highpoint of the protest, threw eggs at the front of the building. The press and city authorities howled at the students and denounced what they described as a socialist or, worse, East German-directed communist attack on the United States and transatlantic relations. The outrage was such among Christian Democratic circles that, three days later, 600 counterdemonstrators gathered to condemn the "student fools" and "crazies" and to demand a hard line against further attacks on the status quo.[90] In a self-published history of the apparent university crisis, Free University students defended the anti-Vietnam protesters with the observation that such "caricatures of violence" as practiced outside the Amerika Haus provoked the state "to abandon its democratic and constitutional forms and undisguisedly 'get down to business,' namely to do violence to people." This overt confrontation, they stated, had contributed "to political enlightenment more than most political podium discussions."[91] Convinced of the authoritarian character of the West German state, the publication's sponsors – and the passage's likely author, SDS leader Rudi Dutschke – conceived of *un*civil disobedience as a way of exposing the always present structural violence that rendered opposition a purely defensive response.[92] By the very nature of the power relations inherent to the system, violence on the part of protesters appeared only as legitimate counterviolence.

[90] "Eier von links," *Der Spiegel* 8 (February 14, 1966): 48. Typically, *Spiegel* gave a rather tongue-in-cheek rundown of events and reactions, mocking *Bild* for reporting that thousands had attended the counterdemonstration. Secondary accounts vary on the details as well. Compare Tilman Fichter and Siegward Lönnendonker, *Macht und Ohnmacht der Studenten: Kleine Geschichte des SDS* (Hamburg: Rotbuch, 1998), 121–2 and Thomas, *Protest Movements*, 73–5.

[91] AStA-FU, ed., *Von der Freien zur Kritischen Universität: Geschichte der Krise an der Freien Universität Berlin*, 2nd ed. (Berlin: AStA-FU, 1967), 31. The publication was undersigned by the Evangelische Studentengemeinde, Freunde der Publizistik, Humanistische Studenten Union, SDS, and Sozialdemokratischer Hochschulbund.

[92] Called before the SDS governing body to defend the previous day's *Plakataktion*, Dutschke made the nearly identical argument and also cited the quoted passage at length in *Rebellion der Studenten*, Dutschke et al., 70. For the *Plakataktion* defense, see Lönnendonker, *Die antiautoritäre Revolte*, 240.

DEMOCRACY IN CRISIS? THE "WHEN" AND "HOW" OF RESISTANCE

On June 2, 1967, a young engineering student named Benno Ohnesorg was shot and killed by a West Berlin police officer not far from where thousands had gathered to protest the state visit of the Iranian Shah.[93] The demonstration's brutal suppression, followed by the city government's refusal to acknowledge any wrongdoing, marked the radicalization of the West German student movement. Many who had previously shown little or no interest in protest were now drawn into the extraparliamentary left milieu. Viewed alongside the Grand Coalition and the Emergency Laws the new government hoped to pass through parliament, Ohnesorg's death was seen as proof of the drastic lengths the state would go to crush opposition. Asked about the current state of democracy in the FRG, many young West Germans answered with a call for open resistance. And they were not alone. The Republican Club (RC), an organization that purposefully excluded students in favor of trade unionists, left-wing Social Democrats, FDP members, and various "left socialists," quickly assembled a university congress in order to discuss both the perceived crisis and the need for action.[94] Convened in Hanover, the congress attracted participants from different generations, all over the FRG, and across the left spectrum – "old" and "new" leftists, "traditionalists" and "antiauthoritarians," Maoists and Trotskyists. Whatever their age differences or political disagreements, these were outweighed at that moment by a shared concern over West Germany's fascist potential and a corresponding commitment to antifascist resistance. The Hanover congress was an event, not unlike the unveiling of the Godesberg Program, where the negative alliance of the extraparliamentary left was made tangible.

Standing before some five thousand participants, esteemed jurist Wolfgang Abendroth pronounced the death of Benno Ohnesorg symptomatic of democracy's precarious position in the FRG. He pointed to current economic and political elites "who had earned their spurs … in the Third Reich" and their efforts to arm the state with special emergency powers. He predicted that – should the long-debated Emergency Laws come to pass – the shooting of Benno Ohnesorg "would become a thousand shootings" and, just as before, German democracy would be destroyed.[95] The strong continuity perceived between pre-1933 and post-1945 politics and society made it possible for Abendroth, in the late 1960s, to argue that a brutal presidential dictatorship followed by openly

93 Find the most thorough account to date in Thomas, *Protest Movements*, 112–23.

94 The Club's Berlin founders capture some of its breadth and character: They included Berlin FDP chair and city councilor William Borm, ex-SPD political scientist Ossip K. Flechtheim, cabarettist Wolfgang Neuß, Hans Magnus Enzensberger, and young sociologist Klaus Meschkat. J. R. Mettke, "Der Club der Linken," *Der Blickpunkt* 165 (December 1967), 21.

95 Uwe Bergmann, ed., *Bedingungen und Organisation des Widerstandes: Der Kongreß in Hannover* (Berlin: Voltaire, 1967), 31–3.

fascist rule was all too possible in the FRG. It also explained how he could be roundly applauded by Germans half or one-third his age. Those who gathered in Hanover were more or less convinced that fascism had yet to be defeated decisively.

Abendroth opened the evening's discussion. Closing it was one of the Republican Club's officers, thirty-one-year-old attorney (and future RAF member) Horst Mahler, who captured what gave postwar opposition its preemptive character.[96] Raising the specter of National Socialism, Mahler stated that the "generation of fathers" was not to blame for its failure to resist a fascist dictatorship. Rather, their failure stemmed from not having acted earlier, when resistance "was still possible and sensible." For those assembled, the question of whether the present situation represented a comparable moment was heartfelt and terrifying and ultimately what brought them to Hanover following Ohnesorg's death. If they answered this question in the affirmative, as Mahler seemed to think they did, then it was time to confront the "ghost of yesterday" with an "active, dynamic interpretation of basic rights." According to the young lawyer, this meant preparing "to confront risks and to give resistance," as was their democratic right and duty.[97] Today, such antifascist vigilance may read as pure delusion, with Abendroth a teutonic Don Quixote. But leftists' fears and those driving authorities' reactions were ultimately two sides of the same coin. Unease over democracy's viability – rational or no – was widespread in the late 1960s.

The Hanover conference is most often remembered as the site of Jürgen Habermas's confrontation with Rudi Dutschke, whose call to action he judged a "voluntaristic ideology" akin to "leftist fascism." In general, Habermas viewed the student activists with great optimism and the events of June 2 only confirmed what he already believed: that student protests helped to compensate for the controls – either absent or ineffective in the FRG – that democracy placed on the violent abuse of state power.[98] But just as he did not hide his unease at the direction state power was taking in the FRG, Habermas openly voiced concern over the growing gap he perceived between theory and praxis on the left – a gap, he argued, that threatened to undermine the students' very ability to effect change. Theory alone, he asserted, prepared the ground for political engagement by mediating a practical orientation with conceptual reflection. Though he could well imagine the impatience students felt at being told to wait and properly prepare, Habermas was emphatic that those who did not

[96] Born in 1936, Mahler established himself as a leading defense attorney in criminal cases brought against leftist demonstrators. Too old for the student movement, his ensuing speech showed he nonetheless understood himself to be among the "generation of children." Ibid., 104.

[97] Ibid. Not unlike Abendroth, Mahler stated that the events just past were an example of "unatoned Nazi justice" – a result of the numerous "old NS-jurists still practicing their evil" in both penal and governmental law – and he directed them to make use of the *Widerstandsrecht*.

[98] Ibid., 42–8.

would end up either swearing off politics altogether or immersing themselves in "actionism," a dangerous practice of mobilizing for mobilization's sake.[99]

However fundamentally Habermas disagreed with Dutschke – and alienated himself from the student movement in the process – he simultaneously expressed his loyalty to the negative alliance. Addressing the audience, he asserted that he had no illusions of a violence-free world.

> But the kind of satisfaction obtained through provoking the transformation of latent violence into manifest violence is masochistic – not satisfaction but instead subjugation to this same violence. The demonstrative violence [*demonstrative Gewalt*] to which student opposition is confined ... the demonstrative violence to which, in our [current] situation, political enlightenment must lay claim, is defined by the goal of enlightenment. Through demonstrations we force attention to our arguments, [arguments] we take to be the better.[100]

Though unpopular, Habermas's intervention attempted to make clear the groundwork of legitimate political action for the students. Specifically, he enjoined them to return to a vision of direct action such as Michael Vester had described and to sensitize society to oppression with their actions. Vital to that task was not so much rendering political action nonviolent as rescuing it from actionism by firmly establishing its ends. For Habermas, *any* action taken without the mediation of theory was unacceptable. Only theory provided political praxis with a definite goal and a contextual understanding of the situation – a roadmap, as it were. Thus only theory could prevent politics' descent into irrationality, oversimplification, and the actionism he associated with fascism. Here, postwar Europe's philosopher of coercion-free communication made a plea for a politics of rational dialogue with a practical orientation. It was, in short, far from a proviolence position. But nowhere is it clear that Habermas rejected the use of force that also succeeded in its communicative mission. If anything, he left the door open to legitimate force, given that protest action's privileged mode was to be, as he put it, "demonstrative violence."

The tensions that Habermas brought to light surrounding the question of praxis only grew as extraparliamentary efforts against the Emergency Laws and Vietnam War intensified. Divergent positions on matters of organization and strategy crystallized around the so-called traditionalists and the antiauthoritarians.[101] As their nickname suggests, the former betrayed a traditional approach to politics, one that focused on parties and coalition strategies and whose crowning achievement was the creation of the umbrella organization,

[99] Ibid., 47.

[100] Ibid., 48.

[101] I use the terms "traditionalist" and "antiauthoritarian" advisedly, categories which largely served the antiauthoritarians' agenda to delimit themselves from everyone else in the extraparliamentary movement. I do not mean to imply that all members of the extraparliamentary left found a spot in one of the two camps, but I nevertheless use the term traditionalist to acknowledge those who allied with the moderate majority against the antiauthoritarians, such as the various Marxist-Leninists, Maoists, and Trotskyists who would come to form the K-Gruppen of the 1970s.

APO. Formed a few months after the Hanover congress, APO made explicit the cooperation of different leftist and left-liberal groups to provide an alternative to the ruling coalition.[102] In particular, this vision of extraparliamentary opposition complemented the self-conceptions of Republican Club left socialists, who understood themselves to not only act under the constitution's legitimate auspices but also as its most determined guardians.[103]

Those who self-identified as antiauthoritarians participated in discussions and demonstrations organized by APO but they themselves privileged an action strategy outside the realm of legality. Rudi Dutschke and Hans-Jürgen Krahl (a student of Adorno) sought to convince SDS members of their position in an "organizational report" they presented to delegates in September.[104] They diagnosed the FRG as a monolithic, oppressive apparatus of "integral statism," drawing explicitly on Horkheimer's earlier "authoritarian state" theory. Reiterating that only provocative, rule-breaking acts could reveal its structural violence, Dutschke and Krahl went on to describe the "agitation inherent in the action, and the sensual experience of the organized solitary fighter in the confrontation with executive state force." The pair used this romantic image of the militant rebel – and theories from the anticolonial struggle – to argue that emancipation relied on the development of consciousness and the will to change, in advanced capitalist societies as in the colonies. Sensitive to the difference between abstract versus manifest violence, they called for a cultural and psychological revolution in the metropoles akin to the third world political revolutions. Che Guevara's "propaganda of the gun" was to be complemented by a "propaganda of the deed" in advanced capitalist countries. The urbanization of rural guerrilla tactics meant, for Dutschke and Krahl, that the SDS had to reorganize if it were to lead the fight against the institutions. Individual actions would be prepared in small, decentralized groups and then carried out in tandem – defying state regulation and thereby exposing the state's vulnerability. This strategy alone would stimulate a mass movement of individuals aware of both the system's illegitimacy and their ability to destroy the authoritarian power structure upon which it rested.

[102] APO members included the SDS, SPD, and FDP student groups, union representatives, the student governments of individual universities, the Humanistic Union, the League for Human Rights, and the West Berlin SED. Lönnendonker, *Die antiautoritäre Revolt*, 489.

[103] Here the constitutional scholarship of Wolfgang Abendroth was particularly influential. On the multiplicity of new lefts in the West German case and Abendroth's influence see Pavel A. Richter, "Die Außerparlamentarische Opposition in der Bundesrepublik Deutschland 1966 bis 1968," in Gilcher-Holtey, *Ereignis zum Gegenstand*, 35–55.

[104] Rudi Dutschke and Hans-Jürgen Krahl, "Organisationsreferat auf der 22. Delegiertenkonferenz des SDS, September 1967," in Rudi Dutschke, *Geschichte ist machbar: Texte über das herrschende Falsche und die Radikalität des Friedens*, ed. Jürgen Miermeister (Berlin: Wagenbach, 1980), 89–95. For in-depth analyses of the report, see Wolfgang Kraushaar, "Autoritärer Staat und antiautoritäre Bewegung," in *Frankfurter Schule*, ed. idem, 3: 15–33; Bernd Rabehl, "Zur archaischen Inszenierung linksradikaler Politik," in ibid., 3: 34–64.

The question of whether and how Dutschke or Krahl can be considered intellectual precursors of the Red Army Faction continues periodically to flare up in German politics and scholarly discussions.[105] It is only relevant here inasmuch as it concerns the shared framework within which they, and the entire extraparliamentary left, worked. Dutschke and Krahl's assertion of the total structural violence integral to postfascist capitalist society demonstrated a new generation's adaptation of an analysis forged during the Nazi era. While the specific appropriation of guerrilla warfare was indeed novel, here too they followed earlier leads. Their call to action not only continued the left's commitment to resistance but also its deep conviction that the very preconditions for resistance lay within popular mentalities. What began as an older generation's struggle to overcome fascist and authoritarian continuities within the FRG had, in the minds of the antiauthoritarians, evolved into an active battle against its globalization. Constant action at the center rather than the mere support of action elsewhere was necessary to emancipate everyone concerned. Key to maintaining the necessary revolutionary drive was also the extralegality of the actions themselves. According to their SDS compatriot Bernd Rabehl, Dutschke and Krahl understood the organizational question to be synonymous with the question of violence. To their minds, if the connection between violence and potential freedom were lost, it was only a matter of time before the extraparliamentary opposition reverted to parliamentarism – before it would literally "social-democratize itself."[106]

The organizational report did not win support from the majority of SDS members, but it established violence as a decisive question for oppositional politics in West Germany. There, as elsewhere, 1968 was a year of dizzying prospects, bitter disappointment, and violent conflict. In Eastern Europe, the Czechs rejected the Soviet model in favor of "socialism with a human face" and, in May, a general strike brought France's economy to a standstill and de Gaulle's conservative government to the verge of collapse. Around the same time, seventy thousand protesters marched on Bonn while thousands of others participated in sit-ins, mass rallies, and worker strikes in the weeks leading up to the Bundestag vote on the Emergency Laws (Figure 2.1). But all this seemingly for naught: The Emergency Laws passed by an overwhelming majority, the alliance between French students and workers collapsed, and, in August, Soviet tanks rolled into Prague's Wenceslas Square to restore the status quo. In the United States, Martin Luther King, Jr. and Senator Robert F. Kennedy were assassinated in April and June, respectively, and the number of body bags returning home from Vietnam spiked as 1968 proved the deadliest year for U.S. troops. And still the war continued. Anger and frustration were palpable, and the effectiveness of current protest strategies hotly contested.

[105] For two prominent, opposing views, see Wolfgang Kraushaar, Karin Wieland, and Jan Philipp Reemtsma, *Rudi Dutschke, Andreas Baader und die RAF* (Hamburg: Hamburger Ed, 2005); Gilcher-Holtey, "Transformation by Subversion?" in Davis et al., *Changing the World*.

[106] Rabehl, "Zur archaischen Inszenierung," 48.

FIGURE 2.1. Former concentration camp inmates were among the thousands who demonstrated against the 1968 Emergency Laws. Protesters' fears were expressed in signs declaring "Once Again Democracy is in Danger," "No N[ational] S[ocialist] Laws," and "Emergency Laws Cause the Emergency" (dpa).

On April 2, Andreas Baader, Gudrun Ensslin, Thorwald Proll, and Horst Sohnlein intervened in this debate. They sought to bring the U.S. war in Vietnam "home" to the FRG by setting fire to two Frankfurt department stores. In 1965, Ensslin had campaigned for Willy Brandt and the SPD as part of an optimistic bid to end the Christian Union's unbroken reign.[107] Three years later, she stood in court and explained that she had most recently acted "in protest against the indifference with which people view the genocide in Vietnam." With an explicit reference to Nazi crimes that foreshadowed things to come, she went on to state that her generation had learned "that speech without action is wrong."[108] Nine days after the department store fires, a young Munich house painter shot Rudi Dutschke outside a pharmacy in West Berlin. In custody, the would-be assassin explained that his was an act of selflessness, an attempt to defend

[107] Ensslin was a member of the Wahlkontor deutscher Schriftsteller, or Election Office of German Writers, whose older and more famous members included Günter Grass and Hans Werner Richter. Daniela Münkler, "Intellektuelle für die SPD," in *Kritik und Mandat: Intellektuelle in der deutschen Politik*, eds. Gangolf Hübinger and Thomas Hertfelder (Stuttgart: DVA, 2000), 222–38; here 227–8.

[108] Ensslin quoted in Stefan Aust, *Der Baader-Meinhof Komplex* (Hamburg: Hoffman & Campe, 1986), 58.

West German interests and democracy from communism.[109] Dutschke miraculously survived, but before this was certain the streets of the FRG had erupted. Protesters smashed windows, destroyed vehicles, and erected barricades, directing the bulk of their fury at the Springer Press, which they blamed for inciting the attack with its negative and often hateful portrayal of Dutschke and student protesters generally. Everywhere demonstrators were met by police, and the widespread and indiscriminate violence that ensued over the course of the long Easter weekend was the worst the FRG had yet seen. In Munich, the rain of stones and other ad hoc projectiles claimed the lives of a photojournalist and a student.

These events inspired celebrity journalist Ulrike Meinhof to write one of her best known columns, in which she offered her readers a deceptively simple definition of protest and resistance: "Protest is when I say that I don't like this and that," whereas "resistance is when I make sure that the things I don't like no longer occur. Protest is when I say I will no longer go along with it. Resistance is when I make sure that no one else goes along with it anymore either."[110] Borrowing the American SDS slogan, "From Protest to Resistance," Meinhof characterized the Easter riots as a positive progression from the verbal and futile to the physical, effective, and – implicitly – heroic. If she criticized the events it was because they had not gone far enough; Springer still existed, as did the previous power relations. By crossing "the boundary between verbal protest and physical resistance" en masse and "not just symbolically, but for real," protesters had, however, achieved something significant. They had broken "the shackles of common decency" to reveal counterviolence as an available strategy. "The fun is over," Meinhof asserted, and closed the essay by repeating, almost as a refrain: "Protest is when I say I don't like this and that. Resistance is when I make sure that the things I don't like no longer occur."

Through her commentaries in the popular left journal, *konkret*, Meinhof became, as Karin Bauer puts it, the spokesperson of a movement she soon surpassed.[111] Here, the two were still in sync, if hardly of one mind. "From Protest to Resistance" captured that which had fueled the Easter riots, namely the mounting conviction among protesters that stronger action had to be taken. The fatal consequences of those riots, however, caused some to publically question whether violence against property could ever remain as free from harming humans as arguments for its legitimate use (versus the illegitimate use of violence against humans) suggested. Others saw the deaths as evidence of state-sponsored murder and thus grounds for civil violence in kind. At least, this is what members of *konkret*'s Berlin Editorial Collective – among them Peter Schneider and Hans Magnus Enzensberger – suggested in a lengthy

[109] For details of the shooting and subsequent riots, see Thomas, *Protest Movements*, 165–81; here, 168–70.

[110] Ulrike Marie Meinhof, "Vom Protest zum Widerstand," *konkret* 5 (1968): 5.

[111] Karin Bauer, Introduction to *Everybody Talks About the Weather... We Don't: The Writings of Ulrike Meinhof*, ed. idem (New York: Seven Stories, 2008), 49.

contribution to the discussion on violence published in June.[112] The coauthored essay argued for the "method and revolutionary legitimacy" of violence as an instrument of political strategy. It did so primarily by asserting the difference between original, oppressive violence and a counterviolence that was emancipatory and enlightening. More novel than the authors' defense of counterviolence's legitimacy – which echoed arguments they had made or come close to making before – was the claim that it, and only it, could overthrow a system that was, by definition, violent and deeply entrenched. Words were ineffectual, they argued, because the "language of capitalism" was violence, a statement that not only underscored the defensive nature of counterviolence but also its discursive character. Speaking nonviolence to violence would never be understood. Using physical force, in contrast, opened up the lines of communication. Protesters' own experience was offered as proof: "only since we began using violence ourselves has a realistic dialogue begun to develop."[113] Violence was thus not only a legitimate political strategy, according to the collective, but a necessary one on several fronts. And limits on its use were not established in principle or categorically, but only relative to the violence being countered.

Whether or not they read the essay, the fact that some agreed with the Berlin Editorial Collective's basic premise is suggested by protesters' actions not only that spring but also later, in what was popularly referred to as the "Battle on Tegeler Weg." On November 4, demonstrators gathered on Tegeler Weg outside the Berlin courthouse, where Horst Mahler stood trial for his participation in the Easter riots. When police attempted to disperse the crowd, a number of protesters chose to resist actively, arming themselves with clubs and stones. Their unprecedented show of force left 131 police officers injured – and sparked a furious debate within APO over the forms opposition could legitimately take in the FRG. Groups like the Social Democratic Student Association (SHB) immediately distanced themselves from the demonstration and publicly criticized the protesters' violent tactics. Many antiauthoritarians, in contrast, embraced the offensive actions taken at Tegeler Weg as part of the radicalized course promoted by Dutschke and Krahl. Before a thousand-person crowd gathered outside the Technical University in West Berlin, SDS member Christian Semler declared that APO's strategy would henceforth include the demonstrated willingness to strike out against police power as well as acts of "individual terrorism."[114] The sharp divergence between these two responses as well as the criticism both positions subsequently received from the majority of

[112] Berliner Redaktionskollektiv, "Gewalt," *konkret* 6 (1968): 24–8 and 35; here, 25. Authorship was also attributed to Rudi Dutschke, Bahman Nirumand, Gaston Salvatore, Jürgen Horlemann, and Eckhard Siepmann. Meinhof was presumably involved.

[113] Ibid., 24.

[114] Quoted in: "An einer wichtigen Markierung," *Berliner Extra-Dienst*, November 6, 1968, 1. The SED-oriented paper offered one of the first overviews of the unfolding debate. The paper did not dismiss what it referred to as Semler's "terrorism thesis" but requested that he back it up with a "theoretical but still readable" position paper.

extraparliamentary leftists proved that there was little agreement over where the limits of resistance lay.

Publicizing this to dramatic effect was the West Berlin Republican Club, whose weekly bulletin launched a debate on "Demonstration and Violence" that quickly consumed its members. In an initial commentary lauding Tegeler Weg for its unprecedented nature, editor Solveig Ehrler argued that the offensive finally put Germans on the same (implicitly correct) trajectory as protesters in other countries.[115] "For the first time, demonstrators did not flee from water cannons, clubs, and horses but instead hit police as they fled ... they were the ones armed with stones, who had water cannons, and who pulled police from horses." Ehrler declared the confrontation a success for its psychologically compensatory and politically strategic function. It proved that students were prepared to fight and that "police could also be hit."[116] Even more, she judged this "step from the masochistic acceptance of violence to concrete counter violence" as having liberated seasoned demonstrators "from the trauma of June 2."[117] The demonstration at Tegeler Weg was thus a "step toward emancipation" and the only ones worthy of criticism, according to Ehrler, were those leftists who distanced themselves from the event and broke solidarity with the demonstrators.

The essay provoked a flood of letters that assumed tidal-wave proportions when the club's executive board issued a statement supporting the editor.[118] The majority of respondents agreed that the militancy advocated by SDS antiauthoritarians and Ehrler was dangerous political folly, though not necessarily for the same reasons. One discussant argued that offensive action was only effective if demonstrators were strong enough to shake the existing power structure.[119] Another predicted – correctly – that greater physical violence would bring greater state repression, arrests, and the end of effective opposition as it was first forced underground and then cut off from the society it hoped to change.[120] Oppositional pastor Helmut Gollwitzer expressed his disappointment over the club's failure to reject violence, suggesting that members had chosen to be a "Trotskyist or similarly titled sect" rather than an "assembly of the radical-democratic left."[121] He drolly observed that, if Ehrler wanted to quickly reduce the RC to a tiny circle of her closest friends, then all she needed to do was keep writing similar commentaries. Others made this point less caustically by underscoring the APO's inability to mobilize mass demonstrations since protest had turned violent that spring. By and large, nonviolence was

[115] Solveig Ehrler, "Demonstration und Gewalt," *RC-Bulletin* 3 (November 7, 1968), 1–3.
[116] Ibid., 3.
[117] Ibid., 2.
[118] "Erklärung des Vorstands des Republikanischen Clubs Berlin zum Thema: Demonstration und Gewalt," *RC-Bulletin* 4 (November 21, 1968), 1–3.
[119] Kurt Fabian, *RC-Bulletin* 4 (November 21, 1968), 4.
[120] T. Ebert, RC meeting on "Demonstration and Violence" from December 5 reprinted in *Berliner Extra-Dienst*, December 11 and 14, 1968.
[121] Helmut Gollwitzer, *RC-Bulletin* 4 (November 21, 1968), 7.

deemed the more effective political strategy, even if several expressed doubts over its long-term sustainability.

Statements condemning the call for militant action did not disagree with assertions that fundamental social change could not occur without violence. They also did not disagree over the basic legitimacy of counterviolence. The main point of contention was not violent versus nonviolent tactics – as is easily assumed – but whether or not the antiauthoritarians' offensive strategy fit the logic of progressive violence. Most members of the left thought not. But its defenders expended a good deal of energy establishing Tegeler Weg's legitimacy: first as class struggle, then as a response to direct police attack. Passions were high precisely because all parties' ability to convince others of their position meant the difference between legitimate and illegitimate violence within the extraparliamentary left. As sociologist Roland Reichwein stated in his "21 Theses on the Use of Violence," the crucial distinction was not between violence against property and violence against people, as some insisted, but rather between offensive and defensive violence.[122] Admittedly, much was left open to interpretation – a police officer, for example, could be understood as either an agent of repressive state power or an exploited wage laborer, provoking disagreements over the legitimacy of attacks on police. But the basic distinction between progressive and reactionary force went uncontested. It was no accident that defenders of Tegeler Weg described acts of offensive violence in terms of liberation and illumination while their critics argued that it clouded public perception and blocked demonstrators' awareness of anything but the fight. In one scenario, Habermas's communicative criterion for legitimate force had been achieved; in the other, it had not. However polemical their debates, leftists within the extraparliamentary milieu agreed that the goal of human emancipation and enlightenment was crucial to distinguishing progressive from retrograde violence. For this reason, leftists unconvinced by antiauthoritarians' attempts to present offensive action as counterviolence interpreted their actions – and simultaneous efforts to limit discussion and criticism in the name of solidarity – as authoritarian or quasi-fascist. And they responded to these developments with corresponding alarm.

What Tegeler Weg and the strategy debate that surfaced and resurfaced at the end of the 1960s exposed was an essentially tactical agreement. The majority of extraparliamentary leftists did not believe the time had come for revolutionary action. Instead, they were convinced that the only violence whose open commission could enlighten West Germans to the contradictions and injustices within the system was that initiated by the state. Just as vividly, though, these discussions confirmed that conceptions of progressive violence and the FRG's fascist or authoritarian potential remained intact,

[122] Roland Reichwein, "21 Thesen zur Gewaltanwendung," *RC-Bulletin* 1 (January 7, 1969), 10–15; here, 12.

across all the emergent fault lines. Even those who rejected a course of radicalization were unwilling to condemn violence altogether or to promote nonviolence as a matter of political principle. As became painfully clear to members of the Republican Club who convened in closed session in early January 1969 to discuss its future in APO, the result was a strategic and moral impasse. Unable to reach an agreement on how to move forward, the extraparliamentary left quickly found its institutions splintering. One by one, APO, SDS, and the RC committed organizational suicide by internal struggles and bickering.

DISSOLUTION: THE EXTRAPARLIAMENTARY LEFT OF THE 1970S

In the wake of APO's demise, extraparliamentary leftists went in myriad different directions. Many turned to reengage mainstream politics and the SPD. After limited gains in 1966, the Social Democrats' electoral victory in 1969 succeeded in ousting the CDU/CSU from government and encouraging a wave of young leftists to join the party ranks. Those leftists disinclined to overlook or forgive the Social Democrats their political differences tended toward one of three routes, each demonstrating a continued commitment to resisting the authoritarian tendencies and systemic violence within society. Many gravitated to one of the various doctrinaire communist splinter groups referred to generically as *K-Gruppen*, or chose the consciously "undogmatic" circles of the *Spontis* and the Socialist Bureau, all of which sprang up at or near West Germany's universities. Moving in the opposite direction were those who rejected overt political struggle altogether and focused their energies on promoting alternative ways of living. By exploring new forms of pedagogy and cooperative or ecologically responsible lifestyles, it has been argued, these leftists sought to regain the antiauthoritarian movement's early emphasis on subjectivity.[123] Finally, a small number decided that the time had come to take up arms against the state and its representatives.

The first militant groups to form drew heavily from the working class, had close ties to the West Berlin drug scene, and took names such as the Hash Rebels and the "Blues," names that captured their outcast, countercultural commitments.[124] Often, early "street battles" with police had less to do with a larger political program and more with the protection of subcultural turf from unwanted state interference.[125] This changed in 1970, with the politically galvanizing effects of Andreas Baader's escape from prison and the subsequent

[123] Sabine von Dirke, *"All Power to the Imagination!" The West German Counterculture from the Student Movement to the Greens* (Lincoln: University of Nebraska Press, 1997).

[124] For a glimpse of this scene, see Bommi Baumann, *How It All Began: The Personal Account of a West German Urban Guerrilla* (Vancouver: Arsenal, 2002).

[125] Dieter Claessens and Karen de Ahna, "Das Milieu der Westberliner 'Scene' und die 'Bewegung 2. Juni'" in Fritz Sack et al., *Analysen zum Terrorismus*, vol. 3 (Opladen: Westdeutscher, 1982), 478–525.

founding of the Red Army Faction. Instead of serving out their sentences for the Frankfurt arson, Baader and Ensslin fled to Paris in late 1969, only to return a short time later at the urging of their lawyer, Horst Mahler. The couple was taken in by Ulrike Meinhof, who, along with the other three, began plans for a guerrilla organization. Baader – though commonly portrayed as a charismatic pretty boy or a hotheaded, even boorish outsider – was indispensable to the project. When he was rearrested, therefore, the group acted. Using her connections as a journalist, Meinhof arranged to meet with Baader at the Free University's Institute for Social Studies under the pretense of conducting research on troubled teens. Near noon, on May 14, three women and a man – two of them armed and masked – charged into the library where Meinhof and Baader sat talking under guard. In the heat of the moment, one of the two masked intruders fired a gun and seriously injured Georg Linke, an Institute employee. Baader and all five "liberators" fled out the window and underground.[126]

In a statement issued shortly after the incident, Meinhof acknowledged that the shooting was unfortunate. She declared the action justifiable, however, by taking Ehrler's previous assertion that "police could be hit" a step further. As Meinhof explained it, "the sort [who wears a] uniform is a pig, not a human being ... and naturally they can be shot."[127] That same day, West Berlin's favorite anarchist rag, *AGIT 883*, printed an anonymous letter to its readers that served to announce the RAF's formation. Scorning "intellectuals, cowards, and know-it-alls" who endlessly debated whether the time for revolution had come, the letter addressed those who had had enough – of being prisoners, of the so-called left's ineffective politics, and of the numbing consumerism that could never compensate them for their daily exploitation.[128] Baader's rescue was reframed as the first step to starting in the FRG what "had already been going on in Vietnam, Palestine, Guatemala, Oakland and Watts, Cuba and China, Angola and New York." Others could debate the point, in other words, but the reader and author knew: The "time to build a red army had come." With its references to the daily grind of industrialized consumer society as well as the pillaging of third world countries, the RAF left no doubt as to its members' rootedness within the extraparliamentary left milieu or about their belief that it was time to bring the international struggle for liberation to its logical, local conclusion in the FRG. Inspired by the RAF's example (if critical

[126] For a scholarly account that pokes significant holes in the popular notion that Meinhof was unwittingly pulled into these events and terrorism more generally, see Sarah Colvin, *Ulrike Meinhof and West German Terrorism: Language, Violence, and Identity* (Rochester, NY: Camden House, 2009).

[127] Ulrike Meinhof, "Natürlich kann geschossen werden," *Der Spiegel* 25 (June 5, 1970): 74. A number of scholars have remarked on the deliberate use of the passive voice, with some attributing it to Meinhof's – or the RAF's – conflicted position on violence. See, e.g., Jeremy Varon, *Bringing the War Home: The Weather Underground, the Red Army Faction, and Revolutionary Violence in the Sixties and Seventies* (Berkeley: University of California Press, 2004), 205–7.

[128] "Die Rote Armee aufbauen," *Agit 883* 62 (June 5, 1970): 6.

of it as well), a number of Hash Rebels and other militant outcasts joined to form the 2nd of June Movement – named in honor of Benno Ohnesorg – and various "Red Cells" not long thereafter. Their members proved equally intent on countering the violence of "pigs" and fascist imperialism with violence of their own.[129]

[129] For the "Revolutionary Cells," a semi-illegal organization founded in the summer of 1972, see ID-Archiv, ed., *Die Früchte des Zorns: Texte und Materialien zur Geschichte der Revolutionären Zellen und der Roten Zora* (Berlin: ID-Archiv, 1993).

3

"Mister Computer" and the Search for Internal Security

Fear is a poor advisor on matters of freedom.

Horst Ehmke (November 1975)[1]

Entering into government with the FDP in 1969, Social Democrats knew they had their work cut out for them. In his first address to the nation as chancellor, Willy Brandt asserted that German democracy was, as yet, incomplete and explicitly linked the country's further democratization to socialism. He did not disparage the very real accomplishments of the past twenty years. Indeed, the SPD was a vocal defender of the "free democratic order" it had helped create. But, Brandt acknowledged, formal political institutions – however critical – were not enough to instill democratic values and assure a just society. Social as well as political equality was necessary to the actual realization of democracy. As the head of the first SPD government since 1930, Brandt underscored the existing deficit in democratic culture in order to draw a line between his and previous conservative governments and, even more crucially, between his party's democratic socialism and the undemocratic communism of the GDR. He proclaimed his government's program of "inner reform" a new beginning for democracy in the FRG and invited all West Germans to take part – to "dare more" rather than settle for good enough.[2]

With Brandt as chancellor and Gustav Heinemann in the president's office, the Social-Liberal coalition did, indeed, promise a new course more in sync with the West Germany of the late 1960s. In contrast to conservatives and even other SPD leaders, Brandt was known for being sympathetic to the political idealism of the student movement, as was Heinemann – a former Christian

[1] Addressing the SPD's convention in Mannheim. *Protokoll über die Verhandlungen des Parteitages der Sozialdemokratischen Partei Deutschlands 1975* (Bonn: SPD-Vorstand, 1976), 103 (hereafter, *Parteitages der SPD 1975*).

[2] Willy Brandt, "Regierungserklärung von 28 Okt. 1969" in *Verhandlungen des Deutschen Bundestages: Stenographische Berichte* (hereafter, *Verhandlungen*), VI. Bundestag, 5. Sitzung (October 28, 1969), 20–34.

Democrat widely admired for having resigned from Adenauer's cabinet in protest over rearmament. Nothing captured the changing of the guard more than the now famous image of Brandt kneeling before the Warsaw ghetto memorial in a spontaneous act that became an official state gesture of remorse for crimes Germany committed under the Nazi regime. Brandt's action was an important step on the road to mastering the German past and also came to symbolize Social Democrats' commitment to *Ostpolitik*, a policy of rapprochement with the Eastern Bloc (including the as yet unrecognized GDR) that Brandt and others saw as the logical complement to Adenauer's policy of Western integration.[3] The chancellor's humble contrition – not well received within the CDU/CSU – was nothing, too, if not a powerful comment on how Social Democrats' conception of state power differed from that of conservatives. At a time when international as well as domestic tension was most often answered with strong-arm tactics and the threat of big sticks, Brandt's government sought strength in the alleviation of those same tensions.[4] At home, it gave legal amnesty to those convicted as participants in the previous years' violent protests, and in one of its first acts of legislation, the new government amended the criminal code so as to exclude demonstrators from charges.[5] By establishing clear legal parameters for demonstrations, Social Democrats sought to regulate civil action and correct state overreaction – showing, too, that the SPD's penchant for legal perfectionism had not waned. Determined to bridge West Germany's political and social divisions, the new government also laid out a plan of democratization that hinged on visions of neutral state intervention and technical progress. It embodied, in other words, Social Democratic conceptions of militant democracy.

The unmistakable cloud darkening Social Democrats' first years at the head of government was the outbreak of terrorism within West Germany's borders. Members of the newly formed RAF used Ulrike Meinhof's personal contacts in the GDR to escape immediate arrest by way of East Berlin's Schönefelder airport.[6] One of the many post-1990 scandals to erupt from the files of East

[3] On its political meanings and legacies as a West German *lieu de mémoire*, see Adam Krzeminski, "Der Kniefall," in *Deutsche Erinnerungsorte*, eds. Etienne Francois and Hagen Schulze (Munich: Beck, 2001), 638–53.

[4] Thomas Basten argues that this approach stemmed from the optimistic belief that the claims of all individuals on the state could be satisfied through the "scientific penetration of all spheres of life." With the proper management of society, legal liberalization posed no security risk. See Thomas Basten, *Von der Reform des politischen Strafrechts bis zu den Anti-Terror-Gesetzen: Die Entwicklung des Strafrechts zur Bekämpfung politisch motivierter Kriminalität in der sozialliberalen Ära* (Cologne: Paul-Rugenstein, 1983), 6.

[5] Members of the CDU/CSU vigorously opposed the bill and sought to overturn it at every given opportunity. For the third StrRG, see *Drucksachen des Deutschen Bundestages* (hereafter, *Drucksachen*), VI. Bundestag, Nr. 139. The Amnesty Law can be found in the *Bundesgesetzblatt* (Bonn: Bundesministerium der Justiz) I:509.

[6] Tobias Wunschik, *Baader-Meinhofs Kinder: Die zweite Generation der RAF* (Opladen: Westdeutscher, 1997), 391; John C. Schmeidel, *Stasi: Shield and Sword of the Party* (New York: Routledge, 2009), 152.

Germany's Ministry for State Security (MfS), this early and relatively common form of assistance was invaluable to those who mobilized against the FRG. It not only allowed the RAF and other militants to flee (and reenter) the country with relative ease, but also provided them access to the Near East and those "world revolutionary terrorists" whom the Soviets had charged the GDR to aid.[7] In June 1970, the RAF's founding members traveled to Jordan along with several new recruits – many of them delinquent youths with whom Ensslin and Baader had previously worked – to train in a guerrilla camp run by the Palestinian liberation party, Al-Fatah. Differences between the militants caused the West Germans' unceremonious eviction and early return to the FRG. But this in no way dampened the RAF's sense of revolutionary purpose – or prevented its future cooperation with the PFLP. Back home, members robbed banks and, invariably, engaged in shootouts with police. Together, these two activities provided the RAF with the funds to secure arms and safe houses and the first fatalities in its declared war.[8] These early skirmishes incited sharp criticism from left journalists at *konkret*, including Meinhof's ex-husband, Klaus Rainer Röhl, who accused the RAF of being "useful idiots," counterrevolutionary, and even fascist, with the potential to empower the state and nothing more.[9] In response, the RAF released two manifestos in April 1971 and April 1972, *The Urban Guerrilla Concept* and *Serve the People*, respectively. Each manifesto took pains to establish the RAF's participation in an international – not merely German – struggle for human liberation and the correctness of violent resistance in the FRG.[10] With a heavy dose of scorn and the expressed wisdom of Black Panther Eldridge Cleaver that one was "either part of the solution or ... part of the problem," the group also did its best to assume leadership over the left as a whole.[11]

[7] Probably the greatest point of connection between the RAF and the GDR was South Yemen and the PFLP, whom the MfS supported (and, in the case of the PFLP, infiltrated) and with whom the RAF cooperated and consorted. If the RAF directly and indirectly benefited from East German aid, the MfS used the RAF to gain information on international terrorism and rescinded its help – to the point of actual subversion – whenever it was in its best interests to do so. Schmeidel, *Stasi*, 142–62 and Wunschik, *Baader-Meinhofs Kinder*, 389–403. Also, idem, "Abwehr und Unterstützung des internationalen Terrorismus – Die Hauptabteilung XXII," in *Westarbeit des MfS: Das Zusammenspiel von "Aufklärung" und "Abwehr,"* ed. Hubertus Knabe (Berlin: Ch. Links, 1999), 263–73. The SED's position was that the RAF posed a risk to internal security and the GDR's international standing, an assessment whose merits the MfS acknowledged. On this as well as the GDR's interest in APO and West German radicalism generally, see Thomas Klein, *SEW – Die Westberliner Einheitsozialisten: Eine "ostdeutsche" Partei als Stachel im Fleische der "Frontstadt"?* (Berlin: Ch. Links, 2009), 171–200.

[8] Three policemen and three armed militants were killed in these early shootouts.

[9] E.g., Claus Fried, "Neubauers nützliche Idioten," *konkret* 12 (1970): 51; Günter Wallraff, "Ulrikes Rote Armee," *konkret* 14 (1970): 7.

[10] RAF, *Das Konzept Stadtguerilla*, reprinted in *Rote Armee Fraktion: Texte und Materialien zur Geschichte der RAF*, ed. Martin Hoffmann (Berlin: ID-Verlag, 1997), 27–48 and, idem, *Dem Volk dienen*, in ibid., 112–44.

[11] For a close reading of these and other RAF manifestos, see Sarah Colvin, *Ulrike Meinhof and West German Terrorism: Language, Violence, and Identity* (New York: Camden, 2009), esp.

True to the RAF's preference for action, however, the group soon exchanged manifestos for bombs in a month-long offensive intended to convince both leftists and the government of its revolutionary intentions. Naming each guerrilla action group after fallen militants, the RAF made explicit the status of its actions as legitimate counterviolence. The first bombs went off on May 11, 1972, in the Frankfurt IG-Farben building where the U.S. Army's Fifth Corps was headquartered. The successful "Commando Petra Schelm" killed one person and injured fourteen others. One day later, two bombs exploded at police headquarters in Augsburg and a car bomb (set by a "Commando Thomas Weisbecker") went off just outside the criminal justice office in Munich, severely harming bystanders and causing significant damage. On May 15, "Commando Manfred Grashof" seriously injured the wife of federal judge Wolfgang Buddenberg, unfortunate enough to be driving his car when it, too, exploded. Buddenberg, whom the RAF blamed for Grashof's death in prison, was not in the car and thus managed to escape harm. The only operation not named for a fallen RAF member, but rather in honor of master martyr Benno Ohnesorg, occurred four days later in Hamburg. The name of the "2nd of June Commando" as well as its target – the Springer Press – underscored the RAF's ties to the 1960s protest movement, both its politics and its hardships. Of the five bombs they planted inside the publishing house's twelve-story building, only two successfully detonated but this alone injured thirty-eight employees and terrified countless more. The final attack of the month took place in Heidelberg, on the base of the U.S. military's European headquarters, and was equally dramatic. Car bombs were once again deployed and this time killed three and wounded five.[12] All told, the wave of violence took four lives – all U.S. soldiers – and injured more than sixty. By the end of May, terrorism had gone from being a relatively minor, if serious, concern to a matter of domestic and international security.

Despite conservative accusations to the contrary, SPD leaders did not hesitate to mobilize state forces against left-wing political violence. They did, however, observe the boundaries for which the party had argued, first in theory (while drafting the Basic Law) and, later, in parliamentary opposition. Faced with the challenge of terrorism, Social Democrats continued to argue that uncontrolled violence and the emotional responses it provoked were best combated by utilizing the resources already available to the state – the law, police, international cooperation, even the people themselves – rather than endangering democracy twice over by violating established norms. True to their conception of militant democracy, they approached terrorism not as an isolated problem but rather as a symptom of larger societal ills that also had to be addressed. As jurist and

80–107. Quote from Eldridge Cleaver, "Stanford Speech," printed in *Post-Prison Writings and Speeches*, ed. Robert Scheer (New York: Random House, 1969), 130. Returning the favor, Cleaver compares the situation in the United States with that of Nazi Germany.

[12] Butz Peters, *Tödlicher Irrtum: Die Geschichte der RAF* (Berlin: Argon, 2004), 285–93.

popular Munich mayor Hans-Jochen Vogel explained, the situation demanded an encompassing "societal policy, indeed, politics as a whole."[13] A formidable force within the SPD, Vogel became the minister of justice in 1974 and was a critical player in the government's fight against terrorism. Convinced that political culture was part of any answer to democratic security, he and other leading officials ensured that counterterrorism policies went beyond their immediate target to take aim at the democratization of state and society.

Crucial to the pursuit of this holistic route was a new rubric of "internal security."[14] Though this notion had appeared in isolated instances in the 1960s, it was not until the Social-Liberal coalition – and the rise of terrorism – that internal security established itself in everyday and official political rhetoric. It provided Social Democrats with an important conceptual hook on which to hang their government's program of counterterrorism by deftly circumventing the language of militant democracy now so closely associated with conservative positions on security. In this way, party leaders created the space to confront terrorism in a manner that the SPD majority, at least, considered within the bounds of established procedures and the rule of law. Despite (or because of) their simultaneous attempts to ward off present and past dangers, civilian and state terror, the SPD found itself caught between two polarized reactions. Government officials and security experts found that their use of new technologies elicited fear among those West Germans concerned, above all, about authoritarian state traditions. At the same time, the government's continued refusal to mobilize extraordinary powers of state to suppress violence emanating from society left them open to attacks from the right – who questioned the SPD's willingness and ability to govern. None of this was helped by the fact that Social Democrats proved increasingly at odds with one another over questions of state power and their government's chosen path to internal security.

MODERNIZATION, PLANNING, AND POLICE

No parliamentary party – in any industrialized nation – was immune to the planning euphoria that first began to catch on in the late 1950s. By the early 1960s, social policy had given way to societal policy – in German, traditional *Sozialpolitik* was replaced by the *Gesellschaftspolitik* called for by Vogel. Far more encompassing than the former, the latter aimed to organize and thereby facilitate individual opportunities and social outcomes as a whole system. It was a shift reflecting the optimism that came with the economic prosperity of the 1950s and the belief that, with the help of technology, humans could

[13] Hans-Jochen Vogel, "Schutz vor Gewalt und Terror – Eine zentrale Aufgabe der Rechtspolitik," speech at the Bavarian Juristentagung, May 25, 1975, Bundesarchiv (Koblenz, hereafter BA) Bundesministerium der Justiz (Hereafter, B141): 48329.

[14] Hans-Jürgen Lange continues to lead the field; for his still current overview, see *Innere Sicherheit im Politischen System der Bundesrepublik Deutschland* (Opladen: Leske & Budrich, 1999).

master their collective fate – or, at the very least, secure it from future disaster.[15] With postwar reconstruction behind them, West Germans thus began to set their sights on the future. The state, once restricted to maintaining order and basic social needs, now sought actively to steer and plan society and to thereby ensure its citizens' general welfare and security.[16] Intertwined with the postwar history of the welfare state in Western Europe, this shift also mapped onto new thinking in the social sciences, particularly in psychology, concerning human development. A new understanding of the individual as a product of society (rather than biology) linked the reform of one to the other, with social harmony hanging in the balance. If society were planned correctly, it was now contended, social ills such as unemployment and crime could be eliminated.[17] Achieving effectiveness and efficiency in public bureaucracies took on new importance; better trained personnel, the technological modernization of equipment, and systematic cooperation with scientists became the order of the day.

West German conservatives were of two minds when it came to technocratic planning. While many came to embrace it as a means of controlling an otherwise unruly mass society, Adenauer's government often swam against this tide, trying, for example, to stall the European Economic Community's adoption of a systematic and long-term economic planning policy.[18] Social Democrats showed no such vacillation. Already predisposed to value experts over public officials and favor optimistic plans of social engineering over the optimism of free market forces, it did not take much to convince the SPD to embrace informed and active planning as the path to a well-formed society.[19] Indeed, Social Democrats' traditional inclination toward centralized uniform power and faith in progress combined with a new embrace of science and technology to create enthusiasm for administrative and governmental reforms at all levels. Championing what they called "modernization," the new SPD government

[15] Gabriele Metzler, "'Wir schaffen das moderne Deutschland': Sozialer Wandel in den sechziger Jahren zwischen Gesellschaftspolitik und Emanzipation," in *Bilanz: 50 Jahre Bundesrepublik Deutschland*, eds. Marie-Luise Recker, Burkhard Jellonnek, and Bernd Rauls (St. Ingebort: Röhrig, 2001), 279–94.

[16] Concerning West German social policy and its shift from managing economic hardships to providing public goods and services, see Hagen Rudolph, "Mehr als Stagnation und Revolte: Zur politische Kultur der sechziger Jahre," in *Zäsuren nach 1945: Essays zur Periodisierung der deutschen Nachkriegsgeschichte*, ed. Martin Broszat (München: Oldenbourg, 1990), 141–51; Hans-Günter Hockerts, "Metamorphosen des Wohlfahrtsstaats," in ibid., 35–45; Dieter Grimm, "Der Wandel der Staatsaufgaben," in *Staatsaufgaben*, ed. idem and Eveyln Hagenah (Baden-Baden: Nomos, 1994), 613–46.

[17] On postwar political planning: Gabriele Metzler, *Konzeptionen politischen Handelns von Adenauer bis Brandt: Politische Planung in der pluralistischen Gesellschaft* (Paderborn: Schöningh, 2005).

[18] Ibid., 237.

[19] For the party's own self-understanding, see Horst Ehmke, ed., *Perspektiven sozialdemokratischer Politik im Übergang zu den siebziger Jahren* (Reinbek: Rowohlt, 1969). See also H. W. Schmollinger and P. Müller, *Zwischenbilanz: 10 Jahre sozialliberaler Politik 1966–1976* (Hanover: Fackelträger, 1980), esp., 123ff.

targeted nearly every public administration perceived as lagging behind the changed social realities of the late 1960s.[20] Their program for domestic reform aimed to restructure and streamline state administrations with the introduction of new management techniques and innovative technologies. This entailed education reform in an effort to bolster math and sciences and, on the whole, bespoke planning's strong orientation to the prevention of social and economic crises.[21] Nothing if not optimistic, the SPD's program for inner reform made the democratization and modernization of society coterminous goals. Though this would change over the course of the 1970s, at the beginning of the decade technology was understood in uniformly positive terms, as an instrument of social progress and social security.

It was from within this established context of planning and reform that the SPD confronted the advent of left-wing terrorism. Often mistaken for the impetus behind the expansive police reforms of the 1970s, terrorism in fact propelled forward already existing plans not only for the modernization of police and intelligence services but also the reform of criminal law and the penal system.[22] In keeping with the state's changing role vis-à-vis society in the 1960s, the police officer lost his position as a kind of domestic soldier, closely identified with the state and trained to preserve and restore order, and took on that of a social engineer whose job was to protect the population (rather than the state).[23] For if criminal behavior was a social problem rather than an individual failing then crime had to be fought differently. Rather than wait to fight crime after it happened, "modernizers" at the state level (many of whom were Social Democrats) pushed for its prevention. Instead of concentrating on the traditional tasks of repelling danger and criminal prosecution, they lobbied for a form of active policing that relied on the accumulation of statistical knowledge concerning what was now seen to be the various demographic, geographic, and other elements that patterned crime.

Of course, as one scholar observes, changes in criminal activity remain the leading inspiration for changes in policing.[24] Beginning in the mid-1960s, an increase in illegal activity, particularly against property, convinced experts that a new form of criminality had come to plague the FRG and other affluent societies. What distinguished the new criminals from the old was their degree of mobility

[20] For the SPD's appropriation of "democratization" and the resulting internal party conflict, see Bernd Faulenbach, "Die Siebzigerjahre – ein sozialdemokratisches Jahrzehnt?" *Archiv für Sozialgeschichte* 44 (2004): 1–38, esp. 14–21.

[21] Peter Katzenstein, *West Germany's Internal Security Policy: State and Violence in the 1970s and 1980s* (Ithaca: Cornell University Press, 1990), 44.

[22] As we have seen, they had long ago pinpointed police power for reform and centralization. See also, Heiner Busch et al., *Die Polizei in der Bundesrepublik* (Frankfurt: Campus, 1985), 440; Lange, *Innere Sicherheit*, 107.

[23] I am indebted to Klaus Weinhauer's work regarding the changing conception of security and police responsibilities by the mid-1960s. See Klaus Weinhauer, *Schutzpolizei in der Bundesrepublik: Zwischen Bürgerkrieg und Innerer Sicherheit: Die turbulenten sechziger Jahre* (Paderborn: Schöningh, 2003), esp. 340–4.

[24] Busch et al., *Polizei in der BRD*, 440.

and professionalism. They were frequently outfitted with the newest technology, well-organized and well-educated, and often from middle-class backgrounds, all of which made it easier for them to blend in and thus escape detection. New, too, was the strong likelihood that they had international connections.[25] This made the new criminal far more difficult to catch than his or her predecessor. And it was the inability of traditional local police practices to effectively combat such crime that inspired reformers' attempts to create a more efficient and modern police force. In the United States, France, and the FRG, the beat cop of the 1950s was gradually replaced by a technologically trained professional with increasingly refined skills of crime detection and law enforcement.[26]

In West Germany, it was the new SPD-FDP government that gave modernizers the opportunity to realize police reform on a large scale. And terrorism gave them the excuse to do so, at a much faster pace than otherwise imaginable. This was because they understood terrorism as simply an extreme form of the new criminality that drove the overhaul of police powers in the first place.[27] Early reports on the RAF noted the group's ability to disappear into "circles" throughout the Federal Republic and thereby elude arrest. Members were considered "extremely intelligent, confident in their carriage, and with access to extensive monetary means" – all characteristics of the new criminal.[28] Consequently, concentrating on the organization, personnel, training, and technological equipping of West Germany's police was seen as necessary from a modernization perspective as well as the government's best possible counterterrorism strategy.[29] Reforming police power was no simple matter, however, given that it lay almost exclusively in the hands of the individual Länder. Federal institutions such as the Federal Criminal Office (BKA) and the Federal Office for the Protection of the Constitution (BfV) were created in 1950 and 1951, but federalist jealousies and memories of the Gestapo prevented either agency from obtaining significant authority. Social Democrats did their best to change this.[30] Under their watch, the BKA went from being what *Der Spiegel*, in

[25] Ibid.

[26] For a survey of police reform in the FRG from the 1950s to the early 1980s, see Reinhard Haselow, Stefan Noethen, and Klaus Weinhauer, "Die Entwicklung der Länderpolizeien," in *Staat, Demokratie und Innere Sicherheit in Deutschland*, ed. Hans-Jürgen Lange (Opladen: Leske & Budrich, 2000), 131–50.

[27] Busch et al., *Polizei in der BRD*, 439–40. Minister of Justice Han-Jochen Vogel's treatise on the legal actions taken to combat terrorism between the years 1974 and 1978 clearly articulates this understanding of terrorism. See Hans-Jochen Vogel, "Strafverfahrensrecht und Terrorismus – eine Bilanz," *Neue Juristische Wochenschrift* 25 (June 21, 1978): 1217–28, esp. 1218.

[28] See, e.g., BA Bundesministerium des Innern (Hereafter, B106): 83800 – 626 310/8.

[29] Haselow, Noethen, and Weinhauer, "Entwicklung der Länderpolizeien," 140–1.

[30] The expansion of federal police power is discussed in several literatures. In addition to Busch and Katzenstein, see Martin Kutscha and Norman Paech, *Im Staat der "inneren Sicherheit": Polizei, Verfassungsschutz, Geheimdienste, Datenkontrolle im Betrieb: Beiträge und Dokumente* (Frankfurt: Röderberg, 1981); Sebastian Cobler, *Law, Order and Politics in West Germany*, trans. Francis McDonagh (New York: Penguin, 1978); Enno Brand, *Staatsgewalt: Politische Unterdrücking und Innere Sicherheit in der BRD* (Göttingen: Werkstatt, 1989).

1969, referred to as merely a "mailbox" in Wiesbaden because its 933 employees did nothing but collect intelligence information, to an agency almost three times that size with the power to intervene in Länder affairs.[31] The BKA gained jurisdiction over international and interstate crimes such as drug and arms trafficking, and, by 1975, both coordinated the nation's fight against politically motivated acts of violence and controlled a new information retrieval system (INPOL) connecting police stations throughout the FRG.[32]

Centrally initiated reforms aimed to unify regular and investigative police forces at all levels and to create a clear, hierarchical command structure. For this reason (as well as local authorities' efforts to maintain control), changes at the federal level were mirrored at the state level. The Länder Criminal Offices also grew in jurisdiction and staff, with sizeable expense going to improve each office's logistical, operative, and personnel infrastructure.[33] The goal was the same here as it was elsewhere: to make police coverage more comprehensive and more specialized. At the same time, the emphasis on prevention made policing more abstract and flexible in response.[34] With each Land office newly outfitted with a security department and integrated into a national system, the agencies were also able to fight crime across state lines – at least in theory. Actual practice always suffered from the fact that the Länder only shared what they wanted, when they wanted, and cooperated with federal or another state's forces in a similar vein. Despite such obstacles, the federal government did more than obtain significant police jurisdiction and clear primacy for the BKA in criminal investigations by the end of the 1970s. Its program of internal reforms also succeeded in streamlining chains of command as well as creating an expanded and technologically savvy West German police force.

The new government's association of technology with not only efficiency but also social justice is essential to understanding this overhaul of police power in the FRG and, specifically, the major expansion of the BKA. Indeed, failing to recognize the radical promise technology held for men such as Horst Herold, the Nuremberg police chief appointed president of the BKA in 1971, is to not understand the modernization project itself. In this, Herold bore little resemblance to his predecessor, Paul Dickopf. Where Dickopf notoriously employed his former SS associates and publicly dismissed the use of computers in police work, Herold was a former KPD member whose championing of technology

[31] The same article noted that the BKA never coordinated interstate police actions or assisted individual Länder. It was, in short, nothing more than an intelligence depository. *Der Spiegel* 15 (April 7, 1969,) 52. As of 1976 the BKA employed over 2,400 people, with the office's annual expenditure charting a similar explosion. Cobler, *Law, Order, and Politics*, 170–1.

[32] These changes were achieved with the 1973 amendment of the BKA law and the 1975 meeting of the Standing Conference of Interior Ministers. For a concise overview of the BKA's history, see Hans Lisken and Hans-Jürgen Lange, "Die Polizeien des Bundes," in Lange, *Staat, Demokratie und Innere Sicherheit*, 151–66.

[33] Katzenstein, *Internal Security Policy*, 10.

[34] Haselow, Noethen, and Weinhauer, "Entwicklung der Länderpolizeien," 131–50. Also Busch et al., *Polizei in der BRD*, 246–50.

earned him the nickname "Mister Computer."[35] Herold and his supporters understood new computer technologies to promise speed, efficiency, and the possibility that unlimited information could be electronically stored, processed, and then rationally applied in areas where human imperfections and emotions were known to interfere with justice. In this way, Herold argued, computer technology held the key to a more democratic policing.[36]

"Cybernetics" emerged in the 1940s as a new interdisciplinary field that studied communication and control in dynamic systems and stressed the importance of feedback for adaptation. Symptomatic of the postwar enthusiasm for technocratic management, it gained wide international currency by the 1960s and strongly influenced the new BKA president's plans for using data processing.[37] An early example of the reform Herold had in mind was known as criminal geography.[38] Using systematically compiled information on the frequency and location of lawbreaking, Herold mapped the city of Nuremberg's criminality in order to identify where police force was most needed and then acted accordingly, rather than distribute units evenly throughout the city as was then the norm. In addition, further analysis of the data provided clues on what made certain spaces attractive to crime and, conversely, how space might be made *un*attractive and eventually crime-free. This, then, was the birth of such crime control innovations as placing security cameras in places with obstructed views and playing (often classical) music in areas popular with teenage loiterers. Genuinely revolutionary at the time, this new form of preventative policing resulted in a significant drop in Nuremberg's crime rates and the widespread adoption of criminal geography by police forces across the FRG.

As president of the BKA, Herold made the expansion of police intelligence and communications a top priority. This did not mean that intelligence gathering was viewed as separate from everyday police measures or intended to be the exclusive province of the BKA. On the contrary, a data-processing system was to be created in which intelligence – collected at all levels – would be centrally held and evaluated for easy retrieval by police officers in the field.[39] Information and technology were simply the means to a more efficient and just form of policing. Due to the resistance of Herold's predecessor

[35] Hans Schueler, "Kein Antwort vom Computer" *Die Zeit*, September 23, 1977, 2. Dieter Schenk, *Der Chef: Horst Herold und das BKA* (Hamburg: Hoffmann & Campe, 1998), 65–74. Schenk's own career as a BKA officer distinguishes his work with an insider's understanding, incomparable access to sources, and personal sympathies.

[36] Horst Herold, "Demokratisierung und Internationalisierung – Zwei Schritte in die Zukunft der Polizei," *Die Neue Polizei* (1967): 145–6; idem, "Gesellschaftlicher Wandel – Chance der Polizei?" *Die Polizei* 63 (1972): 133–7.

[37] The seminal text: Norbert Wiener, *Cybernetics; or, Control and Communication in the Animal and the Machine* (Cambridge: Technology, 1948).

[38] Horst Herold, "Kriminalgeographie – Ermittlung und Untersuchung der Beziehungen zwischen Raum und Kriminalität," in *Grundlage der Kriminalistik*, ed. Herbert Schäfer (Hamburg: Verlag für kriminalistische Fachliteratur, 1968), 201–44. Schenk, *Der Chef*, 52–5.

[39] Horst Herold, "Kybernetik und Polizeiorganization," *Die Polizei* 2 (1970): 33–7; idem, "Informationszentralisten," *Spiegel* 26 (June 19, 1972): 16–19.

to modernizing pressures from below, however, the creation of a centralized computer system linking federal and Länder offices faced significant hurdles.[40] It was not so much a lack of computer technology that was the problem, but rather the fact that the Länder administrators had begun to develop their own distinct electronic databases. These systems served varying goals and were technologically incompatible; they epitomized, in other words, the irrationality and inefficiency that the SPD already associated with a decentralized hyperfederalism. And this did not even take into consideration local and state officials who openly resisted any reform that would transfer new power to the federal administration. More than any other single factor, terrorism helped Herold and the SPD-led government over the hurdles to a unified computer system and greater (if never overwhelming) cooperation between the state and federal levels.

The BKA president argued that terrorism and life underground imposed specific conditions, limitations of mobility, and a unique set of patterns that could be discerned with the perfection of data. By aiming at the terrorists' movements, communications, weapon sources, system of safe houses, and even known sympathizers, police had the power to create from isolated facts a "net" of information that left the terrorists open and vulnerable to capture.[41] Implementing plans he had conceived years before, Herold allocated resources toward the development of computerized catalogs searchable by person or object (a stolen car, for example) and pulled data from a variety of different collection sites to do so – "similar to a clinical examination conducted on a patient."[42] Like doctors, the BKA's agents gathered information not only on the specific pathology but also on the environments conducive to it and the responses triggered by prior police interventions.

Most famous of Herold's innovations was his development of a type of dragnet investigation – the *Rasterfahndung* – whereby a computerized search system scanned enormous data sets to identify overlapping clusters of suspicious traits. Like criminal geography, this system aimed at targeted crime fighting in the hopes of making police work more efficient and accurate. In the BKA's efforts to find terrorists, police accessed utilities records and flagged those customers who paid their bills in cash or through a third party. This group of potential suspects was then checked against residence and automobile registrations as well as data on social security, welfare, or childcare recipients in order to further refine the list of suspects matching the "criminal" profile. Only after such data crunching, in which both human and environmental factors were considered, did those names at the top of the list become the focus of

[40] At a 1968 Bundestag hearing, Dickopf remained firmly against the creation of a computer database, even when Hamburg's senator of interior Heinz Ruhnau promised that the Länder would go it alone. See Schenk, *Der Chef*, 65–74.

[41] Ibid., 57, 108.

[42] Horst Herold, "Organisatorische Grundzüge der elektronischen Datenverarbeitung im Bereich der Polizei: Versuch eines Zukunftsmodells," *Taschenbuch für Kriminalisten* (Hilden: Verlag Deutsche Polizei, 1968), 240–54.

traditional investigative techniques such as surveillance and house searches.[43] Used by the BKA in its "grand search" for terrorists after the RAF's May Offensive, the dragnet proved highly effective. In little more than three days, all leading RAF members had been apprehended, and Horst Herold and his reforms had won widespread admiration.

Though it would eventually provoke sharp criticism, the very impersonal nature of this process was fundamental to the democratic project that Social Democrats such as Herold saw themselves pursuing. In developing and adopting new technologies, these reformers joined police experts in an effort to eliminate more than technical errors. Through consistently and uniformly applied laws and procedures, they sought to remove human bias from the picture as well. Though it is hard to imagine in today's world of identity thieves and privacy advocates, when Herold pioneered the state's use of electronic data processing at the beginning of the 1970s, the debate over data protection and what information could be legitimately collected and stored on an individual was in its infancy.[44] The BKA president's own faith in computer technology left him largely blind to its negative potentials and unable to imagine why anyone would oppose the creation of a comprehensive data-processing system.[45] And his conviction that the cool, impersonal efficiency of computers would help undermine abuses of police power was widely shared by members of government and within the broader ranks of the SPD. Indeed, the modernization and centralization of police power routinely earned Social Democratic leaders the full backing of their party and for this reason alone, no doubt, made it the government's counterterrorism strategy of choice. This, and perhaps the fact that their continued failure to realize these goals (and thus the full potential of the existing counterterrorism forces), could be blamed on conservatives' safeguarding of Länder power. There were, however, limits to Social Democrats' faith in technology. When the internal security program ran up against the boundaries they had erected against traditional, potentially authoritarian abuses of state power, these misgivings proved the stronger. This was nowhere more evident than in the government's relationship with the GSG-9, the elite antiterrorist squad that epitomized the Social Democratic ideal of modern police power.

The history of the GSG-9 starts with the passage of the Emergency Laws in 1968. By strictly delimiting the state agencies responsible for "internal" and "external" emergencies – the police and military respectively – the laws laid the legal groundwork for the reform and demilitarization of the West German police.[46] The organization most immediately affected was the Federal Border Guard (BGS) to which the GSG-9 came to be attached. A quasi-military force,

[43] Katzenstein, *Internal Security Policy*, 44–5; Brand, *Staatsgewalt*, 69.

[44] Hesse was the first in the FRG – and the world – to pass legislation on the proper use and storage of information in 1970; it provided a model for the federal government's own law, the *Bundesdatenschutzgesetz*, which went into effect on January 1, 1978.

[45] Schenk describes Herold's enthusiasm as stemming from a "pioneering spirit" that focused only on the technology's possibilities. Schenk, *Der Chef*, 77–81.

[46] It is worth remembering that this was a delimitation fought for and won by the SPD.

the BGS was established within the Interior Ministry at the height of the Korean War in order to protect the country from external attack and possible civil war. In 1968, it was stripped of its military accoutrements and refashioned into a highly trained and specialized police force. Under the willing oversight of the Social-Liberal coalition, the BGS was heir to the lessons local modernizers such as Heinz Ruhnau had drawn from confrontations between police and student protesters at the end of the 1960s.[47] One of the SPD's leading internal security experts, Ruhnau was an innovator of the "flexible" response unit, a police force less encumbered by traditional, military-style gear and fixed, text-book-style strategies and thus more responsive to unpredictable threats as they developed. Instead of military equipment, the BGS was specially outfitted with the water cannons, tear gas, and plastic shields now strongly associated with crowd control at mass demonstrations the world over.[48] Legally integrated into the federal police system in 1972, the BGS operated as a reserve unit, available to the Länder and to the capital, Bonn.

The BGS was thus clearly redesigned to provide the sort of agile and well-trained police force reformers considered most adept at dealing with tense situations. Yet none of its units were trained in counterterrorism and there were no plans to provide such training until the 1972 Munich Olympics hostage crisis. The inexpert handling of that situation by local authorities resulted in the deaths of the Israeli athletes and their Palestinian captors, and it revealed to West Germans – and a worldwide television audience – how ill-equipped the FRG was to confront the specific problem of terrorism. In a matter of days, the Interior Ministry drew up plans to create a highly specialized and technically advanced unit at the federal level, able to operate undercover, barracked so as to make mobilization possible at any time. Everyone involved emphasized the need for the unit's unsurpassed training, with Horst Herold specifically recommending education in three areas: law, operations and tactics, and what he referred to as an "introduction to contemporary ideologies."[49] In the end, the

[47] On police and the lessons of the 1960s, see Weinhauer, *Schutzpolizei*, esp. 296–332, 345–50. Weinhauer's study stops short of the 1970s and thus does not chart Ruhnau's influence on national policy, but Weinhauer establishes him as one of the key modernizers – a designation I take from him.

[48] Katzenstein, *Internal Security Policy*, 44. These changes required a constitutional amendment and certainly provoked controversy. Busch and his coauthors declare the transformation of the BGS an easy success, however, based on the increasing number of times states used it over the years. See Busch et al., *Polizei in der BRD*, 101.

[49] Horst Herold to Hans-Dietrich Genscher and Dr. Köhler, "3 Lösungsskizze," September 15, 1972, BA B106: 91147 – 625 210/33 Bd. 1. Other recommendations stressed areas of physics, chemistry, and general science over psychology, jurisprudence, and politics. See BMI, "Konzeption für die Aufstellung und den Einsatz einer Bundesgrenzschutz-Einheit für besondern polizeilichen Einsatz," September 19, 1972, BA B106: 88880; Dr. Köhler, "Betr.: Aufstellung einer Bundesgrenzschutz-Einheit für besondern polizeilichen Einsatz (BGS 9)," October 12, 1972, BA B106: 91147 – 625 210/33 Bd. 1; Werner Smoydzin, "Betr.: Aufstellung einer BGS-Einheit für Spezialaufgabe bei politischen Einsätzen (GSG 9); Prüfung der rechtlichen Grundlagen," October 27, 1972, BA B106: 91147 – 625 210/33 Bd. 2.

formation of West Germans' counterterrorism squad, the GSG-9, was strongly influenced by Israeli models – surprising, perhaps, considering the countries' decidedly chilly public relations in the wake of the hostage debacle. At the personal invitation of Israel's defense minister, however, the GSG-9's commanding officer, Ulrich Wegener, spent two weeks training "to fight Arab terrorists with special unit forces" alongside Israeli officers. On his return, Wegener recommended that much of what he had seen in Israel be applied in the FRG.[50]

Far from unusual, international cooperation such as this was very deliberately cultivated by the SPD government as its Western neighbors and allies also developed counterterrorism squads and computerized intelligence systems.[51] Annually, experts and heads of security from France, Britain, Sweden, Italy, and the United States were invited to Wiesbaden in order to discuss organized crime, including terrorism, and the uncharted territories of intelligence technology that each was exploring.[52] Such ventures not only aided information exchange, they also built trust among different states' security experts and confirmed the FRG's place among "civilized" nations. Even historical tensions were cast aside in the common effort to combat terrorism. In addition to Israel offering its own antiterrorist task force as a model for the GSG-9, the French and Germans worked together closely in the hopes of providing a model for Europe-wide cooperation on counterterrorism.[53] International collaboration also confirmed Social Democrats' conviction – not always shared by conservatives – that what was acceptable for some states was not necessarily acceptable for the post-Nazi one. U.S. and British counterterrorism practices in particular were cavalier about civil liberties and police power to an extent that West German experts and officials often judged impermissible.[54] And organized exchanges between French special operatives and members of the GSG-9 provoked a surprised Commander Wegener to comment that the French troops' activism and use of force were outside the bounds acceptable for West Germans.[55] If not always directly applicable, international cooperation nonetheless offered something invaluable: a kind of unofficial standard by which the SPD government could

[50] Ulrich Wegener to Hans-Dietrich Genscher, "Sonderlehrgang bei den israelischen Verteidigungsstreitkräften (ZAHAL) von 30.10.-12.11.1972," November 28, 1972, BA B106: 91147 – 625 210/33 Bd. 2.

[51] Among the comparative studies, see Peter Chalk, *West European Terrorism and Counter-Terrorism: The Evolving Dynamic* (New York: St. Martin's, 1996).

[52] See, e.g., BKA, *Datenverarbeitung: Arbeitstagung des Bundeskriminalamtes Wiesbaden, 13–17. März 1972* (Bonn: Bundesdruckerei, 1972); idem, *Organisiertes Verbrechen: Arbeitstagung des Bundeskriminalamtes Wiesbaden, 21–25. Oktober 1974* (Bonn: Bundesdruckerei, 1974).

[53] Numerous reports on French-German cooperation in the area of internal security can be found in BA B106: 371651.

[54] E.g., BMI, "Betr: Innere Sicherheit und Öffentlichkeitsarbeit des BKA," February 13, 1974, BA B106: 91146–625 210/9 Bd. 2; "Betr.: Terrorismus in Großbritannien," April 24, 1977, BA Bundeskanzleramt (Hereafter, B136): 15685.

[55] Ulrich Wegener, "Bericht über den Erfahrungsaustausch zwischen einer Spezialeinheit der französischen Gendarmerie und der GSG9," May 20, 1977, St. Augustin, BA B106: 3711651.

establish the democratic legitimacy of its actions for itself and, it hoped, for West German citizens.

Despite tremendous success in this arena and continued agreement over the need for a police force specifically trained in counterterrorism, the quasi-military appointments of the GSG-9 raised fears of an unwelcome state force. Most publicly, police union representative (and Social Democrat) Werner Kuhlmann opposed the GSG-9 on the grounds that it was an "amalgamation" of a paramilitary organization and a "close-to-the-citizen" police force that would "tread on human worth and displace officers' rights."[56] Kuhlmann's accusations came directly on the heels of a telephone conversation between Herold and Minister of Interior Hans-Dietrich Genscher, in which the BKA president asserted that a special unit was needed for "near-military situations, where the death of the perpetrator is highly likely or unavoidable."[57] Leaked to the press and quoted out of context, this one line circulated widely to generate considerable outrage over the government's new "extermination" troop. Even time's passage and the concerted efforts of the Interior Ministry to educate the public on the GSG-9's training and skills – in other words, on its very controlled and rational nature – did not diminish the ease with which the antiterrorist task force evoked images of abusive police force and repressive state power.[58] Whether it was because of the GSG-9's negative reception or its failure to fit Social Democrats' determinedly nonemergency vision of militant democracy, even members of government proved unable to accept the troop. Despite the creation of the GSG-9 at their own behest, the relevant cabinet members continually shrank from employing the unit in any function beyond that of glorified bodyguards. This remained true even when the FRG experienced a string of hostage situations beginning in 1975 – the very scenario for which the GSG-9 had been created.

IN SEARCH OF ACTIVE DEMOCRATS

At the same time officials modernized the country's security forces, they also lobbied for the constitution's "positive" protection in order to balance what they

[56] Discussed in an Interior Ministry report, Kuhlmann's critique was published in *Spiegel* 13 (March 26, 1973): 34.

[57] Transcript of telephone discussion between Horst Herold and Hans-Dietrich Genscher, March 19, 1973, BA B106: 91147 – 625 210/33 Bd. 2. See also, "2. Bericht des Bmins des Innern vor dem Innenausschuss des Dt. Btags am 20. März 1973 zu den Vorwürfen gegen den BGS," March 20/21, 1973, BA B106: 91147 – 625 210/33 Bd. 2. According to Genscher, Herold's statement was made in the context of discussing preliminary thoughts on how to deal with a situation in which a wounded terrorist was capable of throwing a grenade.

[58] References to the GSG-9 in the popular media ranged from jokes about expensive state toys to more ominous assessments of "killer teams" that merely opened the backdoor to capital punishment. David T. Schiller, "The Police Response to Terrorism: A Critical Overview," in *Contemporary Research on Terrorism*, eds. Paul Wilkinson and A. M. Stewart (Aberdeen: Aberdeen University Press, 1987), 539.

themselves characterized as repressive police measures.[59] The job of conceptualizing and carrying out such a program fell to the Federal Center for Political Education (BPB), an agency that had grappled with the threat of subversive politics in relative obscurity since 1952.[60] Directed to focus on "confronting the extremism and terror of minority groups" in March 1969, the BPB saw its responsibilities explicitly linked to the field of internal security two years later. The Center for Political Education soon led a coordinated effort involving the whole Interior Ministry to address political radicalism through political education. Less visible than the police reforms, administrative expansion, and legislation widely associated with government efforts to combat terrorism, the role of political education has received no notice from scholars of West German counterterrorism and has been inadequately grasped as psychological warfare in more general studies of the period.[61] But if anything competed with the modernization of police power in terms of the commitment of state resources, it was the attempt to preclude violence and extremism by fostering a political culture in keeping with SPD notions of democratic civil society. In this process, political education was understood as both a means and an end.

In response to a 1968 parliamentary inquiry into "political radicalism" in the FRG, Social Democratic leaders touted political education as the primary solution to the problem.[62] The program they laid out then received the Bundestag's strong approval; when the SPD took over the reins of government the following year, it became policy. The two overarching goals established for and by the Center for Political Education were the prevention of violent radicalism and the enlistment of the population in government efforts to contain it. The former complemented but did not replicate police efforts, as the BPB took a decidedly policy-oriented approach – organizing conferences and engaging the energies of respected scholars in a range of fields with the primary goal of determining the deeper social origins of political unrest.[63] If criminal behavior was a product of specific social and economic conditions, as experts maintained, then – in keeping with their enthusiasm for planning – more than police action was needed to address those conditions. The task was analogous

[59] For early correspondence between BMI and BPB on *positiver Verfassungsschutz*, see BA B106: 53997. This discussion was carried out in the context of the government's "Sofortprogramm." BPB to BMI, "Entwurf! Betr.: Psychologisch und soziologisch zu berücksichtigende Aspekte für die Entwicklung eines Sofort-Programms und eines länger-fristigen von Seiten der politischen Bildung im Rahmen des positiven Verfassungsschutzes," May 12, 1972, BA B106: 53997.

[60] BPB to BMI, "Betr.: Konzeption für den Bereich der inneren Sicherheit," February 23, 1972, BA B106: 53997.

[61] See, e.g., Cobler, *Law, Order and Politics*, esp. 38–51.

[62] The hearing was initiated by members of the FDP and the CDU/CSU. The proceedings of the *Grosse Anfrage* were then printed by Federal Minister of Interior Benda as *Schwarz auf Weiß: Zieler politischer Bildungsarbeit* (Bonn: BMI, 1968). BA B106: 53997.

[63] Published works resulting from these efforts included Manfred Funke, *Terrorismus: Untersuchungen zur Strategien und Struktur revolutionär Gewaltpolitk* (Kronberg: Athenäum, 1977) and the multivolume series *Analysen zum Terrorismus* (Opladen: Westdeutscher, 1981) authored by Fritz Sack, Iring Fetscher, Heinz Steinert, and Herfried Münkler among others.

to the one alluded to by Herold when he compared data processing with a clinical examination. The point was not merely to identify the symptoms ailing the FRG but rather to locate their cause and then direct state resources toward the cure.

Contemporary studies of the RAF and other violent groups typically described them as ideologically confused and, ultimately, lacking any rationale other than the pursuit of violence. It was common for officials to refer to the RAF as "violent anarchists" (or some variation thereof) and thereby convey the opinion that its attacks were ends in themselves.[64] By denying the political nature of terrorism, the government and its experts followed international convention, which defined terrorism as a purely criminal act.[65] They also echoed postwar understandings of fascist violence. Social Democrats were not as inclined as conservatives to see the source of political violence in the student rebellion and the erosion of traditional authority associated with the 1960s.[66] But many prominent party members did view the schools and universities with increasing concern and placed ideological dogmatism, political apathy, and a tolerance for violence – all perceived to be growing at a worrisome rate – on the same path of retrogressive politics that culminated in the RAF.[67] Particularly common among older members of the SPD was the perception that the material affluence and political conformity of the Adenauer years, as well as younger Germans' lack of a historical identity, had left much of the youth politically stunted and with little, if any, sense of connection to the FRG.[68] All of this together prompted comparisons with the political climate of the 1920s and encouraged Social Democrats to conclude that the roots of political extremism lay in sociopolitical malaise. To prevent further deterioration and a potential repetition of Weimar, therefore, members of government

[64] This was true, for example, in deliberations over the 1975 kidnapping of Peter Lorenz by the 2nd of June Movement. See BMI, "Betr.: Entführung v. Peter Lorenz," February 27, 1975, BA B106: 106997.

[65] On building a European Community consensus on this score, see Juliet Lodge, "The European Community and Terrorism," in *Combating the Terrorists: Democratic Responses to Political Violence*, ed. H. H. Tucker (New York: Oxford, 1988), 45–73.

[66] For conservatives' interpretation, see, e.g., Günter D. Radtke, Wolfgang W. Veiders, and Peter Jurecka, *Formen politischer Partizipation in der BRD* (Sankt Augustin: Konrad-Adenauer-Stiftung, n.d.). The authors argued that there was a direct correlation between the importance of family and religion in a citizen's life and the likelihood of illegal political participation (i.e., those with weak family and religious ties were prone to violence, political extremism). BA B141: 48830.

[67] More dismissive than alarmist was the interpretation of extraparliamentary opposition and its demands for direct democracy as a "romantic regression." See Richard Löwenthal, *Der romantische Rückfall* (Stuttgart: Kohlhammer, 1970). The conservative turn of liberal scholars or "integrative republicans" in reaction to 1968 is covered by Dirk Moses, *German Intellectuals and the Nazi Past* (Cambridge: Cambridge University Press, 2007), 186–218.

[68] These fears were expressed repeatedly in letter exchanges, parliamentary speeches, and even memoirs of the party leadership. For a self-critical examination of his generation's unfavorable interpretation of the university scene, see Erhard Eppler, *Das Schwerste ist Glaubwürdigkeit: Gespräche über ein Politikerleben mit Freimut Duve* (Reinbek: Rowohlt, 1978), 91–3.

called for a "political-spiritual confrontation" with terrorism that would do more than sap the RAF of sympathizers. It would also mobilize the population to the active defense of democracy. The BPB, with an explicit mandate to educate West Germans in the art of democratic politics, directed this offensive.

It is not altogether surprising that political education formed a core part of the Social-Liberal government's policy of internal security, recalling the Parliamentary Council debates and the SPD's argument that active democrats were ultimately (militant) democracy's best bet.[69] Now, Social Democrats proposed to strike at the root of political radicalism by cultivating the people's skills of "objective criticism, openness, even of resistance."[70] The operative logic in both 1949 and 1969 was that, properly educated, West Germans would have effectively no choice but to defend the principles of democracy, for both the courage and willingness to do so would have become second nature. Notably, the skills the SPD pinpointed promised to create democrats in the fullest sense of the term – not only active in times of emergency but also able and willing to productively question the status quo in times of peace and prosperity. In fact, when describing the goals of political education before the Bundestag, Social Democrats placed immense importance on citizens fulfilling both of these functions in equal measure.[71] Implicitly they argued that cultivating such dispositions would lay the foundations of a plural and democratic civil society in the FRG.

Surveying the political climate in the early 1970s, officials believed that the most immediate hurdle was the public's lack of information or, just as commonly, its misinformation. It was this, their reports observed time and again, that encouraged West Germans to react irrationally and emotionally. Fear or gut instinct led them to doubt either the regime's legitimacy – and thus sympathize with the terrorists – or its ability to govern – and thus favor more authoritarian leadership and, by implication, the CDU/CSU. According to its self-description, the program for "political education and positive constitutional protection" aimed, therefore, to help orient the citizen politically by facilitating his or her "*rational* – rather than emotional – critical consciousness."[72] If the Center for Political Education was to encourage the public's clear-eyed understanding of terrorism and the government's efforts to contain it, it had to first enlighten the public on existing conditions within the FRG. To do this, the BPB coordinated a multimedia campaign aimed broadly at the

[69] The SPD's influence on the BPB was noted by observant conservatives. Peter Gutjahr-Löser, for example, complained that the office had been turned into a political "Kampforgan" for the SPD and FDP. Peter Gutjahr-Löser, "Selbstbedienung für Volksfrontfreunde? Die Arroganz amtlicher Belehrer wird zum Skandal," *Bayern Kurier*, February 12, 1977.

[70] Vorsitzende der Beratung der Bundesregierung in Fragen der politischen Bildung, "'Zur Deutschen Unruhe' – Überlegungen zur politischen Bildungsarbeit," December 5, 1969, BA B106: 53997.

[71] Ibid.

[72] BPB, "Kapitel F: Politische Bildung und positiver Verfassungsschutz," in the agency's general program from May 12, 1972, BA B106: 53997. Emphasis in original.

politically uneducated and very specifically at the disaffected, that population of Germans whose relationship to the state ranged from willful indifference to open hostility. Its execution relied on BPB experts in mass media, pedagogy, and publicity in consultation with relevant parliamentary committees, experts on constitutional and criminal police matters, and the offices and manpower of both the BKA and the BfV.[73] In short, political education and the positive protection of the constitution involved the entire Interior Ministry.

Much of political education resembled a classic civics lesson on the "free democratic state" in which West Germans lived and the necessary conditions for a functioning civil society. Under the slogan, "Opposition, yes – enemy, no!" for example, the BPB launched a nationwide campaign for tolerance that tried to salvage the distinction between the sort of healthy criticism many argued was necessary to a pluralist society and the antidemocratic opposition the state was busy fighting.[74] To promote this cause, the Center sponsored bus billboards and solicited prominent social scientists' contributions on the subject of tolerance and "public spirit" (*Gemeinsinn*) for a special issue of its magazine, *Aus Politik und Zeitgeschichte*.[75] Well known for scholarly interventions such as this, the BPB's aspirations for political education were, however, greater. The institution's pedagogical commitments were captured best in its use of television, which would not only extend its popular reach but also allow for a more active and entertaining learning format.

In its proposals for television, the BPB promoted news programs similar to the public ARD network's *Pro + Contra* and the development of "who's who" quiz shows and "what if" discussion forums.[76] In the first case, the two-sided presentation of a current controversy did more than promote political awareness. It taught by example critical thinking, civil exchange of ideas, and willingness to compromise, qualities that Social Democrats perceived as essential to democratic civil society and as sorely lacking among extraparliamentary leftists. In comparison, the quiz shows and discussion forums were intended to familiarize their audience in an engaging fashion with the FRG's history and achievements. A particular favorite of BPB officials were programs that sought to convey the well-reasoned construction of the existing political system by asking viewers to contemplate scenarios such as "what if" there were no constitutional rights or "what if" federalism were abolished.[77] Such exercises aimed to combat disillusionment and disaffection – the perceived sources of

[73] Dr. Lewandowski, "Betr.: Konzeption zur politischen Bildung unter besonderer Berücksichtigung des politischen Radikalismus," April 26, 1972, BA B106: 53997.

[74] BPB, "Kampagne: 'Toleranze' der Aktion Gemeinsinn," 1977, BA B106: 70985.

[75] *Aus Politik und Zeitgeschichte* 38 (1977). The contributions included psychologist Bernd Schäfer's "Toleranz – Intoleranz: Anmerkungen zur Begriff, Bedingungen und Beeinflussung;" political scientist Theodor Ebert's "Toleranz und Konfliktfähigkeit;" and theologian Eberhard Müller's "Werbung für die Gemeinsinn – Erfahrungen und Probleme."

[76] BPB, "Betr.: Politische Bildung und positiver Verfassungsschutz," May 12, 1972, BA B106: 53997.

[77] Ibid.

radicalism – by teaching West Germans civic pride as they underscored the need for critical engagement within existing institutions. They recast the frictions and compromises of parliamentary politics as the products of a functioning pluralist society.

In addition to these explicitly didactic programs, the BPB's efforts to undermine political radicalism focused on providing the public with the government's narrative on terrorism and its attempts to contain it. It was this type of work that the Interior Ministry referred to explicitly as the "positive" or "enlightened" protection of the constitution. Through publications, films, and press conferences, the Ministry drew attention to the social and economic cost of violent crime, the government's extensive police reforms, and lingering obstacles to terrorism's successful confrontation. In particular, officials sought to combat the public's demonstrated fascination for individual terrorists, which they considered an information problem because media representations of RAF members – as the personification of German trauma, recent gender transgressions, or even "Hitler's children" – often displaced discussion of their acts and victims.[78] The assumption, of course, behind all these efforts was that the public could not help but support the government's fight against radicalism if made aware of "the facts." As time went on, political education increasingly focused on countering the "panic propaganda" and "misinformation" spread by the government's opponents, from the CSU to the RAF, as well as unflattering media coverage.[79] The intent of "enlightened constitutional protection" had always been to undermine public sympathy for the RAF and win support for the Social-Liberal government – as an arm of militant democracy, after all, it never claimed to be a neutral force. But this more defensive tack notably blurred the line between political education and simple pro-government propaganda, a line crucial to the SPD's own understanding of its policy. The proximity of the two was evident in the Ministry's budgets; the BPB both funded and directed the majority of the Interior Ministry's public relations work.[80]

One of the most basic examples of government efforts to enlighten West Germans was the publication of data on crime and crime fighting in the FRG. Still issued today by Germany's Interior Ministry, these annual reports charted the short- and long-term costs of violent crime in the hopes of making terrorism

[78] Jillian Becker, *Hitler's Children: The Story of the Baader-Meinhof Terrorist Gang* (Philadelphia: Lippincott, 1977). Excellent work has been done on the media's role in mediating events and crafting the RAF legacy. For a selection, see the collected works in *Baader-Meinhof Returns: History and Cultural Memory of German Left-Wing Terrorism*, eds. Gerrit-Jan Berendse and Ingo Cornils (Amsterdam: Rodopi, 2008).

[79] Vogel often referred to Christian Union scare tactics and calls for their "unmasking" met widespread agreement. Hans-Jochen Vogel, "Stellenwert unserer Politik auf dem Gebiet der Inneren Sicherheit," August 3, 1976; idem., "Innere Sicherheit: Ein Schwerpunkt sozialdemokratischer Politik. 10 Thesen," June 9, 1976. Both in Archiv der sozialen Demokratie (Bad Godesberg, hereafter AdsD), Helmut Schmidt Papers 9045.

[80] For budgetary information: BMI, "Betr.: Öffentlichkeitsarbeit auf dem Gebiet der Inneren Sicherheit," March 1977, BA B106: 316279.

relevant to average West Germans – if only to their pocket book.[81] Easy to read graphs also sought to give credit where credit was due by illustrating the decline of certain criminal activity and the redistribution of resources to areas where crime was on the rise. Far more likely to pique the average reader's interest were publications such as *The Baader-Meinhof-Report: Documents, Analyses, Contexts.*[82] Exemplary of efforts to raise public awareness and thereby gain support for the government's cause, it was published immediately following the RAF's 1972 May Offensive. Dedicated to the memory of those killed, the volume deliberately underscored the human victims of terrorism at the same time as it presented information on the roots, networks, and ideology of the "Baader-Mahler-Meinhof-Gang," as the group was initially called. With a fold-out table and appendixes of expert commentary on the RAF's manifestos as well as its connections to Arab terrorists and other criminal associations, the report aimed to instill in the reader an appreciation for the real danger terrorism presented. Just as important, those artifacts of social science expertise were intended to convey the government's command of the situation. A delicate balance to be sure, the overarching goal was to awaken citizens to the state's defense – not to itself terrorize citizens.

As the government's program of internal security came increasingly under attack from the CDU/CSU and extraparliamentary leftists, "enlightenment" became more narrowly self-justifying, focused on countering explicit criticisms. During the in-prison trial of major RAF figures, for example, accusations of torture and state repression made domestic and international headlines. In response, the BPB began plans for a feature film about the country's police forces with the purpose of underscoring how state authority, when backed by the rule of law, did not restrict but rather protected individual liberties.[83] Here, the agency's enlightenment work appears indistinguishable from public relations initiatives on behalf of the police and the BKA.[84] In a similar vein, Horst Herold called for a "counter-information campaign" in 1974 in order to combat what he saw as the media campaign in favor of the imprisoned RAF members.[85] The state, he argued, had no choice but to confront directly accusations of torture and illegality that aimed to discredit it and the justice system. Herold's public relations solution – an "info booth" that could answer

[81] West Germany, *Verfassungsschutzbericht* (Bonn: Bundesministerium des Innern, 1974-); Germany, *Periodischer Sicherheitsbericht* (Berlin: Bundesministerium des Innern, 2001–).

[82] *Der Baader-Meinhof-Report: Dokumente, Analysen, Zusammenhänge aus den Akten des Bundeskriminalamtes, der "Sonderkomission Bonn" und dem Bundesamt für Verfassungsschutz* (Mainz: Hase & Koehler, 1972).

[83] BMI, "Betr.: Zur Vorbereitung des von Herrn Ministern angeordeneten Grundsatzgespräches über das von der Bundeszentrale für politische Bildung vorgelegte Papier zur Auseinandersetzung mit dem Extremismus," September 3, 1975, BA B106: 53999.

[84] The same could be said for its television collaborations with ARD's news magazine, *Panorama*. See BMI, "Betr.: Öffentlichkeitsarbeit – Panorama," February 5, 1974, BA B106: 83805 Bd. 16; Letter from Horst Herold to BMI, November 28, 1973, BA B106: 83805 Bd. 16.

[85] Memo from Horst Herold to BMI, 14 May 1974, BA B106 83806 – 626 310/8 Bd. 18.

the press and the public's questions over the course of the trial – could just as easily have come from the BPB, so similar was its mission to disseminate "the facts" in what the government considered their proper light.[86] Though often remarkably dry, these interventions were far easier and more palatable than the alternative: pressuring the media into covering the government's side, as had been the approach under Adenauer.[87] More than one editor demonstrated who controlled public discourse in the FRG by giving a bullying government official the cold shoulder.[88]

So what, if anything, distinguished education and enlightenment programs from attempts at government propaganda? Those behind the former understood there to be a significant difference – as their dealings with a media expert on their own payroll made clear. The Interior Ministry originally contracted Eduard Zimmermann to create an overarching "concept" for the media's "supportive role in the fight against crime." Opinion polls taken shortly after Baader, Ensslin, and Meinhof were apprehended in 1972 showed that many West Germans did not know who Ensslin was and a significant number considered the arrests purely fortuitous.[89] Zimmermann was hired explicitly to awaken the public to the crimes, the criminals, and the BKA's hard work.[90] In his first report, Zimmermann described various public relations strategies pursued by the U.S. Federal Bureau of Investigations (FBI) and suggested that these might also be used in the FRG.[91] The report was not well received.[92] An in-depth evaluation of Zimmermann's program two years later criticized the media expert for his "ideologization of crime fighting," profit-oriented journalism, and complete lack of concern for legal criteria.[93] The notion that German police officers might model themselves after the FBI simply baffled Zimmermann's superiors:

[86] Memo from Horst Herold to BMI, BMJ, Federal Attorney's Office, and Police, August 8, 1974, BA B106 83806 – 626 310/8 Bd. 18.

[87] On the government-steered "consensus journalism" of the 1950s versus the more "critical public sphere" of the 1960s and after, see Christina von Hodenberg, *Konsens und Krise: Eine Geschichte der westdeutschen Mediaöffentlichkeit, 1945–1973* (Göttingen: Wallstein, 2006).

[88] Shining examples of the media giving as good as it got are captured in Horst Herold's angry exchange with the director of the NDR in February 1973 over what he characterized as the "inaccurate and slanderous" coverage of hunger strikes and the deaf ear *Die Zeit*'s editor-in-chief, Theo Sommer, turned to Ministry of Justice press secretary Sepp Benda's objections over the sympathetic article from February 4, 1977 on Peter-Paul Zahl. Both in BA B106: 106580.

[89] BMI, "Betr.: Terrorismus Bekämpfung," November 1972, BA B106: 91146 – 625 210/9.

[90] BMI, "Anregungen der DKF – Eduard Zimmerman zur Öffentlichkeitsarbeit," March 6, 1974, BA B106: 91146 – 625 210/9.

[91] Deutsche Kriminal-Fachredaktion, "Anregungen zur Öffentlichkeitsarbeit des BKAs unter besonderer Berücksichtigung der Elektronische Datenverarbeitung," n.d., BA B106: 91146 – 625 210/9.

[92] BMI Circular: "Anregungen der DKF zur Unterstützung der Arbeit des BKA bei der Bekämpfung anarchistischer Gewaltverbrecher," November 23, 1972, BA B106: 91146 – 625 210/9.

[93] BMI, "Betr.: Öffentlichkeitsarbeit des BKAs," February 13, 1974, BA B106: 91146 – 625 210/9 Bd. 2.

> The American policeman is never doubted as the bearer of state power. [But] in Germany, the police officer must struggle with his profession's difficult history. He wants to be acknowledged as a normal citizen; to let him show off as a party animal and Superman following the FBI model would destroy whatever trust has been achieved.[94]

In this instance, at least, moving from public education into transparently one-sided advocacy was judged to be fundamentally at odds with the interests of the Interior Ministry.

The officials who responded to Zimmermann's proposed strategies conveyed the opinion that cultivating active citizens required political education to be different from the passive consumption of propaganda. Political education was, at least in its intent, about enabling each citizen to form his or her own opinion by making it possible for West Germans to acquire and critically assess all relevant information. The goal was not simply that citizens side with the state but that they willingly participate in its constitution and support, not mindlessly or patriotically in times of crisis but as part of a habit of political engagement.[95] Here, the SPD demonstrated its ongoing commitment to a civilian defense of democracy and its desire to anchor that popular participation securely within the bounds of parliamentary politics. Party leaders did not reject the claims of resistance but rather the revolutionary ethos, preferring instead a model of pro-state grassroots engagement. In this and its more general pedagogical goals, political education's aims extended considerably beyond the particular threat of the moment. It sought to ensure the state's permanent internal security by achieving actually existing democracy in the FRG's institutions and in its citizens' mentalities.

If the positive side of the SPD's program of political education was the creation of active democrats, however, the negative side was the deliberate exclusion of those who would not conform to its definition of that role. Famous was the 1972 Decree against Radicals, which aimed to prevent so-called radicals from infiltrating the civil service and subverting the existing state. All applicants for public service were screened and whoever refused to profess allegiance to the Basic Law's "free democratic order" was denied employment. The decree likewise threatened everyone from top ministerial employees to professors, teachers, and postal workers with dismissal if they failed a loyalty test. Initiated by the Standing Council of Länder Interior Ministers rather than the federal government, the Decree against Radicals received Willy Brandt's willing signature and strong SPD backing. To be sure, there were those such as deputy chairman Herbert Wehner who, before the law went into effect, expressed unease over the law's potential threat to civil liberties.[96] Mindful of

[94] Ibid.

[95] AG Innenpolitische Grundsatzfragen, "Betr.: Erarbeitung einer Konzeption 'Aufklärender Verfassungsschutz,'" December 17, 1975, BA B106: 53999.

[96] Herbert Wehner was notoriously responsible for maintaining internal party discipline. Thus after the Decree against Radicals was signed, Wehner shifted his energies to squashing its criticism. On Wehner: Christoph Meyer, *Herbert Wehner: Biographie* (Munich: Deutscher Taschenbuch, 2006).

conservatives' enthusiasm for the decree and perhaps his own experiences as a Communist in the 1930s, Wehner specifically warned against misusing the fight against extremism to "abuse and mistrust all that is not conservative."[97] But by and large, Social Democrats defended the decree as a means of ensuring the political loyalties of a particularly important population.

A favorite case study in scholarship on militant democracy, the Decree against Radicals is conventionally explained as following a particularly German practice of binding civil servants to the crown.[98] But rather than a reactionary throwback or a desperate attempt on the part of the SPD to appease conservatives, the law is better understood as part of the postwar struggle to defend democracy – inspired less by authoritarian continuities than by the critiques of authority and democratic militancy of the immediate postwar period. In 1948, memories of *Schreibtischtäter* as well as of the Nazi infiltration of the Weimar Republic's civil service motivated SPD delegates to argue that the state required not a passive or apolitical but an actively loyal bureaucracy responsible to the new democratic order.[99] In 1972, Social Democrats' convictions that the universities and schools were sites of system-threatening extremism and that educators were crucial to West German democratization drove them to a similar conclusion. The striking resemblance between the Land-initiated decree and state ministers' requests forty years before – asking the federal government to use civil service regulations against the Nazis – further solidified their position. In 1931 and 1932, Chancellor Brüning flatly ignored the ministers; the perceived consequences of Brüning's inaction confirmed – for Brandt and many others – the legitimacy of barring radicals' access to state institutions in the early 1970s.[100]

THE RETURN OF THE EXCEPTION: CONSERVATIVES' OPPOSITION

In November 1972, Social Democrats became the strongest party in the Bundestag, a first in postwar history. And the FDP – whose "kingmaker" support vaulted the minority coalition of 1969 into power – likewise experienced record electoral returns. Understood as a vote for *Ostpolitik* and against a return to the status quo ante offered by the CDU/CSU, the elections gave the Social-Liberal coalition a green light to continue its course of domestic

[97] Cited in "Ein Ärgernis," *Die Zeit*, July 21, 1978, 10.

[98] See, e.g., Gerard Braunthal, *Political Loyalty and Public Service in West Germany: The 1972 Decree against Radicals and its Consequences* (Amherst: University of Massachusetts Press, 1990) and John E. Finn, *Constitutions in Crisis: Political Violence and the Rule of Law* (New York: Oxford University, 1991).

[99] *Parl. Rat* 5, 56f., 152f; *Parl. Rat* 2, 226–7n116.

[100] The ministers' request was eventually addressed by Defense Minister Groener with the April 13, 1932 ban on the Nazis and the Communists. Hans Mommsen, *The Rise and Fall of Weimar Democracy*, trans. Elborg Forster and Larry Eugene Jones (Chapel Hill: University of North Carolina Press, 1989), 418–21.

reform.[101] In this context, terrorism and political violence did not hold a primary place in the ruling parties' agenda. Internal security, in fact, failed even to make the list of topics discussed at the 1973 SPD party congress in Hanover.[102] Though the 1972 May Offensive and the tragic events of the Munich Olympics were far from forgotten, the BKA's stunning success at capturing the leading members of the RAF had eased anxieties and returned a sense of relative security to West Germans and their leaders.[103]

By November 1974 much had happened to change this. First, the nation had to contend with the OPEC oil embargo in 1973 and the corresponding global economic downturn. No one anticipated the abrupt end to over two decades of consistent economic growth, least of all the SPD, whose plans for social reform and modernization presumed its continuation. In order to control inflation and stave off deeper crisis, the government saw little option but to switch gears and tighten state expenditures. Second, the SPD-led government was rocked by scandal when Willy Brandt's close aide, Günter Guillame, was revealed to be an East German informant. The discovery was a political goldmine for conservatives who continued to characterize *Ostpolitik* as a national security risk and Social Democrats as communist sympathizers. Against his will, Brandt stepped down as chancellor in favor of Helmut Schmidt, who as a young Bundestag deputy had earned a reputation for his biting attacks on Adenauer's government and the defense policies of Franz-Josef Strauß in particular. It was, however, his accomplishments – his effective handling of the 1962 Hamburg floods as that city's senator of interior and his proven expertise as minister of defense and then minister of finance – that landed him in the chancellery.[104] There was no denying that Schmidt lacked his predecessor's charisma, but his reputation as a *Macher* – someone who could get things done, no matter the obstacles – was considered a boon in suddenly troubled times.[105]

Third and finally, West Germany's "urban guerrillas" again made headlines with the prison death of RAF member Holger Meins on November 9, 1974 and the retaliatory murder of West Berlin judge Günter von Drenkmann by the 2nd of June Movement immediately thereafter. This is not to say that they had ever been absent from the media. In January 1973, the RAF had launched the first of many hunger strikes to protest prison conditions in the FRG, and

[101] The clear message sent by the 1972 elections caused much internal debate within the CDU and ultimately a generational shift, as the young Helmut Kohl replaced Barzel as party speaker. See Hans-Otto Kleinmann, *Geschichte der CDU: 1945–1982* (Stuttgart: DVA, 1993).

[102] *Protokoll über die Verhandlungen des Parteitages der Sozialdemokratischen Partei Deutschlands, Hannover 10.-14. April 1973* (Bonn: SPD-Vorstand, 1973).

[103] The revision of the criminal code to make the "glorification and down-playing of violence" a criminal act paled in importance to the government's efforts to finalize new treaties with the Eastern Bloc and to reform property and family rights, sex crime legislation, and Paragraph 218 of the criminal code banning abortion.

[104] It is worth noting that Schmidt did not hesitate to overstep the law and use BGS and Bundeswehr resources in the 1962 crisis.

[105] Jonathan Carr seconds the stereotype of Schmidt in his biography, *Helmut Schmidt: The Helmsman of Germany* (New York: St. Martin's 1985).

eighteen months later the state sanctioned the first forced feeding of inmates.[106] Since then, West Germans had fought over whether the painful procedure was torture, a violation of rights (either the prisoners' or, as conservatives argued, the doctors'), or a constitutional duty under Article 1 of the Basic Law, which made "human dignity" the state's primary responsibility. This debate reached a crescendo (though not a resolution) with Meins's death after nearly two months on hunger strike. In cities across the country, protesters took to the streets with banners accusing the state of murder while prominent intellectuals such as Ernst Bloch and Martin Walser signed statements protesting prison conditions (Figure 3.1).[107] For many younger West Germans, Meins's death – not unlike Benno Ohnesorg's death seven years earlier – radicalized their perception of the FRG as a uniquely repressive, authoritarian state. It recruited new members to the cause of militant resistance and mobilized a spate of violent attacks, beginning with the murder of von Drenkmann. Among the general public, the state's apparent helplessness before the terrorists – both in prison and outside of it – produced a new consensus on the severity of the threat posed to the Federal Republic by terrorism and the need to actively combat it. In his 1975 New Year's address, Chancellor Schmidt presented a "top five" list of the nation's greatest threats, each reflecting changes in West German security over the previous year. Following global inflation, the oil crisis, the Guillame affair, and unemployment were the "terroristic communists" of the "Baader-Meinhof group."[108]

In the months and years that followed, the BKA was unable to replicate its early successes and the Social-Liberal government seemed constantly on the defensive. Conservatives accused Social Democrats of having failed to take seriously the threat posed by left-wing extremism and suggested that the SPD's own socialist sympathies and fundamental inability to govern were to blame. On the one hand, such exaggerated rhetoric can be chalked up to petty politicking. Members of the Christian Union did not take well to electoral defeat or to being relegated to the opposition.[109] The minutes of the CDU presidium and party meetings reveal a calculated public relations strategy to regain power, as they used each new terrorist attack as an opportunity to assert their identity as the country's proven governors and experts on national security.[110] But the

[106] The first forced feedings took place in early May 1974 when approximately eighty prisoners were on hunger strike.

[107] "Beschuldigungen nach dem Tod von Holger Meins," *FAZ*, November 10, 1974.

[108] Vogel objected to Schmidt's characterization of the RAF as terroristic communists, but the chancellor defended it as a deliberate and correct choice. Personal exchange between Vogel and Schmidt, January 7, 1975 and January 18, 1975, AdsD Hans-Jochen Vogel, Correspondence 400092.

[109] For a study of the CDU/CSU that pays particular attention to this difficult period of transition, see Geoffrey Pridham, *Christian Democracy in Western Germany: The CDU/CSU in Government and Opposition, 1945–1976* (London: Helm, 1977).

[110] This was established as early as 1968, when the CDU struggled to combat its steadily declining returns. See: Protokoll der Bundesvorstandssitzungen, May 10, 1968, Archiv für

FIGURE 3.1. A protest march following the funeral of Holger Meins on November 18, 1974. Meins died in prison nine days earlier during a hunger strike. Second from the left is Helmut Ensslin, a protestant minister and the father of RAF leader Gudrun Ensslin (dpa).

debate that raged between government and opposition over counterterrorism also reflected substantive divergences in their conceptions of state power and democracy's defense. In an early letter to Chancellor Brandt, CDU member Carl Damm explained that conservatives' concerns stemmed from a fundamental uncertainty regarding whether or not the SPD possessed "the courage to act."[111] This singular assertion captured conservatives' unwavering conviction that crises required a kind of decisive action incommensurable with ordinary parliamentary politics. Complaints from members of the Union that the SPD was unable to identify the threat, paid too much mind to procedures and minority rights, or – as Damm suggested – simply lacked the will to decide, ultimately imputed all the long-perceived weaknesses of liberal democracy to the SPD-led government and its program of counterterrorism. The old Schmittian argument returned: Refusing to acknowledge the exceptional, liberal democracy was surely a lame duck.

Christlich-Demokratische Politik (Sankt Augustin, hereafter ACDP) and Protokoll der CDU/CSU Fraktionssitzung, November 12, 1974, BA Karl Carstens Papers N1337/27.

[111] Letter from Carl Damm to Bundeskanzler Brandt, May 24, 1972, ACDP Fraktion AKI VIII-002 79/1.

If Social Democrats understood terrorism as a social problem, then West German conservatives understood it to be a problem of state. As politicians and academics across Western Europe were questioning the status of what they called "governability" in light of the decade's economic crisis and social upheaval, the CDU (with 20/20 hindsight and some strategic blindness) threw up its hands and cried, "no wonder!"[112] Echoing Ernst Forsthoff's predictions of a state tossed about on the waves of modernity's unruly history, a 1973 internal party report alleged that while the state's responsibilities had grown exponentially, the institution had never been weaker.[113] The state's role had been reduced to providing services and gratifying special interest groups at the same time individual citizens – though quick to take the state to task – were increasingly less likely to express loyalty or a willingness to serve.[114] Postwar conservatives were assigned their share of blame for this by younger, more ideologically oriented reformers primed to take over the party. But most of it was reserved for the SPD, whose promised "democratization of the polity," it was argued, had led to the "societalization of the state" whereby the citizen was protected against but still demanded social intervention from the state, while the state was increasingly dependent on corporations, experts, and organizations for its functioning.[115] According to this logic, social conflict and political gridlock were the inevitable result. For the state was unable to guarantee that justice and law be observed, much less to act in its crucial role as sovereign arbiter – that neutral force conservatives asserted was necessary to decide among competing interests and harmonize technology with a mass economy. Thus a new generation of leaders – among them the newly appointed party chairman Helmut Kohl and general secretary Kurt Biedenkopf – argued that the answer to democracy's

[112] For contemporary German scholarship on governability, see, e.g., Erwin K. Scheuch, *Wird die Bundesrepublik unregierbar?* (Cologne: Arbeitgeberverband der Metallindustrie Köln, 1976); Wilhelm Hennis, Peter Graf Kielmansegg, Ulrich Matz, eds., *Regierbarkeit: Studien zu ihrer Problematisierung* (Stuttgart: Klett-Cotta, 1977); and Martin Kriele, *Legitimationsprobleme der Bundesrepublik* (Munich: Beck, 1977). For a prominent left critique: Claus Offe, "'Unregierbarkeit:' Zur Renaissance konservativer Krisentheorien," in *Stichworte zur geistigen Situation der Zeit*, ed. Jürgen Habermas, vol 1, *Nation und Republik* (Frankfurt: Suhrkamp, 1979), 294–318.

[113] Forsthoff himself continued to argue for the return of the emphatically sovereign state, joined by other conservative thinkers who criticized the "societalization of the state" and the vapidness of the West German state. Unlike Forsthoff, these reformers placed new emphasis on the German need for a collective identity. See, e.g., Armin Mohler, *Was die deutschen fürchten* (Stuttgart: Seewald, 1965) and Gerd-Klaus Kaltenbrunner, *Rekonstruktion des Konservatismus* (Freiburg: Rombach, 1972).

[114] "Zweiter Bericht der Grundsatzkommission," August 30, 1973, ACDP Bundesvorstandssitzungen 936.

[115] Richard von Weizsäcker, "Die Starken und die Schwachen: Wie kann die politische Führung ihre Handlungsfähigkeit zurückwinnen?" *Die Zeit*, March 21, 1975. Franz-Josef Strauss offered a more extreme version of this thesis a few years later: "The democratization of society is the beginning of anarchy, the end of true democracy. When democratization has progressed far enough, it ends in Communist dictatorship." *Deutsches Allgemeines Sontagsblatt*, January 11, 1978.

long-term security was to reverse this process by reestablishing a clear conception of the state and its authority, outside and above society.[116] Contrary to what their opponents might contend, conservatives argued that strong state action was not a threat to the freedom of responsible citizens.[117] Rather, the true threat to individual liberty lay in the loss of state authority.

Conservatives' position seemed borne out when the 2nd of June Movement struck again in early 1975 and won what would be armed struggle's biggest victory over the West German state. This time, the group took hostage Peter Lorenz – a popular Christian Democrat and West Berlin mayoral candidate – just seventy-two hours short of the March elections. In exchange for Lorenz's safe return, they demanded the "liberation" of five imprisoned comrades as well as RAF ideologue Horst Mahler. Each prisoner was to receive DM20,000 and air transportation to a secure third world country. The group's success had much to do with its insistence, too, that the government televise all negotiations. It was a brilliant strategic move that both tied the government's hands and placed it, as well as the entire West German media, at the kidnappers' beck and call. The 2nd of June Movement controlled public discourse, and thus events as a whole, for the duration of the crisis.[118] Mahler – the only named prisoner charged with murder – refused to be released, having publicly sworn off the RAF and terrorism at his trial the previous autumn. In retrospect, this was probably fortunate for the others, as it no doubt made their release easier for officials to contemplate. And release them they did. In a concession described by the weekly *Die Zeit* as "humiliating to the West German state," Schmidt's government not only negotiated for the five militants' safe transport to South Yemen, but also agreed to broadcast – live – the newly freed prisoners' prepared statements and departure.[119] The government's willingness to do so was rewarded: On March 4, after the release and extradition of the 2nd of June Movement's members, Peter Lorenz was dumped from a car in West

[116] References to the CDU's contribution to this erosion of "stateness" faded quickly but were present, for example, in the Basic Policy Commission's August 1973 report, which appeared shortly after Kohl became the new party chairman. Kohl appointed Weizsäcker to chair the commission, responsible for formulating a new long-term program that would hopefully breathe new life into the party. See Pridham, *Christian Democracy*; also, the excellent work done more recently by Frank Bösch, *Macht und Machtverlust: Die Geschichte der CDU* (Stuttgart: DVA, 2002).

[117] "Freedom based on responsibility" was, in fact, the new programmatic line set out by Biedenkopf for the next election. As Richard von Weizsäcker explained it, the citizen's level of freedom roughly reflected that afforded the state. The weak distributive state reproduced dependency within the population, turning citizens into "objects of [state] benefice" forced to lobby the same interest groups and elites that propped up the state; a strong state able to ensure democratic responsibility and thus inspire citizens' loyalty and active service, freed them from it. Weizsäcker, "Die Starken und die Schwachen."

[118] As one West German reporter described it, the media simply lost all control to the terrorists at this time. See Richard Clutterbuck, "Terrorism and Urban Violence," *Proceedings of the Academy of Political Science* 34 (Autumn 1982): 175.

[119] *Die Zeit*, March 7, 1975.

Berlin. The politician was given just enough money to call his wife and let her know he was safe.

From the beginning of the kidnapping crisis, the government called for cool heads and the solidarity of all democrats in a public mantra it would perfect over the next few years. Behind the scenes, Schmidt assembled a grand advisory committee – informally referred to as a crisis staff – made up of parliamentary and party heads as well as cabinet members and experts.[120] Intended to promote consensus building between Bonn and the Länder as well as between government and political parties, the advisory committee captured the leadership's preference for decisions based on parliamentary-style procedures and informed agreement. It was also an amalgam of Social Democratic efforts to avoid executive rule and to foist responsibility on all four parties.[121] In the Lorenz case, the crisis staff at the federal level was mirrored by a similar staff at the Land level, as jurisdiction lay not with the federal government and the BKA but with West Berlin authorities. As local officials simultaneously began negotiations for Lorenz's release and conducted an undercover police search for the kidnappers, those assembled in Bonn – most especially, Schmidt's minister of interior, Werner Maihofer – acted as advisers to West Berlin.[122]

The primary question confronting the crisis staff in those first few hours was whether the government had a choice should the kidnappers demand the release of imprisoned terrorists.[123] Constitutional experts said "no." The same foundational principle that required the state to force feed prisoners on hunger strike demanded it negotiate for the life of Peter Lorenz.[124] Minister of Justice Hans-Jochen Vogel said "yes." The question was not a strictly legal one but rather involved "a decision concerning the politics of state" (*eine staatspolitische Entscheidung*). Nowhere, he observed, did the constitution demand that

[120] In this early incarnation, "crisis staff" was used interchangeably with "work staff." Press Secretary Klaus Bölling, however, emphasized the care with which the government avoided using "crisis" publicly in connection with terrorism – maintaining its usage of *große Politische Beratungskreis* or *Beratungsgremium* even when *Krisenstab* had become a household word. See Thomas Mavridis, "Geplante Krise in Public Relations? Eine Studie über umweltsensible, politische und wirtschaftliche Krisenfälle" (M.A. thesis, Otto-Friedrich-Universität Bamberg, 1997).

[121] Recall that one of the conditions for Social Democratic support of the 1968 Emergency Laws had been the legal provision for a "joint (parliamentary) committee" that would consult with (and provide a check on) the executive. The first "crisis staff" was formed (with little effect) by Federal Minister Genscher in 1972 during the hostage crisis of the Olympic Games and became standard practice under Helmut Schmidt. If modeled after the joint committee, these bodies were nonetheless legally undefined by the constitution given the undeclared nature of the emergencies they served.

[122] Given Berlin's special status, the use of federal forces also required consultation with the Allies and entailed certain restrictions on the number of men employed.

[123] The March 3rd cover of *Der Spiegel* reversed the question: "Peter Lorenz – Darf ausgetauscht werden?"

[124] Allgemeine Verfassungsangelegenheiten, "Betr.: Entführung des Berliner CDU-Landesvorsitzenden Lorenz," February 27, 1975, BA B106: 80795.

the life of an individual preempt all other considerations.[125] And, as presider over law and justice in the FRG, Vogel adamantly insisted the others consider this: that legal order would be dangerously compromised if renegade civilians – and not the state – decided how much time violent criminals served in jail.[126] Consulted on whether the terrorists could be trusted to honor their side of the bargain, Horst Herold characterized the 2nd of June Movement as the "SS of the RAF, for whom every humanity had been supplanted by [military] precisionism."[127] Despite this harrowing assessment, the president of the BKA stated that recently confiscated information suggested that the kidnappers would, in fact, release Peter Lorenz if their conditions were met.[128]

Those involved in the deliberations clearly hoped for a win-win situation in which the police would find Lorenz and thus spare the government from having to release prisoners or, alternatively, that the host country could be convinced to detain the prisoners following their – and Lorenz's – release.[129] They did not, however, count on it. Rather, the overwhelming consensus in Bonn, West Berlin, and among the Länder ministers of justice was that the risk to Peter Lorenz's life outweighed the risks to the state.[130] There was no choice but to negotiate with the terrorists. In his address to the public following Lorenz's happy return, however, Helmut Schmidt took a sober tone. He defended the decision to negotiate at the same time he warned that doing so had come at a price. Acceding to terrorist demands encouraged future attacks and would eventually, the chancellor predicted, have a deleterious effect on state authority and the existing constitutional order.[131]

It did not take long for the RAF to prove at least the first half of Schmidt's statement correct. Less than two months later, on April 24, the "Commando Holger Meins" seized the top floor of the German embassy in Stockholm. Holding twelve state employees as hostages, a new generation of RAF members sought to replicate the 2nd of June Movement's success on a larger scale. Before even issuing their demands, the guerrillas shot the FRG's military attaché, Lieutenant Colonel Baron Andreas von Mirbach, in order to convince

125 Ministerbüro, "Gesprächsvermerk: Arbeitsstab im BMI – Lorenz Entführung," March 1, 1975, BA B106: 317905.

126 Ministerbüro, "Gesprächsvermerk: 2. März – Lorenz Entführung," March 2, 1975, BA B106: 317905.

127 Ministerbüro, "Gesprächsvermerk," March 1.

128 Herold reiterated this point at the next day's staff meeting. Ministerbüro, "Gesprächsvermerk," March 2.

129 Foreign Minister Genscher's efforts were reported on in the meeting of March 2, 1975; deliberations over police force and the dangers of widening the search for Lorenz conveyed the hopes placed in finding Lorenz and the kidnappers either during or immediately after events.

130 The Conference of Justice Ministers stated that the conditions allowing for extraordinary action had not been met. Minister Theisen, "Gesprächsvermerk," March 2. See also: "Argumente (für Ablehnung evtl. Austauschforderungen/für Eingehen auf evtl. Austauschforderungen)," 1975, BA B106: 106997.

131 Helmut Schmidt, "Erklärung zur Peter Lorenz Entführung," *Verhandlungen*, VIII. Bundestag, Sitzung (March 5, 1975), 11781.

the Swedish police – who had occupied the building's lower levels – to leave. Once this condition was met, they made the others known. In exchange for the hostages, they demanded the release of twenty-six "political prisoners," among them Ensslin, Meinhof, and Baader. To dissuade rescue attempts and dispel any impressions that the commando might back down, they shot a second hostage, economic attaché Heinz Hillegaart. In this, however, they misjudged. The murders – and their demand for the imprisoned leaders' release – fortified the government's resolve not to negotiate.[132] This turned out to not be their only misstep. During the course of events, the RAF members accidently detonated their own bomb and brought the hostage crisis to an abrupt and, for them, unhappy, end.

More than any incident before or since, the Lorenz kidnapping captured the parties' discordant approaches to crisis management. While Lorenz was still hostage, the outspoken Franz-Josef Strauß rejected the government's plea for solidarity among all democrats – to the applause of his fellow Union delegates. According to the CSU chairman, the call was both hypocritical and weak: hypocritical because "the left" had repeatedly shown itself in solidarity with sympathizers and members of "these criminal organizations;" and weak because the government merely sought to "obscure who really bears responsibility for events."[133] Helmut Kohl seemed to agree. Unconsciously mimicking the RAF's own logic, he pronounced the government's talk of solidarity all fine and good but declared it was action – led by an "aggressive, powerful democracy" – that was required in this "hour of need." It was time to "make clear that [the FRG] is a strong state with authority" and "striking power."[134] Conservatives in and out of parliament argued that energetic measures were necessary to regain the state's monopoly on violence and thereby reestablish law and order. Going further than even Strauß dared, an editorial in the conservative daily, *Die Welt*, pronounced it "shameful" that the "Israel solution" was not up for discussion, referring to that country's categorical refusal to negotiate with terrorists. The West German state had to become harder, he insisted, by replacing the empty talk and grandiose sentiments of its elected officials with "competence and decisiveness in the protection of the *Rechtsstaat*." When he declared that "the end of tepidness … lax liberality … and permissive indulgence had come," his complaints and his call to action could just as easily have been aimed at the SPD government of 1930 as the SPD government of 1975.[135] These were not the words of anticommunism Social Democrats usually confronted but rather the rhetoric of fear concerning parliamentary democracy itself.

Time and time again, the image conservatives conjured up was that of Weimar, a state too weak and dim-witted to protect its citizens from the

132 For more on the government's shift to non-negotiation, see Chapter 5.

133 CDU/CSU, Sondersitzung über die Entführung des Berliner CDU-Landesvorsitzenden Lorenz, February 27, 1975, BA Karl Carstens' Papers N1337/29.

134 DFS, "Bericht aus Bonn" aired February 28, 1975 at 22:05, BA B106: 106997.

135 "Der Kommentar: Für den Staat," *Die Welt*, March 1, 1975.

enemy.[136] Considering that Union representatives were clamoring for the right to bear arms in self-defense, and right-wing groups such as "Death Squadron Berlin" had announced plans for a "counter-action against terror," one could argue that there was good reason to be alarmed at the state's weakened credibility.[137] But the accusations of powerlessness and the party chairmen's explicit rejections of interparty solidarity were rooted in conservatives' general perception of what was required of a state under siege.[138] If Social Democrats had tried, they could not have picked a more fitting symbol than the crisis staff for all that conservatives believed unsuitable in emergency situations. Even in its trim form, the crisis staff did not conjure up decisive action but rather a slow, collaborative decision-making process and all the uncertainty, talking without doing, and potential disaster associated with it. Worst of all, the crisis staff suggested a weak head of state, unable to decide alone. Another *Die Welt* commentator went straight to the point with the headline: "Adenauer Was His Own Crisis Staff."[139] A strong chancellor – like a strong military leader – did not mince words but acted with purpose, instilling confidence in the population and fear in the hearts of enemies.

Accusations of weakness and inaction were not only fueled by the government's humiliation at the hands of Lorenz's kidnappers and the Stockholm crisis immediately thereafter, but also by Social Democrats' seemingly soft position on crime. Conservatives saw them as overly tolerant and too protective of criminals' rights. At least this was how they explained the situation in the prisons, where it seemed that the terrorists not only called the shots but did so with the help of their attorneys. Suspicions concerning the RAF's lawyers began, you might say, with them doing their jobs by advocating their clients' positions. The attorneys voiced the RAF's demands for better prison conditions – including accusations of torture – and pursued a line of defense that not only recognized the militants as political combatants but substantiated their claims against the FRG and the U.S. government to do so.[140] These actions alone provoked open hostility from members of the political establishment and the judiciary in part

[136] Helmut Kohl evoked Weimar's end thus: "the dumbest calves picked their own butcher." Strauß suggested the same in his accusation that the federal government was handing over the country to "criminals and political gangsters." Quoted in DFS, "Bericht aus Bonn."

[137] CDU/CSU, Fraktionssitzung vom 27 Feb. 1975, BA Karl Carstens' Papers N1337/29; BMI, "Betr.: Lagebericht Innere Sicherheit," March 11, 1975, 10:15, BA B106: 85191.

[138] Conservatives, of course, were not the only ones using Weimar as a measuring stick (and political weapon). Willy Brandt directly compared the CDU/CSU's public statements to the accusations of powerlessness made by Hitler against the SPD in 1933. See Willy Brandt, *Verhandlungen*, VII. Bundestag, 155. Sitzung (March 13, 1975), 10762.

[139] Georg Schröder, "Adenauer war noch sein eigener Krisenstab," *Die Welt*, March 6, 1975.

[140] On the lawyers' position between state and "enemy," see Jörg Requate, "Terroristenanwälte und Rechtsstaat: Zur Auseinandersetzung um die Rolle der Verteidiger in den Terroristenverfahren der 1970er Jahre," in *Terrorismus in der Bundesrepublik: Medien, Staat und Subkulturen in den 1970er Jahren*, eds. Klaus Weinhauer, Jörg Requate, and Heinz-Gerhard Haupt (Frankfurt: Campus, 2006), 271–99 and Jeremy Varon, *Bringing the War Home: The Weather Underground, the Red Army Faction, and Revolutionary Violence in the Sixties and Seventies* (Berkeley: University of California Press, 2004), 265–72.

because they defied the existing legal culture. The RAF lawyers roughly followed the Anglo-American tradition of adversarial legalism at fundamental odds with continental Europe's inquisitorial system, where lawyers and the defendants' interests take a backseat to the judge and the state's search for truth. But even according to the rules of American jurisprudence, the defending attorneys went above and beyond the call of duty. In particular, they ran a complex system of smuggled messages that linked RAF prisoners to each other and to the outside world. This "info" network maintained the group's identity and internal hierarchy and kept RAF leaders informed and in control. Hunger strikes were so well coordinated, for example, that Baader was able to monitor the weight loss and thus potential noncompliance of every imprisoned militant.[141] Few members of state or parliament doubted that this free flow of information posed a risk to state security and many understood the RAF lawyers' actions as tantamount to collusion.

Social and Liberal Democrats confronted the problem by targeting the criminal code and court procedure for reform. They newly prohibited a single attorney from representing multiple defendants, made it legally possible to remove and even suspend an attorney based on suspicions of collaboration with a client, and allowed trials to be conducted in the absence of defendants when judged a result of their own actions (as was the case in hunger strikes).[142] Passed by the Bundestag in December 1974, the changes went into effect on January 1, 1975 and were quickly put to use. When the joint trial of Baader, Ensslin, Meinhof, and Raspe began at the end of May, Baader was without legal counsel – his original attorneys, Claus Croissant, Kurt Groenewold, and Hans-Christian Stroeble, had been excluded by the court and his court-appointed replacements rejected by Baader. While many within the legal profession insisted that the new legislation went too far – threatening attorney-client privilege and defendants' right to a fair trial – conservatives argued it did not go far enough.[143] Normal criminal law and procedure, no matter how much they were tweaked, could not adequately address the unique problem of terrorism. What was needed, CDU/CSU delegates insisted, was legislation designed specifically to combat terrorism and reestablish the state's unassailability.

Seizing the initiative, the Christian Union presented four different bills to the Bundestag within a year of Günter von Drenkmann's murder.[144] In order

[141] For insight into "info," see Olaf Gätje, *Der Gruppenstil der RAF im "Info"-System: Eine soziostilistische Untersuchung aus systemtheoretischer Perspektive* (Berlin: Gruyter, 2008) and Pieter Bakker-Shut, *Das Info-System: Briefe der Gefangenen aus der RAF, 1973–1977* (Kiel: Neuer Malik, 1987).

[142] See Basten, *Anti-Terror-Gesetzen*, 119ff.

[143] On left lawyers' opposition and its later influence on the legal profession and justice system: Requate, "Terroristenanwälte und Rechtsstaat," 286–96.

[144] *Drucksachen*, VII. Bundestag: "Gesetz zum Schutz des Gemeinschaftsfriedens," 2854; "Entwurf eines Gesetz zum Schutz der Rechtspflege," 3161; "Entwurf eines Gesetz zur Bekämpfung krimineller terroristischer Vereinigungen," 3661; "Entwurf eines Gesetz zur Erleichterung der Strafverfolgung krimineller Vereinigungen," 3734.

"to prevent civil liberties' misuse," conservatives proposed to supervise all written and oral communication as well as visits between lawyers and prisoners accused or convicted of terrorism. For this reason, too, they targeted political pluralism – as the breeding ground of leftist sympathizers – with a recommendation to restrict free speech and, in an effort to overturn previous Social-Liberal reforms, sharply constrain demonstration rights.[145] Beyond curtailing civil liberties, conservatives advocated stronger deterrents. They were united in their support of harsher sentencing and proposed to lengthen incarceration times, change "support" of terrorism from a misdemeanor to a felony, and prosecute terrorism itself as a unique felony offense. This last was particularly attractive because it would not only win terrorists harsher punishments but also grant police the use of armed force against them.[146] If the idea of empowering police in this manner did not thrill SPD and FDP deputies, it was nothing compared to the outrage they expressed over the possibility of reinstating the death penalty (originally outlawed in 1945) raised in public by Christian Socials Richard Jaeger and Franz-Josef Strauß and up-and-coming CDU leader Alfred Dregger.[147] The Christian Union did not pursue or necessarily even consent to this particular line of discussion, but it is noteworthy that its members also did not reprimand those who did. At the very least, conservatives displayed a comfort with coercive state powers neither shared by Social and Liberal Democrats nor merely attributable to partisan politics.

To be sure, parliamentary debates were full of cheap jabs and partisan bickering. When a member of the SPD referred to the RAF as a "criminal association" or "group" they were interrupted by stomping and the opposition's shouts of "gang!"[148] But even this interaction was predicated on the parties' divergent approaches to crisis management. Social Democrats' rhetoric placed the RAF firmly within an existing legal framework – specifically Article 129 of the Basic Law stating that any group deemed a "criminal association" could be banned and otherwise prosecuted. With their very choice of words, they denied – and would continue to deny – conservative arguments for specific antiterrorist laws. As Hans-Jochen Vogel explained his party's position, a fair

[145] CDU/CSU, *Drucksachen*, VII. Bundestag, 213. Sitzung (January 16, 1976), 4582. This was a blatant attempt to overturn the 1970 reform.

[146] In arguing to designate terrorism a felony, in fact, most of the CDU/CSU's emphasis was placed on police empowerment. See, e.g., Gerhard Kunz (CDU/CSU), *Verhandlungen*, VII. Bundestag, 253. Sitzung (June 24, 1976), 17995; Fritz Wittmann (CDU/CSU), *Verhandlungen*, VIII. Bundestag, 71. Sitzung (January 30, 1978), 5668.

[147] *Der Spiegel* called the reinstatement of the death penalty a "favorite wish" of CSU-Bundestag Vice President Richard Jaeger. "Den Rechtsstaat retten – blodes Zeug," *Der Spiegel* 11 (March 10, 1975), 19; Strauß raised the possibility of the death penalty while publicly criticizing the government's weak and forgiving position across from the terrorists. See his "Sonthofer Rede" reprinted in the same March 10 issue of *Spiegel*; and Dregger admitted his "open-minded" position before Bundestag following the return of Lorenz. He was, however, careful to state his party's ongoing rejection of the punishment. Alfred Dregger, *Verhandlungen*, Bundestag VII. (March 13, 1975), 155. Sitzung, 10741–2.

[148] *Verhandlungen*, VII. Bundestag, 130. Sitzung (November 13, 1974), 8795–7.

trial was "more likely to be achieved if legislative amendments were forced to fit" the basic principles of "an existing constitutional code," than if a special law were passed with nothing more than its own alleged effectiveness to guide and constrain it.[149] The best protection against human fallibility and emotions was, in other words, the existing legal frameworks and justice system. With this in mind, the SPD and FDP repeatedly used their parliamentary majority to restrict legal action to the amendment and reform of existing criminal law and procedure.[150] Taking this tack also shored up the government's position that even the RAF leaders were criminals to be tried as such. In this, they rejected the premise that suspected or convicted terrorists were either enemy combatants or political prisoners, which would have been tantamount to conceding both civil war and the state's political persecution of its own citizens.[151] By refusing to accept the exceptional nature of terrorism and political violence, of course, they guaranteed continued conflict with the CDU/CSU – even at times when proposals of government and opposition differed more in degree than kind.

THE RETURN OF THE POLICE STATE? LEFTISTS' CRITIQUE OF INTERNAL SECURITY

At the same time that conservatives criticized the SPD for its failure to mobilize sufficient state powers, West Germany's extraparliamentary left accused the government of going too far in its counterterrorism efforts. While it would be difficult to find an aspect of internal security of which the extraparliamentary left approved, none was more hated than the Decree against Radicals. It earned leftists' unanimous condemnation and convinced them of the undemocratic nature of counterterrorism in the FRG. Critics referred to the state's attempt to identify and remove radicals from public service as an "occupational ban," a name that deliberately evoked Nazi-era persecutions as well as the right to occupational freedom guaranteed by the Basic Law. Accusations that the ban on radicals violated individual civil liberties – and was thus unconstitutional – seemed borne out as large numbers of leftists came under investigation by the BfV, which received a notable influx of funds and personnel in order to meet the new demands placed on it by the decree. The intrusions on privacy and

149 Hans-Jochen Vogel, "Strafverfahrensrecht und Terrorismus – eine Bilanz," *Neue Juristische Wochenschrift* 25 (June 21, 1978): 1218.

150 This is not to say that there were no proposals for new antiterrorist legislation outside conservative circles or that amendments have little impact. For the former, see, e.g., liberal legal critic (and Bundeshofgericht attorney) Achim von Winterfeld, "Terrorismus – 'Reform' ohne Ende? Konzeption eines neuen Weges zur Abwehr des Terrorismus," *Zeitschrift für Rechtspolitik* 11 (1977): 265–9. See Chapter 5 for more on this debate.

151 For a highly critical read of the government's legal – and decidedly political – definition of the RAF, see Helmut Jennsen, "Der Sicherheitsstaat und die 'RAF' – Wie man mit Recht eine 'terroristische Vereinigung' (be-)gründet und sie (recht wirkungslos) bekämpft," in *Staatssicherheit: Die Bekämpfung des politischen Feindes im Inneren*, eds. idem and Michael Schubert (Bielefeld: AJZ, 1990), 116–39.

the demand for unquestioning loyalty elicited sharp resistance from the extraparliamentary left, who recognized in the Decree against Radicals an attempt to bring leftist teachers and professors to heel and thereby stamp out dissent. More than any other state measure, the "occupational ban" contributed to the widespread sense of political repression on the left – a climate of fear and self-censorship – that many argued had more in common with totalitarian rule than democracy. Leftists of all stripes found or feared themselves subject to investigation and disciplinary action should they be deemed "radical" and therefore, by definition, an enemy of the "free democratic order."

In his 1975 novella ... *and You're Already an Enemy of the Constitution: The Unexpected Expansion of the Personnel File of the Teacher Kleff*, author (and former student activist) Peter Schneider captured the insidious effects of the decree by underscoring the paranoia, fear, and powerlessness produced by even the vaguest of accusations, regardless of one's innocence.[152] The story's protagonist, a high school teacher placed on disciplinary probation for reasons unknown to him, sets out to clear his name and quickly becomes caught up in self-doubt as he is forced to reflect on his past and present actions. Schneider illuminated the consequences of such insecurity, which compelled his protagonist to identify with his faceless antagonists, adopting their perspective and mimicking their practices. Writing to the bureaucrat in charge of his file, the teacher at one point admits to asking himself "whether I really was, without in fact knowing it, an enemy of the Basic Law."[153] Despite the growing file that Kleff, then, manages to assemble on himself, there is no real doubt as to his innocence – at least not in the eyes of the author and his intended audience. Kleff discovers that the charge against him rests on his having opposed the suspension of three students guilty of distributing "radical" pamphlets. Refusing to recant his position, he is denied tenure. He is dismissed, as Kleff/Schneider puts it, for no other reason than because he offered resistance against his illegitimate dismissal. The general sentiment evoked here and shared across the extraparliamentary left was that the Decree against Radicals answered any political nonconformity with repression and criminalization.

Extraparliamentary leftists were not the only ones to denounce the state's actions. Criticism of the ban also came from Social Democrats in displays that ranged from deep ambivalence to outright hostility the longer the Decree against Radicals was enforced. Many party members, particularly those whose formative political years were after 1945, openly rejected the ban. Most emphatic was the party's youth organization, the Young Socialists or "Jusos," who went so far as to lead a public campaign to pressure the government into its revocation.[154] Such breaches of party discipline infuriated its leaders, but the wide

152 Peter Schneider, ... *schon bist du ein Verfassungsfeind: Das unerwartete Anschwellen der Personalakte des Lehrers Kleff* (Berlin: Rotbuch, 1975).

153 Ibid., 22.

154 For a detailed discussion of SPD internal dispute, see Gerard Braunthal, *The German Social Democrats since 1969: A Party in Power and Opposition* (Boulder: Westview, 1994), esp. 95–146.

discrepancies in the decree's implementation between SPD- and CDU/CSU-governed Länder also made them lukewarm in their support of the counterterrorism measure. The sense among Social Democrats that the ban was not doing democracy much good was already apparent at the 1973 party congress.[155] By the 1975 congress, the Decree against Radicals had the air of a bad hangover; those present appeared unanimous in the wish that it would simply fade away. Still, the vast majority proved unwilling to revoke it and give up what they continued to consider an important weapon of the state.[156] Though aware of the coercive and potentially undemocratic effects of the decree, the SPD remained committed to its pursuit of militant democracy. Barring a change of heart, party members were left to pursue a course of damage control. And those who insisted on the ban's revocation had no choice but to work outside of the SPD and its institutions.

Extraparliamentary leftists and dissenting Social Democrats thus came together to defend civil liberties from what they understood to be the state's overreaction to political violence. Political impotence at home encouraged them to direct their efforts at mobilizing international opinion against the situation in West Germany. The convening of a third International Russell Tribunal to investigate civil liberties in the FRG attested to the overwhelming success of such a strategy.[157] A "people's court" founded by Bertrand Russell and Jean-Paul Sartre with the goal of investigating those injustices that went unexamined by existing institutions, the Russell Tribunal first convened in 1967 to examine the genocidal dimensions of American military actions in Vietnam. Without legal status and "uncompelled by state reason," it aimed primarily to "prevent the crime of silence."[158] Its decision to assess human rights violations in the FRG spoke to the currency of prisoners' rights as a barometer of a society's democratic commitments as well as the continued relevance of social and political networks born of earlier, transnational protest. Above all, however, the concern awakened outside of the FRG for the country's counterterrorism tactics built on fears of latent fascism. Doubts over Germans' ability to break free of authoritarianism or fascism were voiced most shrilly by the French media, but "friends" in the United States and Britain also expressed alarm at recent developments in West Germany.[159] Lingering international and domestic concerns over the German past proved mutually reinforcing. And this, together with the

155 Braunthal, *Political Loyalty*, 54–5.

156 *Parteitages der SPD 1975*, 816–30, 843–52.

157 Important to this decision were accusations regarding West Germany's prisons, discussed in the next chapter.

158 For a new understanding of the Russell Tribunal as an expression of popular justice and the French Maoists' emphasis on the method of investigation, see Julian Bourg, *From Revolution to Ethics*: May 1968 and Contemporary French Thought (London: McGill-Queen's University Press, 2007), 51–4, 68–78; quote: 71.

159 See, e.g., Jacques Guillerme-Brulon, "Ist der Satan Deutscher?" trans. from *Le Figaro* October 6, 1977; Karl Carstens, Protokoll der CDU/CSU Bundesvorstandssitzung, September 12, 1977, ACDP 07–001–982. Also, "Die Stunde der Anti-Germanen," *Stern*, September 22, 1977, 252–3.

rising scrutiny drawn by citizens' rights movement's efforts to hold governments accountable, is one explanation for why the Russell Tribunal turned its attention to the FRG and not one of the more established democracies similarly accused of inhumane prison conditions or, as Rudi Dutschke demanded, to human rights violations in the Eastern Bloc.[160] The Third International Russell Tribunal was rightly perceived as a powerful vote of no confidence in West German democracy. And there was little doubt that the international community's intervention lent further legitimacy to allegations of political persecution and extralegal action on the part of the West German state.[161] It is unsurprising, then, that the planned tribunal was denounced by Willy Brandt as "transparently propagandistic and slanderous" in its intent and generally scorned by the FRG's political class.[162]

The Third Russell Tribunal proved that even if conservatives made life difficult for the coalition government, they were still easier for the party and its leaders to contend with than its critics on the left. This was true not only because of their ability to mobilize international opinion but because members of the SPD were clearly not immune to concerns typical of the extraparliamentary left – with the party's left wing often appearing closer to the protesters than to its government when it came to matters of state power. For a party whose leadership was intent on overcoming not only terrorism but also longstanding doubts over its political loyalties and its ability to govern, this proved a significant problem. To the SPD's embarrassment and the CDU/CSU's delight, for example, resistance broke out within the SPD over the 1976 government-sponsored bill to further amend the criminal code so as to criminalize both "support of violence" (§88a) and "incitement to violence" (§130a).[163] Rather than closing a legal loophole as the bill's supporters claimed it would, critics

[160] A rare discussion of the multisided controversy surrounding the Third Russell Tribunal at the time it occurred can be found in Hugh Mosley, "Report: Third International Russell Tribunal on Civil Liberties in West Germany," *New German Critique* 14 (Spring 1978): 178–84. Its inclusion of sample cases brought before the Tribunal makes it valuable for anyone interested in the Degree against Radicals.

[161] Aside from the Russell Tribunal and Amnesty International, external intervention also came – notoriously – in the form of Jean Paul Sartre's December 1974 visit to Baader in Stammheim. Though the visit was brief and confined to a visitor's area, Sartre made several subsequent statements affirming the RAF's allegations of torture. Stefan Aust, *The Baader-Meinhof Group: The Inside Story* (London: Bodley Head, 1987), 277–8. The chapter on "Sartre in Stammheim" was cut from the newest English language edition, though notably not from the 2009 and 2010 German editions. For an example of how the visit was used to link Sartre to terrorism, see Hans Egon Holthusen, *Sartre in Stammheim: Zwei Themen aus den Jahren den großen Turbulenz* (Stuttgart: Klett-Cotta, 1982).

[162] SPD-Vorstand, Protokoll über die Sitzung des Parteivorstandes, October 13, 1977, Bad Godesberg, AdsD.

[163] Bundesregierung, "Entwurf 13. StÄG," *Drucksachen*, VII. Bundestag, 3030. Attempting to address party members' concerns, what was originally proposed as the singular amendment to §130StGB was revised with the introduction of §88a making the support of violence a separate offense with its own set of delimitations. This, then, ultimately made up the 14th StrÄG passed in June 1976.

like Freimuth Duve saw it as opening the door to censorship and the repression of cultural and intellectual freedom.[164] The proposed law included a list of criteria by which to determine "support" for violence, but Bundestag member Manfred Coppick proved this brought little comfort to its critics. How, he questioned, was the state's prosecution system – hardly filled with academic experts – to determine the difference between an "apparent" and "real" work of scholarship?[165] While both Duve and Coppick had supported previous legislative measures against the incitement, encouragement, threat, and glorification of violence, they were unwilling to back the newest attempt to control the discourse. "Support" for violence was simply too undefined and thus the potential for unchecked abuse of power was too great. Before the Bundestag, Dieter Lattmann formally registered the dissenting voice and aimed his critique directly at the heart of SPD strategy – at the "dangers and delusions" of searching for security in the perfection of laws. However noble the intent, he warned, "what might be achieved is a climate of intimidation, opportunism, and that particular brand of self-censorship that has suppressed moral courage in Germany far too often."[166]

For leaders of the SPD, internal dissent was not only politically embarrassing. It also smacked of the anti-establishment position they had sought to purge at Godesberg. More than any other West German party, the SPD experienced a significant demographic makeover following the influx of new members in the late 1960s and early 1970s. By 1973 two-thirds of the party membership had joined after 1960, with seventy-five percent of those who joined in 1972 under forty years of age.[167] As the debates within the party attested, one result of these changes was a widening gap in age and experience between the rank and file and the leadership and, corresponding to this, the emergence of new and divergent understandings of social democracy. Despite Willy Brandt's explicit warnings, clear left and right factions formed, highlighting the members' very different relationships to Marxism and to the FRG itself.[168] While tried-and-true antagonisms hearkening back to the days of Weimar – and the more recent desire to distance themselves from the politics of the GDR – made older Social Democrats the most rabid of anticommunists, a new generation of SPD members demonstrated a willingness to enter into coalitions with communists and,

[164] *Parteitages der SPD 1975*, 841–4. Duve underscored that the SPD would be empowering all future governments, not just its own, by asking his fellow Social Democrats to envision this law in the hands of a "Federal Minister of Interior Dregger" or a "Chancellor Strauß."

[165] Ibid., 841–2.

[166] *Verhandlungen*, VII. Bundestag, 213. Sitzung, (January 16, 1976), 14739.

[167] Heinrich Potthoff and Susanne Miller, *Kleine Geschichte der SPD: Darstellungen und Dokumentation 1848–1990* (Bonn: Dietz, 1991), 226.

[168] Theory discussions played a much larger role in the SPD during the first half of the 1970s than in the 1960s. In addition to the Seeheimer Kreis, Herbert Wehner and other members with strong ties to labor tried to counteract the strong academic character of the left by reactivating worker organizations, such as the Arbeitergemeinschaft für Arbeitnehmerfragen (AfA) formed in 1973. See Faulenbach, "Ein sozialdemokratisches Jahrzehnt?" 27–30.

increasingly, to return to the anticapitalist, Marxist positions the party had rejected. The Jusos declared themselves a Marxist youth organization while a number of party colleagues revived the "state monopoly capitalism" (or *Stamokap*) thesis, disparaging the FRG – in rather orthodox Marxist-Leninist style – as an antidemocratic fusion of monopoly economy and imperialist state.[169] In response, the leadership strongly asserted its understanding of the FRG as legitimate and explicitly bound the fate of the SPD to the preservation and expansion of its democratic foundation.[170] Though it guaranteed the membership freedom in questions of theory and praxis, the executive stressed that the fundamental values of social democracy made all Social Democrats duty-bound to defend the free and democratic order as it existed in the FRG. Those who clung to revolutionary ideas and rejected the possibility of constructive reform were seen to be at odds with the SPD and democracy itself. Peter Glotz, whose willingness to engage the extraparliamentary left placed him solidly in the party's left camp, summarized the situation thus: "whoever wants to overcome or blow up the system cannot hope that he will thereby remain gentle, democratic, and parliamentary."[171]

Over the course of the 1970s, then, the party leadership became increasingly intent on finishing what it had started at Bad Godesberg. It aimed not merely to quash the Marxist resurgence – expelling those who persisted in their *Stamokap* theories – but to reform Social Democrats' lingering distrust of the state. Ruminating over the division within the SPD on the matter of internal security, Hans-Jochen Vogel observed:

> [S]ections of our party ... and those intellectuals sympathetic to us – continue to have a conflicted relationship to the state and its legitimate sovereign and defense functions. They see genuine danger sooner in the state and its activities or, at the very least, in the ... possibilities for abuse within existing or proposed state authority. The fact that the concrete state is no longer the capitalist authoritarian state of the past but rather a corporation shaped by us in fundamental areas and after ideas with which we can ourselves identify – regardless of all its deficiencies – is not yet sufficiently realized by them.[172]

The result, in his estimation, was threefold. First, party members displayed little willingness to occupy themselves with questions of security, refusing even to recognize the successes of Social Democratic security policy as such, much less to actively defend them. Second, they were inclined to meet state organs – including the justice system – with distrust and criticism, to the point of favoring the person against whom the state had a grievance. And third, they showed

[169] For the Jusos' doctrinal views, see Braunthal, *German Social Democrats*, 121–46.

[170] Hans Koschnick, "Vorlage für den Parteivorstand: Zur weiteren Diskussion um Stamokap-Theorien und ihre Anhänger in der SPD," August 26, 1977, AdsD Helmut Schmidt Papers 9403.

[171] Peter Glotz, "Systemüberwindende Reformen?" in *Beiträge zur Theoriediskussion*, ed. Georg Lührs (Berlin: Dietz, 1973): 205–44.

[172] Hans-Jochen Vogel, "Stellenwert unserer Politik auf dem Gebiet der inneren Sicherheit," March 8, 1976, AdsD Helmut Schmidt Papers 9045.

a latent readiness to paint Social Democrats in executive or judicial state positions as reactionaries or opponents of the rule of law.[173] If pushed, Vogel might simply have accused left-wing Social Democrats of acting like extraparliamentary leftists. And, just as he did with those disaffected leftists, the minister of justice regarded Social Democrats' continued distrust of state power to be a serious obstacle to the left's ability both to govern successfully and to protect democracy.

In order to combat these internal fissures, SPD leaders launched a campaign for party solidarity and self-confidence among the rank and file not unlike "enlightenment" efforts carried out elsewhere.[174] Above all, they insisted on the relevance of Weimar, reminding Social Democrats that fascism was not the only evil to be guarded against: State *in*action could also be deadly for democracy. In this vein, Willy Brandt reminded Social Democrats of their duty to uphold the state's ability to function and defend the constitution: "The Social Democrats of Germany will never again – like in the unhappy year 1930 – relieve themselves of responsibility. A retreat into resignation will not occur. The SPD will not catapult itself from government and thereby leave the area of civil rights to the ideologues.... The consequences [of such actions] are known."[175] Vogel proved similarly indefatigable in his monitoring of party morale and attempts to counteract "radicalism." Repeatedly, he intervened through open letters as well as private reprimands to shape a consistently positive treatment of the government's security program in articles and editorials printed in party periodicals.[176] However they sought to achieve it, Brandt and Vogel demanded the same thing: that members give the government and its internal security program their full, undivided support and agree to help them *govern*. The leaders' response and their ongoing struggle with internal dissent made clear the SPD's schizophrenic relationship to state power and its increasing relevance to the party's future.

173 Ibid.

174 The need for the SPD to gain self-confidence and to assert itself was the dominate theme of the 1975 Mannheim party convention. See, in particular, the opening and closing speeches made by Willy Brandt and Peter von Oertzen's introductory report on the party's ten-year program: *Parteitages der SPD 1975*, 35–77, 984–1005, and 264–88.

175 Willy Brandt, ibid., 76.

176 Vogel justified his actions in "Stellenwert unserer Politik."

4

The Security State, New Social Movements, and the Duty to Resist

It is not quiet but democracy that is the citizen's first duty.

Dieter Lattmann (1976)[1]

My concern is not only a concern for the environment [or] for health, but also a concern for democracy ... because this energy and these forces ... are so dangerous that everything must be guarded and everyone watched.

Robert Jungk (February 19, 1977)[2]

Both contemporaries and later scholars have examined West Germany's new left in order to confirm or dispute its sympathies for violence and terrorism.[3] Needless to say, the political stakes involved in such a debate were – and still are – considerable. And, as Social Democratic leaders scrutinized by their more conservative counterparts discovered, the identification of "terrorist sympathizers" is very much in the eye of the beholder. The question of blame that energizes both sides of this debate casts more shadow than light on the subject of terrorism; it encourages the defenders of "1968" to hastily dismiss terrorism

[1] Dieter Lattmann (SPD), *Verhandlungen des deutschen Bundestages: Stenographische Berichte* (hereafter, *Verhandlungen*), VII. Bundestag, 213. Sitzung, (January 16, 1976), 14739.

[2] Robert Jungk speaking before antinuclear demonstrators at Itzehoe on February 19, 1977. Quoted in *Der Spiegel* 10 (February 28, 1977), 29.

[3] Among the more recent, see, e.g., Hans-Jürgen Wirth, ed., *Hitlers Enkel oder Kinder der Demokratie? Die 68er, die RAF und die Fischer-Debatte* (Giessen: Psychosozial, 2001); Gerd Koenen, *Das rote Jahrzehnt: Unsere kleine deutsche Kulturrevolution, 1967–1977* (Cologne: Kiepenheuer & Witsch, 2001); Gerd Langguth, *Mythos '68: Die Gewaltphilosophie von Rudi Dutschke: Ursachen und Folgen der Studentenbewegung* (Munich: Olzog, 2001); Belinda Davis, "Activism from Starbuck to Starbucks, or Terror: What's in a Name?" *Radical History Review* 85 (Winter 2003): 37–57; Wolfgang Kraushaar, *Die Bombe im Jüdischen Gemeindehaus* (Hamburg: Hamburger Ed., 2005); idem, Jan Philipp Reemtsma, Karin Wieland, *Rudi Dutschke, Andreas Baader und die RAF* (Hamburg: Hamburger Ed., 2005); Bernd Rabehl, *Linke Gewalt: Der kurze Weg zur RAF* (Schnellroda: Antaios, 2007); Götz Aly, *Unser Kampf 1968 – ein irritierter Blick zurück* (Frankfurt: Fischer, 2008). Kraushaar's many contributions have prompted a debate forum in the *taz* and responses such as Markus Mohr's "Die dummen Einfälle des Dr. Kraushaar," *Streifzüge* 39 (April 2007): 27.

and violence as a sideshow and its opponents to illegitimately attribute a proviolence position to the left. One thing is certain: the relationship between the extraparliamentary left and the RAF was anything but uncomplicated or trivial. Radicals and activists addressed the RAF and the violence it perpetrated with difficulty; theirs was an uneasy relationship that mirrored their long-standing relationship to the FRG and its National Socialist past. For postwar leftists were not so convinced of West Germany's democratic character that they could categorically rule out the need for and thus legitimacy of violent resistance. This did not mean, as some have suggested, that the left (specifically the '68ers) actively supported the use of political violence.[4] For most, it remained a hypothetical discussion about the potential need for armed resistance – inspired by the past but kept alive by events in the present. Just as in the organizational debate of 1968, many regarded such action as unwarranted (if not morally abhorrent) under the given conditions and saw the RAF's war on the state as, therefore, politically indefensible.

Yet whether members of the extraparliamentary left openly disavowed the violence perpetrated by the RAF, remained silent (implicitly condoning it), or celebrated it – as some certainly did – they continued to perceive solidarity as critical to the future of progressive politics. And their experience of counterterrorism did not help to persuade them otherwise. For their part, RAF members were conscious of their dependency on a broader extraparliamentary milieu at the same time as they voiced disgust with a legal left quick to criticize, quick even to sympathize, but unwilling to take militant action. The relationship between the extraparliamentary left and the RAF was thus not only ambiguous but often tense. How, then, can one make sense of the ties that linked the RAF and members of the extraparliamentary left together even in the face of sharp disagreement and discord? Surely a common commitment to resisting the authoritarian tendencies of a society in which they still saw pervasive structural violence and proto-fascist potentials played a not insignificant part.

The persistence of the negative alliance explains the RAF's ability to count on the continued solidarity, however critical, of extraparliamentary actors. Each new skirmish between the RAF and the state tugged at the logic of counterviolence and resistance and in this way helped to renew allegiances. For, just as understandings of violence had deeply influenced the left's relationship to the state in the 1960s, these same concerns continued to shape extraparliamentary leftists' perception of the political stage in the next decade. If most were unconvinced by the RAF's self-stylization as revolutionaries in the fight against capitalist imperialism, they could still understand individual members of the RAF as victims of state-initiated violence who acted to defend themselves and the cause of progress from the forces of reaction. As foolhardy and theoretically flawed as many understood the RAF to be, extraparliamentary leftists could not simply turn their backs on its members as victims and fighters of

[4] See, for example, Stephen Eisel, "Angebliche 'Gewaltfreiheit' als Gründungsmythos," *Die Politische Meinung* 376 (March 2001): 60–4.

oppression. Indeed, with counterterrorism measures feeding suspicions of the state's authoritarian nature, many concluded there was no option but to support the guerrillas, if not their actions – a fine line that sometimes got blurred. Significantly, this solidarity and the perpetrator–victim schema upon which it rested prevented the majority of the radical left from effectively confronting left-wing political violence as anything but reactive counterviolence. This theoretical blind spot encouraged leftists to deflect questions of violence onto the state and helped maintain the negative alliance when little else remained to do so.

Of course, all did not revolve around the confrontation between the RAF and the state. In their efforts to create the conditions for their understanding of modern democracy in the FRG, Social Democrats introduced plans for urban renewal, a massive new energy program, education reform, and a revision of marriage and family legislation. Counterterrorism was thus one of many areas in which the government actively sought to intervene in the average citizen's life to further the common good. As with the internal security policy, many West Germans were critical of these extensions of state power and moved openly to contest them. In this context, numerous leftists forged new protest networks that straddled the traditional left–right divide and, in many instances, national borders as well.[5] For this reason alone, it is unsurprising that it was here, at what we might call the extraparliamentary left's periphery, that a space first opened up to confront the implications of the left's historical relationship to violence. The antinuclear and women's liberation movements in particular embraced conceptions of violence, power, and resistance often at odds with long-standing currents within the postwar extraparliamentary left. As these protesters found their activities undermined by their association with violence and, increasingly, with terrorism, the differences became impossible to ignore. Reaching an agreement on political strategy was more difficult than ever given the diversity of actors. For this same reason, it was also rightly seen as essential to any progressive future. This, and the risk of government repression, on the one hand, and alienating the public, on the other, prompted a number of self-identifying leftists to interrogate long-held assumptions regarding West German democracy and the legitimate tools for its defense. They publicly questioned the notion of progressive violence, the easy but ultimately inadequate equation of antimilitarism and pacifism, and the lack of attention to the private sphere. It was, to be sure, a hairline crack in the negative alliance and critical to leftists' later reorientation. But in the short term, the result was an extraparliamentary left simultaneously paralyzed and in flux, unable to move forward because its members grew increasingly at odds over the means to do so.

[5] For a critical review of the literature on NSMs and the movements' possible global implications, see Donatella Della Porta and Mario Diani, *Social Movements: An Introduction*, 2nd ed. (Malden, MA: Blackwell, 2006). On NSMs in the FRG: Ruud Koopmans, *Democracy From Below: New Social Movements and the Political System in West Germany* (Boulder: Westview, 1995).

THE RAF AND THE QUESTION OF LEFT SOLIDARITY

It is not a coincidence that when the RAF and other violent militants appeared on the pages of the alternative and underground press it was often as victims of state violence – either as objects of torture or prisoners of war denied their legal rights. In prison, members of the RAF cited solitary confinement (or "isolation torture"), lack of stimulation ("sensory deprivation"), and around the clock surveillance (including all written and oral communication) as confirmation of West German torture. When the first forced feedings occurred in May 1973, they were added to this list and to the evidence for what the RAF argued was the state's coordinated effort to destroy it and all leftist domestic resistance. Though prison conditions varied by Land and changed over time, the abuses enumerated in the first years of the founding core's incarceration remained fairly constant. The accusations of torture and demands for prisoners' rights worked to mobilize left sympathies and to confirm the RAF's position in the broader anti-imperialist struggle.[6]

Reaching for Germany's Nazi past in order to describe their present circumstances, the imprisoned RAF members demanded the attention of the left. Ulrike Meinhof famously detailed in verse her eight-month experience in the "dead wing" (*toter Trakt*) of a Cologne prison. Her poem, which first circulated among prison inmates in January 1974 and then widely within the extraparliamentary left, described the psychological confusion and mental distress that came with living in an undifferentiated environment with minimal human contact.[7] When removed from the isolation wing the previous May, she provocatively summarized her experience: "the political concept for the dead wing, cologne, i say quite clearly, is gas. my auschwitz fantasies were ... real in there."[8] Statements issued by the RAF in response to the first round of forced feedings made equally explicit comparisons with the victims of the Third Reich. They accused authorities of resurrecting the "methods of the recent past" in order to "openly terrorize a section of the proletariat" with the prospect of "Treblinka, Majdanek, Sobibor" and thereby break "the resistance of the great majority of the people against exploitation."[9]

[6] For a sensitive discussion of the RAF's incarceration – the conditions and, ultimately, its effect on RAF politics – see Jeremy Varon, *Bringing the War Home: The Weather Underground, the Red Army Faction, and Revolutionary Violence in the Sixties and Seventies* (Berkeley: University of California Press, 2004), 215–30 as well as Martin Jander, "Isolation oder Isolationsfolter: Die Auseinandersetzung um die Haftbedingungen der RAF-Häftlinge," in *Der "Deutsche Herbst" und die RAF in Politik, Medien, und Kunst: Nationale und Internationale Perspektive*, ed. Nicole Colin (Bielefeld: Transcript, 2008), 141–55.

[7] Ulrike Meinhof, "Brief einer Gefangenen aus dem toten Trakt," reprinted in *Ulrike Marie Meinhof und die deutschen Verhältnisse*, ed. Peter Brückner (Berlin: Wagenbach, 1976), 152–4. The poem originally appeared in the informational brief that functioned as prisoners' internal communication system.

[8] May 20, 1973 "info" letter, reprinted in *Das Info – Briefe der Gefangenen aus der RAF, 1973–1977*, ed. Pieter H. Bakker Schut (Kiel: Neuer Malik, 1987), 21.

[9] "Hungerstreikerklärung vom 8. Mai 1973," reprinted in *Rote Armee Fraktion: Texte und Materialien*, ed. Martin Hoffmann (Berlin: ID-Verlag, 1997), 187–8. Though I leave examinations of the RAF itself to others, I do understand its decision to take up arms against the West German state firmly within the German debate on democracy, counterviolence, and resistance.

The ease with which RAF prisoners compared their treatment at the hands of the West German state to the persecution and mass murder of European Jewry is potent evidence of the postwar left's problematic memory politics.[10] Their description of the forced feedings also provides a striking example of how the entire spectrum of parliamentary and extraparliamentary left struggled to prevent the same thing – Nazism's repetition – and came into direct conflict over how to do so. While Social Democrats understood the forced feeding of prisoners as crucial to distinguishing the FRG from the Nazi state, the RAF's evocation of Nazi death camps mirrored extraparliamentary leftists' convictions regarding the state's ongoing fascist potential and the need to actively guard against it. Keeping the latter updated on the prisons was the *Information Service for Undisclosed News*, or *ID*, an information sheet whose reports – printed and reprinted in an array of radical left newsletters and papers – served to connect extraparliamentary leftists throughout the FRG.[11] In this particular case, *ID* helped to document torture and the state's illegitimate use of force by regularly detailing the prisoners' conditions and publicizing the RAF's messages. Over the course of 1973, committees against torture and legal aid organizations such as *Rote Hilfe* were founded across the country. While *Rote Hilfe* was invaluable in the external circulation of RAF texts, the committees led a public campaign against what they called the state's program of "exterminatory incarceration."[12] Both worked with prisoners' family members to inform human rights organizations and the United Nations of the situation in the FRG.

Crucial to all these endeavors were the RAF's lawyers. They ran both the prisoners' "info" network and the committees against torture, making their offices a veritable hub for information moving between the prison and the outside world as well as for persons eager to help with the cause.[13] In court and out of it, the lawyers defended their clients' constitutional rights against the state – including the use of their bodies (in the form of hunger and thirst strikes) as a means of protest. And no one, it seems, did more to substantiate claims of torture and abuse and thereby drum up sympathy for the militants than their

[10] On memory and Germans' secondary or latent antisemitism, see Theodor Adorno's 1959 lecture, "Was bedeutet Aufarbeitung der Vergangenheit?" in *Eingriffe: Neun kritische Modelle* (Frankfurt: Suhrkamp, 2003) and Jeffrey Herf, *Divided Memory: The Nazi Past in the Two Germanys* (Cambridge: Harvard University Press, 1997). On how this played out on the left and in younger generations: Kraushaar, *Bombe im jüdischen Gemeindehaus*; Martin Kloke, *Israel und die deutsche Linke: Zur Geschichte eines schwierigen Verhältnisses*, 2nd ed. (Frankfurt: Herg & Herchen, 1994).

[11] The International Institute for Social History (Amsterdam, hereafter IISG) houses an ID-Archiv that is a treasure trove for those interested in the West German extraparliamentary left.

[12] See, for example, Komitees gegen Folter an politischen Gefangenen in der BRD, *Der Tote Trakt ist ein Foltersinstrument* (Köln-Ossendorf: Komitees gegen Folter, 1974). For a brief overview: Butz Peters, *Tödlicher Irrtum: Die Geschichte der RAF* (Berlin: Argon, 2004), 314–15.

[13] On the RAF's internal and external communication networks as well as the well-orchestrated performance involved in the group's hunger strikes, see Leith Passmore, "The Art of Hunger: Self-Starvation in the Red Army Faction," *German History* 27, no. 1 (2009): 32–59.

lawyers. Evidence suggests, for example, that RAF lawyers Klaus Croissant and Kurt Groenewold helped to publicly disseminate the autopsy photo of Holger Meins, knowing that words could not compete with the image of Meins's emaciated body.[14] The photo elicited anger and fear, as viewers almost reflexively associated the RAF member's starved remains with the skeletal victims of the previous German regime.[15] Suspicions of willful neglect and even murder in West German prisons raised the question of just how far the state would go to suppress political opposition – and just how different it was from its Nazi predecessor. The image of Holger Meins's dead body thus helped to renew leftists' commitment to antifascist vigilance and solidarity, not only among the fringe few who took up arms at this time, but generally.[16] Rudi Dutschke might have spoken for the negative alliance as a whole when he raised his fist at Meins's funeral and swore: "Holger, the struggle goes on!"

As time passed, however, the specter of Nazi terror increasingly competed with that of an Orwellian surveillance state in the imaginations of the extraparliamentary left. Student newspapers, underground literature, and social scientific scholarship registered mounting fears of a society in which the pursuit of cold technological perfection (rather than racial domination) enslaved humanity.[17] Though not absent from earlier public discourse, the presence of "Big Brother" received a boost from the state's own emphasis on state-of-the-art technologies. Months before their trial was to begin in May 1975, Baader, Ensslin, Meinhof, and Raspe were moved to Stammheim prison outside of Stuttgart (Figure 4.1). A high-security facility built ten years earlier in accordance with the day's "most modern security research" (as is still advertised today), Stammheim was specifically retailored to hold the suspected terrorists while they stood trial.[18] Intended to deflect rescue attempts and instill a sense of security among the West German public, the prison instead redoubled concerns for inmates, rights, and prison conditions across the country. Confined to their own floor behind the reinforced concrete walls, electrified fences, and guard towers of Stammheim, the RAF leaders might have let the ominous structure speak for itself. Their addition of "brainwashing" – a notion introduced into popular Western consciousness by accounts of American POWs in

[14] See Petra Terhoeven, "Opferbilder – Täterbilder: Die Fotographie als Medium linksterroristischer Selbstermächtigung in Deutschland und Italien während der 70er Jahre," *Geschichte in Wissenschaft und Unterricht* 58, no. 7/8 (2007): 380–99; here, 392.

[15] Passmore, "Art of Hunger," 52–5; Terhoeven, "Opferbilder – Täterbilder," 392–3.

[16] Compelling arguments have been made that Meins's actual death was less important than the photo of his emaciated body when it came to recruiting the next generation. See, in particular, Carrie Collenberg, "Dead Holger," in *Baader-Meinhof Returns: History and Cultural Memory of German Left-Wing Terrorism*, eds. Gerrit-Jan Berendse and Ingo Cornils (Amsterdam: Rodopi, 2008), 65–81.

[17] I am not alone in noting this change. See Klaus Weinhauer, "'Staat zeigen': Die polizeiliche Bekämpfung des Terrorismus in der Bundesrepublik bis Anfang der 1980er Jahre," in *Die RAF und der linke Terrorismus*, ed. Wolfgang Kraushaar (Hamburg: Hamburg Ed., 2006), 945.

[18] Justizvollzugsanstalt Stuttgart, "Geschichte und Gebäude," accessed June 24, 2010, http: www.jva-stuttgart.de.

FIGURE 4.1. The high-security prison outside of Stammheim-Stuttgart, retroactively outfitted to hold leading members of the RAF while they stood trial (ap).

the Korean War – to the list of torture accusations, however, assured that the prison evoked the newest visions of totalizing state control.[19] The industrialized killing of Auschwitz and the behavior modification techniques of Communist China could be – and often were – read as simple variations of the same Cold War nightmare, namely the totalitarian state.[20] Or, for those who rejected the totalitarian framework given its blanket stigmatization of nonliberal, noncapitalist regimes, the methods cited by the RAF resonated also with the new work of French philosopher and historian Michel Foucault, who called attention to the technologies developed by modern states to manage and control (both positively and negatively) individual bodies and whole populations.[21]

Indeed, the success of the RAF's torture campaign owed much to the transnational prisoners' rights movement (whose critical edge seems to have inspired Foucault's analysis of the disciplinary society).[22] The struggle to

[19] Meinhof, in particular, took pains to insert the term into the discourse of the RAF's lawyers and prison aid committees. See Passmore, "Art of Hunger," 49.

[20] On how Chinese "brainwashing" came to be a universal characteristic of totalitarianism, see Abbott Gleason, *Totalitarianism: The Inner History of the Cold War* (New York: Oxford University Press, 1994), 89–107.

[21] Most famously in *Discipline and Punish: The Birth of the Prison* (originally published in 1975 and translated into German in 1976), Foucault offered a history of the prison as the exemplary institution of a disciplinary society.

[22] It is hard not to see *Discipline and Punish* as an extension of Foucault's intense engagement with prisoners' rights beginning in 1971, when he cofounded the Prison Information Group (*Groupe d'information sur les prisons*). See James Miller, *The Passion of Michel Foucault* (Cambridge:

protect prisoners from unchecked state control began in the early 1960s and continued to grow as conflict between states and civilian protesters escalated and large numbers of leftist militants entered the prisons, unused to incarceration and equipped with an external support network and their previous experience as activists.[23] The prisoners' rights movement reached its height in the early 1970s, when prison administrators in the United States, France, Great Britain, Sweden, and the FRG – eager to regain control of their inmate populations – implemented various new pacification programs.[24] These experiments in "rehabilitation" drew directly on American and Canadian research of Chinese behavior modification techniques and made the U.S. federal penitentiary in Marion, Illinois famous for its segregation of inmates and its permanent Control Unit, in which "disruptive" inmates were treated to extreme forms of isolation and sensory deprivation.[25] Prisoners' rights movements in different countries joined in solidarity with the explicit purpose of opening up prisons to public inspection – and thus to common standards of civil liberties and human rights.[26] West German leftists were active in the movement before the RAF launched its antitorture campaign, with connections to the Black Panthers and Black Liberation activists like Angela Davis drawing them into more than one international campaign to free the wrongly incarcerated and to improve U.S. prison conditions.[27] In 1973, *Kursbuch* dedicated a volume to the discussion of torture in the FRG, in which Dutch psychiatrist Sjef Teuns did more than any other individual to raise West German awareness of behavior modification techniques – their origins and further development through the international cooperation of governments and scientists. In particular, he informed his readers about a superior German version of the Control Unit,

Cambridge University Press, 1993), 185–93 and Julian Bourg, *From Revolution to Ethics: May 1968 and Contemporary French Thought* (London: McGill-Queen's University Press, 2007), 79–95.

[23] The transnational nature of the movement is referenced in the national literatures on prisons and prison protest but currently lacks its historian. Among the most helpful, see James B. Jacobs, "The Prisoners' Rights Movement and Its Impacts, 1960–80," *Crime and Justice* 2 (1980): 429–70; Dylan Rodriguez, *Forced Passages: Imprisoned Radical Intellectuals and the U.S. Prison Regime* (Minneapolis: University of Minnesota Press, 2005); Bourg, *From Revolution to Ethics*, esp. 68–95; Marie Gottschalk, *The Prison and the Gallows: The Politics of Mass Incarceration in America* (Cambridge: Cambridge University Press, 2006), 165–96.

[24] Jon Vagg, *Prison Systems: A Comparative Study of Accountability in England, France, Germany, and the Netherlands* (New York: Oxford University Press, 1994).

[25] See Mike Ryan, "Solitude as Counter-Insurgency: The U.S. Isolation Model of Political Incarcerations," in *Cages of Steel: The Politics of Imprisonment in the United States*, eds. Ward Churchill and J. J. Vander Wall (Washington, DC: Maisonneuve, 1992), 83–109. Also, Alan Eladio Gómez, "Resisting Living Death at Marion Federal Penitentiary, 1972," *Radical History Review* 96 (Fall 2006): 58–86.

[26] In examining the immediate impetus behind the multinational prison reforms of the 1970s and 1980s, Jon Vagg provides a rare glimpse of this transnational movement. Vagg, *Prison Systems*, esp. 43–85.

[27] Martin Klimke, *The Other Alliance: Student Protest in West Germany and the United States in the Global Sixties* (Princeton: Princeton University Press, 2009), 108–42.

the "silent cell," designed in Hamburg.[28] One did not have to believe (as some did) that international forces were aligning to crush progressive opposition in order to perceive what was going on in the world's most "civilized" prisons as an offense. The West German left could easily denounce the actions of the RAF and still defend its members as victims of gross human rights violations.[29]

Related to the attention given to torture in West German prisons was the campaign begun in 1974 to recognize imprisoned RAF members as prisoners of war, with all the rights afforded them under the Geneva Convention. The line of argumentation used by the defense in the Stammheim trial followed a political logic with widespread currency among the extraparliamentary left. In their evidentiary motions, attorneys Otto Schily, Hans Heinz Heldman, and Axel Azzola attested to the violation of the U.N. Convention on Genocide by U.S. forces in Vietnam, the natural right and duty to resist as last resort (*ultima ratio*), and the legitimacy of violent acts perpetrated by international liberation movements.[30] When viewed together, they argued:

> The statement of the prisoners and the [individual] motions of the attorneys make clear that, from the standpoint of international law, the actions of the RAF were justified resistance against genocide and that the imprisoned fighters must be recognized as prisoners of war.[31]

If one believed in each person's moral obligation to resist undemocratic and repressive regimes, the lawyers continued, the true crime would have been *not* to fight the state and political order that condoned genocide in Indochina.[32] In order to establish the West German state as the instigator of violence through its complicity in the unjust and criminal U.S. intervention in Vietnam, Ensslin's attorney (and later minister of interior), Otto Schily, joined the court-appointed Heldmann in calling Helmut Schmidt and U.S. president Richard Nixon to the stand. The motion was, unsurprisingly, thrown out but even without the heads of state's testimonies the attorneys hit their mark. Notions of counterviolence and the moral obligation to resistance underwrote the solidarity of the extraparliamentary left with the RAF over and against the state, whose representatives insisted on trying the members of the RAF as simple criminals rather than grant them special recognition as political combatants.

[28] Sjef Teuns, "Isolation/Sensorische Deprivation: Die programmierte Folter," *Kursbuch* 32 (1973): 118–26. For recent work on this: Gerd Koenen, "Camera Silens: Das Phantasma der 'Vernichtungshaft,'" in Kraushaar, *Die RAF*, 994–1010.

[29] Accusations of torture and comparisons of the FRG to criminal regimes were often implicit, such as when the feminist (and not radical) magazine *Courage* reprinted Meinhof's "Death Wing" poem as a sidebar in an article on torture in Chile. See Traude Bührmann, "Folter an Frauen in Chile," *Courage* 3 (March 1977): 31–4.

[30] Otto Schily and Hans Heinz Heldman, *"Einen Revolutionär können sie töten, aber nicht die Revolution": Beweisanträge im Stammheimer Prozess* (1976). IISG ID-Archiv Bro 2224/19.

[31] Ibid., 4.

[32] The interpretation of Vietnam as *Völkermord* was neither new nor particularly fringe. See, e.g., the 1968 interview with famous writer and artist Peter Weiss: "Amerika will den Völkermord," *Der Spiegel* 32 (August 5, 1968), 66–74.

The trial's opening salvo and the well-coordinated torture campaign that accompanied it suggest that the RAF – at least its leaders and key lawyers – grasped better than anyone the concerns around which the extraparliamentary left's diverse membership cohered. They were not the only ones, however, to recognize that conceptions of counterviolence could lock members of the left into an overdetermined logic of friend and foe – one in which solidarity was necessary for the struggle against oppression. Several prominent leftists, including sociologist Oskar Negt, proved keenly aware of this and, in the wake of the RAF's 1972 May Offensive, moved to counter the uncritical sympathies involved in understanding the militants as victims of state violence without examining their violent deeds. Negt famously – and very publically – repudiated the RAF at a congress honoring Angela Davis as she and activists everywhere awaited her trial's verdict.[33] He argued that its members did not practice progressive politics but instead equated politics with "individual tests of courage" and "mistook the fear that they spread for political success."[34] Through their actions, the "desperados" had isolated themselves from society with the result that both their understanding of the world and their politics derived from confrontations with the police rather than from interactions with regular people, who were the true object and subject of socialist politics. In this Negt was certain:

> The police truncheon is no more the center of reactionary violence than the skillful bomber has anything to do with revolutionary violence. The portentous flares that they want to set with their bombs are in reality will-o'-the-wisps.[35]

The RAF had, in other words, fallen victim to its own illusions, becoming a danger to itself and to the left as a whole. For Negt, the fate of the RAF was important in as much as it could affect the fate of genuinely progressive politics. If what he called the "mechanism of solidarity" at work among the extraparliamentary left were not dismantled, he feared for socialism's future.[36]

Negt's condemnation of the RAF was reported on with fury and a sense of betrayal in the underground alternative press. Contrary to what one might assume, however, Negt had not cast himself outside the negative alliance's political universe. Indeed, the very tenacity of counterviolence as a framework for the politics of the extraparliamentary left was evident in Negt's refusal to reject political violence per se, even as he distanced himself from its practitioners.

[33] About ten thousand people attended the conference held for Davis in Frankfurt, where she studied for two years before following Herbert Marcuse to the University of California, San Diego. After she was arrested as an accomplice in the Soledad brothers' August 1970 abduction and murder of a California judge, a number of prominent West German intellectuals – Negt among them – joined the international "Free Angela Davis" campaign. See the chapter on "black and red panthers" in Klimke, *Other Alliance*, 108–42.

[34] Oskar Negt, "Sozialistische Politik und Terrorismus" reprinted in *Frankfurter Schule und Studentenbewegung: Von der Flaschenpost zum Molotowcocktail, 1946–1995*, vol. 2, *Dokumente*, ed. Wolfgang Kraushaar (Hamburg: Hamburger Ed., 1998), 752–7.

[35] Ibid., 755.

[36] Ibid.

Before opening up his critique of the RAF, he firmly established the build up of the state's means of violence and its coercive measures against all groups and factions on the left. He reminded those professing moral outrage at the militants' recent violence that "before there were the desperados of the Baader-Meinhof group," there were "the murderous actions" of the United States in Vietnam – going so far as to assert that the American "mechanical destruction of human life" threatened to "overshadow the governmental mass killings of the Third Reich."[37] This state-initiated violence was not limited to the physical. Negt insisted that dispositions toward mental "illness, psychological break-down, aggression, and violence" were bred by capitalist social relations, the bourgeois family, and a repressive educational system. West German politicians and police would do best to look to contemporary society for the source of their troubles. In all this, he himself maintained an understanding of the guerrillas as fellow victims of structural violence, framing their motivations – if not their methods – in terms of justifiable counterviolence and the duty to resist oppression. Indeed, Negt's efforts to distance terrorism from socialist politics in general and genuinely revolutionary violence in particular can be seen as an attempt to keep open a space for what he considered fully legitimate civil violence.

Oskar Negt's speech has been credited with beginning a debate on terrorism and violence within the left.[38] This is true only at a certain level, and not the more fundamental one relevant here. True, several older extraparliamentary leftists echoed Negt's assessment of the RAF and were subsequently denounced by younger radicals as weak and traitorous.[39] But, just like in 1968, a rigorous engagement of some foundational assumptions did not occur. Those who participated in the discussion rehashed old debates from the days of APO's demise and addressed not the basic question of counterviolence's legitimacy in general but rather the strategic utility of its particular manifestations. What did differentiate this particular go around from its predecessor was the central importance of solidarity, both in the immediate dispute and in the more diffuse and informal discussions of the coming years. Extraparliamentary leftists who railed against Negt did not do so because he dared to criticize the RAF – not when so many of them had also critiqued the RAF for its "loss of reality," vanguardism, and dangerous abstractionism.[40] The anger – and the ensuing debate – instead stemmed from his attack on left solidarity, exacerbated by the public nature of his critique. However much they may have disagreed with one another or disavowed the actions of certain of their fellows, radical leftists considered a united front vital to their political survival in the current state of

[37] Ibid., 754.

[38] E.g., Gerd Koenen, *Das Rote Jahrzehnt*, 392.

[39] Herbert Marcuse, for example, described the RAF's actions as explicitly "counter-revolutionary." See his interview in *Konkret* 18 (1972): 15.

[40] E.g., *Bewaffneter Kampf: Texte der RAF: Auseinandersetzung und Kritik* (Graz: Rote Sonne, 1973).

repression. Solidarity remained a privileged stance for those who hoped to preserve the possibility of critique within the FRG.

What consistently eluded the extraparliamentary left was how to reject the RAF's political praxis without rejecting either counterviolence or RAF members and leaving the left vulnerable. Negt's friend, Jürgen Seifert, attempted to resolve at least part of this problem by distinguishing political solidarity from the solidarity felt for a victim of political struggle (*Solidarität der sozialen Sensibilität*) and the solidarity born of a common fate and purpose (*Solidarität in der Sache*).[41] Even though he denied the RAF the first, he insisted this did not rule out the other two forms – not when the state's inhumane treatment of RAF prisoners could establish a precedent for the repression of all left opposition. Seifert, moreover, understood basic humanist commitments to demand a certain solidarity. Countering Negt's unpopular conclusions, he thus made a case against the ostracism of armed militants and for leftists' qualified solidarity with the "political prisoners." Unsurprising, members of the RAF – who were very much participants in the debate on violence – rejected Seifert's suggestion that solidarity could be anything but complete and political. And given the continued anger directed at those said to be "distancing" themselves from the RAF, many on the radical left seemed to agree. The negative alliance remained intact and, as subsequent years would show, possible to mobilize. The incomplete confrontation with violence in this 1972 debate became clear to some of the era's activists, but it did so only in retrospect, under the influence of later events.[42]

MAKING ENEMIES OF THE STATE: COUNTERTERRORISM AND THE MEDIA

It was not only the treatment of imprisoned RAF members that convinced extraparliamentary leftists of the need for continued solidarity, but also their own encounters with counterterrorism and public acrimony. Indeed, for these West German citizens, police checkpoints, apartment raids on suspected sympathizers, and armed guards in Bonn's diplomatic quarters became evidence of the state's own terroristic deformation. The pages of the popular press similarly suggested to them that the FRG had not yet mastered the rudiments of democratic tolerance; headlines attacked universities as breeding grounds of radicalism while politicians went on record accusing left intellectuals of "fertilizing the soil of violence." Ironically, too, the government's political education program, which intended to reduce the field of so-called sympathizers and woo disaffected intellectuals to the cause of the existing order, only further alienated

41 Jürgen Seifert, "Plädoyer gegen die Ächtung des politischen Gegners," *Kursbuch* 32 (August 1973): 129–35.

42 See, e.g., the interview with former militant "Carlo," taped in 1987 for the unfinished documentary *Projekt Arthur: Die Gewaltfrage – 1968*. IISG ID-Archiv, Projekt Arthur Collection, Interview "Carlo."

this part of the population. In fact, by targeting this very group, the government unintentionally solidified the negative alliance by promoting a common sense of persecution within the extraparliamentary milieu. Critical old leftists joined former student radicals in feeling themselves to be the favored objects of state control and a new generation of anticommunist scare tactics.

After the June 1976 amendment of the criminal code, extraparliamentary leftists experienced their basic freedoms of expression increasingly subject to violation in the name of counterterrorism. Just as critical Social Democrats had feared, the amended Paragraph 88a (criminalizing the "support of violence") was coupled with Paragraph 129 (concerning support for or membership in a criminal organization) in order to legally justify the censorship of books ambiguously defined as aiding terrorism. In this way, storeowners who displayed or sold texts by any militant group or by their current and former members could be – and were – accused of supporting a criminal organization. Police also carried out sting operations in order to confiscate supposedly subversive materials. On August 18, 1976, in one of the country's biggest coordinated raids, police in seven different cities searched bookstores, storeowners' homes, and a book distribution center.[43] Of the books targeted by the state, none better captured the fear and intolerance terrorism inspired than Michael "Bommi" Baumann's *How It All Began*.[44] An autobiographical account of a working-class youth's experiences of rebellion, life in the West Berlin anarchist scene, and, eventually, membership in the 2nd of June Movement, *How It All Began* captured the initial romance of the underground – but also that it was a decidedly short-lived affair. The narrative force behind Baumann's book is his growing disenchantment and final rejection of armed resistance. While the book was defended by left-wing commentators for its insight into the origins and appeal of violence in the FRG, government officials joined right-wing politicians in condemning it. Read only for its descriptions of bomb making and open antagonism toward the state, Baumann's autobiography was judged a threat to the democratic order and banned at the federal level.

Nobel Prize winner Heinrich Böll proved that one did not have to be a "radical," communist, or former urban guerrilla to be ensnared in the vitriol of counterterrorism. A vocal pacifist and public, if critical, supporter of the SPD, Böll caused a scandal in January 1972 when, in an effort to combat the media's sensationalist approach to terrorism, he wrote a piece for *Der Spiegel* observing that the war between the RAF and the FRG was "six against sixty million" and hardly warranted current reactions.[45] This and his suggestion that Germans confront the current crisis with mercy and restraint rather than a

43 Gerard Braunthal, *Political Loyalty and Public Service in West Germany: The 1972 Decree against Radicals and Its Consequences* (Amherst: University of Massachusetts, 1990), 161.

44 First published in 1975, Bommi Baumann's memoir is available in English, as *How It All Began: The Personal Account of a West German Urban Guerrilla*, trans. Helen Ellenbogen (Vancouver: Arsenal Pulp, 2002).

45 Heinrich Böll, "Will Ulrike Gnade oder Freies Geleit?" *Der Spiegel* 3 (January 10, 1972): 54–7.

declaration of emergency, was widely read as an attempt to minimize, possibly even excuse, the terror of the RAF. Readers flooded the magazine with impassioned letters, spewing hate and accusations of treason in response. A commentator on the popular radio show, *Tagesschau*, labeled Böll an "attorney of anarchistic violent criminals." And conservative politicians joined the Springer Press in roundly demonizing Böll, declaring him a terrorist sympathizer as the radio commentator had done. Even those who disavowed the attacks on Böll heftily criticized the author for dangerously downplaying the RAF's activities. According to one of his more judicious critics, Böll – "intending to call for reason" – had instead "written unreasonably himself."[46]

All this gave Böll materials for his novel *The Lost Honor of Katharina Blum; or, How Violence Develops and Where It Can Lead.*[47] The novel depicted a heartless police and press campaign against a young, initially apolitical woman who unwittingly falls in love with a suspected terrorist and then helps him to escape police clutches. Her poor treatment at the hands of the authorities and money-hungry tabloids suggested that the true threat to democratic civil society in the FRG was not terrorism but rather the police's lack of accountability and the media's enthusiastic contribution to a terrorist scare. Indeed, both *Katharina Blum* and the controversial 1972 essay offered scathing critiques of the sensationalist and profit-orientated reporting surrounding terrorism. Böll attacked the tabloids' blatant disregard for accuracy – declaring murder without evidence and assigning guilt outside the court of law – not only because it violated a certain code of decency presumed to exist but because of the press's very real influence on events. Böll perceived then what terrorist specialists have since elucidated, namely that modern terrorism is a media event. The average citizen experiences terrorism almost entirely through media representations, meaning reporters – who are the first to respond to a terrorist attack and the first to profit from one – are uncommonly well-positioned to shape reality for their readers or viewers.[48] To Böll, the media's misrepresentation of the RAF – as well as anyone who offered a dissenting opinion – was a calculated abuse of power that escalated the current violence by exaggerating people's sense of threat and encouraging "lynch justice." It was an incitement of fear, hate, and witch hunts for the sake of good copy – and more violence – that amounted, in Böll's words, to "naked fascism."[49] His was not an argument to win new friends; conservatives criticized the author and his new novel for being overtly sympathetic to radicals and terrorists. But it was an argument intended for a wider audience – a heartfelt warning that the media's reckless fearmongering

[46] Diether Posser, *Der Spiegel* 5 (January 24, 1972): 40–1. Posser, a jurist, was North-Rhine Westphalia's minister of federal affairs at the time.

[47] Heinrich Böll, *Die verlorene Ehre der Katharina Blum oder: Wie Gewalt entstehen und wohin sie führen kann* (Cologne: Kiepenheuer & Witsch, 1974).

[48] Annette Vowinckel, "Skyjacking: Cultural Memory and the Movies," in *Baader-Meinhof Returns*, 251–68; here, 258, 263. Also, Alexander Spencer, *The Tabloid Terrorist: The Predicative Construction of New Terrorism in the Media* (New York: Palgrave, 2010).

[49] Böll, "Gnade oder Freies Geleit?" 76.

did not just threaten the left but, as the story of innocent Katharina showed, all West Germans.

In real life, it was a middle-aged engineer rather than a pretty young woman who grabbed headlines due to the unwarranted – and ultimately illegal – attentions of West Germany's counterterrorism forces. Nuclear expert Klaus Traube was a manager of the Siemens subsidiary, Interatom, in charge of developing a fast breeder reactor at Kalkar, in North Rhine-Westphalia. His contact with individuals identified by the state as terrorist sympathizers raised the suspicions of Cologne's Office for the Protection of the Constitution; in mid-1975 he was put under close scrutiny by the Federal Intelligence Agency (*Bundesnachrichtendienst*, BND). Given Traube's particular expertise and access to nuclear reactors in the FRG and abroad, he was deemed a "unique" threat to domestic and international security.[50] Unique enough, in fact, to justify illegally bugging his private residence when a man loosely connected to Traube, Hans-Jochen Klein, helped carry out an armed raid on OPEC's headquarters in Vienna in December. Led on behalf of the PFLP by notorious international fugitive Carlos the Jackal, the OPEC attack led to the loss of numerous lives and prolonged hostage negotiations. Having found no evidence of Traube's complicity through legal means (namely round-the-clock surveillance and the interception of mail and telephone communications), BfV president Richard Meier authorized the wiretaps with the knowledge and support of Interior Minister Werner Maihofer. *Der Spiegel* exposed the story to the West German public in late February 1977; its headline – "The Constitutional Guardian Broke the Constitution" – said it all.[51]

In his defense, Maihofer emphasized the genuine sense of emergency caused not only by the OPEC raid but the close succession of attacks preceding it: the assassination of von Drenkmann in November 1974, followed by the Lorenz and Stockholm hostage incidents that spring. The moment in late 1975 had been a "decisive situation," where unusual circumstances and the potential dangers warranted, in his words, "exceptional" actions by the state.[52] Unfortunately for him, the West German minister received about as much sympathy as President Nixon had for Watergate a few years earlier. All three parliamentary parties unanimously agreed on the need to create a mechanism for parliamentary oversight of the BND while critical leftists speculated that the "Traube Affair" had more to do with the government's investment in nuclear energy than with counterterrorism.[53] The few who defended Maihofer stood fairly far to the right and

[50] Werner Maihofer, before the Bundestag interior committee on March 1, 1977 reprinted in *Der Tagesspiegel*, March 2, 1977. Before taking a position at Interatom, Traube worked as a nuclear reactor specialist for AEG in Germany and General Dynamics in San Diego.

[51] Cover title from *Der Spiegel* 10 (February 28, 1977). See the lead article, "Der Minister und die 'Wanze,'" 19–35.

[52] Werner Maihofer, "Erklärung zur Traube/Abhöraffäre," in *Verhandlungen*, VIII. Bundestag, 17. Sitzung (March 16, 1977), 957–61.

[53] In October, the three parliamentary parties held a joint press conference announcing a new bill to create a supervisory commission over the BND, the BfV, and the FRG's counterespionage

argued that the constitution's framers were to blame for having created a weak, "introverted" state with no emergency powers.[54] When the intelligence tapes failed to prove a conspiratorial link between Traube and terrorism, Maihofer had no choice but to resign his post. Klaus Traube, too, found himself out of a job, due to the suspicions cast on his reputation as a faithful employee and a loyal citizen. A one-time champion of nuclear energy, Traube went on to have a highly acclaimed career as an advocate for alternative energy sources.[55] He, like many others at the time, had begun to reevaluate the nuclear program. And this development went hand in hand with his involvement in popular politics. By Traube's own account, his experience of government paranoia politicized him and convinced him to reject nuclear energy.[56]

CHALLENGING THE NUCLEAR STATE

"Nuclear state or Rechtsstaat?" ran a headline of the time by critical journalist and *Spiegel* editor Rolf Augstein.[57] Was this the choice confronting citizens in Western industrialized nations as governments pushed for the adoption of nuclear energy? For many West Germans, incidents like the "Traube Affair" certainly suggested that civil liberties as well as the environment were at stake in the rise of a newly expansive, technologically equipped state. Indeed, the SPD's pursuit of nuclear power rivaled its program of internal security for breeding insecurity among those it ostensibly sought to protect. In September 1973 – just before the decade's first major oil shock – Brandt's government announced plans to expand the number of nuclear plants in the FRG from eight to fifty by the year 1985.[58] Social Democratic leaders embraced the alternative energy source as a means to growth and employment amid rising oil prices and the onset of global recession. Given their conviction that unemployment and dwindling economic prospects encouraged political extremism, government leaders understood nuclear power to contribute to national security in a more narrow sense as well.

Over the course of the 1970s, however, the SPD's love affair with technology and state planning became increasingly less palatable for wide swaths of the

service. Critical leftists' response to events is nicely summed up in: Wolf-Dieter Narr, ed., *Wir Bürger als Sicherheitsrisiko* (Reinbek: Rowohlt, 1977).

54 See, e.g., Roman Schnur, "Zurück vom Mond," *Die Welt*, March 23, 1977. Maihofer undoubtedly had the support of other security officials but, with public opinion against them, they remained largely silent.

55 In addition to writing hundreds of articles, Traube was the official speaker of BUND (Association for Germany's Environmental and Natural Protection). In March 2009 he was awarded Germany's Service Cross, First Class.

56 "Klaus Traube im Gespräch mit Wolfram Wessels," Südwestrundfunk 2 *Zeitgenossen*, February 20, 2005, 14:05, accessed March 2, 2010, http://www.swr2.de.

57 Rolf Augstein, "Atomstaat oder Rechtsstaat?" *Der Spiegel* 10 (February 28, 1977), 29–31.

58 Christian Joppke, *Mobilizing Against Nuclear Energy: A Comparison of Germany and the United States* (Berkeley: University of California Press, 1993), 93; Dorothy Nelkin and Michael Pollack, *The Atom Besieged* (Cambridge: MIT, 1981), 15–16.

West German population – including many of the party's own members. The 1973 oil crisis burst the postwar faith in unlimited economic growth and, with it, Social Democrats' reform agenda. But the death knell on Social Democratic visions of a "growth society" (*Wachstumsgesellschaft*) had, in actuality, tolled a year earlier, with the publication of the Club of Rome's *Limits to Growth* report.[59] Commissioned by an international think tank dedicated to global political issues, the report presented evidence of undeniable ecological limits to growth. Its authors argued that heavy industry and construction – the origins of postwar prosperity – had accelerated environmental destruction to such an extent that, if their expansion continued at their current rate, humans would face early extinction rather than the long hoped for utopia.[60] Like global warming today, the notion of environmental and ecological constraints to economic expansion had its share of naysayers. By the mid-1970s, however, these skeptics were increasingly pressed to take note of public interest in ecological problems and the suspicion, voiced by diverse citizens' groups, that the unceasing pursuit of economic growth was responsible for many other ills. Such suspicions were only made worse by government leaders' reliance on experts for policy making and the ensuing overlap between government officials and top-level administrators in the very industries benefiting from public investment. As state intervention became both more pronounced and shrouded in bureaucracy and technical lingo, government policy became less and less transparent, and large numbers of citizens expressed growing insecurity due to a notable loss of control. The result was a powerful critique of Social Democratic policy and the shortcomings of representative government in the seemingly spontaneous birth of hundreds of local citizens' initiatives (*Bürgerinitiativen*, CIs). Not willing to sit idly by and let their government take calculated risks with their lives and livelihoods, these West Germans moved to challenge the state's definition of internal security and democracy with ones of their own.

In their ideal form, citizens' initiatives exemplified grassroots democracy in action. As such, they questioned the legitimacy of current government practice at both the local and federal levels. From the start, the extraparliamentary left was well represented, with those who had turned to community organizing at the end of the 1960s frequently taking the lead in local initiatives. But the CIs proved that middle-class radicalism was not confined to the left or to the youth. Defying left–right political frameworks, individuals from diverse social and ideological backgrounds came together to oppose administrative plans they considered contrary to local communities' interests, such as the construction of a coal-fired power plant, a new airport runway, or the speculative land practices driven by urban renewal. Government bureaucrats and corporate managers were the enemy, and technocracy (more than capitalism) was the system

[59] Donella H. Meadows et al., *The Limits to Growth: A Report for the Club of Rome's Project on the Predicament of Mankind* (New York: Universe, 1972).

[60] Ibid., 23. The report also cited the arms race and the world's population explosion as major contributors to resource depletion and environmental degradation.

to be countered. As one West Berliner described the problem, "elected officials [had] become caricatures," defending decisions made by their administrations "whose contents, let alone whose consequences, they could not understand."[61] The majority of CI activists were politically moderate and, at least initially, sought to act as a cooperative, plebiscitary complement to official, technocratic, bureaucratic politics.[62] But their emphasis on participatory democracy and defense of a reproductive (rather than an exclusively productive) sphere that valued family and ecology brought them into alliance with activists from a more explicitly leftist background.[63]

Of all the causes championed by citizens' initiatives, the fight against nuclear power most successfully escaped the organizational confines typical of single-issue movements. The citizens' ability to gain public and even elite sympathy against nuclear energy and, as a result, successfully contest government policy transformed local initiatives into a national and even international protest movement. Most histories of West German antinuclear protest begin with Wyhl, a small town situated on the upper Rhine near the French border in Baden-Württemberg.[64] Selected in 1972 as a possible site for a nuclear reactor, the town was already sensitive to the risks such an honor entailed thanks to the campaign against a planned reactor on the other side of the river, in Alsace.[65] When the Land government and the utility company, *Kernkraftwerk Süd*, announced in July 1973 that Wyhl would indeed be the future site of construction, the Citizens' Initiative Weisweil immediately formed. Over the next nine months, residents collected over one hundred thousand signatures opposing the proposed reactor and won support from farmers, winegrowers, the educated middle class, and university students from Freiburg (some twenty miles away) as well as from notable CDU politicians (in defiance of their

[61] Bürgerinitiativ Kraftwerk Oberhavel, "Das Phänomen Bürgerinitiative: Reichen unsere Parteien als 'Willensbildungsorgane' nicht aus?" October 1976, cited in: Carl J. Hager, "Democratizing Technology: Citizen and State in West German Energy Politics," *Polity* 25 (Autumn 1992): 48.

[62] According to one study, 36.4 percent of CI members came from the professional sector, 27.3 percent were civil servants (predominately in positions requiring an advanced degree), and 24.2 percent held management positions in the service industry or clerical segment of the German economy. Wolfgang Rüdig, "Bürgerinitiativen im Umweltschutz: Eine Bestandsaufnahme der impirischen Befunde," in *Bürgerinitiativen in der Gesellschaft*, ed. Volker Hauff (Villingen-Schwenningen: Neckar, 1980), 163–4.

[63] Peter Mayer-Tasch, *Die Bürgerinitiativenbewegung* (Reinbek: Rowohlt, 1985), 18–25; Andrei S. Markovits and Philip S. Gorski, *The German Left: Red, Green and Beyond* (New York: Oxford University Press, 1993), 101.

[64] The best account of Wyhl and the unfolding antinuclear movement remains Dieter Rucht's *Von Wyhl nach Gorleben: Bürger gegen Atomprogramm und nukleare Entsorgung* (Munich: Beck, 1980). Stephen H. Milder is currently working on a much welcome update: Stephen H. Milder, "'Today the Fish, Tomorrow Us': Anti-Nuclear Activism in the Rhine Valley and Beyond, 1970–79" (PhD diss., University of North Carolina at Chapel Hill, forthcoming).

[65] Both sites were, in fact, part of a large-scale development plan to industrialize the upper Rhine region of Germany, France, and Switzerland that envisioned a total of seventeen new nuclear plants. Roger Karapin, *Protest Politics in Germany: Movements on the Left and Right Since the 1960s* (University Park: Pennsylvania State University Press, 2007), 126.

own state government), Protestant pastors, and the SPD mayor of Weisweil.[66] Formal public hearings one year later only succeeded in escalating existing tensions when they exposed the collusion between government officials and company representatives to reveal how little local concerns mattered.[67] These failed attempts at negotiations eventually prompted the citizens to expand the scope of their opposition. In the summer of 1974, an estimated two thousand demonstrators marched to the proposed construction site. Once there, West Germans joined with French activists across the river to form the International Committee of Bad-Alsatian Citizens' Initiatives (*Internationales Komitee der Badisch-Elsässischen Bürgerinitiativen)*, an umbrella organization whose original membership of twenty-one CIs more than doubled over the next three years.[68] Together, the protesters publically disavowed the corrupt tactics employed by government officials and declared their willingness to occupy the site if necessary.[69] These members of the early antinuclear movement insisted that greater citizen participation and a socially responsible energy policy were the preconditions for a secure and democratic future.

Despite continued opposition, construction began at Wyhl on February 17, 1975.[70] Thirty CIs convened a joint press conference condemning the action while several hundred citizens occupied the site and successfully brought construction to a halt. Though police managed to disperse the demonstrators, it was a fleeting victory for nuclear advocates. An outpouring of support for the antinuclear protesters brought an estimated twenty-eight thousand people to the construction area on February 23. Determined to hold the site, local organizers drew inspiration from recent demonstrations in France, in particular the occupation of a proposed lead factory in the town of Marckolsheim, which was just winding down as the mass occupation at Wyhl took off.[71] The citizen initiative did more than occupy the building site; activists built an "alternative" settlement that eventually included a "friendship house" and an adult education center. For a significant number of the participants and the movement's later chroniclers, the cooperative and nonviolent nature of these sorts of projects defined their experience of Wyhl. Their efforts appeared to pay off when, a month and a half after the first bulldozer rolled onto the site, an administrative court ordered a halt to construction. The decision was soon overturned,

[66] Ibid., 127.

[67] Among other things, it was disclosed that four members of the government oversight committee were actually on the utility's board of directors. Rucht, *Wyhl*, 83.

[68] Hans-Christian Buchholtz, "Chronologie der Widerstandsbewegung gegen Atomkraftwerke am Oberrhein von 1971 bis 1977," in *Widerstand gegen Atomkraftwerke*, eds. idem, Lutz Mez, and Thomas von Zabern (Wuppertal: Hammer, 1978), 121–40; here, 126.

[69] "Erklärung der badisch-elsässischen Bürgerinitiativen," reprinted in *Für eine bessere Republik: Alternative der demokratischen Bewegung*, eds. Heinrich Billstein and Klaus Naumann (Cologne: Pahl-Rugenstein, 1981), 172–6.

[70] For more, see Nina Gladitz, ed., *Lieber heute aktiv als morgen radioaktiv* (Berlin: Wagenbach, 1976), 56.

[71] Rucht, *Wyhl*, 83–4.

however, and it was not until March 1977 that the plant's building permit was officially suspended (at least for the next five years, when another court changed the ruling once more).

Wyhl is remembered fondly as a triumph of organized citizens' action and a model for nonviolent protest.[72] However much such an interpretation papers over or leaves out entirely, there is little doubt that the mass occupation of the Wyhl site became both symbol and catalyst for broad antinuclear opposition, not only in the FRG but in other countries as well.[73] Indeed, Wyhl introduced the extraparliamentary left to the ecological scene, which most had previously dismissed as too narrow in outlook and agenda.[74] When they did embrace the antinuclear movement, however, they brought their own interpretative frameworks. For extraparliamentary leftists, nuclear energy was not an isolated issue but symptomatic of the state's authoritarian relationship to power and undemocratic disregard for the people's opinions and true interests. These activists, particularly those from K-Gruppen and Sponti circles who participated in the occupation of construction sites, understood antinuclear demonstrations as a matter of political resistance in the postwar sense of the term. They sought nothing more or less than to defend democracy (if not liberal democracy) by putting an end to what they regarded as the state's abuse of power. In a pamphlet explaining "why we fight," the West German Communist League (*Kommunistischer Bund Westdeutschland*, or KBW) echoed sentiments common within the antinuclear movement: resentment over being ignored, fear of being treated as guinea pigs, and disbelief over nuclear technology furthering the public good.[75] The conclusion they drew from Wyhl was that two "democracies" existed within the FRG. There was the "apparatus" (parliament, state bureaucracy, courts, army, and police) that used the "free democratic order" and the formal rule of law to prop up the "capitalist classes against the people." And then there was the "genuine" democracy of the people, which was being trampled. Rather than submit to laws and rules that served only the interests of the first, repressive democracy, the KBW argued that "the people must ... answer the entire apparatus of power and violence ... with its own violence."[76] Though hardly a call to immediate armed rebellion, it clearly articulated the continuing belief in the potential need for

[72] This is essentially how both Dieter Rucht and Roger Karapin frame their discussions of it.

[73] As Stephen Milder observes, for those unaware of the years of struggle preceding the February 23 mass occupation, the antinuclear movement "seemed to explode onto the stage with ... Wyhl." For the international nature of Wyhl and the ecological movement, see Stephen Milder, "Thinking Globally, Acting (Trans-) Locally: Petra Kelly and the Transnational Roots of West German Green Politics," *Central European History* 43 (2010): 301–26.

[74] In 1973, for example, Hans Magnus Enzensberger was still able to observe that the left "remained skeptical of the ecological hypothesis and avoided alliances" with those groups he assessed as "purely ecological" in orientation. *Kursbuch* 33 (1973): 7.

[75] KBW, *Warum kämpfen wir gegen das Kernkraftwerk in Wyhl? Eine Antwort auf die Broschüre der Landesregierung*, (Freiburg: KBW, 1975).

[76] Ibid., 16.

violent resistance against the originary violence of the system. And this belief influenced the direction of the antinuclear movement by helping to intensify confrontations between demonstrators and authorities, who had drawn their own conclusions from recent events. If Wyhl symbolized the power and potential of grassroots intervention, then Brokdorf – the next major demonstration site – came to symbolize the movement's potential for violence as well as for political disaster.

A small village in West Germany's northernmost state of Schleswig-Holstein, Brokdorf was declared the future site of a nuclear reactor in the fall of 1973. Shortly thereafter, the Lower Elbe Environmental Protection Citizens' Initiative (*Bürgerinitiative Umweltschutz Unterelbe*, BUU) was founded in order to coordinate the opposition efforts of surrounding regional groups. From the beginning, tensions between the citizens of the affected area and nuclear energy advocates ran high. Attempts by representatives of the Schleswig-Holstein government and the power company to buy off locals with public works projects failed as did a public referendum on the proposed plant. The nuclear power company, however, chose to ignore the popular vote and proceed as planned – a decision that all but guaranteed conflict. Seeking to prevent the occupation tactics that had proven successful at Wyhl, authorities cordoned off the proposed site in October 1976, before construction even began. One published account captured the highly charged lens through which many viewed such preventative policing:

> It was just like in a movie: when you looked down from the dam, you saw the KZ – equipped with about 12 water guns, an encampment at its center, and mercenary soldiers everywhere. On the surrounding dirt roads the assailants wandered in slow troop movements. This, at the same time the citizens' initiative gathered ... a small group in the distance.[77]

Referring to the site as a *KZ*, the German abbreviation for concentration camp, the writer invoked Nazism to convey both the extreme criminality and the magnitude of state force confronting demonstrators in Brokdorf. By doing so, he or she also implied the legitimacy of counterviolent measures to halt construction as a form of antifascist resistance.[78]

For their part, state officials acted in such a way as to convince a broad spectrum of demonstrators of the need for open resistance. Though construction had been halted by court order, the minister president of Schleswig-Holstein, Gerhard Stoltenberg (CDU), ordered heavy machinery onto the site under police

[77] This *ID* report Nr. 152 was reprinted in abbreviated form as: "Die Schlacht von Brokdorf," *Grosse Freiheit*, December 1976, 8.

[78] Others interpreted the antinuclear movement as part of the larger struggle against imperialism, whose relationship to fascism, for dogmatic communists at least, was taken as a given. According to one Brokdorf flyer, nuclear energy aimed at nothing less than the submission of the third world to its former colonizers' whims. In this case, they sought to force oil-rich countries to forgo the rules of capitalism and lower their prices. See KBW, *Nieder mit Imperialismus und Reaktion: Kein KKW in Brokdorf*, (KBW, 1976).

protection and the cover of night.[79] Even Helmut Schmidt – no great friend of the antinuclear movement – voiced disgust at such a "night and fog" action.[80] In protest, an estimated thirty thousand to forty-five thousand people gathered alongside the Elbe on October 30, shouting "Where justice becomes injustice, resistance becomes a duty" and "No nukes in Brokdorf or anywhere!"[81] Several angered protesters broke off from the main demonstration, forded the moat, and – under the fire of water cannons – tore down a segment of wall to successfully occupy the construction site. From this point on, events rapidly escalated. A second group of demonstrators reached the construction site equipped with helmets, shovels, rocks, and other makeshift "tools of defense." There, they encountered unprecedented police force, with local units bolstered by the BGS, whose members were now trained in the shields, tear gas, and truncheons of crowd control. In keeping with recent police reforms, police officers and border guards avoided frontal attacks in order to focus their energies on the crowd's violent elements. The strategy met with mixed results, both in terms of the many peaceful protesters who came under police clubs and the increased violence caused from directly engaging radicals.[82] According to eyewitness reports released by the BUU, over 500 people sustained injuries from "various toxic gases," flying stones, and cudgels.[83] The violent clash between police and protesters left more than casualties, however. It set the tone for the occupation attempt at Grohnde, 180 miles away in Lower Saxony, and for the fatal demonstration in Malville, France not long after.

THE ECOLOGICAL MOVEMENT AND THE CHALLENGE OF VIOLENCE

One of the most significant consequences of Brokdorf was the association it forged of antinuclear protest with political violence – and the danger this posed to the movement. Indeed, after Brokdorf, officials at the state and federal

[79] Stoltenberg previously served as the federal minister of research and technology under Chancellors Erhard and Kiesinger.

[80] "Redeauszug des BKs in seiner Ansprache vor den Delegierten der SPD-Kreisdelegiertenversammlung," Bergdorf, November 7, 1976, Archiv der sozialen Demokratie (Bad Godesberg, hereafter AdsD), Helmut Schmidt Papers 9226. The chancellor's choice of "Nacht und Nebel" deliberately conjured Nazi police actions against political opponents.

[81] BUU (Brokdorf), *Der Bauplatz muß wieder zur Wiese werden!* (Hamburg: BUU, 1977), 102.

[82] Though police brutality was widely noted – and endured – by contemporaries, later scholars argue that if the policing of the mid-1970s was harder and more repressive than before, it was also more selective and less likely to escalate the situation. As one indicator: even when physical force was greatest, nobody was killed. See Heiner Busch et al., *Die Polizei in der Bundesrepublik* (Frankfurt: Campus, 1985), 328–42 and Donatella Della Porta, *Social Movements, Political Violence, and the State: A Comparative Analysis of Italy and Germany* (New York: Cambridge University Press, 1995), 63–9.

[83] "Presseerklärung der Bürgerinitiativen Umweltschutz Unterelbe: Betr.: verletzte KKW-Gegner vom 13. November 1976," in *Augenzeugenberichte aus Brokdorf* (Brokdorf/Wewelsfleth: BUU, November 20, 1976), Dokumentationsstelle für unkonventionelle Literatur (Stuttgart, hereafter Dokumentationsstelle) D 097.

levels approached antinuclear demonstrations like they did terrorism – as intertwined threats to be contained. It was not only the impression of uncontrolled violence that linked the two in their minds but also the government's position that nuclear energy was critical to the West German order. Mindful of his need to walk a fine line, given the SPD's continued (if seriously circumscribed) commitment to popular resistance, Helmut Schmidt nonetheless made clear his position that an attack on nuclear power plants was an attack on the FRG. He and other like-minded politicians distinguished between "convinced democrats," who legitimately made use of their civil liberties, and "small groups of terrorists and militant enemies of our constitution," who "hoped to strike the free democratic order with their violent actions against nuclear energy sites."[84] By connecting rowdy demonstrators to terrorists and extremists, the chancellor publicly limited legitimate resistance – and every West German's constitutional right to resistance – to nonviolent, peaceful protest and folded the destruction of property into the definition of illegitimate violence.[85] Those who rejected this definition or, like Traube, associated with those who did, became legitimate objects of investigation as suspected enemies of the state. As such, antinuclear demonstrators were subjected to surveillance, apartment searches, and possible dismissal from public sector positions under the Radicals Decree.

The popular media encouraged these same, violent associations. The daily newspaper, *Tagesspiegel*, for example, ran a headline proclaiming that Brokdorf and the antinuclear movement were "linked with terrorists in a common fight against the state."[86] In case the Molotov cocktails, steel helmets, and other sundry weapons with which the "militant Brokdorf groups" were said to be equipped was not enough to convince readers of this shared agenda, the article made explicit reference to the RAF. Citing responsible security officials, the paper announced that "the terrorists in custody were also discussing the events at Brokdorf and their possible significance for a 'new solidarity campaign.'"[87] Whether or not the majority of the reading public swallowed the terrorist-like portrayal of antinuclear activists, it was a nightmare for a movement that relied on public favor to affect political change. Polls showed that the population was strongly torn over the question of nuclear power, concerned but not

[84] Helmut Schmidt to minister president of Schleswig-Holstein, February 3, 1977, AdsD Helmut Schmidt Papers 6523. Schmidt's perception of violent demonstrators as state saboteurs came through clearest in a letter to all SPD and FDP members of the Bundestag, in which he directly referenced the RAF in relation to the violence surrounding antinuclear protest. See Helmut Schmidt, "An die Mitglieder der Fraktionen der SPD und der FDP im Deutschen Bundestag," March 24, 1977, AdsD Helmut Schmidt Papers 9402.

[85] "Erklärung der Bundesregierung zu den am 19. Februar 1977 in Brokdorf vorgesehenen Demonstrationen gegen die Errichtung eines Kernkraftwerkes," February 7, 1977, AdsD Helmut Schmidt Papers 6523. See, too, a different draft of the speech from February 12, 1977, AdsD Helmut Schmidt Papers 9226.

[86] Horst Zimmermann, "Brokdorf/Anti-AKW mit Terroristen verbunden im gemeinsamen Kampf gegen den Staat, nicht nur KKW," *Tagesspiegel*, February 17, 1977.

[87] Ibid.

convinced of an alternative.[88] Faced with stories of violence and a media barrage of "experts" who only canceled each other out, West Germans registered a growing disinterest in the politics of nuclear energy and the hope that the whole controversy might simply go away.[89]

Very quickly, then, fear of their own political isolation forced citizens' initiatives to place violence at the forefront of discussion, a move that predictably exposed the stark differences between activists' backgrounds and political orientations. Demands for the categorical rejection of all physical aggression from the movement's pacifist elements as well as from members concerned to recoup public support were rejected by those who were convinced that nonviolent protest could neither eliminate violent confrontations nor bring about change given the violence of the system itself. The majority took a middle ground; they conceded the illegitimacy of violence against humans but insisted that the destruction of property, a frequent practice in site occupations, was an acceptable – and vital – form of resistance. While events in late autumn certainly got people talking, it was the preparations for a reoccupation of Brokdorf on February 19, 1977 that pressed the demonstrators to address violent resistance explicitly. Immediately following the November demonstration, BUU representatives issued a public statement laying bare the simmering tensions within the movement. In it, they declared their rejection of "radicals" and fear of those who sought to use antinuclear protest for their own ends. This fear, they stated, was "not simply an expression of conservative and anti-communist opinion," as some suggested, but rather "the product of real experience with the organizationally bigoted, out-of-touch behavior of various leftist groups."[90] When the time came to organize a new demonstration, however, the BUU proved far from unanimous. In particular, the organization's Hamburg constituency refused to exclude the possibility of violent resistance at the next demonstration. Heavily influenced by Spontis, the Hamburgers were adamant that whether or not violence occurred depended not on protesters but on measures taken by police. In an effort to push through plans by bypassing the subject of violence altogether, they called on all "honorable" opponents of the nuclear program to demonstrate their ongoing will to fight – "regardless of [their] respective conceptions regarding what form protest should take" – by showing up at Brokdorf on

[88] By December 1976, seventy percent of those polled believed nuclear energy posed a risk to human health (versus forty-eight percent in June 1973); at the same time sixty-five percent expressed optimism in humans' ability to gain control of this and other technology as well as the belief that nuclear energy was a condition of living in an advanced industrial society. Elisabeth Noelle-Neumann, ed., *Allensbacher Jahrbuch der Demoskopie* (Vienna: Molden, 1977), 182, 184, 186.

[89] As one scholar noted at the time, the public discussion over nuclear energy had "ossified into ritual: the arguments and counterarguments were known by all and quotes from experts of every stripe were swung like clubs according to the set rules of war." See Jürgen Dahl, *Auf Gedeih und Verderb: Kommt Zeit, kommt Unrat: Zur Metaphysik der Atomenergie-Erzeugung* (Ebenhausen: Langewiesche-Brandt, 1977).

[90] Barbara Michael, "Noch ein Brokdorf und wir können die Kernenergie Abschreiben," *Große Freiheit*, December 1976, 6–7.

February 19.[91] They did so, moreover, in the name of the entire BUU. Furious, the Wilster Marsh and West Coast action groups refused to participate in an occupation they considered flawed from the start.

As a result, two demonstrations came to be planned for the same day, one at the Brokdorf construction site and one in the nearby town of Itzehoe. The latter, billed as a protest "festival," was an unabashed attempt to persuade would-be protesters away from Brokdorf and what many saw as certain violent conflict. Organized by Social Democrats, Free Democrats, and Communists associated with the antinuclear movement, the counterdemonstration at Itzehoe became an opportunity for Schmidt's government to isolate so-called rowdies from the main body of the movement.[92] A week and a half before the demonstrations, Bonn publicly asked that CIs and other "engaged citizens" not let themselves "be misused" by "terrorists" and others intent on provoking violence against the state.[93] The government officially banned demonstration activities at Brokdorf while it simultaneously presented Itzehoe as a model of civil disobedience compatible with democracy. In various speeches, Schmidt made it clear that the right to resistance would be tightly constrained at the same time Minister of Justice Hans-Jochen Vogel publicly asserted that demonstrators' actions at Brokdorf were not legitimate expressions of Article 20, Section 4 of the Basic Law.[94] For, if one accepted the legitimacy of the existing constitutional order – as the parliamentary parties and members of government most certainly did – then *Widerstand* could only be waged to defend or restore it, not against the state order itself. Emphasizing civility over disobedience, in other words, a democrat was defined as someone committed to open dialogue with government officials and the German public.[95] Since any act of physical aggression – including the destruction of property – was deemed incompatible with such a course, well-intentioned protesters were explicitly encouraged to separate themselves from those engaged in *un*civil (and thus undemocratic) action at Brokdorf.

Despite politicians' wishes, however, individuals' decisions to attend one or the other demonstration could not be read as a straightforward

[91] Cited in: Hans Jürgen Benedict, "Bürger, Linke und Gewalt: Ein subjektives Plädoyer für einen radikalen Pazifismus der Bürgerinitiativen," *Kursbuch* 48 (June 1977): 143.

[92] The heaviest push for an alternative demo came from the Schleswig-Holstein SPD, who showered the region with seventy thousand pamphlets on February 14. The Land SPD and Klaus Matthiesen, in particular, used Itzehoe to announce their opposition to violence and to critique the CDU government in power. AdsD Helmut Schmidt Papers 10088.

[93] "Erklärung der Bundesregierung zu den am 19. Februar 1977."

[94] See, e.g., Hans-Jochen Vogel to Herbert Bruns (Bundesverband Deutsche Bürgerinitiative für Umwelt und Lebensschutz), March 31, 1977, AdsD Hans-Jochen Vogel Correspondence 4; ARD, "Pro und Contra: Bürgerinitiative – Recht auf Ungehorsam?" February 1977, AdsD Hans-Jochen Vogel Papers 512.

[95] "Erklärung der Bundesregierung zu den am 19. Februar 1977." Also, Dieter Lasse, "Protokoll über die Sitzung des Präsidiums am 15. Februar 1977," February 23, 1977, AdsD Helmut Schmidt Papers 9442; Schmidt, "An die Mitglieder der Fraktionen."

affirmation or condemnation of either violent resistance or democracy in the FRG. Activists went to Brokdorf or Itzehoe based on a variety of calculations. In Frankfurt, a teach-in was held specifically to weigh the pros and cons of the two February demonstrations. Those gathered there agreed that an occupation attempt would be "extremely dangerous" and that the antinuclear movement did "not want or need any martyrs."[96] In general, it could be said that participants expressed a clear desire to avoid violent conflict. But the question of violence remained, first and foremost, a matter of strategic consideration – as the argument that put an end to the evening's deliberations made clear. Given the negative press and division within the movement, it seemed that Brokdorf was fated to remain only a "minority demonstration." Sidestepping questions of violence as a political principle, the Frankfurters concluded that no protest was preferable to one that weakened the movement "in the eyes of the West German population." Though with some regret, the teach-in participants – which included not a few Spontis – decided to stay home.

Perhaps because of meetings such as this, one observer noted that, despite all the noise, the question of violence was not actually being discussed. Violence, he lamented, was only being considered "for its strategic-functional aspects."[97] Strategy did, in fact, dominate the debates and decisions of early February, though ethical and philosophical discussions were not wholly absent. Angry over the attempts to forgo the original demonstration plans, many Brokdorf supporters dismissed nonviolence and Itzehoe as so much propaganda aimed at destroying opposition and left solidarity. It was not an accident, one activist argued, that the loudest calls for "no violence" came from outside the movement, from the same people who were also "gathering together their modern Cossacks" in order to demonstrate the counterrevolution's monopoly on power.[98] Echoing what Marcuse had argued a decade earlier, he and others planning to occupy Brokdorf insisted that nonviolence was merely a tool used by the ruling classes to maintain the status quo. As a principle, nonviolence was an "absurdity" and as a (winning) strategy, impossible.[99] In a last appeal before the February demonstrations, the Hamburg Spontis asked all would-be protesters to refuse to be "called to order:"

Do not let yourselves be provoked into listening to the Gang of Four – the state, parties, unions, science – because there is only one thing you can believe of them. Yes, they are serious when they speak of peace and order. But it is the peace of the cemetery and the order

[96] AStA-Frankfurt, ed., *Brokdorf Info: Teach-in, Donnerstag 17.2., 19.00* (Frankfurt: AStA, 1977), IISG ID-Textarchiv 62/3 612.

[97] Hans Jürgen Benedict, "Bürger, Linke und Gewalt," 144.

[98] "Kolonne" Klaus Störtebecker, Hamburg Brokdorf flyer, reprinted in *Pflasterstrand* 5 (March 2–15, 1977), 5.

[99] "Es geht nicht ohne 'Gewalt,'" *Arbeiterkampf*, April 4, 1977, 1.

of walls, barbed wires, prisons, suburbs, single-family homes, factories, high rises, reform schools.[100]

In their linkage of nuclear death to both overtly and covertly repressive social institutions, the discussion of structural violence was, in fact, quite present. But the legitimacy of violent resistance rarely received such sustained attention.

If Brokdorf supporters did not spend much time addressing the question of violence, however, it was because they did not perceive it to be a genuine point of dissension. Like with nonviolence, several members argued that raising the question itself was purely a distraction, a technique employed by state agents to derail the antinuclear movement. As the Bremen Citizens' Initiative described the situation, the government was deliberately slandering the movement in Brokdorf to divide protesters and promulgate the "fairy tale" that opposition to nuclear energy came only from "chaotics and terrorists."[101] Both before and after February 19, a number of activists insisted that the movement was sorely underestimating itself, overestimating the influence of the K-Gruppen, and allowing itself to be convinced of a divide that did not exist.[102] Here, as in their dismissal of nonviolence, Brokdorf's defenders sought to redirect protesters' attention to the state as the real source of division and fear besetting the movement and society more generally. Their discussion of Brokdorf and future strategy was peppered with descriptions of the BGS, the massive police force used to defend nuclear construction sites, and other accounts of state repression in order to make clear to all that the state was the true instigator of violence. Those activists who announced their intention to attend the counterdemonstration at Itzehoe were accused of forgetting this fundamental fact or, worse – of still being obedient Germans. As one described it, the Itzehoe-bound were caught in the same "bourgeois and intellectual" fantasy of "state-condoned radical reform" that had prevented revolution in Germany since 1848.[103] The occupation attempt at Brokdorf on February 19 was thus presented, first, as a rejection of state attempts to break protesters' solidarity and, second, as resistance to the state in an ongoing German struggle for individual autonomy and an alternative future.

While the defenders of Brokdorf argued for solidarity and a near exclusive emphasis on state violence, those leftists who threw their weight behind the counterprotest at Itzehoe chose to do so largely because of their inability to control the conditions at Brokdorf. In announcing their decision to go to Itzehoe, the Wilster Marsh and West Coast CIs stressed two strategic considerations. First, they stated, "no one believes in a peaceful rally." This was not

[100] Quoted in *Pflasterstrand* 5 (March 2–15, 1977), 5.

[101] Bremer-Bürgerinitiative-Gegen-Atomenergieanlagen, *Was war wirklich los in Brokdorf?* (Bremen, 1977), IISG ID-Textarchiv 62/3 612.

[102] This position was expressed with sheepish remorse, for example, by the editors of *Pflasterstrand* who, along with a large contingent of Frankfurter Spontis, had decided against the demonstration at Brokdorf. See *Pflasterstrand* 5 (March 2–15, 1977), 2.

[103] Störtebecker, "Brokdorf flyer."

because it was impossible to occupy a nuclear power plant peaceably – they understood Wyhl to prove it was – but rather because authorities were looking to provoke a "decisive battle" in the hopes of shifting public attention away from nuclear energy to civil violence. Demonstrating at Brokdorf therefore risked a level of violence that could play into the state's hands. This raised the BUU members' second consideration, namely the maintenance of the movement's broad base and public support. The Hamburgers' refusal to skip an unavoidably violent occupation was problematic for this very reason. The groups' official spokesperson, Lars Hennings, was adamant that protesters' common goal – captured in the slogan "No nuclear power plant in Brokdorf or anywhere" – could not be achieved "without a consensus over the methods [to be used] in this confrontation."[104]

Those who favored the Itzehoe demonstration did not rule out all violent action as illegitimate, but their participation in a diverse social movement and concern for protesters' safety required that that violence be strictly limited. Without the Hamburgers' agreement and the state's cooperation on this score, Brokdorf was understood to risk lives and the movement's future. If the Wilster Marsh and West Coast CIs refused to be bullied by the Hamburgers, however, they acted similarly toward the state. Rather than agree to the government's assertion that the destruction of property involved in site occupations disqualified them as legitimate resistance, the BUU countered with its own definition of civil disobedience. By that time, it was probably the most widely used definition within the antinuclear movement and the West German left as a whole: Illegitimate civil action was that which targeted or risked human life. All other avenues of resistance remained open.

If the question of violence as strategy seemed to dominate the Brokdorf-Itzehoe debate in much the same way as it had the final months of APO, there was a critical difference. This time, extraparliamentary leftists involved in the antinuclear movement had achieved notable success at Wyhl, and had done so with the help of nonviolent means. This experience fed optimism as well as the knowledge that demonstrators actually had something to lose. While the majority of extraparliamentary leftists defended their long-standing conceptions of counterviolence and resistance and the negative alliance these entailed, a number of dissenters reconsidered them in the hope that new answers might – finally – bring real change. Making this move did not require them to abandon their critique of society's structural violence. Like the antiauthoritarian wing of the student movement, these leftists argued that power structures would not change until mentalities and social relations changed. They denied, however, that violence could potentially play a productive part in bringing this about, however extreme the conditions. From within the antinuclear and women's movements, these leftists voiced disillusionment with counterviolence

[104] Lars Hennings (BUU press secretary), "Marschenkonferenz: Presseerklärung," February 6, 1977, Hamburg, Dokumentationsstelle DO1220.

as a progressive force and accorded a newfound importance to nonviolent resistance in achieving the left's traditional goals of emancipation and peace.

FANTASIES OF PEACE AND VIOLENCE

The heavyweight in the fight against nuclear energy was the Federal Association of Citizens' Initiatives for Environmental Protection (*Bundesverband Bürgerinitiativen Umweltschutz*, BBU), representing nearly 400 CIs by 1977.[105] Since its founding in 1972, the BBU had come to champion an ethos of "ecological humanism," with which traditional pacifists, Christians, and a growing number of feminists and socialists also publicly identified. Although its diverse membership harbored a range of perspectives, the election of pacifists Petra Kelly and Roland Vogt to the BBU's board in January 1977 was indicative of a growing trend within the organization by the time of the Brokdorf controversy. In increasingly unequivocal terms, the BBU held that the use of violence was antithetical to the campaign against nuclear energy. For the struggle to free West Germans and the natural environment from nuclear destruction could not be won by answering violence with more violence. As far as the organization's leaders were concerned, at least, there were no exceptions to this rule. Spokesman Hans-Helmuth Wüstenhagen clarified that their goal was not "revolution" but rather "the protection of life," and he proclaimed Wyhl the symbol of the BBU's principled commitment to "nonviolent resistance."[106] The BBU, then, openly refuted the heritage of progressive counterviolence. But it was adamant that nonviolent resistance did not equal passivity. On the one hand, it demanded a sustained refusal to be drawn into physical conflict that experience showed required more than good intentions and lucky circumstances. On the other hand, nonviolent resistance relied on open opposition in forcing attention to specific injustices. Resonating as this did with the direct action strategy of the 1960s, the BBU found support from a number of leftists who had, over the course of the decade, come to agree that violent resistance was a moral and strategic dead end.

If this group of activists rejected the notion of emancipatory violence, they did not exchange it for the pacifist's dream of a violence-free world. The immensely popular antinuclear activist and songwriter Walter Moßmann, for instance, was skeptical of the BBU's categorical rejection of violence, asserting that the denial of violence's omnipresence verged on "middle-class self-delusion."[107] But his experiences as an anti-Vietnam War and then antinuclear demonstrator led him to embrace nonviolence as the only path to peace. Certain as he was that the media's "war reporters" exaggerated the violence and "militaristic

105 Markovits and Gorski, *Red, Green and Beyond*, 102.

106 BBU, "Rundschreiben an alle Mitgliedsgruppen des BBU am 19.2.77 Demonstration in Brokdorf," February 2, 1977, AdsD Helmut Schmidt Papers 9442.

107 Projekt-Arthur, "Protokolle: Interview von Walter Moßmann," September 29, 1987, ISIG ID-Archiv, Project Arthur Collection.

flag-waving" of the K-Gruppen and Spontis, Moßmann was equally convinced that the aggressiveness and militancy ascribed to activists was not pure fiction. Both ran rampant among the radical left, he argued, and would continue to do so unless members took the time to examine their own actions – and even their fantasies – for all the ways they fell short of the politics they espoused.[108] Hoping to inspire further self-reflection, Moßmann pointed out certain undercurrents of leftist culture. He noted, for instance, a widespread preference for action movies in which Viet Cong rebels blew up American bombers over documentaries on everyday life in Vietnamese towns. He then related this to the casual way that demonstrators violated the homes of villagers and townspeople with spray-painted slogans, while at the same time ridiculing the residents' provincial customs and concerns. The conclusions he drew were unequivocal: Such behavior smacked of the same distant, uncaring elitism displayed by the politicians and businessmen they criticized. This was not simply hypocrisy but rather symptomatic of the very mentality on which the activists blamed "wars, ecological disasters, and radioactivity."[109]

Moßmann did not condemn armed resistance or deny his own complicity in what now disturbed him about radical culture. Indeed, his critique of violence came very much from inside, and he held up the same mirror to his own actions that he put before those of his associates. He recounted sitting before a television in May 1972, cheering the RAF's bombing of U.S. military bases, sure of the parallels between Germany's urban guerrillas and the Vietcong. And he recalled how, a few years later, he still argued that the RAF and what he referred to as the "great sit-in" at Wyhl were rooted in the same antiwar movement.[110] Looking back, these recognitions fed his desire to save the left from a series of distinctive blind spots, specifically militant attitudes, undemocratic habits, and elite disinterest in regular people. He insisted that the path was as crucial as the goal. He was not the first to link the ends of social progress and peace to the cultivation of caring, personal interactions along the way. But he was among the first postwar leftists to publically reexamine notions of progressive violence for their destructive and inhumane consequences – and to reject them as a result. This represented a break with the negative alliance, one that Moßmann himself understood as having developed out of (rather than in opposition to) the extraparliamentary left. For if he turned his back on violence and thereby dealt a blow to the victim–enemy dichotomy, his commitment to nonviolence rested on critiques of elitist politics, state power, and militarism common to that milieu. If the left wanted to close the gap between its actions and its politics, it would have to close the gap between itself and the people in whose name it spoke; it would have to confront the implications of its violent fantasies and spend at least as much energy analyzing itself as it did analyzing

[108] Walter Moßmann, "Der lange Marsch von Wyhl nach Anderswo," *Kursbuch* 50 (1977): 1–22; here, 13–14.

[109] Ibid., 16.

[110] Ibid., 12.

the state. In more ways than one, the path envisioned by Moßmann was one of rejuvenation and not departure.

Moßmann's position echoed discussions within the autonomous women's movement, where a similar sense of disillusionment and a gendered understanding of violence opened the doors to its critique. Born of, yet also in open opposition to, the antiauthoritarian student movement of the 1960s, the West German women's movement first gained mass proportions in the summer of 1971, when women from across the FRG joined in protest against the continued criminalization of abortion.[111] In these early years, feminists concentrated on consciousness raising and creating a decentralized, grassroots movement that would counter the repressive hierarchies and delegative politics of modern patriarchy.[112] This loose organizational structure and rising numbers encouraged a plurality of positions, particularly after 1975, when abortion was largely decriminalized and thus no longer served as a cohesive issue.[113] Particularly troubling for early (socialist) feminists and cultural feminists like Alice Schwarzer, who stressed gender's purely constructed nature, this plurality risked the return of "biology as destiny."[114] Increasing numbers of women found difference empowering and embraced the "new femininity" in ways that intentionally and unwittingly mixed essentialist and constructivist understandings of gender distinctions. Regardless of the conflict over the origins and mutability of gender difference, feminists tended to reach the same conclusions regarding violence, namely that it was male and to be condemned as an intrinsic part of the reigning patriarchal system.

[111] Most histories date the movement's birth to the rebellion of female SDS members, especially one woman's hurling of tomatoes at male leaders in West Berlin. For a nuanced discussion of the women's movement's origins, see Gisela Notz, "Die autonomen Frauenbewegungen der Siebzigerjahre: Entstehungsgeschichte – Organisationsformen – politische Konzepte," *Archiv für Sozialgeschichte* 44 (2004): 123–48. For a comparative perspective: Kristina Schulz, *Der lange Atem der Provokation: Die Frauenbewegung in der Bundesrepublik und in Frankreich 1968–1976* (Frankfurt: Campus, 2002).

[112] Maria Mies claims that the feminist movement was first to reject *Stellvertreterpolitik* in the FRG, with the other social movements later following suit. Maria Mies, *Patriarchy and Accumulation on a World Scale: Women in the International Division of Labour*, 2nd ed. (London: Zed Books, 1998), 43n9.

[113] For the history of the movement, see Herrard Schenk, *Die feministische Herausforderung: 150 Jahre Frauenbewegung in Deutschland* (Munich: Beck, 1980); Ilse Lenz, ed., *Die Neue Frauenbewegung in Deutschland: Abschied vom kleinen Unterschied. Eine Quellensammlung* (Wiesbaden: VS-Verlag, 2008). Belinda Davis has shown that many women came to feminism via the 1980s peace movement; a similar phenomenon seems to have emerged a decade earlier as well, enabled by women's strong presence in citizens' initiatives and the movements' common critique of technocratic society. Belinda Davis, "'Women's Strength Against Crazy Male Power:' Gendered Language in the West German Peace Movement of the 1980s," in *Frieden, Gewalt, Geschlecht: Friedens- und Konfliktforschung als Geschlechterforschung*, ed. Jennifer A. Davy (Essen: Klartext, 2005), 244–65; here, 251.

[114] Alice Schwarzer's frustration over these developments is narrated in her ten-year retrospective: *So fing es an! 10 Jahre Frauenbewegung* (Cologne: Emma, 1981).

In a move that precipitated their split from SDS, left feminists insisted that the overthrow of the repressive, capitalist system had to begin at home and in private, with the "internal dictatorship" between men and women, husbands and wives, parents and children.[115] Their emphasis on the private, subjectivity, and women's right to become fully actualized individuals defined second-wave feminism. The attention to domestic production and reproduction as well as women's specific oppression under existing political and socioeconomic structures echoed earlier feminists, however, in as much as they tended to associate women with the rejection of violence. In truth, the average feminist spent little time contemplating the matter of counterviolence, secondary as it was to the more immediate concern of violence against women. Rather than problematized explicitly, nonviolence seems – more often than not – to have been assumed as female, recapitulating the same binary public-private, head-heart, male-female, perpetrator-victim logic for which feminists criticized capitalist patriarchy.[116] Even as they rooted gender differences in social or cultural conditions, which the majority of early feminists did, they tended to discuss the world in dualistic terms whereby women were freed – by dint of their historical and ongoing experiences of violence and repression – of all destructive impulses.[117] Radical- or ecofeminist critiques of patriarchal society, for example, understood violence, whether against women, the environment, or other nations, as the product of a male culture that prized instrumental thinking and was characterized by alienated and exploitative relationships.[118] These women argued that an ecologically sustainable and peace-loving society could only be realized with the thorough feminization of society. By the mid-1970s, matriarchy was thus something of an antidote for everything that threatened not only subjective freedom but humans' very existence.

West German feminists acted as part of a transnational movement, reading translated works, taking inspiration from actions in other countries, and joining women from around the world in staging critical events.[119] Comparatively

115 See Helke Sander's February 1968 essay, "1. versuch: Die richtigen fragen zu finden," reprinted in Lenz, *Neue Frauenbewegung*, 55–9. She expanded on the essay's core premises later that September: idem, "Rede des 'Aktionsrates zur Befreiung der Frauen,'" reprinted in *Autonome Frauen: Schlüsseltexte der Neuen Frauenbewegung seit 1968*, ed. Ann Anders (Frankfurt: Athenäum, 1988), 39–47.

116 Mies, *Patriarchy and Accumulation*, 35. First published in 1986, *Patriarchy and Accumulation* is peppered with insights and observations from Mies's time as an active member of the West Berlin scene in the 1970s and her understanding of feminism as the rejection of all dualistic and hierarchical divisions created by capitalist patriarchy.

117 This is where intent and conscious theory were often at odds with one another, as feminists soundly attacked the dualistic culture – the separation of mind and body, work and home, private and public – associated with modern rational society.

118 A leading example of the ecofeminist critique can be found in Gabrielle Kuby, "Ende der patriarchalen Herrschaft," *Frauenoffensive* 2 (April 1975): 3–13.

119 The 1976 Brussels conference was conceived as an international tribunal on violence against women in response to the United Nations' 1975 "Year of the Woman" campaign. Lenz, ed., *Neue Frauenbewegung*, 286.

speaking, however, the West German women's movement was a late bloomer, and, in the present context, it is worth noting that women first moved to confront the problem of domestic violence and rape in the FRG at the same time violence verged on becoming a national obsession. Though several groups concerned with violence against women appeared in major cities by 1974/75, the first safe house for battered women and their children was not founded until November 1976, in West Berlin.[120] Quickly imitated in other cities across the country, these shelters aimed not only to provide the victims of domestic abuse with much needed support but also to break through the stifling silence that prevailed on the subject.[121] At the same time, women organized telephone hotlines, aggressive information campaigns, and street protests in order to draw attention to the victims and perpetrators of rape. On April 30, 1977, for instance, feminists across the country gave new life and meaning to Walpurgis Night – a festival traditionally given over to the celebration of witches and general revelry – by marching in the FRG's first "take back the night" demonstration.[122] As one participant later commented, in this and other events women publicly gave the lie to the notion that the state monopolized the legitimate use of physical force – exposing how in the privacy of the family and under the cloak of darkness the state still permitted the individual patriarch a certain degree of violence.[123]

Local initiatives and the creation of women-only spaces dominated the movement after 1975 and further encouraged feminists' understanding of violence as specifically male.[124] In their efforts to raise the status of "reproductive work" – the unpaid female labor sustaining patriarchal society and capitalism – a number of feminists emphasized women's singular ability to bear life as a source of power, a move that asserted both women's natures as peace-loving (because life-giving) and reproduction as a fundamental difference between the genders. Pursuing this logic in the national campaign against violence against women, these feminists argued that men were biologically as well as culturally programmed to abuse and rape women.[125] Many feminists

[120] Though the first such shelter was founded in the United States in 1964, both Schenk and Lenz credit the British example and, more specifically, Erin Pizzey, who opened the first woman's refuge in London in 1971. Her 1974 book, *Scream Quietly or the Neighbors Will Hear*, was translated into German in 1976, followed, not long after, by German-language studies on domestic violence. Of particular mention: Sarah Haffner, ed., *Gewalt in der Ehe und was Frauen dagegen tun: Frauenhäuser* (Berlin: Wagenbach, 1976); Erica Fischer, Brigitte Lehmann, and Kathleen Stoffl, *Gewalt gegen Frauen* (Cologne: Kiepenheuer & Witsch, 1977).

[121] Alice Schwarzer judged the success of the campaign based on the fact that even the *Bild-Zeitung* acknowledged domestic violence in a series entitled, "My Husband Hits Me." See Schwarzer, *So fing es an!* 80.

[122] Schenk, *Die feministische Herausforderung*, 99; Schwarzer, *So fing es an!* 82.

[123] Mies, *Patriarchy and Accumulation*, 26–7.

[124] Lenz argues the movement's first phase ended in 1975, with the turn to feminist "projects," the cultivation of specifically female spaces and culture, and a "new femininity" that considerably muddied the line between culture and biology. Lenz, ed., *Neue Frauenbewegung*, 29–32.

[125] Ibid., 29, 180.

staunchly opposed such arguments and instead located sexual violence firmly within the existing social system. In her bestseller, *The "Little Difference" and its Huge Consequences*, Alice Schwarzer blamed the fact that from birth onward men and women were cast as perpetrators and victims and argued, in effect, that both were victimized by the current gender regime.[126] Theoretical differences faded to the background, however, when it came to feminists' concrete efforts to combat domestic and sexual violence. Even if men were victims, women were the "victims of the victims," and feminists were unanimous in the desire to expose their male aggressors and the sexual politics that legitimated violence against women.[127]

With violence coded directly or indirectly as male, feminists could collectively reject it with relatively little difficulty. As with extraparliamentary leftists, however, their opposition to repressive violence did not necessarily lead feminists to identify as pacifists or to actively pursue nonviolence. Indeed, strategy discussions clearly indicated that counterviolence and armed resistance were not off the table for many feminists frustrated by the resilience of patriarchal institutions. According to one woman's analysis, however, they necessarily ranked low on the list due to the fact that overwhelming force was "on the other side."[128] This not uncommon assessment of counterviolence's futility suggests, perhaps, that feminists' distancing of women from violence made even left feminists less prone to the fantasies of successful revolution maintained by their male counterparts. Their autonomous position against traditional socialism certainly gave feminists within the extraparliamentary left the room to explicitly criticize counterviolence as a macho myth.[129] But it did not translate into the dismissal of violence as a potentially liberating form of resistance. Many women activists agreed, for example, with the editor of *Courage*, Sibylle Plogstedt, who criticized Irish feminists for their too docile peace march and carefully equivocated on whether Ulrike Meinhof had erred in taking up arms – admiring her for having defended herself, in contrast to most women.[130] Far from advocating violence, Plogstedt was deeply committed to overcoming its systemic presence. Like other critical leftists at the time, however, it was hard if not impossible for her to imagine doing so without recourse to some form of counterviolence.

[126] Alice Schwarzer, *Der"kleine Unterschied"und seine großen Folgen* (Frankfurt: Fischer, 1975).

[127] Ibid., 178.

[128] Susanne Kahn-Ackermann, "Verschiedene Ebene von Gewalt," *Frauenjahrbuch '76* (Munich: Frauenoffensive, 1976): 179–86; here, 182.

[129] The "Männerbund" and elite mythos promoting violent resistance was one of several reasons Antje Vollmer, the later Green Party politician, gave for her final rejection of political violence. Antje Vollmer, "Die Faszination der Gewalt und die eigene Geschichte," *Links* 9 (1986): 18–20.

[130] Sibylle Plogstedt, "Irland: Frauen, die pfeifen," *Courage* 2 (October 1976): 31–2; idem, "Vom Protest zum Widerstand: Der Tod an Ulrike," *Courage* 0 (June 1976): 22–3; here, 23. *Courage* ran from 1976–84 and was, like *Emma*, a critical organ for West German feminism as a whole.

Ambivalent, to be sure, left feminists were nonetheless discussing the broader implications of violence for the achievement of their goals. After a series of high-profile rape acquittals, for instance, the delegates to the March 1977 National Women's Conference in Munich unanimously concluded that the task of defense and self-protection fell to them.[131] In planning the coming year, however, the matter of "direct actions" was hotly debated, particularly the proposal to publicly "out" the fathers, husbands, boyfriends, and brothers accused of rape by attaching special decals to their cars and homes. Though the majority of women present found the idea "terribly good," a few protested loudly against such an act of social stigmatization. These women objected to the decal action on the grounds that it would incite organized violence, comparable "to the Ku-Klux-Klan, known for taking the law into their own hands and [being] quite violent."[132] As no one, least of all its supporters, understood the decal action itself to be violent, the debate that ensued did not center on the legitimacy of counterviolence per se but rather on the legitimate provocation of violence. A consensus was not reached. But as members of a politically diverse alliance, those extraparliamentary leftists present were pressed to reconsider – if only to better defend – one of the '68er movement's core commitments.

On the pages of *Courage*, the importance of language as well as action to the realization of the movement's long-term goals was raised by the magazine's censorship policies. When the editorial collective refused to allow the word "bulls" (*Bullen*), a derogatory term for police commonly used among leftists, the antinuclear activists who had contributed a piece on their recent demonstration experiences took umbrage. The collective did not back down, and the authors conceded the point, as evidenced by the unfamiliar references to the "blues" scattered throughout their published article.[133] True to the magazine's interest in providing a discussion forum for feminists of various persuasions, however, the editors did not hide the conflict but instead allowed the offended authors a postscript in which to air their grievances and argue for the legitimacy of their original words.[134] The odd use of uniform colors to refer to the police and BGS (the "greens") drew at least momentary attention to activists' language. And, like the proposed decal action, objections to their rhetorical dehumanization of opponents raised questions regarding their own contribution to the very cycle of violence they hoped to break.

If feminism offered a space for the incipient critique of counterviolence, efforts to delegitimate the movement by connecting women's liberation to the rise of international terrorism complicated those same discussions. The

[131] "Vergewaltigung" (workshop on rape and violence at the National Frauenkongreß in Munich, March 5–6, 1977), reprinted in Lenz, *Neue Frauenbewegung*, 299–301.

[132] Ibid., 301.

[133] Vier Berliner Frauen, "In Grohnde," *Courage* 5 (May 1977): 27–9.

[134] Ibid., 29. The open airing of conflicts was normal in *Courage*, which purposely embraced a nonprofessional format and authorship and even designated a regular column covering the debates, conflicts, and dilemmas surrounding its publication.

unprecedented number of women militants was an object of titillating media coverage from the beginning, but female RAF members' open disavowal of feminism and the movement's relative infancy guarded against an initial association.[135] Awash in traditional stereotypes, mainstream and left-leaning media depicted female militants as dependent on their male counterparts – hangers on rather than partners in terrorism.[136] Common were references such as *Bild*'s "Baader Terror-Girls" or *konkret*'s admiration for RAF member Horst Mahler's position as "a Clyde" to "very many Bonnies." The notion that love motivated women to act violently was also widely circulated in articles speculating on love triangles (particularly between Baader, Meinhof, and Ensslin) or in *Quick*'s report on the life of "The Band, Bombs, and Love."[137] As participation in the West German women's movement reached new heights and female criminality began to command the attention of social scientists and governments in the industrialized world, however, new explanations arose blaming the penchant for violence on women's liberation.[138] In pursuit of equality, these women were portrayed as having gone too far, either by adopting mannish characteristics or by seeking "emancipation 'with a gun in the hand.'"[139] It was not the first time such a connection was made. As early as February 1971, when media and officials were still ruminating about the formation of the RAF, Bonn security chief (and future BfV president) Günther Nollau noted that there must be "something irrational" behind the involvement of so many young women, suggesting that "an excess of emancipation" was the cause.[140] But it was not until the escape of four RAF women from prison in 1976 and the murder of Dresdner bank president Jürgen Ponto a year later that Nollau's statement was picked up and widely quoted by supporters and critics alike. The image of female terrorists on the run followed by the news that one of Ponto's assailants, RAF member Susanne Albrecht, was well known to him opened the floodgates to feminism's association with terrorism.

[135] On female RAF members' often hostile relationship to feminism, see Sarah Colvin, *Ulrike Meinhof and West German Terrorism: Language, Violence, and Identity* (New York: Camden House, 2009), 188–224. The Rote Zora, the feminist faction of the Revolutionary Cells, and a few short-lived women-only groups differ in this respect and West German feminists' relationship to them, though not taken up here, is certainly worthy of study.

[136] On the media's portrayal of female violence: Brigitte L. Nacos, "The Portrayal of Female Terrorists in the Media: Similar Framing Patterns in News Coverage of Women in Politics and Terrorism," *Studies in Conflict & Terrorism* 28 (2005): 435–51.

[137] *Der Spiegel* ran an early retrospective on media coverage, particularly the argument that women's dependency explained their violence. See the headline story: "Ausbruch der Frauen: Die Terroristen machen mobil," *Der Spiegel* 29 (July 12, 1976).

[138] An unprecedented level of female criminality was observed and analyzed by sociologists, criminologists, and political scientists in several Western nations, many of whom saw a direct link to female emancipation. See, e.g., psychoanalyst Friedrich Hacker's *Terror, Mythos, Realität, Analyse* (Vienna: Molden, 1973) and U.S. sociologist Freda Adler, *Sisters in Crime: The Rise of the New Female Criminal* (New York: McGraw-Hill, 1975).

[139] "Ausbruch in Berlin," *Der Spiegel* 29 (July 12, 1976), 17–18.

[140] Nollau cited in: "Meinhof/Baader: Löwe los," *Der Spiegel* 9 (February 22, 1971), 26–34; here, 27.

Following the prison break, the *Berliner Tagespresse* provided its readers with a list of characteristics by which to recognize the female terrorist: self-confident, intelligent, aggressive, and, of course, lesbian.[141] At the same time (and in an expanded version a year later), *Der Spiegel* presented the Japanese Red Army's Fusako Shigenobu, Irish Republican Army member Marre Drumm, Leila Khaled of the PFLP, and American heiress Patty Hearst alongside the 2nd of June Movement's Gabriele Kröcher-Tiedemann as evidence that an international movement such as feminism had international terroristic consequences.[142] "Exactly there, where guerrillas are most active, women have the finger on the trigger and they pull it again and again."[143] Far from being weak or male-dependent, then, these women were cold and calculating murderers very much in the driver's seat. In short, they were everything a woman was traditionally *not*, and female violence was unnatural – an aberration brought on by women acting like men or, in sociologist Erwin K. Scheuch's words, like "female supermen."[144] A frequently quoted voice of authority, Scheuch himself asserted that female militants were either lesbians or inclined toward lesbianism and that the women's "leadership and use of guns" could be seen as the "decisive and manifest break with their rejected female selves."[145] That Ponto was killed by a pretty young woman who used her close relationship with the victim to gain access to his home epitomized the perfidy of the crime. West Germans' horror at actual violence was paralleled by a horror around manly and insensitive women (and, by implication, effeminate and emotional men).[146]

Whether they were referred to as "Bonnies," supermen, or cold-hearted seductresses, the portrayals of female militants were all sexist. At their extreme, they implicated every woman who abandoned traditional female roles by arguing, as American criminologist Freda Adler did, that women's violence was the "shady aspect of liberation."[147] Using humor to protest the conflation of feminism with terrorism, the editors of *Courage* parodied the nation's coverage of the prison break with headlines such as "Man-Eaters from Duisburg: 6 New Victims" and "Terror-Girls: Prison Break – Because They Are Lesbians?"[148] Feminists' ability to better protect themselves and female militants from the gendered demonization was, however, hampered by their own disagreement

[141] Cited in "Fahndung nach Frauen," *Courage* 1 (August 1976): 9.

[142] "Ausbruch in Berlin," 17–18 and "Frauen im Untergrund: 'Etwas Irrationales,'" *Der Spiegel* 33 (August 8, 1977), 22–33. The 1977 article was the title story for the cover headline "The Terrorists: Women and Violence."

[143] "Frauen im Untergrund," 23.

[144] Quoted in: ibid., 25.

[145] Erwin K. Scheuch, "Von der Banalität des politischen Terrorismus," *Merkur* 8 (1975): 779–85; here, 781.

[146] On the gendered panic and condemnation surrounding Ponto's murder, see Patricia Melzer, "'Death in the Shape of a Young Girl': Feminist Responses to Media Representations of Women Terrorists During the 'German Autumn' of 1977," *International Feminist Journal of Politics* 11 (March 2009): 35–62.

[147] Adler, *Sisters in Crime*, 13, 15.

[148] *Courage* 1 (August 1976): 9.

over women's relationship to violence. If pacifism seemed to go hand in hand with feminism in the 1980s, we have seen how this was not the perspective of many feminists in the 1970s.[149] A minority at least responded to assertions that women taking up arms was "irrational" by pointing to the quite rational reasons for them to do so – namely the unbearable systemic repression that had not been moved to change by legal means.[150] The question of whether there was something more unnatural about women touting guns than men, moreover, touched a raw nerve among feminists wedded to the fully constructed nature of gender. They refuted portrayals of female terrorists as aberrations just as resolutely as they refuted other feminist's claims that women's life-bearing functions made them nonviolent.[151] In this instance, questioning counterviolence took a backseat to the battle against essentialism. Many more left feminists simply had trouble seeing how women's categorical rejection of political violence would not play into the hands of the movement's enemies. As Susanne von Paczensky described the dilemma that she and others faced at the time:

> When female suspects are persecuted and branded not only for their delinquencies but also as insubordinate women, then this persecution is aimed at me, too, and at my efforts for change.... If the rejection of violence, the horror at a group that wants to destroy itself and our society, is at the same time reinterpreted as a rejection of active women, a renouncement of protest and necessary rage, then this conflict leaves me paralyzed between two solidarities.[152]

Here, as elsewhere, the ideological use of terrorism to arm the established order against anyone who threatened the status quo made the categorical rejection of armed resistance and solidarity with alleged terrorists difficult. Left feminists may have had an easier time starting the conversation on violence, but they were far from done debating the subject.

"The left relates to the question of the guerrilla or, concretely, the RAF, just like a large part of the population related to the Nazi trials. They simply don't want to hear about it any more."[153] This was a comparison clearly meant to provoke, but it was also hard to refute. Terrorism functioned like a virus, ready to infect the efforts of the extraparliamentary left. Still, distancing oneself from the RAF was no simple matter, even for those who openly disavowed their decision to opt for armed resistance. The death of Ulrike Meinhof, found hanged in her prison cell on May 8, 1976, laid bare this fact. Meinhof had always stood apart from her fellow guerrillas, first due to her celebrity status and then as someone to whom many attached a particular moral and intellectual integrity – a purity

[149] For the naturalization of women's activism as nonviolent amidst the peace movement of the 1980s, see Davis, "Women's Strength Against Crazy Male Power."

[150] On this very point: Melzer, "Death in the Shape of a Young Girl," 48–50.

[151] See Alice Schwarzer, "Terroristinnen," *Emma* (October 1977): 5.

[152] Susanne von Paczensky, ed., *Frauen und Terror: Versuche, die Beteiligung von Frauen an Gewalttäten zu erklären* (Reinbek: Rowohlt, 1978), 11–12.

[153] Uncle Tupa, "Texte zur Frage der revolutionären Gegengewalt," *Radikal* 2 (July 1, 1976): 8.

of purpose that separated her from the "desperados" and "female supermen." Sarah Colvin has shown the tremendous effort that went into constructing this image of Meinhof; already before her death, Klaus Rainer Röhl and powerful writers like Stefan Aust and Peter Rühmkorf worked to enhance Meinhof's public reputation – or, as Colvin puts it, "to locate Ulrike Meinhof on the side of the angels."[154] Their success, of course, depended on Meinhof's own journalistic talents and her well-established commitment to social justice. As early as 1958, she had inspired comparisons to Rosa Luxembourg.[155] And precisely because Meinhof's path to armed resistance seemed principled and sympathetic, her death prompted soul searching among many within the extraparliamentary left milieu. Guilt and anger were the sentiments most commonly expressed: guilt for one's own waning solidarity, and anger at the state, which was held, in some way or another, responsible for Meinhof's death. However much leftists may have criticized the RAF and the group's specific acts of violence, Meinhof again made clear that the extraparliamentary left had yet to confront the politics of revolutionary violence that linked it to the guerrillas.

If counterterrorism measures, public attacks on "sympathizers," and repeat clashes with police reinforced solidarity on the left, these same pressures also worked to convince a growing minority that the only way to escape criminalization and isolation was to rethink their relationship to violence in principle. There was no singular path to doing so, but one of the earliest such moves came in direct response to the violence and street riots that followed the news of Meinhof's death. At a conference in Frankfurt, an unidentified Sponti – the as yet unknown Joschka Fischer – expressed genuine horror over the direction the radical left might take if it continued to follow the logic of violence and counterviolence.[156] In their anger over Meinhof's death, he charged, activists had reached the outer bounds of justifiable militant action and now threatened to make the same mistakes as the urban guerrillas – namely to lose sight of the connection between their violent militancy and their political isolation. The fateful decision made by the RAF, for which Fischer criticized it, was the completeness with which it severed negative notions of resistance from the positive need to create a new way of living. Had he stopped there, Fischer's speech would have differed little from Negt's and others before him. But animating his critique of the RAF was a clear refusal to break with it, to denounce its members as "desperados" who had nothing to do with the left. Where others had sought – and, for all intents and purposes, failed – to confront the problem of solidarity by simply denying any relationship between the RAF's violence and the broader agendas of the left, Fischer succeeded by resisting such a move. Instead, he called for solidarity with their comrades underground, all the while

154 Sarah Colvin, "Ulrike Marie Meinhof as Woman and Terrorist: Cultural Discourses of Violence and Virtue," in *Baader-Meinhof Returns*, 83–101; here, 96.

155 Colvin, *Ulrike Meinhof*, 4.

156 Frankfurter Spontis, "Uns treibt der Hunger nach Liebe, Zärtlichkeit und Freiheit..." *links* 8 (1976): 11.

urging his audience to reconsider its conditions. Solidarity, he argued, could not be a one-way street. In the present situation, it demanded that the urban guerrillas put a stop to their "death trip" and their "armed self-isolation," to "put aside their bombs and their stones," and return to a form of resistance that promised life. In this, Fischer managed a critical balance. By affirming the importance of solidarity among the extraparliamentary left, he relieved many extraparliamentary leftists from having to make an all-or-nothing decision at odds with their emotional attachment to the RAF and their sympathy for its members as victims of terrible state repression. He also opened the door for them to refute the legitimacy of counterviolence as resistance without having to distance themselves from the dream of radical change and a more just tomorrow, one they recognized as the RAF's basic motivation as well.

5

The German Autumn, 1977

> Help, now, to decisively deny terror ground! Help, so that our country does not have to become a police state!
>
> Willy Brandt (September 6, 1977)[1]

West German terrorism and counterterrorism escalated dramatically in the year 1977. In retaliation for Meinhof's death and the April sentencing of Baader, Ensslin, and Raspe to life in prison, the RAF launched a series of attacks. Meanwhile, state repression and an intensified hunt for sympathizers produced a terror all their own. Indeed, as each side repeatedly moved to respond to the other, the cycle of violence produced an air of oppression now synonymous with West Germans' experiences of that year and that autumn in particular. Terror and counterterror – violence and counterviolence – reached an abrupt crescendo on the night of October 18. In something approximating a final faceoff, the federal government and the RAF each pushed their defense of democracy to its outer limits, with the former mobilizing armed force and members of the latter taking their own lives. But before these dramatic events, actors of every political persuasion influenced events to the best of their abilities. Conservatives used the newest wave of violence to assert their position as the nation's natural leaders and to attack those policies long associated with state weakness. To be sure, all the doom-and-gloom rhetoric could not hide the glee with which those on the far right greeted the autumn's crisis. Extraparliamentary leftists, meanwhile, sought to combat what more than one contemporary observer described as the McCarthyist political climate produced by politicians' common efforts to "dry up" sources of terrorist sympathy.[2] Their efforts to safeguard civil liberties from an overzealous state were

[1] Willy Brandt's appeal published in *Vorwärts* on September 6, 1977; reprinted the next day in the *Frankfurter Rundschau.*

[2] See, e.g., Peter Weiss, "Joe McCarthy is Alive and Well and Living in West Germany: Terror and Counter-Terror in the Federal Republic," *New York University Journal of International Law and Politics* 9 (1976): 61–88.

seriously inhibited, however, by the continued ambiguities in their relationship to the RAF and other militants. No matter how clear leftists believed their position to be, their vocal defense of publicly offensive antics such as the "Buback Obituary" – whose violent fantasies infuriated many – did little to clarify it to the average West German. Fuel to the flames, it only encouraged the left's association with violence and terrorism. In a sober effort to reverse the situation, a growing number of critical leftists advocated self-critique and thereby helped to move questions of solidarity and progressive violence from the periphery to the center of extraparliamentary discussion. As that autumn heated up, the left thus found itself faced with the task of having to confront the postwar pillars of resistance and militant democracy simultaneously.

Despite significant mobilizations of state power and indications that SPD leaders were increasingly open to measures they had previously ruled out, postwar boundaries they had set on democracy's defense remained in place throughout the spring and summer of 1977. Not until the kidnapping of Hanns-Martin Schleyer and the October hijacking of a Lufthansa airliner did the SPD-led government reach for forces it had previously rejected as illegitimate or too problematic given Germany's fraught history. The SPD had already shown itself willing to employ censorship in its fight against terrorism and the party majority came to support the further suppression of civil liberties with a ban on imprisoned and suspected terrorists' contact to the outside world. In even more of a departure from its traditional stance on state power, the SPD strengthened the executive by freeing it to act without either the approval of parliament or full public disclosure. So empowered, the coalition government pursued a path of non-negotiation and, at the height of the crisis, chose finally to deploy paramilitary force in the form of the GSG-9. Crucial to all this, however, was Social Democrats' ability to distance the new strategies they pursued – to their satisfaction, at least – from authoritarian and militarist traditions. The SPD's internal security program, which simultaneously enhanced and democratized state power, went far toward achieving this, not only by reshaping the police and attendant institutions but also by rhetorically connecting the (social) state with the people. Even as they embraced new levels of coercion, Social Democrats very consciously fashioned an image of democracy around the state they empowered.

THE HUNT FOR SYMPATHIZERS

Both the extraparliamentary left's ability to mobilize international opinion against the FRG and the conflict around nuclear energy were taken by authorities as confirmation that their early concerns regarding the disaffected left had been well warranted. By 1977, members of government displayed palpable resentment for this particular population, and security experts began to lose their previously dispassionate tone. Their mounting frustration was captured in the Interior Ministry's January review of the success, failure, and ongoing potential of its political education program. The document described terrorism as an extreme outgrowth of the so-called sympathizer scene, rather than the other way around, and concluded that it was in fact these "anti-groups" that posed the greatest threat to democracy.[3] According to the report's authors:

> Sympathizers should be viewed ... as the primary pathological symptom, as a group that, for various and certainly not uniform reasons, takes a negative to hostile stance toward the democratic state, *Rechtsstaat*, free order.... They weaken the population's will to resistance and alter – when permitted to do so – the consciousness of the people and, in particular, broad segments of the intellectual elite.[4]

Though security experts cited numerous weaknesses in the way political education had been pursued over the previous five years, they did not question its essential value. On the contrary, their report lent a new urgency to the government's attempts to gain control of a population increasingly understood as the "enemy within."[5]

This same sentiment was expressed by a number of liberal scholars who, once sympathetic to the political left, increasingly entered the public fray in order to defend the existing system from it. By the mid-1970s, for example, political scientist Kurt Sontheimer – who previously supported the student movement against conservative vitriol – joined political scientist Dolf Sternberger, social philosopher Hermann Lübbe, and historian Golo Mann (among others) in criticizing left intellectuals for what they saw as their destructive tendency to throw out the baby with the bathwater. Leftists, the disgruntled liberals complained, dissected the West German system for its deficiencies, without ever acknowledging its achievements.[6] Loyal SPD supporters at the start of the decade, many of them now blamed Social Democrats for contributing to the current crisis. In their unhappy estimation, efforts to democratize West Germany's universities had merely politicized them by making education an obvious means to a political end – in this case, that of progress. For evidence that this "overburdening of politics" was not only socially subversive but, in its tendency to subordinate the present to a utopian future, potentially totalitarian, liberal critics looked no further than the political extremism of the 1970s.[7] Having once protected democracy from Adenauer and a conservative

[3] BMI Circular, "Programm zur Bekämpfung des Terrorismus durch politische Bildung," 1977, Bundesarchiv (Koblenz, hereafter, BA) Bundesministerium des Innern (hereafter, B106): 70996.

[4] Ibid.

[5] The vital nature of political education in preventing further sympathizers was reiterated in that summer's overall program for internal security. See BMI, "Gesamtausbauplan für den Bereich Innere Sicherheit, Hier: Arbeitsgruppe: "Extremismus," July 18, 1977, BA B106: 70996.

[6] See, e.g., Kurt Sontheimer, *Das Elend unserer Intellektuellen: Linke Theorie in der Bundesrepublik* (Hamburg: Hoffmann & Campe, 1976).

[7] Peter Graf Kielmansegg, "Die Überforderung der Politik: Ein Beitrag zur Frage nach dem Verbindlichen heute," *Merkur* 30 (October 1976): 901–10. He was far from alone. See, e.g., Hermann Lübbe, "Freiheit und Terror," *Merkur* 31 (September 1977): 819–29; idem, "Fortschritt als Orientierungsproblem im Spiegel politische Gegenwartssprache," Also, Kurt Sontheimer, "Gewalt und Terror in der Politik," *Neue Rundschau* 1 (1977): 1–12.

resurgence, this group of scholars now felt called upon to secure it from leftist radicals and the SPD's social engineering efforts. They narrowly defined democracy as the liberal order they helped build and, in so doing, embraced the cause of conservatism for the first time.[8]

In the fight against terrorism, these "liberal conservatives" moved to block the very path critical theorists had pursued to create resistance-capable citizens. Kurt Sontheimer famously sparred with Jürgen Habermas over critical theorists' responsibility for left-wing terrorism, but it was Hermann Lübbe who most fully articulated this line of the liberals' defense. Lübbe criticized left theorists not only for failing to achieve their goal but for making Germans even less capable of resistance in the process.[9] By helping to destabilize core values and popular trust in existing institutions, he argued, left intellectuals had deprived the younger generation of the very tools necessary to weather crises and successfully confront antidemocratic forces. "The ability to resist does not [naturally] follow from a critical habitus," Lübbe explained, "but rather from a firmly established identification with that which, if attacked, can then be experienced as worthy of defense."[10] It was an argument that easily complemented the Interior Ministry's assessment of "anti-groups" and sympathizers, the differences between the two being mostly one of emphasis. But when liberal conservatives voiced their fears in the mainstream media, their alarmist rhetoric was closer to that of traditional conservatives than it was to that of the Social-Liberal government. Tilting the lance of militant democracy, the scholars actively demanded strong state action in the fight against extremism and helped to significantly raise West Germans' collective blood pressure while they were at it.

The spring murder of Attorney General Siegfried Buback and the notorious Buback Obituary penned shortly thereafter acted like a match to this tinder of mounting government paranoia and liberal resentment. The immediate context of the murder was the impending conclusion of the Stammheim trial. After nearly two years of courtroom combat, few observers felt justice had been served. The trial's slow and complicated procedures alone were antithetical to the swift ruling and decisive punishment that conservatives understood the state to require, as well as to the humane conditions leftists and many liberals believed were necessary to a fair trial. With the dismissal (and even arrest) of RAF attorneys, the defendants' refusal to recognize the court, the wiretapping of prisoners' cells, and – after some eighty-four attempts – the removal of chief presiding judge Theodor Prinzing, the circus quality of the proceedings was

[8] Arguing this point as well, Dirk Moses describes the neoconservative turn as one of integrationist liberals versus redemptive republicans in a struggle to maintain cultural hegemony in the aftermath of 1968. See A. Dirk Moses, *German Intellectuals and the Nazi Past* (Cambridge: Cambridge University Press, 2007), esp. 201–18.

[9] For more on Lübbe and the "liberal secessionist" core of this unwieldy group, see Jens Hacke's *Philosophie der Bürgerlichkeit: Die liberalkonservative Begründung der Bundesrepublik* (Göttingen: Vandenhoeck & Ruprecht, 2006).

[10] Hermann Lübbe, "Solidarität und Leistung," *Merkur* 32 (February 1978): 120–9; here, 124.

hard to deny.[11] It was also difficult to dispute *Der Spiegel*'s observation that "a fortress with a graduated ring of defense, bulletproofing, and a net on the roof to protect against bombs, is not a courthouse built for acquittals."[12] The Stammheim trial, in short, seemed to raise far more questions than it settled. Was there any possible verdict other than guilty? And if not, what was the point? Was this democratic justice or merely a rationalization for vengeance? On April 28, 1977, Ensslin, Baader, and Raspe were found guilty on four counts of murder, at least thirty attempted murders, and several bombings. None of the defendants were present to hear their sentence of life in prison.

Before the sentence was even delivered, RAF members unleashed a new offensive against the FRG. On April 7, fifty-seven-year-old Siegfried Buback was gunned down by two motorcyclists who pulled up alongside his car at an intersection. His driver and bodyguard were also killed in the torrent of gunfire. The explanation given by the RAF for Buback's "execution" was his role as an "agent of the system." Specifically, the "Commando Ulrike Meinhof" judged him complicit in the proceedings at Stammheim as well as the ostensibly system-induced deaths of Meinhof and Holger Meins.[13] The egregious and unprecedented attack on the state shocked the West German public. Politicians and members of the press immediately compared the violent murder to the 1922 murder of Foreign Minister Walther Rathenau, not only because both victims represented the state but also because of the nearly identical manner in which the men were murdered. If public discourse focused on the specters of Germany's past, members of government found equal cause for alarm in contemporary comparisons – specifically, the 1976 murder of Genoese chief prosecutor Francesco Coco by members of the Red Brigades. One of many violent crimes carried out in Italy against politicians, lawyers, and judges over the course of the 1970s, the murder had successfully stalled legal proceedings against suspected terrorists and all but brought the Italian justice system to its knees.[14] Hans-Jochen Vogel in particular kept the Italian example in mind when assessing the latest developments at home.[15] His statement to Willy Brandt that it had taken some four years "after the first critical appearance" for the Italians

[11] For a detailed legal discussion of the trial, its legality, and how a state of law defends itself against its enemies, see Ulf G. Stuberger, *In der Strafsache gegen Andreas Baader, Ulrike Meinhof, Jan-Carl Raspe, Gudrun Ensslin wegen Mordes u.a.: Dokumente aus dem Prozess* (Frankfurt: Syndikat, 1977).

[12] *Der Spiegel* 19 (May 2, 1977), 35–41. In a similar vein: "Die Materialschlacht," *Der Spiegel* 21 (May 19, 1975), 32–46.

[13] RAF Kommando Ulrike Meinhof, "Erklärung vom 7. April 1977 zur Erschießung des Generalbundesanwalts Buback" reprinted in *Rote Armee Fraktion: Texts und Materialien zur Geschichte der RAF* (Berlin: ID-Verlag, 1997), 267–8.

[14] The violence would culminate with the 1978 kidnapping and assassination of Italian prime minister Aldo Moro. See Leonardo Sciascia, *The Moro Affair* (London: Granta, 2002); Donatella della Porta, *Social Movements, Political Violence and the State: A Comparative Analysis of Italy and Germany* (New York: Cambridge University Press, 1995).

[15] The Foreign Ministry kept Vogel abreast of developments in Italy as they developed throughout the summer and fall of 1977, particularly in regards to new laws passed in August and

to reach their present situation conveyed Vogel's sense that the murder of his attorney general introduced a new and ominous stage to West Germany's own fight against political violence.[16] Determined to prove that terrorism would not usurp the rule of law, the government demanded that the public support their judicial officers and clearly disavow the terrorists and the violence they perpetrated. Those who expressed sympathy for the RAF's political aims or sought to downplay the severity of the group's crimes were not to be tolerated.

One did not have to condone the murder of Siegfried Buback, of course, to have a very different reaction to it and the public outcry it produced. Hermann L. Gremliza, the editor of *konkret* since 1974, commented on the uproar and expressed the thoughts of many extraparliamentary leftists at the time.[17] Making clear his wish that Buback had not been murdered, Gremliza nonetheless defied those who suggested that he – and every West German – should openly mourn his loss. His reasons for doing so rested on the conviction that the existing order was responsible for the recent tragedy as it "first created the atmosphere of violence that made Buback's violent death possible. The first dead person was named Benno Ohnesorg, and Kurras was the name of the shooter, who was acquitted." Gremliza's emphasis on the state as the originator of violence as well as his claim that terrorism was insignificant in comparison to the violent crimes committed near the Frankfurt train station were surely meant to redirect attention away from the fear and fury of the moment to the roots of the problem.[18] But it – and the many responses like it – could only achieve the opposite because it offered no sympathy for the victims – not for Buback and his family and not for a stricken West German public. Indeed, to a general reader (much less one already critical of the left) Gremliza's commentary could only be viewed as a callous dismissal of both Buback's life and the violence that terrorized the country. As such, it was yet more evidence that leftists like him were more foe than friend.

It was the anonymously written article "Buback – An Obituary" and not common expressions like Gremliza's, however, that provoked the full fury of mainstream political commentary and open government repression.[19] Printed in the student-run *Göttinger Nachrichten* and subsequently in university papers across the FRG, the obituary offended many readers with its overblown rhetoric and casual malice. The author, an "urban indian" (*Stadtindianer*) using the pseudonym "Mescalero," half confessed, half declared his unorthodox response to Siegfried Buback's death:

> Balance, stringent argumentation, dialectic, and contradiction – I couldn't care less about any of it. This Buback story caused me to belch quite a bit and these burps should be put

past – apparently ineffective – legislation against terrorism. Archiv der sozialen Demokratie (Bad Godesberg, hereafter, AdsD), Hans-Jochen Vogel Papers 449: Italy/Greece.

16 See, e.g., Hans-Jochen Vogel to Willy Brandt, June 7, 1977, AdsD Hans-Jochen Vogel Papers, Correspondence 3.

17 Hermann L. Gremliza, "Trauer um Buback?" *Konkret* 5 (May 1977): 12.

18 Ibid.

19 Mescalero, "Buback-Ein Nachruf," *Göttinger Nachrichten*, April 27, 1977, 10–12.

down on paper; perhaps they will add a little to public debate. My immediate reaction, my "shock" after the execution of Buback, is quickly described: I couldn't, didn't want to (and still don't want to) deny a clandestine joy.[20]

Mescalero's "clandestine joy" over Buback's death was all the average West German likely read or heard about the text in the ensuing months. Politicians, the mainstream media, and government officials took the obituary as proof that an antidemocratic and nihilistic culture had taken root within universities and the left scene. Even the more sympathetic among them expressed horror at the author's dehumanizing language, unconcealed hate for the existing political system, and affirmation of "joyful" violence; comparisons to early Nazi hoodlumism were widespread if not always explicit. In response, the federal government mobilized to defend democracy by making use of the recently amended criminal codes. It banned the Buback Obituary for abetting terrorism, raided student newspapers and alternative presses to suppress its further publication, and brought up the editor of the *Göttingen Nachrichten* on criminal charges for refusing to divulge the author's identity.[21] The Christian Union once again demanded new counterterrorism legislation, while prominent Christian Democrats like Baden-Württemberg's minister president, Hans Filbinger, also called for the dissolution of universities' state-funded student governments (AStA). Among other things, AStA was responsible for the campus newspapers that first printed and then widely circulated the Buback Obituary. The need to "drain the terrorist swamp" on university campuses became the CDU's excuse to crack down on an organization that had long used its podiums and pages to attack the state and conservative politicians in particular.

Ironically, had the mainstream political public not attacked the Buback Obituary with such ferocity, the RAF would have had to.[22] For, if read in its entirety and not merely mined for its provocative rhetoric, the obituary was in fact an explicit statement against the RAF and its use of political murder in the fight against the state. The author described how his initial affirmative reaction to the murder of Buback eventually gave way to open critique, not of the state or of Buback but rather of his own scene's willingness to condone and even to use violence.[23] Though it was lost on the majority of West Germans, who did not engage the text beyond its initial offense, the obituary can be read as a working through of violent fantasies that ends by rejecting political murder. Mescalero admitted that he, "like so many of us," admired the "armed fighters" for doing what he only daydreamed about doing. But as he went on to imagine what his life would be like if he lived underground and planned actions such

[20] Ibid., 10.

[21] For a critical assessment of events, see Peter Brückner, *Die Mescalero-Affäre: Ein Lehrstück für Aufklärung und politische Kultur* (Hannover: Internationalismus, 1978).

[22] Dany Cohn-Bendit, interview with the author, Frankfurt, November 25, 2002.

[23] There are a number of extensive literary analyses of the text. Among them: Sabine von Dirke, *"All Power to the Imagination!" West German Counterculture from the Student Movement to the Greens* (Lincoln: University of Nebraska, 1997), 95–103.

as the murder of Siegfried Buback, appreciation turned into sober reflection. Mescalero concluded that no one had the right to decide whether someone lived or died, or who was guiltier than whom. Such thinking led to a society of terror and repression and was therefore antithetical to the political goals and ethics of radical left opposition. The author's language, his cynicism, and his avowed search for a "happy" practice of "force/militancy" (*Gewalt/Militanz*) – a form of violence he defined only insofar as it was "blessed by the masses" and distinctly different from the violence of the establishment – opened the door to all kinds of questions and obscured his critique.[24] But when all was said and done, Mescalero denied both state and citizen the right to take a life – no matter how well grounded in social theory or moral tradition.

The underground and leftist literature of the 1970s had never wanted for discussions of political violence, but the novelty of the Buback Obituary was immediately attested to by prominent members of the left community. Erich Fried, a poet and frequent social commentator, for example, countered mainstream fury by declaring the Mescalero text "one of the most significant documents of the present-day German left against political murder."[25] While the state mobilized the powers of militant democracy, extraparliamentary leftists reached for resistance in its mildest form – namely civil disobedience – to defend Mescalero and combat that very mobilization of state power. In July, forty-three professors and teachers from across the country joined forces to publish the (now) illegal obituary.[26] They did not comment on the text itself, but, like Gremliza, sought to draw West Germans into a critical examination of the social and political conditions for present-day violence. It was to facilitate this overdue discussion, the professors stated, that they reprinted the Buback Obituary – along with Rosa Luxembourg's 1905 essay on "Terror," select newspaper articles, and other public statements against the demonization of AStAs and student culture more generally. Though doubtless sincere, the chosen texts and lack of commentary on Buback's murder and the unorthodox obituary demonstrated again the limited nature of leftists' own discussion of violence. The professors certainly got a response but not the one they had hoped.[27]

[24] Mescalero, "Buback-Ein Nachruf," 12.

[25] Erich Fried, "Zur Veröffentlichung des 'Mescalero'-Textes 'Buback-Ein Nachruf,'" *Das da* 9 (1977). Fried's own response to Buback's murder displayed a give-and-take dynamic similar to that of Mescalero, speaking out against political murder while simultaneously describing Buback as a "piece of flesh" guilty of being human – both lovable and hateful. It ended on the thought that it would perhaps have been best had Buback never been born. Erich Fried, "Auf den Tod des Generalbundesanwalt Siegfried Buback," *Diskus* (April 10, 1977).

[26] "*Buback-Ein Nachruf*": *Eine Dokumentation* (Berlin, 1977), Außerparlamentarische Opposition Archiv (Freie Universität Berlin, hereafter, APO-Archiv), Mescalero Affair. See also: "Gemeinsame Erklärung der Berliner Herausgeber der Dokumentation 'Buback-Ein Nachruf'" (Berlin, August 15, 1977).

[27] In an interview with *Der Spiegel*, three Bremen professors involved in the republication admitted that they had misjudged its reception. See "Nur Anstandsregeln verletzt? Bremer Professoren Preuß, Kneiper und Heide Gerstenberg über ihre 'Mescalero'-Aktion und die Gewalt," *Der Spiegel* 34 (August 15, 1977), 26–31.

Despite the solidarity and even praise Mescalero received, the obituary was not particularly remarkable as a statement against political violence, and it is doubtful that anyone on the left would have defended it as such, had the mainstream political public ignored it. It was this demonstration of support, however, that had repercussions for the extraparliamentary left, for it pushed public outrage to even greater heights and forced political violence from the periphery to the center of debate within the left. This did not occur because the obituary's republication had the desired effect but rather for quite the opposite reason: it served to distract from conversations that might have taken shape around the subject of violence and counterviolence in the FRG. Most notoriously, the professors – as civil servants appointed and paid by their Länder governments – breathed new life into the otherwise stale crusade against radicals' infiltration of state institutions. Left-wing Social Democrat Peter Glotz – who also had the distinction of being West Berlin's minister of education – denounced the professors' republication of the obituary and openly questioned why those who considered West Germany so devoid of democratic legitimacy would want to stay in its employ.[28] Convinced that one in five West German youth felt as Mescalero did toward the existing system, Glotz concluded that open debate on the subject was the only way to combat their tacit opposition.[29] Toward this end, he initiated – with admittedly limited success – a public dialogue with the Berlin professors involved in the "Mescalero Affair."[30] Things looked much different in Lower Saxony, where the article was first published and from whence a large number of its supporters came. There, Glotz's ministerial equivalent, Christian Democrat Eduard Pestel, showed no such interest in facilitating communication between the two warring sides. In a letter to the local newspapers, Pestel instead declared that "a state which tolerates such as these, a state which keeps paying high sums to such 'state servants' rather than fire them, might as well take a long walk off a short pier!"[31] He demanded that all professors distance themselves from the author of the Buback Obituary and sign a written declaration of their loyalty to the state and its constitution.[32]

[28] Peter Glotz, "Offener Brief," *Die Welt*, July 9, 1977.

[29] "'Jeder fünfte denkt etwa so wie Mescalero,'" *Der Spiegel* 41 (October 3, 1977), 49–63; here, 53. He announced this before the Berlin parliament on August 25, 1977.

[30] Glotz's original letter was reprinted alongside a response from Claus Offe in the *Frankfurter Rundschau*, July 30, 1977, 14, (hereafter, *FR*). Glotz followed up with another letter on August 3: "Schlampig gedacht und im Ergebnis katastrophal," *FR*, August 9, 1977, 9. He also released another on August 19, this time in response to a letter written by Berlin college professors to him. Both letters were printed in *FR*, August 27, 1977.

[31] Wissenschaftsminister Eduard Pestel, "Offener Brief," *Deutsche Nachrichten*, July 22, 1977.

[32] The form issued by the Lower Saxon Ministry of Education read as follows:

> In connection with the investigations of the Lower Saxon state government concerning the publication of the documentation "Buback – An Obituary" I declare:
>
> I reject murder or kidnapping or any use of violence in our liberal democratic constitutional state under any condition. Therefore I condemn terrorist actions and all attempts that justify them.
>
> I know that I, as an official, have a special duty of allegiance toward the state. This duty of allegiance requires more than a cool, internally distant attitude toward the state and the

The most immediate result of all this was to turn the Mescalero text overnight into a symbol of the extraparliamentary left's fight against the Decree against Radicals and the government's counterterrorism policies more generally. Almost as quickly, Peter Brückner, whose career as a resister began in the Third Reich, became the campaign's poster boy. As the author of several exceptional nonfiction works attempting to grapple with the left's relationship to the RAF and to political violence on the whole, Brückner was no stranger to state surveillance and persecution under the "occupational ban."[33] A professor of psychology at the University of Hanover since 1967, he had been suspended from teaching in 1972 under suspicions that he had sheltered Ulrike Meinhof. Now, in addition to being an editor of the reissued Mescalero text, Brückner defied the authorities by openly refusing to sign Pestel's pledge of loyalty.[34] He was suspended once again, this time indefinitely as his case bounced around courts and disciplinary committees – and became a magnet for the pent-up outrage of conservatives and radical leftists alike.[35] Brückner was exemplary, but not alone. On besieged university and college campuses, the most oft-floated thesis was that the Mescalero article was being used as a pretext to eliminate leftist elements within the student body and the faculty.[36] Here, too, the conviction that the Buback Obituary had led to still further unjustifiable repression kept the left's attention focused on the state and away from difficult self-examinations and the actual victims of terrorism.[37] By late summer, the gulf separating the extraparliamentary left and the government in the fight to protect German democracy had never been wider.

constitution; it requires particularly that the official distance themselves explicitly from groups and tendencies that attack, combat, and defame this state, its constitutional authorities, and the effective constitutional order. I will comply with my political duty of allegiance. This duty of allegiance has to prove of value particularly in times of crisis and in serious conflicts, in which the state is dependent on the official taking sides with the state.

I distance myself in due form from the author and the content of the so-called Buback Obituary.

Reprinted in *Sozialistischer Hochschullehrer Bremen* (Bremen, 1977). International Institute for Social History, (Amsterdam, hereafter, IISG) 1 P Js 676/77.

33 E.g., Peter Brückner and Barbara Sichtermann, *Gewalt und Solidarität: Zur Ermordung Ulrich Schmückers durch Genossen. Dokumente und Analysen* (Berlin: Wagenbach, 1974); Peter Brückner, *Ulrike Meinhof und die deutschen Verhältnisse* (Berlin: Wagenbach, 1976).

34 Peter Brückner, "'Nein:' Eine Begründung. Kritik der Pestel-Erklärung" and "Warum ich die Erklärung nicht unterschrieben habe," *Diskus* 4/5 (October 25, 1977): 10–11.

35 He was not reinstated until 1981, shortly before his death the following year.

36 See, e.g., SB-Hochschulegruppe Göttingen, *links* 90 (July–August 1977), IISG ID-Archiv Bro 604/6 fol.

37 Typical of student engagement was a Darmstadt documentation of the events surrounding Buback's murder. The students did not waste much time discussing their position or the Mescalero article, which they dismissed as one of the "many idiocies" found in AStA publications. Instead, the Darmstadters focused on what they called the state's "singular concentration" on the murder. Far from warranted, they argued, it was part of a general ploy to distract the West German public away from the everyday violence that the oppositional left worked to reveal. See AStA/Technische-Hochschule-Darmstadt, *Dokumentation: Buback und seine Folgen* (Darmstadt: AStA 1977), IISG ID-Archiv Bro 604/6 fol.

Leftist accounts of the German Autumn often begin with the "Mescalero Affair," as the start of a crisis – characterized by blanket intolerance and the left's isolation – that lasted months not weeks. For a small but vocal minority, however, the Buback Obituary was first and foremost a study in political folly. They blamed their fellow leftists for alienating the broader public with incomprehensible actions and internalist dialogue as well as for inadvertently empowering the state – for contributing, in other words, to the current intolerable situation. For this reason, members of the "undogmatic" left in Frankfurt's Socialist Bureau refused to support either Mescalero or his defenders and instead seized upon the entire affair as an opportunity to take collective aim at the extraparliamentary left's present course. Out of a self-professed desire to reestablish the left once again as a trusted force against social injustice and state oppression, Socialist Bureau members such as Detlev Claussen, Helmut Gollwitzer, and Wolf-Dieter Narr censured its blind solidarity and illusions about legitimate violence. Claussen, in particular, criticized the victim–perpetrator schema that continued to mobilize leftists behind the kind of "political stupidity" exhibited in the Buback Obituary by underscoring its lack of progressive political content: "Solidarity at any price, only to demonstrate one's own radicalness, fetishizes a unity that we all know is not to be had. What unifies us cannot be opposition alone."[38] Instead of focusing on the oppressor, Claussen argued, the left needed to reorient itself to the interests and goals of the larger, oppressed population. Only in this way might the extraparliamentary left once again find a properly socialist program and, with it, genuine solidarity.

Wolf-Dieter Narr argued along similar lines in addressing what he claimed was the potentially fatal absence of self-critique on the left.[39] It was not enough, he asserted, to let acts of opposition stand alone and unexamined, for doing so ultimately undermined the left's ability to act on its own terms. The Buback Obituary offered a perfect example. As Narr described it, the left had, first, naïvely discounted public reaction to the text and, then, in a panic and solely because "the ruling groups banded together against" the Mescalero obituary, exerted formidable pressure on its members to defend something that was, to his mind, indefensible. If the left was to take control – to chart a course of thoughtful opposition – they needed to actively (not reactively) engage problems. Seconding Claussen, Narr urged the left to "justify itself with its own actions and positions, not legitimate itself according to the negative standards set by the rulers' reactions and by reactionaries."[40] In short, a positive and self-reflective politics was the solution to the left's current conundrum. For only this would free the left to take an unambiguous position against violence and

[38] Detlev Claussen, "Solidarität oder Distanzierung: Falsche Alternative," *links* 40 (July–August 1977): 40.

[39] Wolf-Dieter Narr, "Diese Gesellschaft ist keine pädagogische Provinz: Zur Kritik und Selbstkritik der Linken am Beispiel des 'Buback-Nachrufs,'" *links* 43 (October 1977): 18–20.

[40] Ibid., 20.

terrorism while at the same time allowing – even demanding – solidarity where and when it was needed most.

If Narr and Claussen focused on the once and future politics of left solidarity, Helmut Gollwitzer did what perhaps only he could as a member of the oppositional Confessing Church under the Third Reich and, more recently, a close friend to Dutschke and former pastor to Meinhof. The theologian openly attacked the notion that the left's humanitarian commitments required solidarity for the RAF.[41] In an unrelenting run through of the RAF's crimes, Gollwitzer sought to force members of the extraparliamentary left to judge the RAF on its own actions and not those of the state. The group's demonstrated contempt for humanity proved to the radical minister, at least, that the "self-appointed 'guerilleros'" were "allies and tools of reaction," not socialism. The left's continued gestures of solidarity with the RAF – as political prisoners and victims of state repression – were symptoms of self-delusion, he argued, not humaneness. A collective statement issued later that autumn underscored the Socialist Bureau's position that there was no middle ground. Socialism and terrorism were diametric opposites and those who "contemplated terrorist methods in a playful and tactical way" discredited socialist politics.[42] The members were not insensitive to the left's fears – quite the opposite – but they nonetheless insisted that "despair concerning the conditions of this society cannot make us doubt the very search for [society's] humanization. This is why we reject terror with the same radicalism as we challenge authoritarian, repressive, and police methods."[43] The Socialist Bureau, in short, opened a two-front struggle against terror, declaring the inhumane and violent strategies of the far left just as abhorrent and retrogressive as the state violence they professed to fight. And the first step toward realigning left practice with its humanitarian goals was for this group of undogmatic leftists to unambiguously deny the legitimacy of counterviolence as resistance.

Alternative papers within the anarchist and Sponti scene such as the West Berlin *Radikal* – a descendant of *Agit 883* – and the Frankfurt weekly *Pflasterstrand*, also signaled a new interest in confronting radicals' relationship to West Germany's urban guerrillas. *Pflasterstrand*, in particular, committed itself to opening up a space for self-critique, a soul searching sympathetic to the Socialist Bureau's position even if it was too subjective and tinged with lingering solidarity for their taste. The impetus came in part from developments internal to the scene. Joschka Fischer's speech from the previous autumn, as well as his follow-up article in *Autonomie*, were printed and reprinted in radical journals and functioned as a touchstone for a broader critical engagement.[44] But just as this discussion was touched off by the summer's violent

41 Helmut Gollwitzer, "Gegen falsche Solidarisierung," *links* 40 (July/August 1977): 39.

42 "Sozialismus und Terrorismus: Stellungnahme des Arbeitsausschusses des Sozialistischen Büros," *links* 41 (September 1977).

43 Ibid., 2.

44 Joschka Fischer, "Verstoß in 'primitivere' Zeiten: Befreiung und Militanz," *Autonomie* (February 1977): 52–5.

riots, subsequent events were also influential. In particular, conflicts within the antinuclear movement and the murder of Siegfried Buback made members of the scene feel increasingly like pawns in a politics not of their making.[45] The desire to reestablish a standpoint clearly independent of the militants' was palpable. For the editorial board of the *Pflasterstrand* and its readership in the Frankfurt Sponti scene, a crucial break in the emotional push-and-pull cycle of solidarity with armed resistance came in May, with the public renunciation of revolutionary violence by Red Cells member Hans-Jochen Klein.[46] In a letter to *Der Spiegel*, Klein made known his desire to leave a life of resistance that he had come to see as "almost fascist" at its core.[47] Providing novel – and for many, indisputable – insight "from within," the repentant guerrilla detailed the group's single-minded, cynical, and wholly intolerant pursuit of its ends. It was, he now recognized, a politics and way of life antithetical to the just and humane world for which he originally fought. The moral corruptness and sheer "insanity" of the guerrillas' "revolutionary politics" had reached intolerable heights when, according to Klein, the RZ initiated plans to murder the leaders of the West Berlin and Frankfurt Jewish communities for their supposed advocacy of Zionist imperialism.[48] By sending his letter to the mainstream press, Klein hoped to prevent the two deaths. But he insisted he was no traitor, simply returning to sanity: "I have hardly changed from Saul to Paul. But from Saul to once again being a sensible, politically thinking and acting person."[49]

Klein's insider experience and his exposure of RZ plans to turn the anti-imperialist fight against West German Jews did more than rob armed struggle of romance or heroism. His tale implicated extraparliamentary leftists by pointing a finger at their own cynical weighing of human lives and help rationalizing the death of innocents with the argument of counterviolence. Rather than shrink from Hans-Jochen Klein's criticisms, the editors of *Pflasterstrand* publicly embraced them and the repentant urban guerrilla – in order to repent themselves. "Klein-Klein is a comrade whom many of us know and who shares with us a common history. [His] is the history of Frankfurt's left-radical

[45] One essayist covered the full gamut of resentments and common critiques while exploring the "fully unclear" character of his solidarity with the urban guerrillas. Anonymous, "Solidarität," *Pflasterstrand* 8 (April 20–May 3, 1977), 20.

[46] This was the same Hans-Jochen Klein with whom Klaus Traube had briefly come into contact earlier in the decade. See Chapter 4.

[47] First printed in *Der Spiegel* 20 (May 9, 1977), *Pflasterstrand* reprinted Klein's letter in its entirety shortly thereafter. See "Brief von Jochen Klein," *Pflasterstrand* 10 (May 18–31, 1977), 20–1.

[48] Of the urban guerrillas, the RZ maintained the closest contacts with Palestinian militants. Some of the cells participated in PFLP attacks on Israeli targets, and the RZ's biggest actions were cooperative missions. The 1976 Entebbe hijacking in particular – in which Jews were separated from the other passengers, evoking, for many observers, Nazi practice – inescapably raised questions about latent antisemitism in the anti-imperialist politics of West Germany's new left. On this particularly dark chapter of West German militancy, see Wolfgang Kraushaar, *Die Bombe im Jüdischen Gemeindehaus* (Hamburg: Hamburger Ed., 2005).

[49] "Brief von Jochen Klein," 21.

movement."[50] The anticipated objection that airing Klein's experiences was counterrevolutionary – a response to his having "deeply disturb[ed] the left's internal solidarity taboo" and opened it to self-critique – was soundly refuted by the editors. They instead presented their paper as a forum with the assertion that Klein had set in motion "an incredibly important process.... It is distressing that it took the statement issued by Klein-Klein to push us finally to declare what we have thought and assumed for some time. Now, however, we will very decidedly not remain silent."[51] Touting the slogan, "only the dead remain silent," the editors joined other members of the Frankfurt scene to protest their previous failure to speak out and to prove that, from then on, their politics would be dictated by neither the state nor the urban guerrillas.

The pages of the alternative and underground press demonstrated the stark black-and-white terms in which the Frankfurters' decision to distance themselves from violence and terrorism was interpreted by significant swaths of the extraparliamentary left. For those who saw themselves as part of a broader radical movement and agreed that the "criminalization, political isolation, and finally liquidation of the most militant part of revolutionary movements" was a common establishment strategy to destroy the left as a whole, nothing less than full solidarity for the RAF and other guerrillas was acceptable.[52] Those leftists who publicly disavowed the Buback Obituary, criticized the imprisoned terrorists, or rejected the legitimacy of violent resistance were attacked as supporters of the state and enemies of the left. Some argued (not for the first time) that the very question of whether violence was justifiable was misplaced. In an editorial entitled "SB – Penitents on Pilgrimage to Godesberg?" the daily *Arbeiterkampf* – produced by the Hamburg-based Communist League – accused the Socialist Bureau of "turning Social Democrat" and mocked it for its professional tone and misreadings of Marx. The only time Marx "distanced himself from terrorism," the editors instructed, was in opposition to structural "violence that was, in theory, 'cowardly, concealed, deceitful' and, in practice, 'brutal contemptible, mean.' In both instances [violence was] completely without honor."[53] The violence of the left, by implication, was everything that the violence of the bourgeois state was not, namely honorable and legitimate. The communists were adamant that to distance oneself from violent protest, from terrorism, from the fantasies of the Buback Obituary – or to encourage others to do so, as the Socialist Bureau had done – was nothing short of counterrevolutionary.

[50] Editors, "Nur Tote schweigen," *Pflasterstrand* 10 (May 18–31, 1977), 22.

[51] Ibid.

[52] From a 1972 interview of Wolf Biermann reprinted in *Über die Produktion von Terror – Urteilen!* (Bochum: Rote Hilfe Bochum, n.d.), 96.

[53] Editors, "SB – Reuige Sünder auf Wallfahrt nach Godesberg?" *Arbeiterkampf*, October 17, 1977, 8. For a less bombastic argument along these lines, see Elmer Altvater, "Komitee zur Verteidigung der demokratischen Grundrechte," *Radikal* 2 (July 1976): 10. A reprint of Altvater's speech at the West Berlin Technical University on May 20, 1976; he, too, argued for a definition of violence and terrorism as an exclusively right-wing, conservative phenomenon.

The perspectives of those extraparliamentary leftists who had long disdained theoretical battles were more directly influenced by the urban guerrillas and, as a result, decidedly shriller in tone. The RZ, for example, responded to the *Pflasterstrand*'s criticism with a letter of its own. It attacked the Spontis for the hypocrisy of their swift and unjustified withdrawal of support and their unwillingness to "confront them as human beings" or "understand the political content or logic" of the urban guerrilla.

HJK's letter is the so-called "evidence" for the dirt that these left-wingers emit in order to avoid the conceptual debate on armed resistance as well as a debate with us, with themselves, about the fear inherent in this system.... The respective contributions made to this paper from "Krankfurt" ["sick city"] bear witness, sentence for sentence, to the self-deception, the colonized brain, the disturbed memories of past experiences (with themselves, with us, with HJK), to the planned destruction of the urban guerrilla, to the bull mentality wherein HJK acts as the means of their psychological and practical warfare against us.[54]

Pulling on the analytic tropes – and heartstrings – of the extraparliamentary left, the RZ hoped to reestablish its legitimacy and turn leftist criticism back onto Klein and the Frankfurter Spontis. Demonstrating how high it believed the stakes to be, the RZ ended its barrage using the most powerful weapon in its arsenal. It accused Klein, the *Pflasterstrand*, and all other disloyal leftists of attempting "to end resistance" in Germany.[55]

The RZ's criticism of the *Pflasterstrand* and those loyal to it was, by nature, exceptional. The earnestness with which the latter's editorial board and readers engaged the former's critique, however, established the parameters for discussions of violence and solidarity in the FRG. True to its word, the *Pflasterstrand* facilitated an ongoing conversation with and on the urban guerrillas as well as on the left's loyalties to them by printing the RZ's letter and all subsequent communications.[56] The personal histories and common cause that tied critics and defenders together generated a highly internalist, emotionally charged discourse. Here, as in the theoretical debate, the critique of violent resistance inspired rabid personal attacks on those distancing themselves from their leftist comrades and too often drowned out substantive dialogue on violence. But by autumn, the left had become painfully aware of the obstacles to social change thrown up by its romance with revolutionary violence and its refusal to confront the RAF's violence as violence (rather than as counterviolence or bad strategy). The consequences of such a course – the threat to the goals of the antinuclear movement, the increasing ease with which all activists were

[54] Revolutionäre Zellen, "Zum Brief von Hans Joachim Klein: 'Die Hund bellen, und die Karawane zieht weiter,'" May 24, 1977. Printed in *Pflasterstrand* 11 (June 2–15, 1977), 26–7.

[55] Ibid.

[56] The issues in which they published Klein and the RZ's original letters were devoted largely to this discussion. The RZ letter, for example, was printed under the heading "Armed Leftists...a couple of essays for discussion." Topics taken up were: solidarity, armed struggle, urban guerrillas, revolution, myths, and resistance – "for and against." Ibid.

criminalized, and the repressive effect of solidarity with the RAF – pushed growing numbers of extraparliamentary leftists to question resistance as they had conceived and practiced it.

Not without some irony, just as they began to articulate an effective critique of terrorism and political violence as a whole, their words were all but lost to the greater public. True to the lessons Walter Moßmann took from antinuclear demonstrations and the Socialist Bureau from the Buback Obituary, the left had effectively isolated itself from the population. Its insular and jargon-laden language, inattention to what preoccupied (and terrorized) those outside its circles, and constant infighting silenced it when the state's efforts to do so may have failed. In the terrorist crisis of the German Autumn, the extraparliamentary left found itself powerless to break through its isolation and thus unable to combat the new levels of fear and intolerance displayed by the West German state and public alike.

THE GERMAN AUTUMN

In early August, Hans-Jochen Vogel wrote historian Karl Dietrich Bracher to ask for reading recommendations.[57] West Germany's minister of justice wanted to learn more about universities and high schools in the Weimar Republic between the years 1928 and 1932 when, in his own recollection, the Nazis first came to dominate the institutions. In particular, Vogel hoped to discover whether "there was a comparable relationship to political murder, say to the Potempa murder" – the final act in the SA terror campaign of August 1932 – as that demonstrated in "the wake of the so-called Buback Obituary."[58] Far from dismissing Vogel's line of inquiry as paranoid or alarmist, Bracher was sympathetic to the other man's fears and voiced his strong support for the minister's efforts to control rampant extremism.[59] As he provided the requested bibliographic help, Bracher noted with grave concern the number of similarities he, too, saw between the political cultures of the late Weimar Republic and the 1970s. Where previously he had perceived right-wing radicals to pose the greatest threat to liberal democracy, his knowledge of history and politics

[57] Hans-Jochen Vogel to Karl D. Bracher, August 4, 1977, AdsD Hans-Jochen Vogel Papers, Correspondence 3. Bracher is the author of numerous works on the Weimar Republic, Third Reich, and twentieth-century politics. If there is a thread that runs through his work, it is the problem of democracy's preservation in light of its inherent weaknesses. Karl Dietrich Bracher, *Die Auflösung der Weimarer Republik: Eine Studie zum Problem des Machtverfalls in der Demokratie* (Stuttgart: Ring, 1955).

[58] In addition to researching developments on the colleges, Vogel also researched the "President's Decree against Political Terror and the Extension of the Death Penalty (August 9, 1932)" and the "Government Decree for the Creation of Special Courts, Presidential Decree for the Protection of Domestic Peace, and Presidential Decree against Political Riots (June 14, 1932)." AdsD Hans-Jochen Vogel Papers 449.

[59] Karl Dietrich Bracher to Hans-Jochen Vogel, September 15, 1977, AdsD Hans-Jochen Vogel Papers, Correspondence 3.

now convinced him – like Sontheimer and the other anxious liberals – that the radical impulses of an extraparliamentary left were the far graver danger.[60]

Despite the seriousness with which the ruling few (and their intellectual interlocutors) interpreted the present in light of the past, government members still did not revise their approach to democracy's defense. In the aftermath of Buback's death, Schmidt, Vogel, and other government officials did signal a new willingness to consider measures they had previously blocked.[61] And each subsequent attack – most notably the July assassination of Dresdner Bank president Jürgen Ponto – won such measures additional supporters (Figure 5.1). But roundtable discussions indicate that, as late as August, the chancellor's cabinet members and fellow party leaders refused to implement major changes to existing counterterrorism policy. Rather than "risk alienating the core constituency of the SPD and FDP, as new laws and other 'strong-arming tactics' would," they once again chose to emphasize counterterrorism's dependence on a uniform legal code and improved police technologies.[62] On August 31, Interior Minister Werner Maihofer introduced a massive DM950 million domestic security program that remained fully in line with the course laid down in 1969. In addition to a unified computer system, the bill called for five thousand new security positions and the introduction of, among other things, forgery-proof license plates and new traffic controls. As cabinet members anticipated, the proposed security bill did not meet with significant resistance from within the ruling parties. Länder authorities and members of the Christian Union, however, made their displeasure known and moved to block the release of funds.[63]

It was the RAF kidnapping of Hanns-Martin Schleyer in Cologne just five days later that encouraged many to rethink their position – on federal police powers and other counterterrorism practices as well. Once Bonn was informed and the chancellor briefed on the bloody events in Cologne, federal officials moved to contain the crisis by assuming direct control of the criminal

[60] Bracher took particular aim at the expansive fascism theory of the new left as opposed to which he pleaded for "totalitarianism" as a category. See, e.g., Karl Dietrich Bracher, *Zeitgeschichtliche Kontroversen: Um Faschismus, Totalitarismus, Demokratie* (Munich: Piper, 1976); idem, *Zeit der Ideologien: Eine Geschichte politischen Denkens im 20. Jahrhundert* (Stuttgart: DVA, 1982).

[61] E.g., "Erklärung der Bundesregierung zur inneren Sicherheit und zur Terrorismusbekämpfung am 20.4.1977," *Verhandlungen des deutschen Bundestages: Stenographische Berichte* (hereafter, *Verhandlungen*), VIII. Bundestag, 22. Sitzung (Bonn, 1977), 1444–9.

[62] Kanzlerbüro, "2. Sicherheitsgespräch beim Herrn Bundeskanzler: Überlegungen für eine offensive Taktik," August 16, 1977, AdsD Helmut Schmidt Papers 10014.

[63] Herold followed up the announcement at a special joint meeting of the Bundestag's interior and justice committees, with a report that used the frustrated search for Ponto's killers as evidence for the ongoing need for cooperation and technological uniformity between the federal and state levels. "Verstärkter Kampf gegen Terrorismus mit mehr Personal bei Sicherheitsbehörden," *Süddeutsche Zeitung*, September 1, 1977, 1; (hereafter, *SZ*). "Herold beklagt Fahndungspannen," *SZ*, September 2, 1977, 2; "Die Innenminister beraten die Terrorismus-Bekämpfung," *Frankfurter Allgemeine Zeitung*, September 3, 1977 (hereafter, *FAZ*).

FIGURE 5.1. On July 30, 1977, Dresdner Bank Chairman Jürgen Ponto was murdered by members of the RAF in his home outside Frankfurt. Here, around three thousand mourners march through the city of Frankfurt to show solidarity for the victim and demand the state put an end to the violence. The far-off banner asks: "How Many More Must Die?" (dpa).

investigations already under way and any future hostage negotiations. Within hours, Vogel and Maihofer joined State Minister Hans-Jürgen Wischnewski and North Rhine-Westphalia's interior minister, Burkhard Hirsch, at the scene of the crime (Figure 5.2). With Hirsch's consent, the GSG-9 was ordered to Cologne later that same evening.[64] Back in Bonn, Horst Herold took control of all police and constitutional protection measures relating to Schleyer's rescue, as the newly appointed head of a centralized command center hastily set up in the Chancellor's Office as events unfolded.[65] One of the security chief's first acts was to confirm each Land's success in implementing "full control" over traffic, borders, and possible escape routes (by auto, train, and air), as well as search and surveillance operations targeting those persons identified as suspects or

[64] Burkhard Hirsch, "Erklärung zu den am 5. September in Köln Geschehenen," November 2, 1977, BA Bundesministerium der Justiz (Hereafer, B141): 85348.

[65] Werner Maihofer, "fernschreiben an alle länderinnenminister und -senatoren; schleyer," September 6, 1977, BA B106: 107327; ÖS 9/MR Dr. Bochmann, "Befugnisse der Zentralen Einsatzleitung," October 5, 1977, BA B106: 106647; Smoydzin, "Betr.: Struktur einer Fahndungs-Einsatzzentrale beim Bundeskriminalamt," September 13, 1977, BA B106: 106690

FIGURE 5.2. On September 5, 1977, the RAF ambushed industrialist Hanns-Martin Schleyer near his Cologne apartment. Killed in the blaze of gunfire were Schleyer's chauffeur, Heinz Marcisz, and the three men following in the car behind: his bodyguard, Reinhold Brändle, and police officers Roland Pieler and Helmut Ulmer (ap).

sympathizers.[66] At 9:30 P.M., Helmut Schmidt addressed the country in a televised speech that emphasized calm determination and the strength of democratic solidarity. Terrorism, he explained, had no chance of triumphing, "for it is not simply the will of the state that stands against it. Against terrorism stands the will of the entire nation." The chancellor tied the fate of West Germans to the fate of the state, adamant that an attack on the FRG was tantamount to an attack on every citizen. What was needed now – Schmidt's one request – was everyone's active support for the police in their current search and for "state institutions, in all possible situations."[67] Not far away, in Stammheim prison, Baader, Ensslin, and Raspe were among the few West Germans not glued to their televisions. Though each had been privy to the initial reports coming out of Cologne, by prime time all three inmates had had their radio and television sets confiscated and were in the middle of having their cells turned upside down for evidence on Schleyer's whereabouts.[68]

[66] Horst Herold, "fernschreiben an alle im, alle lka, bonn bmi, koeln bfv: entfuehrung schleyer; hier: masznahmen zur umsetzung des ak roem. 2-beschlusses vom 21.2.1975," September 8, 1977, BA B106: 106647.

[67] "Erklärung des Bundeskanzlers am 5. September 1977 nach der Entführung Schleyers" reprinted in *Dokumentation der Bundesregierung zur Entführung von Hanns Martin Schleyer* (Augsburg: Goldman Sachbuch, 1977), 229–30.

[68] Stefan Aust, *Baader-Meinhof: The Inside Story of the RAF*, trans. Anthea Bell (New York: Oxford University Press, 2009), 311–12.

From the moment events in Cologne became public, conservatives of every persuasion went to great lengths to demonstrate just how unimpressed they were by Schmidt's call for solidarity or his government's display of leadership. One of these was Golo Mann, a one-time speechwriter for Willy Brandt who demonstrated the particular vehemence with which liberal conservatives called for state action. Mann mocked officials for continuing to talk of "cool heads," the need to exhaust "all existing means," and a "moral" confrontation with terrorism. These were, he implied, the weak weapons of an all too weak government. "The murder bandits' – or no! the 'suspected terrorists' – newest ... atrocity makes clear for justice and politics what should have already been and must now be clear: we are in a state of emergency. We find ourselves in a savage and thoroughly new type of civil war."[69] That which security experts and government officials had studiously denied the RAF and other armed militants – namely recognition as enemy combatants – Mann happily accorded them.[70] And he was far from alone in doing so. Indeed, after September 5, there was "a proper boom" in war metaphors used to describe the terrorist attacks and their threat to the FRG.[71] Ever the shadow chancellor, Helmut Kohl preempted Schmidt's public address by thirty minutes in order to demand aggressive action. The Christian Democrat announced that the day's events "proved once again" that a "trigger-happy band of murderers" had declared war "on our people and civilization, and free democracy as we choose to call it and live it." Explicit in his critique of government inaction, Kohl insisted that every West German grasp that it was "five minutes to midnight" – long past time to use all available powers of state so as to "finally end this unbearable threat to our domestic freedom."[72] As he put it a few days later: "in the fight against terrorism there can no longer be any taboos."[73]

By suggesting that the current state's struggle to contain terrorism was nothing less than a fight for democracy's survival, this type of rhetoric played to Germans' historical fears and, indisputably, made good media copy.[74] It also conveyed conservatives' uncalculated conviction that current conditions were exceptional and thus warranted the kind of state force normally reserved for times of war. A week after Schleyer was taken hostage, the CDU's general

69 Golo Mann, "Quo usque tandem?" *Die Welt*, September 7, 1977.

70 This was not the first time Mann spoke of terrorism in terms of war. In a television interview shortly after Buback's murder, he compared the "war in the FRG" with that between Britain and the IRA. For excerpts: "Dokument zum Tage: Wenn gesetze nicht ausreichen, müssen sie geändert werden," *Union-in-Deutschland* 16 (April 21, 1977).

71 Andreas Musloff, "Bürgerkriegs-Szenarios und ihre Folgen: Die Terrorismusdebatte in der Bundesrepublik, 1970–1993" in *Die RAF und der linke Terrorismus* vol.2, ed. Wolfgang Kraushaar (Hamburg: Hamburger Ed., 2006), 1180.

72 *Dokumentation der Bundesregierung*, 19.

73 "Kohl: Bei der Terrorismus-Bekämpfung darf es kein mehr Tabu geben," *Die Welt*, September 15, 1977.

74 A case in point: *Die Welt* asked other experts to weigh in on Mann's thesis, thus guaranteeing its repetition and more sales. *Die Welt*, September 13, 1977. For an unsolicited response to Mann, see Erich Böhme, "Mann, o Mann," *Der Spiegel* 31 (September 12, 1977), 18.

secretary publicly proposed mobilizing the West German army against the terrorists.[75] And Alfred Dregger and Franz-Josef Strauß grabbed headlines (once again) by proposing to bring the "people's war" to the urban guerrillas who waged it. They suggested this could be achieved with capital punishment (a move that the CSU argued would prevent future hostage takings) and an "antiterrorist *Jagdkommando*" whose sole purpose would be to hunt down the terrorist "vermin." In order to secure Schleyer's release, they further intimated that imprisoned RAF members, too, could be shot.[76] All this operated on the simple but absolute assertion of two opposed groupings: "us" and "them," friend and enemy. And, in case West Germans were confused as to just where the lines should be drawn, the CDU published a "black book" of quotations offering evidence of prominent Social Democrats and public intellectuals' terrorist sympathies.[77]

For its part, the mainstream media commonly portrayed the newest hostage situation as a moment when the government had to regain control of the state's monopoly on violence – or risk history repeating itself. The history to be avoided was, of course, democracy's destruction. But what was not entirely clear to West Germans – judging by the number of editorials and media exposés raising the specters of both Weimar's end and Nazi authoritarianism – was whether the terror of the RAF or a relapse into the police state would cast the decisive blow. Officials cursed the media for helping to ensure that "apprehension and distrust of state agents is more deeply entrenched in the heads of many than the fear of terrorism."[78] And yet, Social Democrats' own internal dialogue suggests that the uncertainty was not entirely of the media's making. If conservatives interpreted the threat as essentially one-sided (the government could, of course, be weak or traitorous but this did not change the fact that terrorists were the enemy), members of the ruling party did not. Even the most conservative of them continued to perceive a dual threat, in no small part because they commonly interpreted the ultimate threat posed by terrorism to

[75] "Geissler will Terror mit der Bundeswehr kämpfen," *FR*, September 16, 1977.

[76] On the measures called for by Strauss and Dregger as reported on by the popular media, see: J. H. Darchinger, "Pflege des Zusammenhalts," *Die Zeit*, September 23, 1977; "Fall Schleyer: 'Die Dramatik muß raus,'" *Der Spiegel* 39 (September 19, 1977), 21–4; DLF, transcript of interview with Alfred Dregger, "Zum Terrorismus Bekämpfung," September 13, 1977, 06:20, Archiv für Christlich-Demokratische Politik (Sankt Augustin, hereafter, ACDP), Pressearchiv Schleyer S 7e. Government members feared the popularity of the death penalty enough to devote considerable time to drawing up legal arguments against it. See, e.g., Hans-Jochen Vogel's formal response: "Die Tödesstrafe – ein Irrweg" *Bulletin* 105 (1977): 958–62 and in *Recht* 52 (September 20, 1977).

[77] *Terrorismus in der Bundesrepublik Deutschland – Eine Auswahl von Zitaten* (Bonn: CDU-Bundesgeschäftsstelle, September 1977).

[78] The government's ongoing battle with the media is well documented in the archives of the BfV, BMI, and BMJ. Here: BfV to BMI, "Betr.: Bekämpfung des Terrorismus, hier: Mitarbeiter Presse," June 13, 1977, AdsD Hans-Jochen Vogel Papers 449: Behandlungen des Terrorismusproblem in den Medien.

be that of a right-wing fascist resurgence. Not long after Schleyer's kidnapping, for example, the party presidium released the following statement:

> The terrorist murderers are not incorrectly described as the late children of Hitler. If given the chance, they would renew fascism among us with their guns. Our young democracy ... is clearly supposed to be pushed to destroy much of what we have built of a democratic, liberal, and social constitutional state. This we must not allow.[79]

It seemed little had changed in the past thirty years. In this newest attack on the FRG, Social Democrats understood their party as the critical buffer against the antidemocratic extremism to both its left and right.

In an address countering recent conservative attacks, Helmut Schmidt referenced the influx of letters that he, the BKA, and various other state agencies had received from angry citizens either willing to take law and order into their own hands or demanding vengeance from the state.[80] Countering the emotional calls for action – and perhaps to spite Golo Mann – the chancellor once again insisted on the "cool head" he and his government would maintain toward terrorists *and* toward those who advocated measures incompatible with the rule of law:

> Many citizens believe that the constitutional state [*Rechtsstaat*] is simply too weak. That the state must strike back with draconian measures. I take these concerns very seriously.... And nevertheless I say with a cool head: the *Rechtstaat* is an indispensable good. Even if the individual citizen does not regularly think to appreciate its merits and therefore can easily entertain dispensing with "a little *Rechtsstaat*," all historical experience teaches: that path ends in lunacy.[81]

Hans-Jochen Vogel wrote Mann personally to express his particular displeasure over the latter's hyperbolic rhetoric. He argued that Mann's description of the current situation as a state of war played directly into the hands of the RAF – for whom "nothing would be more welcome than to be recognized as an army" – and was unduly sensationalist. This last particularly concerned him: the justice minister explained to Mann that it was especially important for the German people, "whose nerves are not the best for a number of reasons," to be given the "correct dimensions of the problem."[82] With this, Vogel reiterated the reason the SPD government had made the Center for Political Education a key component of its counterterrorism program. Though they were not above raising specters, Schmidt and his cabinet demonstrated their continued com-

[79] SPD, "Kommunique über die Sitzung des SPD-Präsidiums am 13. 9. 1977," AdsD Helmut Schmidt Papers 9445.

[80] "Erklärung der Bundesregierung zum Terrorismus, 15.9.1977," *Bulletin* 86 (September 16, 1977): 805–8. Helmut Schmidt's correspondence housed in Bad Godesberg as well as BKA and BMI files at the federal archive in Koblenz substantiate the number and troubling nature of letters received after September 5.

[81] Ibid.

[82] Hans-Jochen Vogel to Golo Mann, September 19, 1977, AdsD Hans-Jochen Vogel Papers, Correspondence 15.

mitment to balanced and informed dialogue. Instead of picking up the rhetoric of war, they heavily favored a discourse of democratic solidarity.

While officials continued their attempts to convince citizens that they were partners in the struggle to contain both terror and state overreaction, the "solidarity of democrats" was institutionalized in the immediate reconstitution of the grand advisory committee. Whereas Kohl and Strauß as well as Bundestag president Karl Carstens had pointedly declined past invitations to discuss internal security with the chancellor and his security experts, they could not refuse to join that autumn's crisis management team.[83] Though Helmut Schmidt personally orchestrated the state response, the advisory committee was charged with making all emergency decisions. When, in the midst of the autumn's hostage situation, police chief Manfred Schreiber questioned the government's use of the crisis staff, Schmidt explained its value in pragmatic terms: "If each of the state's leaders and party heads is personally bound to all operations, party-colored squabbling does not occur as much or in its full degree."[84] Here, the target was the kind of political irresponsibility Carlo Schmid once connected to Weimar's collapse, namely politicians' penchant for feuding obstinately rather than resolving problems. Theoretically, at least, the nonpartisan crisis staff absolved one party from having to accept full responsibility for life and death decisions; the state, relieved of paralyzing party politics, could then present its citizens – and its terrorist opponents – with a united democratic front. Still, the symbolic importance of the crisis staff was paramount. One of the legal experts in the room summarized the key point: "proof must be given that our free basic order is stronger than a strong man. All decisions must be subordinated to this postulate."[85]

To be sure, the rhetoric of solidarity that the government employed was not as warm and cuddly as the SPD pretended. Schmidt's preference for making decisions without the consultation of party leaders and self-styling as a "chancellor above parties" was well established. Indeed, it was this that endeared him to voters and in many ways won the 1974 election for the SPD even as it greatly strained internal party relations.[86] The government, too, divided up the population and promoted new levels of intolerance by defining not only the terrorists but also alleged sympathizers as outside of and at odds with the

[83] See, e.g., Helmut Kohl and Franz Josef Strauß's responses to an invitation to attend a talk on internal security and terrorism in the Chancellor's Bungalow on April 26, 1977 found in BA Bundeskanzleramt (hereafter, B136): 31610. Speaking to his fellow party members a month earlier, Kohl was blunt: He was not willing to join a "Krisenstab" to help the government out of its acute difficulties. CDU/CSU Bundesvorstandssitzung, March 21, 1977, ACDP 07–001–979.

[84] "Niederschrift über ein Gespräch des BKs mit Sicherheitsexperten in Kanzlerbungalow," September 13, 1977, BA B136: 31610.

[85] Former interior minister and retired CSU representative Hermann Höcherl voiced this typically SPD position on executive power at the same time as he called for strong, decisive action in response to the public's desire for "strong leadership" even in particularly difficult cases. Ibid.

[86] For more on Schmidt and tensions within the party, see Gerard Braunthal, *The German Social Democrats Since 1969: A Party in Power and Opposition*, 2nd ed. (Boulder: Westview, 1994), 100–1, 245–6, 290–3.

democratic community of citizens. And the refusal to declare an official state of emergency – an act that would have fanned fears and given legitimacy to conservatives and urban guerrillas alike – meant that the crisis staff was constitutionally undefined.[87] In 1975, the grand advisory committee served mainly to open up communication between the federal and Länder governments and provide the chancellor with cross-party backing. In 1977, it effectively became the ruling body of the nation for nearly six weeks. With each party represented and the relevant Länder spoken for, the need to consult the legislature on matters of national importance was circumvented. Decision-making powers were concentrated in the hands of the executive.

The first decision to confront members of the newly assembled grand advisory committee was, indeed, a matter of life and death. One day after the incidents in Cologne, the "Commando Siegfried Hausner" made the terms of Schleyer's ransom known. In exchange for Schleyer's safe return, the RAF demanded the release of ten of its imprisoned members – including leaders Ensslin, Baader, and Raspe – as well as media coverage, money, and safe passage out of the FRG. The communiqué also repeated the kidnappers' threat from the night before, which promised Schleyer's death if the nationwide police search were not called off. The crisis staff's first order of duty, then, was to decide whether or not the West German state would concede to the demands. In the case of Peter Lorenz, the majority had agreed that giving in to the terrorists' demands was a necessary evil; the constitutional commitment to human dignity required protecting the hostage's life even at the state's expense. When the grand advisory committee met late on September 6, 1977, however, its members were of a different mind. Within an hour and a half, they agreed to orient all future decisions around three goals: to free Schleyer alive; to arrest and try the kidnappers; and to avoid endangering either the state's ability to act or its domestic and international credibility. This last, the committee openly acknowledged, meant not allowing the state to be pressured into freeing prisoners.[88] Negotiating for Schleyer's life was off the table from the very beginning.

In the years since the Lorenz kidnapping, two developments occurred to explain the crisis staff's newest decision. A U.S. government report by Secretary of State Henry Kissinger on Bonn's handling of the Lorenz case found the FRG "too precipitate in immediately yielding to all [terrorist] demands." Endorsing the opposite approach, he asserted that experience showed that "the use of imaginative delaying tactics" caused kidnappers "to become more and more concerned with their own safety and less and less preoccupied with their

[87] Though reminiscent of the joint committee (*Gemeinsamer Ausschuß*), the crisis staff violated the separation of executive and legislative powers it was intended to protect in times of crisis. Adopted in accordance with international security standards, the crisis management team is a great example of the failure to reconcile European and domestic law – and the SPD's continued reticence to confront a state of emergency via extraordinary legislation.

[88] *Dokumentation der Bundesregierung*, 26–8.

political objectives."[89] Though not without its risks, such an approach was clearly seen as preferable to West Germans' continued willingness to negotiate with terrorists. When the RAF seized the Stockholm embassy in April 1975 and demanded the release of twenty-six imprisoned terrorists, this, then, was the strategy the Social-Liberal government pursued. Whether because of pressure from the American and British governments, the fact that the location of the hostages was known, or the negative fallout after Lorenz's release, the assembled crisis staff voted unanimously against negotiations.[90] Whatever the reasons, the decision greatly simplified things in Stockholm by bringing the FRG in line with the Swedish government's own policy of non-negotiation. Unintentionally, the RAF members helped Schmidt's government assume this new position by murdering two of their twelve hostages. The murders squared the government's new hard line with the state's duty to protect life by confirming that the release of the RAF's hard core from prison would lead to the deaths of more innocent West German citizens.[91]

The events in Stockholm did more than solidify the government's new position on hostage negotiations, however; they also prompted Schmidt to advocate strenuously for antiterrorism legislation at the international level. In July 1976, the FRG requested that the United Nations Security Council establish international standards for counterterrorism. Though this met with little immediate success, a similar proposal within the framework of the Council of Europe did. Due in large part to West German prodding, the European Convention on the Suppression of Terrorism was adopted by the Council on November 10, 1976.[92] If read against the SPD's general approach to militant democracy, the government's sudden interest in international antiterrorism laws (legislation it refused to support domestically) can be seen to have achieved two goals. It further legitimated the government's policy of non-negotiation by establishing the practice as an international legal standard. At the same time, it protected against rash and undemocratic action in the heat of future crisis by, once again, submitting counterterrorism measures to the scrutiny of West Germany's international peers.

89 Secretary of State Washington, DC to American Embassy, Bonn et al., March 1975, Margaret P. Grafeld Declassified/Released U.S. Department of State.

90 One interesting case made *for* negotiations emphasized the hostages' position as civil servants to essentially argue that the flipside of having to declare loyalty to the state was the state's heightened responsibility to protect them. Internal communication from BMJ to AL IV, April 25, 1975, AdsD Hans-Jochen Vogel Papers 523. On international pressure: Stephen M. Sobieck, "Democratic Responses to International Terrorism in Germany," in *The Deadly Sin of Terrorism: Its Effects on Democracy and Civil Liberty in Six Countries*, ed. David Charters (Westpoint, CT: Greenwood, 1994), esp. 55.

91 "Regierungserklärung, 25. April 1975," 11782. The chancellor explicitly noted that the "core RAF members" were responsible for at least nine deaths and more than 100 injuries.

92 For an overview of West German efforts to combat international terrorism, see Miklos Radvanyi, *Anti-Terrorist Legislation in the Federal Republic of Germany* (Washington, DC: Library of Congress Law, 1979), 89–104.

The kidnapping of Hanns-Martin Schleyer was the first incident to test Bonn's new resolve on German soil. Over the weeks that followed, Schmidt's inner circle of advisers discussed a wide range of alternatives only to dismiss them in favor of the course originally agreed upon by the crisis staff. The policy of non-negotiation received support from intelligence information confirming that the five prisoners released in exchange for Lorenz had all returned to the FRG and each had been involved in further acts of violence.[93] Verena Becker, for example, helped plan the murder of Siegfried Buback, while less than a year after her release Gabriele Kröcher-Tiedemann participated in the attack on OPEC's Viennese headquarters. The crisis staff also conveyed the conviction – undoubtedly encouraged by Horst Herold – that, given enough time, police could find and rescue Schleyer. Thus, despite the threat of retribution, the BKA continued its manhunt while government officials pursued Kissinger's "imaginative delaying tactics." Swiss lawyer Denis Payot was chosen to mediate between the commando and the West German government in what became a series of ultimatums and missed deadlines, with the government alternately insisting on more time, blaming the kidnappers for responding too late, and repeatedly demanding evidence – personal letters, photos, and video recordings – that Hanns-Martin Schleyer was still alive (Figure 5.3). To buy the government even more time, those prisoners named for release were surveyed as to their preferred escape destination. State Minister Wischnewski then spent weeks flying to and from South Yemen, Iraq, and Vietnam in order to verify whether or not the countries were amenable to accepting the militants.[94] The fact that they were not only worked to the government's advantage.

All of this relied on word not reaching the kidnappers as to the government's true intentions. To facilitate its chosen course of action, therefore, Schmidt's government placed several restrictions on the media. At the formal request of government press secretary Klaus Bölling, members of the West German press agreed to limit coverage of the Schleyer affair and to refuse the RAF access to print space or air time.[95] These constraints sought to prevent the media from inadvertently jeopardizing the state's efforts to locate Schleyer while depriving terrorists of the publicity they required to successfully pressure the state. Presented by Bölling as a regrettable but necessary expedient, the restrictions

[93] AL II, "Betr.: Entführung von H. M. Schleyer," September 5, 1977, BA B141: 85348. This information was emphasized in the Ministry of Justice's legal weighing of the state's obligations to hostages, whose arguments against negotiations far outnumbered those in favor.

[94] These negotiations and Wischnewski's travels are documented in the government's account of events: *Dokumentation der Bundesregierung*, esp. 88–9, 92, 97, 99, 105, 107, 111. More detailed versions can be found in "Dokumentation der Schleyer Entführung," BA B106: 107119.

[95] "Schreiben des Regierungssprechers an Chefreakteure vom 8. September 1977, mit der Bitte um zurückhaltende Berichterstattung," "Appell des Deutschen Presserates vom 8. September 1977," both reprinted in *Dokumentation der Bundesregierung*, 236–8. The coalition government originally sought to establish parliamentary control over media coverage pertaining to terrorism but efforts toward this end were thwarted by the CDU/CSU.

FIGURE 5.3. Government authorities entered into negotiations with RAF Commando Siegfried Hausner in the hopes of buying police enough time to find Hanns-Martin Schleyer. The risks involved in such a strategy increased dramatically when members of the PFLP (Commando Martyr Halimeh) hijacked a Lufthansa airliner on October 13, in solidarity with the RAF and its demands (dpa).

went beyond the acknowledged curtailment of press freedom.[96] It empowered the crisis staff to act without public disclosure – a fact that did not go unremarked upon. Not two weeks into the search for Schleyer, the *Süddeutsche Zeitung*'s Klaus Dreher sharply questioned how an unconstitutional body such as the crisis staff could possibly have the right to refuse to negotiate with the Bundestag and the West German people.[97] To this and criticism coming from his own party, Schmidt responded with the assertion that if critics had the security information he and his advisers possessed, there would be no question that their actions were warranted. In an address to the SPD, the chancellor explicitly

[96] As noted, there is a large literature on the media and the particular dilemma it poses to democratic governments during terrorist crises. For more on this particular case, see Andreas Elter's study *Propaganda der Tat: Die RAF und die Medien* (Frankfurt: Suhrkamp, 2008).

[97] Klaus Dreher, "Eine Institution, die keine Statuten kennt," *SZ*, September 17, 1977.

requested his fellow party members' trust and promised to fully divulge suppressed information and minutes of staff meetings once the crisis ended.[98]

Not that Schmidt and members of his cabinet understood all media coverage to be bad. Indeed, in the days immediately following Schleyer's kidnapping, newspaper reports on the hurdles encountered by the police investigation did much to convince the public and conservative politicians of the need for the government's proposed security program. Topping the list of problems was "Nadis," the information and communication system maintained by the West German secret service, which bogged police down with incomplete data and missing cross-references. Already something of a public joke, Nadis took a fatal hit with the kidnapping investigation. The newspaper *Die Welt* obtained precise information on the crime scene before the police did, as its computer network demonstrated clear superiority over that used by local investigators.[99] Slow, unclear information about the exact crime scene and the perpetrators delayed and impaired police activity in those vital first minutes.[100] In a litany of failure, every mainstream daily described in detail how police ignorance allowed the criminals to escape without any kind of chase. A lack of police communication and coordination, many pointed out, could win the war for the terrorists.[101] It was, in short, a coup for security experts and modernizers. In the words of FDP deputy chairman Wolfgang Mischnick, Schleyer's kidnapping crystalized the need to place "federalist prestige behind the goal of optimal police work."[102]

As days passed without any knowledge of Schleyer's whereabouts, however, it became less clear whether better police intelligence could act as more than a preventative force against terrorism. As one commentator put it, the hard truth of the matter was that all the computer technology and tools of criminal investigation were of no use without the help of Kommisar Zufall – "Commissioner Chance."[103] The new search techniques also shaped the FRG's

[98] Following the crisis, Schmidt once again promised that the forthcoming documentation of events would "at the very least make clear for members of the SPD why we had to ask for a demonstration of trust and how we came to be willing to ask for such a thing." "Diskussionsbeitrag von Bundeskanzler Helmut Schmidt in der Sitzung der SPD-Bundestagsfraktion," October 25, 1977, AdsD Helmut Schmidt Papers 10018.

[99] "'Eigentlich müßte jeder verdächtig sein:' Das Dilemma der Terroristen-Fahndung," *Der Spiegel* 38 (September 12, 1977), 22–33; here, 27.

[100] Not only was there a significant lag in time before police arrived at the scene, a half hour passed before a dragnet was ordered, another passed before airport security was alerted, and it took nearly the full hour for officers to confirm that they were dealing with a kidnapping. All the while, nearby Autobahn entrances were never closed.

[101] E.g., "Schwarze Stunde," *FZ*, September 5, 1977, 1; "Schwächen der Fahndung in den ersten Stunden," *FR*, September 8, 1977, 3; Michael Wesener, "Am Tatort: 300 Patronenhülsen," *Die Zeit*, September 9, 1977, 4.

[102] Wolfgang Mischnick quoted in *FR*, September 7, 1977, 4; Karl-Heinz Kumm, "Nach Köln gab es keinen Widerspruch mehr," *FR*, September 15, 1977, 3.

[103] "Auch die ausgefeilteste Kriminaltechnik braucht den Zufall," *FAZ*, September 8, 1977; Hans Schueler, "Ratlose Fahnder hoffen auf den Zufall," *Die Zeit*, September 9, 1977, 3.

image ever more in the mold of the police state that terrorists and leftist critics accused it of being. Headlines such as "Police Checks Become the Rule" and photographs of police inspecting automobiles on major roads reflected the tangible impact Schleyer's kidnapping had on West Germans' everyday lives.[104] Commuters and weekday travelers listening to their radios on the morning of September 6 were warned of traffic jams resulting from police controls. Stopping traffic at alternating checkpoints throughout the FRG, police officers examined drivers' licenses and personal identification cards, comparing them to computer data on the suspected terrorists.[105] Allusions to George Orwell's *1984* were made by *Der Spiegel* in an article on new measures proposed jointly by Maihofer and the Länder interior ministers. The technology behind "Action Red Light" would allow police to change all traffic lights to red with the push of a button and effectively freeze traffic within a fifty-kilometer radius of a terrorist attack. In its dramatization of the newest technique in car chases, the magazine unfolded a scene wherein the state's controlling hand constrained the population by way of various science fiction-like technologies.[106] Media and crime experts alike viewed such an attempt at "full control" as bordering on the absurd. As another article pointed out, if the 1,003 traffic lights in West Berlin were simultaneously changed to red, it would take somewhere between three and four months for police to check every car.[107] Though the very use of the phrase "full control" could not help but conjure up fascist attempts at "total" control, the *Spiegel* article is an excellent example of how – not unlike its extraparliamentary counterparts – the media's references to the Nazi past were increasingly tangled in nightmares of a future technological dystopia.

Even if the new police technologies startled citizens, their mobilization and continued innovation was the sort of counterterrorism one had come to expect from Social Democrats in government. The same cannot be said of the SPD's overwhelming support for new antiterrorism legislation. In its advocacy of the 1977 Contact Ban Law (*Kontaktsperregesetz*) the party charted a new – and, for many of its supporters, distressing – course. The Contact Ban was unprecedented in a number of ways. With unparalleled conviction and efficiency, the Bundestag took only three days to lay the finished bill on the table for the final signature of Federal President Walter Scheel. The new law empowered the minister of justice and his colleagues in the Länder to bar all contact between prisoners and the world outside their cells. Most significantly, this suppression of rights applied to visitation with defense attorneys and all written

[104] Hans-Jürgen Bidermann, "Polizeikontrollenwerden die Regel," *FR*, September 7, 1977, 15.

[105] Harry Koch, "Fahndung auch im Münchner Raum," *SZ*, September 7, 1977, 17; Christian Schütze, "Wirklich kein Polizeistaat," *SZ*, September 9, 1977, 17; "Autofahrer wissen, wo es blitzt," *FR*, October 5, 1977, 16.

[106] "Ran an die Kästen," *Der Spiegel* 42 (October 10, 1977), 25–7.

[107] Volkmor Hoffmann, "Nach einen Anschlag sämtliche Amplen auf Rot?" *FR*, October 9, 1977, 2. Also: Carl-Christian Kaiser, "Den Mördern keine Chance lassen," *Die Zeit*, October 28, 1977, 4.

communications as well.[108] The condition established for the ban's enactment was a strong belief that the prisoner posed a "present danger to life, limb, or liberty." It could only be issued by a Land government or the federal justice minister and required an affirming judicial decree within two weeks, or it expired. Nothing in the law, however, prevented the ban's continual renewal.[109]

Though the parliament's debate on the law was extremely brief – taking barely more than a day's time – it culminated years of agonizing over whether and where to draw the line between prisoners' rights and the state's prerogative of self-defense. Earlier, criminal procedure had been amended in order to curtail suspects' ability to disrupt court proceedings, but the state had never figured out how to legally prevent defense attorneys from cooperating with their clients. Lawyers for suspected terrorists, it is true, found many ways to raise the state's hackles, including their unending attempts to defend their clients as political prisoners rather than criminals. But above all, the attorneys' key role in moving information between imprisoned terrorists and the outside world was considered most detrimental to state security and to the government's public image. When the Christian Union first proposed to legalize the monitoring of written and oral communication between attorneys and their clients in 1974, however, the SPD argued that such legislation and the suppression of civil liberties it entailed were not only ineffective means of counterterrorism but also undemocratic. With the help of the FDP, Social Democrats successfully killed the bill.

Their position provoked conservatives' strong criticism and caused friction between the Ministry of Interior and other government ministries. For the terrorist crises of 1975 demonstrated that its officials were considerably more willing than others to tread on civil liberties. In addition to the invasion of Klaus Traube's home, the interior minister authorized the secret wiretapping of suspected criminals in "nonresidential" cells and in conversation with their lawyers.[110] When word of the prisoners' treatment reached Hans-Jochen Vogel, the minister of justice wrote Werner Maihofer personally to express his "surprise" over the latter's position that such actions were permissible without a court order or the knowledge of those under surveillance. He described his "considerable legal concerns" against such a view and demanded that the two ministers meet as soon as possible to discuss the matter.[111] The cells' uninterrupted surveillance suggests that little came of the meeting. Perhaps Vogel himself ceased to object. Evidence collected on Stockholm proved that a number of RAF attorneys were more than communication conduits and public

108 Sobieck, "Responses to Terrorism," 55.

109 Radvanyi, *Anti-Terrorist Legislation*, 82.

110 News of the Stammheim tapings came out shortly before the trial's end, in March 1977. Baden-Württemberg's interior minister Karl Schiess (CDU) and justice minister Traugott Bender (CDU) admitted that bugs were installed with the aid of the BfV and BND and the full knowledge of the Chancellor's Office. See "Abhör-Affäre: Die Koalition schlingert,"*Der Spiegel* 13 (March 21, 1977), 21–9.

111 Hans-Jochen Vogel to Werner Maihofer, June 25, 1975, AdsD Hans-Jochen Vogel Papers 584.

relations headaches. Siegfried Haag, who once represented Holger Meins and Andreas Baader, organized the Stockholm action in conjunction with the RAF's imprisoned leaders, obtaining the necessary weapons and recruiting the commando members from the antitorture committees.[112] Haag, in fact, recruited many of the RAF's second generation – and went underground himself a few months after Stockholm. He was not the first RAF attorney to have done so.[113] Another of Baader's lawyers, Claus Croissant, may not have conspired to commit violent crimes but he certainly hired many who did. RAF member Siegfried Hausner, who killed the two attachés in Stockholm (and for whom Schleyer's commando was named), worked for Croissant, as did Elisabeth van Dyck and Hans-Joachim Klein. Van Dyck helped Haag plan the embassy raid while Klein participated in the attack on OPEC later that year.[114] Still, cutting off the information network that made much of this possible required violating the most basic of civil liberties. When the governing coalition convened a joint meeting at the beginning of 1976, party leaders and ministers insisted that they would continue to oppose infringements on attorney-client privilege.[115] The CDU/CSU's renewed efforts in this area were thus defeated when presented to the Bundestag in February.

In an interview with the news magazine *Stern* two years before his murder, Siegfried Buback voiced the question that militant democracy raised about attorney-client privilege and the rights of the accused: "Does the principle of a fair trial apply even if a defense lawyer misuses his privileges and if the client knew about [the abuse] or even incited it?" The attorney general answered emphatically, "no."[116] Following the kidnapping of Hanns-Martin Schleyer, Social and Liberal Democrats reached this conclusion as well. As dominant members of the crisis staff, they immediately mobilized Article 34 of the Criminal Code in an attempt to cut off prisoners' contact with the outside world. This proved to have its drawbacks, however. Article 34 allowed for the overriding of laws in situations of "justified emergency," but different judges handed down different verdicts on the justifiability of this particular measure. To resolve this problem, the Constitutional Court advised the government to create the necessary legislation, which would, in effect, become the Contact Ban Law.

On September 29, each of the parliamentary parties argued before the Bundestag in support of the new antiterrorist legislation. Though the lines

[112] For a detailed report on the lawyer-client network and early evidence of collusion, see BKA/TE 13, "Bericht zur Materialsammlung BMI. Terrorismusbekämpfung. Hier: Info-Zentral der RAF im Büro des RA Groenwold, Hamburg," September 15, 1975, BA B106: 83808.

[113] Jörg Lang, who first brought RAF clients to Claus Croissant's law firm, went underground in 1974 after previously securing safe houses and other logistical support for RAF members. Lang is suspected of playing a key role in the 1977 offensive. Jeremy Varon, *Bringing the War Home: The Weather Underground, the Red Army Faction, and Revolutionary Violence in the Sixties and Seventies* (Berkeley: University of California Press, 2004), 267–8.

[114] Ibid.

[115] Coalition leaders were unanimous in their opposition to any such infringement of civil liberties. "Koalitionsgespräch," January 12, 1976, AdsD Helmut Schmidt Papers 9370.

[116] Peter P. Born, "Achtung Garage!" *Stern* (June 5, 1975), 128–38; here, 128.

of argument did not differ dramatically from one another, each party added emphasis according to their respective political philosophies. Members of the Christian Union declared that only a state able to reconcile "liberality and the well-equipped use of lawful power," a state, in other words, that could distinguish friend from foe, could end the current crisis and recurring fears of democracy's collapse.[117] For their part, Social Democrats justified the Contact Ban on two counts. First, they argued for the rights of the many law-abiding citizens over those of the few lawbreakers.[118] And, second, they stated that the new law was a necessary corrective to existing legislation, which lacked uniform judicial procedures for serious acts of state intervention.[119] Largely responsible for the imprecise and vague nature of the Emergency Laws, Social Democrats now moved to allow the state that which they had earlier denied it, namely the right to restrict civil liberties and to differentiate terrorists from other citizens before the law.

Support for the Contact Ban was not unanimous. Many of the same Social Democrats who had protested the violence protection paragraphs (§88a and §130a) the year before took a firm stand against the Contact Ban as well. This time, however, they refused to conform to the majority position. On behalf of the dissenters, Manfred Coppick openly declared the ban a "cog in the wheel of terrorism" – a repressive dismantling of freedom that would only produce new terror in response.[120] Not unlike critical members of the extraparliamentary left, Coppick called on his colleagues to help break the cycle of violence by rejecting the Contact Ban. He only succeeded in provoking their fury. When the votes were cast, the parliamentarians demonstrated their overwhelming support for the new law. Of the 392 Bundestag members, 371 voted for the law, 17 abstained, and 4 – Social Democrats Karl-Heinz Hansen, Dieter Lattmann, Klaus Thüsing, and Manfred Coppick – voted against it.[121] The next day, the Bundesrat approved the Contact Ban and Scheel signed it. The law went into effect at midnight on October 2 and not two minutes later, Vogel used it to deprive seventy-two prisoners of all contact with the outside world.[122] Despite the ease and speed with which the bill became law, those deputies who voted against it or abstained were pressured to change their votes with a force disproportionate to their small numbers, revealing the threat perceived in their critique. The four dissenting Social Democrats were condemned by party leaders for pursuing "individualist interests" at the party's expense and for breaking the ruling coalition's united front.[123] What leaders resented most, of course,

[117] Klaus Hartmann in *Verhandlungen* VIII. Bundestag, 44. Sitzung (September 29, 1977), 3366–7.
[118] Hubert Weber in ibid., 3368–9.
[119] Hans-Jochen Vogel in ibid., 3370.
[120] Manfred Coppick in ibid., 3371–3.
[121] Ibid., 3384.
[122] *Dokumentation der Bundesregierung*, 114.
[123] Protokoll über die Sitzung des Parteivorstandes, October 13, 1977, AdsD Helmut Schmidt Papers 9477; Protokoll über die gemeinsame Sitzung von Parteirat, Parteivorstand und Kontrollkommission, October 14, 1977, AdsD Helmut Schmidt Papers 6290.

was the ammunition they gave members of the Christian Union – who immediately broadcast the lack of consensus within the SPD as evidence of weak leadership and ideological sympathy with the terrorists.

If the kidnapping of Hanns-Martin Schleyer convinced the SPD government to revise a number of positions – on executive power, civil liberties, antiterrorism legislation, and undeclared states of emergency – it still shied away from the most elementary state power: armed force. This included a reluctance to deploy the GSG-9, the counterterrorist task force it had created in 1972. To be sure, the attacks on Buback, Ponto, and, finally, Schleyer, had turned Bonn into a city of closely guarded officials, with the GSG-9 playing the role of glorified bodyguards. But the government hesitated to utilize this force in more overt confrontations with terrorism out of concern for Länder opposition and the need to avoid resembling the FRG's fascist predecessor – in the eyes of its own citizens and the international community.[124] As one ministerial adviser so baldly put it, "because of Auschwitz" the FRG could not do what other countries might.[125] Indecision affected officials' actions even after Schleyer's kidnapping. Having immediately ordered the GSG-9 to Cologne – the first such call the special task force had received in all its five years – the government just as quickly dismissed the unit upon its arrival. While the search for Schleyer began in earnest, Bonn's "terrorist hunters" were benched.[126] One month later, *Der Spiegel* ran a short piece entitled "Police-Rockers in Bonn," describing the mystery and suspense surrounding the antiterrorism task force:

> They sit two to a powerful BMW motorcycle, with civilian license plates, wearing black boots; black, logo-decorated, leather suits; and white helmets: the young officers of the GSG-9.

It was not only the agents' "rocker gear" that attracted the magazine's attention but also the state's evasive behavior. Though the GSG-9 had been guarding politicians' cars for the last fourteen days, the BGS, Interior Ministry, and the chief of police all denied knowing anything about the FRG's "false Hell's Angels."[127]

Officials' attempt to keep the GSG-9 out of action and its profile low ended with the second terrorist attack of the German Autumn. On Thursday, October 13, four members of the PFLP hijacked Lufthansa Flight 181 on its return to Frankfurt from the Spanish island of Majorca. Just after 1:00 A.M. on Friday, an ultimatum was delivered linking the fate of Hanns-Martin Schleyer to that

[124] Strong federalist sentiments against using the special task force were dramatized in the nationwide police action, "Winter Travel." Planned as a major showdown with the RAF in January 1977, the GSG-9 was uninvited due to opposition from coordinating interior ministers. The incident was retold in *Stern* (September 15, 1977), 218.

[125] MR Keller, "Niederschrift über ein Gespräch des BKs mit Sicherheitsexperten," Kanzlerbungalow, September 13, 1977, AdsD Helmut Schmidt Papers 10014. His comment is ample evidence that new left radicals were not the only ones to conflate police terror with genocide.

[126] "Feuerwehr auf der Reservebank," *Stern* (September 15, 1977), 216–17.

[127] "Polizei-Rocker in Bonn," *Der Spiegel* 42 (October 10, 1977), 27.

of the eighty-six passengers and five crew members aboard the *Landshut* airliner.[128] Declaring themselves partners in the fight against the "expansionist racism" of the "new Nazis in Bonn and the Zionists in Tel Aviv," the "Martyr Halimeh Commando" reiterated the demands of the "Siegfried Hausner Commando" and added some of its own.[129] At the same time, the RAF issued its seventh and final ultimatum. After forty days of playing cat and mouse with Schmidt's government, it had had enough. The group stated in no uncertain terms that if the demanded prisoners were not released and each given DM100,000 by 8:00 A.M. on Sunday, October 16, the hostages would die. The stakes in the struggle between the FRG and the RAF suddenly and spectacularly changed. If there had been any doubt, the hijackers' ultimatum made palpable to the world the power held by governments over the lives of their citizens. As one newspaper reported, the terrorist crisis turned Bonn into a site of pilgrimage for those inexplicably drawn to the center of decision making (Figure 5.4).[130] For Willy Brandt, Social Democrats' willingness to accept this responsibility was a historical hurdle they had yet to overcome. In a meeting later that Friday, he reminded SPD members once again of their binding "contract with the population to govern" and of the need for this to outweigh other considerations. Brandt was emphatic: What was demanded of Social Democrats in this moment was their "conscious willingness to seize and exercise state power."[131]

Members of Schmidt's inner circle required no such prodding; before the hijackers had time to make their demands known, the government mobilized the GSG-9.[132] The task force was to await word from Hans-Jürgen Wischnewski (later dubbed West Germany's "Lawrence of Arabia" by the conservative French daily, *Le Figaro*), who with several security experts followed the flight path of the hijacked *Landshut*. After refueling the plane in Cyprus and then again in Bahrain (having first found airports in Syria, Jordan, and Kuwait "closed" to them), the "Martyr Halimeh Commando" pressured officials in Dubai into letting it land on the morning of October 14. The United Arab Emirates' defense minister, Sheik Mohammed Bin Rashid, took over responsibility for the airfield and attempted to convince the hijackers to release women, children, and the sick. His requests were denied. Wischnewski arrived in Dubai close to midnight in Bonn, empowered by the crisis staff some twelve hours before to exhaust all diplomatic means to free the hostages from his position in the Middle East.

[128] The three statements – the ultimatum written to the chancellor and each commando's separate declaration – are reprinted in *Dokumentation der Bundesregierung*, 136–44.

[129] They demanded the release of two Palestinian prisoners in Turkey and a ransom of fifteen million U.S. dollars.

[130] Klaus Dreher, "Noch mehr Sicherheitsvorkehrungen in Bonn," *SZ*, October 18, 1977, 2.

[131] SPD, "Protokoll über die gemeinsame Sitzung von Parteirat, Parteivorstand und Kontrolkommission," October 14, 1977, AdsD Helmut Schmidt Papers 6290.

[132] *Dokumentation der Bundesregierung*, 135. The following account draws heavily on the government's own documentation of events as well as Butz Peters, *Tödlicher Irrtum: Die Geschichte der RAF* (Berlin: Argon, 2004), esp. 430–59.

FIGURE 5.4. Outside the Federal Chancellor's Office on October 15, 1977. Crowds gathered while Federal Border Guard tanks patrolled the government district and police stood watch (ullstein bild).

Contrary to what Wischnewski's airborne pursuit and presence in Dubai implied, the decision to authorize an armed rescue attempt had not yet been made. Schmidt first sought to gauge international receptiveness to a West German action by consulting his fellow European heads of state James Callaghan and Valéry Giscard d'Estaing. Multiple phone conversations between the chancellor and the British prime minister revealed an excellent working relationship based on political affinities – both men the head of embattled labor governments – and Callaghan's clear support for the planned initiative.[133] The French president, on the other hand, would not officially advise Schmidt on the current terrorist situation. Expressing his "entirely personal opinion," however, Giscard d'Estaing left no doubt that, if he were in Schmidt's shoes, he would neither give up the chase nor release the demanded prisoners. Offering up the cold hard calculus of sovereign statecraft, the French leader stated his belief that "an action" was "the only solution:"

One must take care to keep the state in mind, whereby the concern is not only for the German state but also the authority of [all] European states. It is, however, important that

[133] Transcript of telephone discussions between Chancellor Schmidt and Prime Minister Callaghan, October 14, 1977, 14:15–14:30 and 16:00–16:20, AdsD Helmut Schmidt Papers 10016.

this action be carried out by a good team. This situation will perhaps result in a few deaths but certainly not all the passengers will be killed.[134]

After receiving a green light (officially and unofficially) from the British and the French, two developments further cinched the government's decision to use paramilitary force. The first was the Constitutional Court's ruling on October 16 in favor of the government in the suit brought against it by Hanns Eberhard Schleyer.[135] Having successfully raised the money demanded for his father's release, Hanns Eberhard hoped to force the government's hand by suing the state for violating its constitutional mandate to protect life by refusing to negotiate with the RAF. The court, however, ruled that the state's duty to the individual did not trump its duty to ensure the security of the majority. The significance of this for the passengers of the *Landshut* was explicitly addressed by Press Secretary Bölling in his announcement of the court ruling on the same day as the RAF's deadline.[136] The government's official position was (and unofficially had already been) that this interpretation of the constitution applied not only to Schleyer but to the newest hostages as well.[137] Though members of cabinet and the grand advisory committee had not considered conceding the terrorists' demands, the court's ruling offered welcome public legitimation for their policy of non-negotiation. Indeed, having received word of the court's decision early that morning, Schmidt and his advisers once again ruled out the release of prisoners and moved to continue plans for a police rescue mission in Dubai .

At approximately the same time that the Constitutional Court announced its ruling, however, the hijackers announced their intentions to leave Dubai, having spent two days there taking on provisions and awaiting a generator to aid the airliner's failing oxygen and cooling systems. The commando's leader, Zohair Yousif Akache (alias Mahmud), demanded fuel and threatened to kill the Lufthansa pilot, Captain Jürgen Schumann, and then two passengers every five minutes unless authorities complied. They did, and the *Landshut* departed that afternoon for Aden, despite Yemen's block on air traffic. Wischnewski, unable to follow suit, flew instead to the Saudi Arabian port city of Jeddah. He was not there long, however. Shortly before dawn on October 17 – a day after the commandos' deadline – the *Landshut* landed in Mogadishu. Within an hour, the Somali government contacted the West German embassy to inform them that Captain Schumann had been murdered and his body tossed down an escape chute.[138] They also reported that the hijackers had extended their

[134] Transcript of telephone discussion between Chancellor Schmidt and President Giscard d'Estaing, October 14, 1977, 14:30–14:45. AdsD Helmut Schmidt Papers 10016.

[135] For an analysis of the court case, see Carsten Polzin, "Kein Austausch! Die verfassungsrechtliche Dimension der Schleyer-Entscheidung" in Kraushaar, *Die RAF*, 1026–47.

[136] Klaus Bölling, "Gemeinsames Bemühen zur Rettung der Geiseln im Flugzeug und des Lebens von Dr. Schleyer," *Bulletin* 102 (October 18, 1977): 933.

[137] *Dokumentation der Bundesregierung*, 148–50.

[138] Schumann was shot and killed by Akache in Aden the day before. For details: Peters, *Tödlicher Irrtum*, 445–6.

deadline to later that day. Bonn immediately opened up communications with the Somali government and ordered Wischnewski and accompanying security experts (including GSG-9 commander Ulrich Wegener) to Mogadishu. After several hours on the phone discussing everything from strategic concerns to future economic concessions, Schmidt, Maihofer, and Foreign Minister Hans-Dietrich Genscher were met with the second and decidedly critical development for the deployment of West German armed forces: Somalia's military dictator, President Mohamed Siad Barre, agreed to support a rescue action. Upon his arrival, Wischnewski met with Barre to confirm that preparations to free the hostages would be made in cooperation with his government. In order to give the two countries' security forces the necessary time, negotiators in the air tower convinced the hijackers to extend their deadline yet again – to 3:30 A.M. local time. Meanwhile, a third Lufthansa airliner landed under cover of darkness, this one carrying the officers of the GSG-9.

However much they consulted and prepared with security experts on the ground, government officials in Bonn could not deny the potential for events to go terribly wrong. If anyone needed reminding, not two hours after the GSG-9 landed in Mogadishu an urgent message went out over the Reuters newswire from Tel Aviv:

> a west german boeing 707 reported to be carrying a squad of crack anti-guerrilla police landed this evening at mogadishu airport where hijackers are holding 86 hostages aboard a lufthansa jet. israeli radio monitors, who tracked the plane as it flew south towards somalia, said it touched down after dusk using only navigation lights and that it was believed to be carrying an anti-guerrilla squad for a possible attempt to storm the hijacked boeing 737.[139]

To West German officials' horror, it took barely ten minutes before news of the planned police action was broadcast over the American Forces Network, British Broadcasting Corporation, Europe I, and Radio France. Reuters' editors – and the entire wire service – were quickly reminded of Klaus Bölling's earlier appeal for cooperation. Doing what he could in terms of damage control, the West German press secretary now emphatically requested that the international news media "not, repeat not, report anything concerning the movements of the anti-guerrilla squads."[140]

Except for this minor media drama, the night's events went as planned. With the unanimous support of the crisis staff and Somali forces providing reinforcement, Schmidt ordered the military police action "Fire Magic" – the first mobilization of German forces abroad since 1945.[141] Even if the Israelis had observed the GSG-9's arrival, the hijackers apparently had not, nor had they caught wind of the news. After being briefed by Wegener, the team's members waited until 2:05 A.M. (just after midnight in Bonn) for the signal to storm the

[139] Reuters im/haa, "urgent: hijack—squad," Eun394 epc 329, 21:07, BA B106: 106684.

[140] Reuters nm/ng, "note to editors" Eun410 epa 138, 21:31 and Reuters im/arp, "note to editors," Eun411 epb 402, 21:31, both in BA B106: 106684.

[141] Feuerzauber (fire magic) happens to be the title of the third act in Richard Wagner's *Valkyrie*.

Landshut. Using a flare gun to temporarily disorient the four hijackers and moving with meticulous precision, the task force took all of seven minutes to gain complete control of the airplane. They killed three of the commando's members and badly wounded the fourth, while successfully leaving all eighty-six passengers unharmed. As if this alone did not capture the cool efficiency that the SPD government hoped to project, Wischnewski's telephone call informing the West German chancellor of the mission's success was just as calm and to the point. Betraying no emotion, the state minister informed Schmidt that "the situation is resolved."[142] If there was a message to be found in such bureaucratic brevity it was this: that the West German state – a legitimately democratic state – had acted appropriately and with deadly force. But unlike its enemies past and present, it would not glorify or delight in that violence .

AFTER MOGADISHU

News of the successful rescue mission broke the next morning, awakening a sense of giddy euphoria in the FRG and apparent pride from the country's previously "concerned" international friends. One swift action seemed to relieve many West Germans of doubts not only concerning democracy's ability to defend itself but also about its future in Germany. If not everyone came naturally to this conclusion, then the British prime minister helped them. In a speech he delivered from Bonn the very next day, Callaghan declared: "Bonn's lawful action stands in the interests of the protection of freedom." Accordingly, "the Germans should have self-confidence. With this they have proved themselves to be on the right path."[143] U.S. president Jimmy Carter, Israel, and even the French press concurred, praising the West Germans for having won a victory against terrorism on behalf of all democratic peoples.[144] For members of government, however, it is likely that none of the responses pleased them more than the laudatory conclusions drawn by the *New York Times*, whose unnamed correspondent cautioned against taking from Mogadishu the lesson "that the way to succeed against terrorists is simply to be tough." Not only was such a conclusion false, the author stated, but it demeaned "what West Germany has, in fact, proved. Tough, yes, but also prepared, flexible, smart."[145]

[142] *Dokumentation der Bundesregierung*, 112–14. "Die Arbeit ist erledigt" was quoted widely in both the domestic and international reporting of events. The *New York Times*, e.g., closed its detailed account of the "106 hour" hijacking crisis with Wischnewski's words. "4 Days of Fear, Then 7 Minutes for the Rescue," *New York Times*, October 19, 1977, A1 (hereafter, *NYT*).

[143] Quoted in "Callaghan: Bonn fügt Terrorismus eine wichtige Niederlage zu," *SZ*, October 19, 1977, 1.

[144] "Eine Flut von Glückwünschen für Bonn," *SZ*, October 19, 1977, 5; *FR*, October 19, 1977, 4; "Israel Praises Bonn for the 'Salvation' of Plane Hostages," *NYT*, October 19, 1977, A14. *Der Spiegel* ran a retrospective comparing international coverage of West German counterterrorism before and after Mogadishu: "Deutsche können stark und menschlich sein," *Der Spiegel* 44 (October 24, 1977), 4–9.

[145] "Terrorism: The Battle and the War," *NYT*, October 19, 1977, A24.

Given that armed force was so heavily associated with the crimes of Germany's past, the rehabilitative effects of international praise was evident in the media buzz celebrating not merely the victory of the GSG-9, but the GSG-9 itself. The joyful homecoming ceremony held for the paramilitary unit was unprecedentedly patriotic, and an outpouring of articles and readers' letters conveyed pleasure at the celebration of young West Germans in uniform to the accompaniment of their national hymn.[146] It was, it would seem, a historic moment. And the question that hung on everyone's lips, according to one reporter, was "who were these men that, in the blink of an eye, turned the nightmare oppressing an entire people into the triumph of a republic?"[147] The popular media answered with portraits of an engaging group of unpretentious heroes, casually dressed twenty-somethings who "looked around shyly and gave a few embarrassed smiles before slipping into formation." When asked how it felt to return a hero to jubilant Germany, one twenty-year-old responded as the professional police officer he was trained to be: "Who's a hero here? I get paid to do this sort of thing."[148] Wischnewski could not have said it better.

Further demonstrating the country's changed mood, headlines about weak national leadership were replaced overnight with an image of an SPD-led government and, by association, a West German state that exuded strength and certitude. Throughout the mainstream media, terrorists were warned to pay heed: democracy and the German state would not be forced to their knees by violent outlaws.[149] News pages were emblazoned with photographs of Schmidt standing solitary and strong – not only in the suit and tie of his office but, more striking, in the uniform of the Federal Border Guards, the GSG-9's umbrella organization.[150] However similar this was to the "strong man" image of leadership associated with conservatives, at the end of the day Schmidt elicited no fears from the mainstream. As the cover of *Der Spiegel* put it, he was "the admirable German."[151] His studied desire to stand above partisan politics now won Schmidt deep respect at the same time that his level-headed calm was lauded as evidence of his humanitarian nature. Schmidt, it seems, was delightfully boring – not a militarist reactionary or an authoritarian leader but rather a man of decidedly liberal values. Even better, perhaps, was how his image as an ordinary pragmatic "doer" (versus a charismatic leader or a genius) could be generalized

[146] See, e.g., Karl Feldmeyer, "Die Spezialtruppe von Mogadiscio: Zu Hause stolpert sie über viele Drähte," *FAZ*, October 19, 1977, 5; Winfried Didzoleit, "Die Beschützer waren die Beschützten," *FR*, October 19, 1977, 5; Theo Sommer, "Frisch gewagt – erst halb gewonnen," *Die Zeit*, October 21, 1977, 1.

[147] Adelbert Weinstein, "Der Chef der GSG 9," *FAZ*, October 19, 1977, 12.

[148] Herbert Riehl-Heyse, "Die lässigen, schüchternen Befreier," *SZ*, October 19, 1977, 6.

[149] See, e.g., Werner Holzer, "Mogadischu und Stammheim," *FR*, October 19, 1977, 3; Fritz Ulrich Fach, "Zwischenbilanz des Verbrechens," *FAZ*, October 19, 1977, 1; Hans Heigert, "Ein Wendepunkt," *SZ*, October 19, 1977, 4; Carl-Christian Kaiser, "Müde, froh und auf der Hut," *Die Zeit*, October 21, 1977, 3; *Stern* 39 (October 27, 1977), 212–18.

[150] *Stern* 39 (October 27, 1977), 211–12.

[151] "Nach Mogadischu: Der bewunderte Deutsche," *Der Spiegel* 44 (October 24, 1977), cover.

so as to apply to West Germans as a whole. Here, the *Wall Street Journal* captured it best, with the comment that against all expectations, Mogadishu had demonstrated that "Germans can be both strong and humane."[152]

True to form, government officials took pains to emphasize that the crisis was not yet over and avoided all appearances of renewed hubris in Germany. Until Schleyer was also safely home "Bonn would not jubilate."[153] The end, however, came quickly. On October 19, news came that "after 43 days" the kidnappers had, in their words, "put an end to [Hanns-Martin Schleyer's] miserable and corrupt existence."[154] That evening, police found his body in the trunk of a green Audi outside the Alsatian town of Mulhouse. Schleyer's death was not the only one to cast an immediate shadow over the success of Mogadishu. In a final act of resistance, Baader, Ensslin, and Raspe took their own lives shortly after learning of the *Landshut*'s rescue. Even without the accusation of murder issued by their fellow imprisoned RAF militant Irmgard Möller (after she regained consciousness from the multiple stab wounds that she herself sustained), there was ample room for speculation over the government's role in the triple suicide. Short wave radios and the handguns with which Baader and Raspe killed themselves were found in their cells, implying, at best, severe police incompetence and, at worst, the state's direct responsibility. The fact that the Contact Ban had isolated the prisoners since the beginning of the hijacking crisis only made matters worse. This and other questions concerning the government's actions over the course of the German Autumn quickly tempered the public's praise for Schmidt's government. The state of exception had passed and politics as usual resumed.

The confrontation with terrorism that culminated in the events of the German Autumn did, however, have lasting consequences. The success of the rescue mission to widespread acclaim ensured, for example, Social Democrats' (retroactive) support for their government's decision to utilize what was, by that point, the last of several coercive state powers they had traditionally refused. Though many have argued otherwise, neither the success of the GSG-9 nor the widespread panic of that autumn are sufficient to explain the party's revised position on state power, much less its maintenance of that position in subsequent decades.[155] At each step, Social Democrats' decisions to empower the state they led hinged on their perception that it was not only significantly

[152] Quoted in "Deutsche können stark," 8.

[153] Thomas Meyer, "Bonn nach dem Sieg von Mogadiscio: Das Bangen der letzten Wochen bleibt," *FAZ*, October 19, 1977, 3.

[154] *Dokumentation der Bundesregierung*, 190.

[155] For interpretations that emphasize mass fear or the state's inherently reactionary nature, see, e.g., Klaus Hartung, ed., *Der blinde Fleck: Die Linke, die RAF und der Staat* (Frankfurt: Neue Kritik, 1987); Sebastian Scheerer, "Deutschland: Die ausgeburgerte Linke," in *Angriff auf das Herz des Staates*, Henner Hess, et al. (Frankfurt: Suhrkamp, 1988); Tatjana Botzat, Elisabeth Kiderlen, and Frank Wolff, eds., *Ein deutscher Herbst: Zustände 1977* (Frankfurt: Neue Kritik, 1997); Heinrich Breloer, *Todesspiel: Von der Schleyer-Entführung bis Mogadischu. Eine dokumentarische Erzählung* (Cologne: Kiepenheuer & Witsch, 1997).

FIGURE 5.5. Following the discovery of Hanns-Martin Schleyer's body on October 19, 1977, the Federal Criminal Office launched its biggest dragnet. Here, a woman hands out flyers bearing the pictures of the suspected kidnappers to customers and passers-by at Hamburg's weekly farmers' market (dpa).

different from the National Socialist state but also from what the West German state had been just ten years before. They were, in other words, believers in their own democratization programs, and the change in Social Democratic conceptions of legitimate state action necessarily mirrored a change in their assumptions regarding the viability of West German democracy. Problematic though it may have been, the crisis staff represented a deliberate rejection of conservatives' proposals to centralize power in the hands of "one strong man" during a national crisis. With each party represented by its parliamentary speaker, the implicit presence and authority of the Bundestag acting as a check on executive power legitimated their course of action. In this way, the crisis staff was understood by many Social Democrats to avoid the worst abuses of power by enabling efficient state action through representative institutions.[156] Similarly, party leaders' argument that the Contact Ban protected the average citizen from both untimely death (by preventing further terrorist attacks) and unwarranted state intervention (by creating clear and fixed procedures for suspending civil rights) was not simply a political expedient. It also furthered and expressed their reconceptualization of state power as democratic. To Social Democrats, their government's attention to the protection of human life and the control of

[156] See, e.g., Jens Fischer, "Mogadischu oder: Wie ein sozial-demokratischer Kanzler eine Krise bewältigte," *Vorwärts*, October 27, 1977, 3.

FIGURE 5.6. The return of State Minister Hans-Jürgen Wischnewski and the GSG-9 to the Frankfurt airport after the successful rescue of the hijacked *Landshut* on October 18, 1977. Bundesarchiv, B 145 Bild-F051866-0010 / photo: Ludwig Wegmann.

arbitrary state power demonstrated the sharp distinction between its actions and those taken by the authoritarian regimes of the past.

The SPD's democratization of state power in this sense was, of necessity, most vividly on display where coercive force was physically manifest. The government's decision to deploy paramilitary power required countering Social Democrats' ingrained distrust by distancing such a move from past abuses. The GSG-9 did just that. Returning from Mogadishu, the GSG-9 – truly in the public eye for the first time – realized the image of the nonmilitaristic military that security experts had set out to create in 1972 (Figure 5.6). Dressed in blue jeans and black leather jackets, the men of the GSG-9 did not evoke comparisons with Prussian or, worse, Nazi soldiers. Instead, accounts of modest heroism and technical efficiency abounded in descriptions of these "rocker-cops" with "honed 007 skills that made the use of weapons redundant."[157] Clothing GSG-9 members both literally and figuratively in the trappings of Hollywood heroes allowed many Social Democrats and other West Germans to conceive of this newest, formidable deployment of state power as distinct from the excesses of the past and, at some basic level, democratic in character. Regardless of its

[157] Riehl-Heyse, "Die lässigen, schüchternen Befreier;" Karl-Heinz Krumm, "Die lange verschmähte Elite-truppe," *FR*, October 19, 1977, 3; Holzer, "Mogadishu und Stammheim;" "Die Spezialtruppe von Mogadishu," *FAZ*, October 19, 1977, 5; Sommer, "Frisch gewagt."

accuracy, it was this sense that state power had been significantly democratized – and not simply the fear provoked by terrorism – that convinced many Social Democrats that a German state could indeed manifest strength without being authoritarian.

Writing in the party organ, one Social Democrat attempted to explain the emotional significance of Mogadishu for the SPD. To him, the successful hostage rescue was not only about "the chancellor, the federal government – a democratically legitimated executive – fulfilling their sworn duties with calm and luck." It concerned more, even, than "the democratic state having proved itself capable of action." The experience that the author underscored for his readers was the collapse of the "stereotypical conservative-reactionary slander" that claimed "Social Democrats have no relationship to the state and power."[158] For many in the SPD, the lasting importance of the autumn's events was the conviction not only that their government had demonstrated the decisive yet democratic use of German state power but also that its actions had once and for all established Social Democrats as effective statesmen. That they celebrated this despite the fact that the government had overstepped the bounds that the party long maintained on state power spoke directly to a change in their perception of German democracy itself.

As one might guess, not all members of the SPD took pride in their government and chancellor. The tensions and internal fissures that had publicly announced themselves in debate over the Contact Ban, the government's complicity in the "hunt for sympathizers," and the increase in police power were not resolved by the successful hostage rescue. For those Social Democrats who already had one foot out the party door, in fact, the display of paramilitary power in Mogadishu only sealed their belief that the SPD had taken a wrong turn. Hans-Jochen Vogel's response to criticisms voiced earlier that year perfectly conveyed the gulf across which the party's left and right wing now regarded one another over precisely the issue of state power:

> In light of the most recent events, how is it possible to so one-sidedly maintain the thesis that the freedom and life of a citizen is first and foremost endangered by the state and its organs? I can also hardly understand with what reason one would want to accuse Helmut Schmidt and the federal government of epitomizing "the rule of strong-arming efforts at authority." Sometimes I fear that you really don't see an essential part of reality and, as a result, fully over-interpret other parts of it.[159]

By October, Vogel's incomprehension and unwavering confidence in the rightness of his position was shared by the party majority. Many older critics remained loyal to the SPD, arguing that Schmidt and his government had, at the very least, protected German democracy from a far worse fate, namely

158 Fischer, "Mogadischu," 3.

159 Hans-Jochen Vogel to Dieter Lattmann, April 15, 1977, AdsD Helmut Schmidt Correspondence 6397.

overreaction and militarism by the Christian Union.[160] But for many leftists who had joined the SPD in the late 1960s on a wave of reformist optimism, this was simply not enough. In the end, the events of the German Autumn encouraged disillusioned members such as these to finally retract their support and transfer their political energies elsewhere.

160 Throughout the terrorist crisis, Schmidt and Vogel received numerous declarations of support for the government's cool-headed approach from otherwise critical Social Democratic supporters. The chancellor, for example, received both thanks and constructive criticism at a meeting with literary notables Heinrich Böll, Max Frisch, Siegfried Lenz, and Siegfried Unseld. See Herbert Ehrenberg, "Notiz im Anschluss an das Gespräch beim BK mit H. Böll, M. Frisch, S. Lenz und S. Unseld am 16.10.77," November 8, 1977, AdsD Helmut Schmidt Papers 8744.

6

Civility, German Identity, and the End of the Postwar

> I have never understood how one can seriously believe that ... core concepts can change other than by absorbing complex forms of argumentation; they reflect innovations and processes of learning.
>
> Jürgen Habermas (1979)[1]

> There is only violence or freedom from violence. There is nothing else.
>
> Uli Fischer (June 2, 1987)[2]

Was the terrorism of the 1970s a sideshow that receives attention more because of its sensational nature – and a resurgence of interest in terrorism after September 11 – than because of any real significance for postwar Germany?[3] There is no denying that the media was influential in framing the way West Germans experienced the terrorism of the 1970s and that its dramatizations shaped a public rhetoric that played to the heightened emotions – and historical fears – of the moment. It would, without a doubt, be mistaken to uncritically accept the claims for the German Autumn's watershed importance made by contemporaries, especially those made in immediate response to Mogadishu.[4] The media circus that accompanies – and, yes, defines – all modern terrorism,

[1] "Einleitung," in *Stichworte zur "Geistigen Situation der Zeit,"* ed. Jürgen Habermas, vol 1, *Nation und Republik* (Frankfurt: Suhrkamp, 1979), 21.

[2] Uli Fischer, transcribed recording of the Green Party session, "Schwerpunktthema: Gewalt," June 2, 1987, 57. Archiv Grünes Gedächtnis (Berlin, hereafter, AGG), Christa Nichels Papers 64.

[3] Eminent historian Detlef Siegfried expressed this opinion, to wide audience agreement, in his concluding remarks at the VW-sponsored conference, "The 'Other Alliance': Political Protest, Intercultural Relations, and Collective Identities in West Germany and the United States, 1958–77," Heidelberg, May 22, 2005.

[4] Arguments for the media-exaggerated significance of terrorism and the German Autumn can be found in: Klaus Weinhauer, Jörg Requate, Heinz-Gerhard Haupt, eds., *Terrorismus in der Bundesrepublik: Medien, Staat und Subkulturen in den 70er Jahren* (Frankfurt: Campus, 2006); Hanno Balz, "Gesellschaftsformierungen: Die öffentliche Debatte über die RAF in den 70er Jahren," in *Der "Deutsche Herbst" und die RAF in Politik, Medien und Kunst: Nationale und internationale Perspektiven*, ed. Nicole Colin (Bielefeld: transcript, 2008), 170–84.

however, does not alone refute the German Autumn's rightful place in the annals of postwar history. Here, actions may not always have spoken louder than words, but they do help to grasp the significance of the experience of terrorism for German political culture, especially when viewed within the broader context of the twentieth century.

For, if the terrorist crisis encouraged Social Democrats to revise their position on democracy and state power and to act to contain terrorism accordingly, it also had long-term effects on the extraparliamentary left. The political impotence and disillusionment they felt prompted many to actively reengage the political mainstream and, correspondingly, to express an explicit and unprecedented appreciation for nonviolent politics. From the German Autumn onward, leftists translated the lessons of the previous decade – both positive and negative – into a growing list of constructive political activities predicated on the conviction that the FRG could be reformed internally. The fact that the Federal Republic did not collapse in the autumn of 1977 settled doubts about its viability on the other side of the political spectrum as well. This was particularly critical for a new generation of conservatives, galvanized by the decade-long fight against terrorism and more ideologically committed than their predecessors. By making German patriotism palatable and traditional values commonsensical, Mogadishu and the outrage of liberal conservatives helped mainstream conservatives pursue a course of moral and national rejuvenation. Taken together, these shifts in political sensibility suggested a consensus on the polity's legitimacy heretofore denied the West German state. However imperfect, Bonn had proved it was neither unsteady Weimar nor authoritarian Berlin, and in response, Germans stopped watching their backs and agreed to move forward on newly shared ground.

LETTERS IN DEFENSE OF THE REPUBLIC

As we have seen, the autumn terrorist crisis inspired new levels of intolerance for those judged to be enemies of the "free democratic order." Popular television series contributed to the poisonous atmosphere, with exposés on the "torturous path to terrorism" allegedly paved by prominent left intellectuals such as Herbert Marcuse, Heinrich Böll, and Helmut Gollwitzer, on the one side, and an indifferent SPD government on the other.[5] Böll, having already gained an undeserved reputation as a terrorist sympathizer, became the man conservative politicians and many regular citizens loved to hate. Over the course of the German Autumn, Böll was publicly reviled, and although there was a counterdialogue – defending the writer from injustice and criticizing the FRG for its persecution of anyone who did not support the new antiterrorism

[5] For example: "ZDF-Magazin: Verharmloster Terrorismus," aired September 29, 1977 and "Im Brennpunkt: Terrorismus: Protokolle eines Irrwegs zum Terrorismus in Deutschland," aired October 5, 1977. Complete transcripts found in Archiv der sozialen Demokratie (Bad Godesberg, hereafter, AdsD), Hans-Jochen Vogel Papers 449.

program – it was disturbingly ineffective in the face of a shrill majority.[6] Böll also suspected he was victimized during the state's search for Schleyer, citing phonetapping, surveillance, and the search of his and his son's homes by police intent on finding evidence of anything that could be construed as sympathetic activity.[7] All this seemed of a piece with what he and other members of the West German intelligentsia – older critical leftists who did not resemble the violent radicals of conservative imaginings in the least – feared was the average West German's mental swing to the right.[8]

Determined to protect themselves and basic civil liberties from attack, a number of the government's citizens – a wide array of left-wing Social Democrats, independent socialists, and feminists – refused to be silenced. More specifically, they refused conservatives or the government the right to define what it meant to be a loyal citizen and democrat in the FRG. In what was ultimately a fight over public discourse and public perception, these leftists moved to defend democracy by opening up avenues of social critique that did not tacitly approve of armed resistance in the FRG, regardless of the circumstances. In letters and statements issued in quick succession, they took great pains to dispel all ambivalence on the subject of terrorism and the left's relationship to it by openly renouncing the RAF and the use of political violence on principle.[9] At the same time, they also warned that the threat to the republic was not one-sided and specifically criticized the politically motivated attacks on intellectuals and independent leftists for, among other things, undermining democratic pluralism.[10] They assured that their voice would be heard, moreover, by

[6] The *Stern* issue of October 6, 1977 ran an article on Böll and his present treatment in the FRG. The flood of letters from readers in response provides an example of the dialogue surrounding the pacifist intellectual. See, "Briefe," *Stern* 45 (October 27, 1977): 7. An example of the wider hunt for sympathizers is captured in *Der Spiegel*'s serial, "Terrorismus: Wer sind die Sympathisanten?" 41 (October 3, 1977). For reader responses to it, see "Briefe," *Der Spiegel* 43 (October 17, 1977): 7–10.

[7] In response to Böll's list of grievances, Maihofer expressed "surprise and concern" over the writer's accusations but could only state that the police chief responsible for Böll's neighborhood denied that any action had been taken against Böll or his son. Heinrich Böll to Werner Maihofer, December 15, 1977 and Werner Maihofer to Heinrich Böll, December 20, 1977, copied to the desk of Helmut Schmidt. AdsD Helmut Schmidt Papers 6807.

[8] Böll expressed just this at a private meeting between the left literati and Schmidt at the height of the fall crisis. Herbert Ehrenberg, "Notiz im Anschluss an das Gespräch beim BK mit H. Böll, M. Frisch, S. Lenz und S. Unseld am 16.10.77," November 8, 1977, AdsD Helmut Schmidt Papers 8744.

[9] "Erklärung von September 7, 1977," *Frankfurter Rundschau* (hereafter, *FR*), September 12, 1977; Heinrich Böll, Bishop Kurt Sharf, Pastor Heinrich Albertz, Dr. Helmut Gollwitzer, "Appell an die Entführer," *FR*, September 12, 1977; Sozialistisches Büro, "Mit wenigen Schüßen den mühsamen Kampf zunichte gemacht," *FR*, September 13, 1977; "Erklärung von Hochschullehrern und wissenschaftlichen Mitarbeitern anläßlich der Entführung von Hanns-Martin Schleyer," *FR*, September 17, 1977.

[10] In addition to the general statements, see the Humanist Union's letter to Federal President Scheel sent on September 9 and reprinted as "Erklärung der Humanistischen Union," *FR*, September 9, 1977, 4.

directing it at an international as well as domestic audience. The Jusos joined the Humanist Union and several other organizations, for example, in issuing a letter of public support for the International Russell Tribunal and its investigation of civil rights violations in West Germany.[11] In the letter, they called for an open discussion of violence and strengthened their critique of the current repressive atmosphere.

Among the most visible and high-profile statements made by leading figures of the extraparliamentary movement were those issued by Rudi Dutschke and Herbert Marcuse and printed in *Die Zeit*. Both men emphatically distanced themselves from the RAF and, more significantly, defined the group's violence not as a wrongheaded strategy but as an illegitimate form of oppositional politics. Dutschke now stressed the need for democratic limits on civil disobedience and used himself as a counterexample to the RAF. The struggle could go on, he argued, but it had to be carried out within the institutional channels of the extraparliamentary and parliamentary opposition. Marcuse, like many on the left, had long regarded the RAF as counterrevolutionary and reiterated that the end goal of resistance, namely the liberated individual, must necessarily appear in the means toward liberation. He did this in the hopes of finally dispelling the notion that the RAF was an agent of progress for no other reason than that it aimed its weapons at the state. Conspiracy and assassination were not the acts of revolutionary movements but rather, Marcuse asserted, those of "isolated individuals and small isolated groups." Human liberation could only be won through an open struggle that, due to its very nature, relied on mass support; the senior voice of Critical Theory wanted no more ambivalence on this point. Though he left the door open to a truly popular revolutionary transformation, Marcuse very deliberately closed it in the face of the RAF and all other "self-appointed desperadoes" living in the FRG.[12]

In a rather different vein, that autumn's experience of heightened violence and repression also prompted a group of feminists to issue a public "Call to All Women for the Invention of Happiness" at the annual Frankfurt book fair – a frequent venue for political position takings in the FRG. However whimsical in style, it explicitly rejected the logic of violence and counterviolence and the solidarity it entailed. The women portrayed the state and the armed rebels as cut from the same cloth, both responsible for the current "reign of terror" due to the treacherous abstraction of their politics from human life. The text gave vent to a shared sense of powerlessness that, if not new, had been made worse by that autumn's showdown, and it expressed a commitment to end that condition. The authors announced their refusal, from that moment on, to take part either actively or passively in the ongoing "death dance," proclaiming that

[11] Humanistische-Union,Jungdemokraten,Jungsozialisten-in-der-SPD,Liberaler-Hochschulverband, and Sozialistische-Jugend-Deutschlands, "Presseerklärung über ihre Unterstützung von dem Russell-Tribunal," September 23, 1977, AdsD Helmut Schmidt Papers 9477.

[12] Rudi Dutschke, "Kritik am Terrorismus muss klarer werden" and Herbert Marcuse, "Mord darf keine Waffe der Politik sein," both in *Die Zeit*, September 16, 1977.

they were done with "the gravediggers'" standard. They rejected the "market places and politics" of liberal democracy as well as the left's romance with violent struggle and instead proposed that women "form a resistance against general unhappiness!" using the weapons of laughter, dance, and a love for life.[13] Theirs was not a call to "raise the Red Army" and it therefore did not resemble one. It smacked more of fantasy than a plan of action and approached the problem of violence and terrorism from a simple life-affirming position rather than from the vantage point of Marxist theory. But for all that, it was no less expressive of extraparliamentary leftists' determination to change their current direction and regain control over the substance of their politics.

In many ways what is most striking about these interventions is not only the leftists' open break with the potential legitimacy of armed resistance but also the difference a decade had made to their perception of the FRG – inseparable as the two were. As with Social Democrats, fear alone does not explain why members of the extraparliamentary left acted as they did. Key to escaping the negative alliance, the compulsory nature of left solidarity, and renouncing political violence was their reassessment of the FRG's fascist potential. However odd it sounds, at the same time that West Germans proved more than willing to tread on civil liberties and to mobilize coercive force against certain segments of the population, this collection of leftists and left-liberals expressed their conviction that democracy had in fact established a defensible stronghold in the FRG. Recall that the shooting of Benno Ohnesorg in June 1967 compelled leftists of different ages and theoretical bents to attend a conference dedicated to ascertaining whether or not the time for committed, active resistance had come. That is, they asked whether, as Horst Mahler summarized it, theirs was a moment comparable to 1930 when fascist dictatorship could still be prevented and the republic saved. In September 1977, by contrast, many of those same actors contributed to a thin volume entitled *Letters in Defense of the Republic*, either by including an individual letter to a real or imagined audience or by reprinting position statements issued at the beginning of the autumn crisis.[14] Diverse in themes and authorship, the texts sought to defend the political order's basic framework by mobilizing readers to the side of tolerance and plurality – to display civic courage despite (or precisely because of) their fears. Read against the Hanover Congress, the overall position cobbled together in these letters and collective statements expressed an optimism that had been absent ten years earlier. Though references to Weimar's crisis abounded, fascism was no longer presented as an immanent threat and thus the call for antifascist resistance was correspondingly absent. If one or two letters betrayed an accusatory tone, the editors explicitly denied that the volume was either an indictment or a counterattack. They did so not only to anticipate critics but

[13] "Aufruf an alle Frauen zur Erfindung des Glücks," Frankfurt, October 1977. Printed in: *Courage* 12 (1977): 10.

[14] Freimut Duve, Heinrich Böll, Klaus Staeck, eds., *Briefe zur Verteidigung der Republik* (Reinbek: Rowohlt, 1977).

also to deny the left its habitual defensive position: "Terrorists and their many political beneficiaries appear to have one fundamental conviction in common: that this society is neither needful nor capable of reform."[15] Aimed at conservatives – traditional or liberal, Social or Christian Democrat – whom they blamed for undermining democratic political culture in the FRG, this observation also pointed a way out of the left's current crisis. The path to an offensive defense of democracy was cleared by the recognition of the West German order – its population as well as its institutions – as a legitimate project of reform.

REDIRECTION AND THE ROAD TO TUNIX

From a few months distance, Peter Schneider noted the exceptional character of these declarations. They were exceptional not only in their specific content but because they were made at all; what he remembered about the German Autumn was leftists' overwhelming silence.[16] Like many others, Schneider attributed this silence to fear, but he asserted that it was not a fear of repression but rather a "fear of furthering the opposing argument" that kept leftists quiet about "the Cologne assassinations."[17] Lingering uncertainty about the legitimacy of violent resistance in the FRG "kept [the left] stuck in a whirlwind of ambivalent emotions," avoiding "the political and moral questions" posed by events so that they remained silent not only about Schleyer and the murder of his driver and bodyguards, but also about Stammheim. They could do nothing in their outrage, he claimed, but "count the dead." With the easing of the autumn crisis this changed, and the majority of leftists, like Peter Schneider, found their voice and began to reflect on what did and did not happen during the weeks just past – and what this meant for the future.

One of the best known commentaries on that autumn's crisis is the 1978 production *Germany in Autumn*.[18] A landmark of New German Cinema, the film presents a pastiche of sequences by thirteen directors and writers that drew on and shaped the left's collective memory of events. Those by Rainer Werner Fassbinder, in particular, present an autobiographical vignette that seems to stand in for the paranoia, despair, and utter disorientation commonly associated with the extraparliamentary left's experience as a whole. Bookended by the state funeral for Schleyer and the more personal funeral held for Ensslin, Baader, and Raspe, the film reserved emotional sympathy for the latter but ultimately located both the actions of the state and the terrorists beyond the

[15] Ibid., 9.

[16] Peter Schneider, "Der Sand an Baaders Schuhen," *Kursbuch* 51 (1978): 1–15.

[17] Ibid., 11–12. For another take on the left's silence that includes (rather than excludes) the autumn's declarations, see Tilman Fichter and Siegward Lönnendonker, "Nihilistischer Terror, links etikettiert, und die Sprachlosigkeit der Neuen Linken," *Der Lange Marsch* 29 (October 1977): 2.

[18] Henrich Böll, Alf Brustellin, Hans Peter Cloos, R. W. Fassbinder, Alexander Kluge, Maximiliane Mainka, Beate Mainka-Jellinghaus, Edgar Reitz, Katja Rupe, Volker Schlöndorff, Peter Schubert, Bernhard Sinkel, and Peter Steinbach, *Deutschland im Herbst* (Munich, 1978), 123 min.

democratic pale. The restriction of civil liberties and the left's experience of persecution is brought home by the anger and paranoia with which Fassbinder's character refuses to house his lover's acquaintance – afraid of bringing the "hunt" for sympathizers to *his* door. Out of work (because "blacklisted") and isolated (because too afraid to leave his apartment), Fassbinder's inability to control his situation makes him – and by extension, the extraparliamentary left – self-absorbed and infantile. Accepting the role of victim, the left rendered itself ineffective. The theme of powerlessness is followed up in another sequence suggestive of the terrorizing quality of the road barricades set up by police to search the population for suspected terrorists. The joking banter of one guard with the occupants of a stopped car points to the state's potential for small and random acts of cruelty. The border guard – immediately pegged as unsophisticated and likely conservative by his provincial accent – makes jokes and derisive comments that simultaneously evoke the criminal profiling being used to track terrorists and the callous exercise of power by even the state's most petty agents.

The film's creators did not restrict their gaze to the state or to the German Autumn of 1977. In one sequence, for example, choppy stock footage of turn-of-the-century communist organizers in the workplace is interspersed with shots of present-day directors staging recreations of flag-waving, flag-burning, and bloody-fisted revolt in order to critically juxtapose the revolutionary enthusiasm of the postwar youth against the actual revolution of workers' movements. Similarly, the shots of domestic violence between Fassbinder and his lover – whom he in turn beats, throws out, and then clings to in desperation – suggest that even extraparliamentary leftists were not immune to the violent and authoritarian relations for which they attacked the existing system. From beginning to end, the film pays visual homage to the inescapable presence of Germany's flawed history and a younger generation's almost desperate desire to find it – if only to free themselves by finally burying it. Images of Rosa Luxembourg shortly before her death reminded viewers that the radical left had good reason to distrust the state (and the SPD in particular) and possibly conjured up the memory of another female writer-revolutionary.[19] Other documentary footage, taken from the Nazi funeral for Field Marshal Erwin Rommel, alluded to Schleyer's past as a member of the SS and one-time assistant to Reinhard Heydrich.[20] Showing the two funerals side by side, the directors not only denied the industrialist the role of innocent victim but also implied that the government's refusal to negotiate for Schleyer's life was akin to Rommel's state-ordered suicide – that Schleyer, like Rommel, had been

[19] In January 1919, the SPD government called on the Freikorps to crush a communist uprising in Berlin. More than happy to oblige, they assassinated Rosa Luxembourg along with Karl Liebknecht and murdered hundreds of others.

[20] Though Schleyer's Nazi past became a major topic of conversation when "weighing" the crime of his murder, RAF members were ignorant of it at the time of the kidnapping. For a biography of Hanns-Martin Schleyer, see Lutz Hachmeister, *Schleyer: Eine deutsche Geschichte* (Munich: Beck, 2004).

sacrificed for the collective. Stringing together these seemingly disparate scenes are the lilting strains of Germany's national anthem and the film's opening and closing refrain: "There comes a point when the horror is such that it is no longer a matter of who began it: it must simply stop." Manifested in this black-and-white statement was the artists' sense that politics needed to evolve beyond its current preoccupation with casting blame – through the left's categories of violence and counterviolence and the state's insistence on crime and punishment – and begin anew.

As the film anticipated, the experiences of the German Autumn proved decisive for propelling oppositional politics down a new path. Mogadishu may have symbolized terrorism's defeat for the mainstream public, but for most leftists the RAF's defeat was self-inflicted and the decisive blow, the murder of Hanns-Martin Schleyer. After five weeks with his captors, Schleyer had been shot at close range in the back of the head and stuffed in the trunk of a car. It was both cold-blooded and personal, a callous execution-style killing that West Germans strongly associated with Nazism. The RAF's actions had long degenerated into a single-minded pursuit of their leaders' liberation and their blatant disregard for the "rules of revolutionary pragmatism" (i.e., the consequences of their actions, especially as they pertained to the build up of state powers) criticized from day one. But that year's string of assassinations – and Schleyer's murder in particular – undermined the guerrillas' cultivated image as victims as well as the moral justification for their armed struggle. "What would have happened if the kidnappers had released the *person* Schleyer!" asked former SDS member, doctor, and historian Karl Heinz Roth (a.k.a "Leo Kerrner").[21] It was a rhetorical question with the power to provoke self-reflection should the reader, like the RAF, find the scenario unimaginable. For by killing Schleyer or, as Roth put it, by making an "unperson" of the "person Schleyer," members of the RAF proved that they operated with the same abstract hate and easy exchange of victims as the institutional forces they fought. Rather than offering hope or some semblance of the freedom to come, the RAF's armed struggle was seen to resemble the violence of the state or, worse, the violence of a future despotic system.

Though they were in no way willing to condone the state's clear overstepping of constitutional boundaries in its fight against terrorism, extraparliamentary leftists began to confront the moral bankruptcy of the RAF and the implications of their own previous ambivalence toward the question of counterviolence. For many, this process entailed definitively rejecting the legitimacy of violent resistance in the FRG. As one leftist declared, "my problem was never distancing myself from the RAF and their 'suicidal politics,' but rather the feeling of inadequacy that I *myself* was unable to conduct my war with this state at that level."[22] This was also true for Peter Schneider who, having

[21] Leo Kerrner, "Terror und Unperson," *Autonomie: Materialien gegen die Fabrikgesellschaft* 10 (January 1978): 4–12; here, 12.

[22] "Jupp Heynckes," "Erwiderung," *Pflasterstrand* 18 (November 3–16, 1977): 23–5; here, 23.

declared violence a legitimate political strategy in 1968, observed nearly ten years later that "most of us still only instinctively know what we think of the strategy of armed struggle." Any convincing condemnation of "political terror" depended on the FRG not being fascist, something Schneider suggested the left would continuously struggle to determine until it understood there to be a "qualitative difference between fascist and democratic capitalism" and the "forms of anti-capitalist struggle" appropriate to each.[23] In this instance, what counterterrorism hid, leftists' own silence and emotional turmoil helped reveal, namely that the FRG was not, in fact, fascist and that the left's ability to effect change relied on this revised assessment of its opponent. Casting off their previously accepted role as victims was equally important to the reevaluation of violent resistance. As many younger radicals, in particular, assumed a certain amount of responsibility for recent events, they conveyed a simultaneous sense of empowerment that came with recognizing their own political agency and – after a decade of its disparagement – the power of discourse. Indeed, a significant number ultimately concluded that, despite the highly imperfect nature of the West German system, working with it was the best way to achieve their goals and to protect civil liberties from the terrorism of misguided militants and the state.

Of course, none of this happened overnight and some were far more reticent than others. Many radicals first responded to that autumn's attempts to distance the left from the RAF and violence much as they had before. For many within the extraparliamentary milieu, the RAF could not be reduced down to a matter of violence. Sympathy for the RAF was "the wish to no longer put up with things, to more effectively defend oneself, to accomplish more aggressive resistance, to no longer enter into compromises, to give back oppression and pain to those from whom it came."[24] And it was this myriad of desires that was difficult for them to let go. As ever, though, the affront had less to do with the actual content of the critique and more with its public and overly penitent character, seeming to come from leftists too willing to break rank and appease the mainstream. A podium discussion with Peter Brückner, Daniel Cohn-Bendit, Otto Schily, Alice Schwarzer, and Frank Wolff at the annual Frankfurt publishing expo, for example, concluded that Marcuse and Dutschke were digging their own political graves by remaining silent on the fact that they were victims of a new level of state persecution.[25] Those who violated the solidarity of the left were accused of masochism, self-delusion, and a "deadly stupidity" attributed to their fear, their psychological identification with the "overly powerful collective aggressor," and their sense of guilt over "having done or desired something improper" in the eyes of the system. The

[23] Schneider, "Sand an Baaders Schuhen," 15.

[24] Heynckes, "Erwiderung," 24.

[25] Verband des Linken Buchhandels, "Sympathy for the Devil: Hexenjagd auf die Linke. Podiumdiskussion auf der Frankfurter Buchmesse," October 1977, International Institute for Social History (Amsterdam, hereafter, IISG) ID-Textarchiv 66/1 714.

podium discussants demanded that such pointless self-sacrifice be replaced by "cunning and courage."[26] On the other side of the country and in the aftermath of the crisis, a new collective forming within West Berlin's alternative scene showed a similar disdain for those who sought to deny their radical political identity by distancing themselves from the RAF: "We experienced the reaction of the left to the events surrounding Schleyer and Mogadishu as cowering before an imagined attack by the state. Many were taking cover as they would from an approaching thunderstorm ... crying 'don't get me wet!'"[27]

Despite the derision heaped upon those who publicly turned their backs on the urban guerrillas and disavowed all violence, the Frankfurt podium discussants and the West Berlin collective were charting a practical path not unlike that of those they criticized. At the very same time that they made these statements, these leftists were busy plotting their own way out of the isolation and identity crisis besetting the nearly defunct negative alliance. The Frankfurt discussants were at the center of an initiative to create an alternative daily newspaper with national distribution. Though there had long been talk of such a project, the desire to protect local "scene" papers and to avoid competing with *ID* had prevented any movement on this front.[28] According to the initiative's members, however, the conditions of that autumn were such that they no longer had a choice – it was imperative to establish a "counter-public sphere" (*Gegenöffentlichkeit*) and the *tageszeitung*, or *taz*, was a major step in that direction. Unabashedly oppositional in conception, the newspaper nonetheless privileged communication over confrontation. The editors maintained that even in the "midst of the media machines of the ruling class, a public sphere requires discussion, so that reason has the force of truth behind it."[29] They sought to introduce critical views and information into a pluralized public opinion by not only discarding the self-referential "elitism" that, in their opinion, plagued the existing alternative press, but also by introducing the left to

[26] Ibid., 3. *Der Lange Marsch* ran a forum on terrorism that captured this initial polarization and the resulting exchange of verbal blows. See, e.g., Dirk Müller, "Legenden auf Sand," and Thomas Fischer and Adam Josef Szell, "Übertotengräber," *Der Lange Marsch* 30 (November 1977): 4–7 and the scathing response by Erich Fried, "Über politische Leichenschändung," followed by each author's response, in *Der Lange Marsch* 32 (January 1978): 19–24. Also, Karl Heinz Roth, "Moral Gehirnwäsche und Verrat" with responses from Peter Brandt, Bernd Rabehl, and the paper's editors Tilman Fichter and Siegward Lönnendonker, in *Der Lange Marsch* 42 (March 1979): 4–5; 7–9.

[27] Autorenkollektiv: Quinn der Eskimo, Frankie Lee, Judas Priest, "Zum Tango gehören immer zwei, wenn ich gehe, kommst du mit!" in *Zwei Kulturen? Tunix, Mescalero und die Folgen*, ed. Dieter Hoffmann-Axthelm, et al. (Berlin: Ästhetik & Kommunikation, 1978), 127.

[28] For background, roundtable discussions and general correspondence on the subject beginning in 1976, see IISG ID-Textarchiv 66/1 714.

[29] "Herbst 77: Es wird ZEITung," in *Dieses obskure Objekt unserer Begierde: Die Tageszeitung: Diskussionspapiere und Leserbriefe April 1978-Januar 1979*, ed. TAZ (Frankfurt: taz, 1979), 5. For the canonical theoretical treatment of *Gegenöffentlichkeit* within the left milieu, see Oskar Negt and Alexander Kluge, *Public Sphere and Experience: Toward an Analysis of the Bourgeois and Proletarian Public Sphere* (Minneapolis: University of Minnesota Press, 1993).

ideas foreign to it. As the newspaper initiative evocatively put it, "the *taz* will have ears for melodies played outside the left."[30]

For their part, the Berliners were planning a January meeting of all "freaks, friends, and comrades" interested in leaving behind "Model Germany" and traveling south "to the beach of *Tunix*" – a play on the imperative *tu nichts* or "do nothing."[31] Somewhere between a flight into fancy and a determined effort to rediscover a radical left in the midst of the recent chaos and confusion, Tunix pronounced a continued commitment to resistance even as it turned its back on old resistance forms. Organizers and participants conveyed their utter exhaustion as both the victims and perpetrators of violence and, as such, negatively coded counterviolence as a reaction rather than a liberating or self-initiated action.[32] The road to Tunix was unclear for these young leftists, but the events of the "three-day party" indicated that it would be paved not only with a negative aversion to violence but also by the positive advances visible in the growing diversity of the left scene as well as the everyday life politics its members pursued. The sure knowledge that they had had enough of death and state repression and that there had to be a better way to banish the powerlessness they felt signaled the increasing currency of a previously marginal belief: that violence of any sort could not bring them closer to the alternative society of "Tunix." Both here and in the case of the *taz*, violence was explicitly rejected as a legitimate mode of opposition.

The desire to reestablish communication and trust with a broader segment of the West German population was the stepping off point for many radicals' political makeover. Members of BUF (*Bewegung Undogmatischer Frühling*, or the Undogmatic Springtime Movement), the student anarchist group responsible for printing the notorious Buback Obituary, were newly critical of their past actions. In ironic reference to the year's events and their own, contentious part in it, they announced the need to call it a day and start over in an article entitled, "BUF – An Obituary." In the context of its self-dissolution, the BUF editorial board acknowledged its failure to clearly disassociate itself from terrorist violence; earlier, their words of well-crafted cynicism had been too opaque and too tongue in cheek to be fully intelligible to outsiders and they now identified their politics as self-interested and destructive: "We provoked the rotting of the system, but then just watched it rot."[33] Similar self-critiques could be heard elsewhere. One group of communists – the Marxist Group (MG) – admitted that its love of jargon had only been outdone by its rhetorical style – an aggressively ironic tone that came to dominate everything its journal published, such that only "violent bitterness and acid cynicism" remained. And even that, the

[30] Initiativgruppen für eine Tageszeitung, eds., *Prospekt: Tageszeitung* (Frankfurt: Zeitungsinitiative-Verlag, 1978), 5.

[31] Flyer for "Treffen in Tunix," IISG ID-Textarchiv: Projekt Arthur.

[32] For a summary of the events and conclusions of the three-day meeting, see "Tunix O-Ton," in Hoffmann-Axthelm, *Zwei Kulturen*, 94–109.

[33] "BUF – Ein Nachruf," *BUF Info* 5 (1977): 1.

group remarked, had required the reader to translate from "MG German" into "normal German." This was all clearly intolerable, its members asserted, given that their goal was the necessarily popular one of socialist humanism.[34] For this reason the MG too disbanded – to reappear in 1983 with the explicit goal of facilitating open and wide-ranging dialogue.[35]

Change was born not only of a renewed commitment to communication but also a clearer sense of how anger and disillusionment had come to poison the left's relationship to society and politics. If Fassbinder's filmic self-representation personified the crisis experienced by the extraparliamentary left generally, then it was not enough to escape the prison of his apartment. Self-obsessed and destructive behavior – as well as romantic and idealized notions of armed revolt – had to give way to a constructive reorientation toward the needs and interests of the general population. Developments in the ecological movement offered one possibility. Shortly after they were elected to the board of the BBU in January 1977, Petra Kelly and Roland Vogt published an article that not only extolled the values of the movement's pacifist wing but planted the seeds for its emergence as a new, national political party.[36] The first Green/Alternative List candidate entered state elections in Lower Saxony in December of that year; less than three years later, a spectrum of sixty-eighters, environmental activists, radical leftists, and disillusioned Social Democrats founded the West German Green Party. Indicating the conscious importance of the question of violence to the movement's history and goals, nonviolence joined ecology, grassroots democracy, and social welfare as one of the party's "four pillars."[37]

[34] Freie-Arbeit-Union, "Einige Anmerkungen zur Marxistischen Gruppe (MG)," *Große Freiheit* 63 (1983): 20–1.

[35] For further exemplary reflections from members of the alternative information "scene," see Redaktion, "Fragmente aus unsere Köpfe," *Pflasterstrand* 17 (October 20–November 2, 1977): 27–31 and Ulrich Mückenberger, "Thesen zu 'Terrorismus, Repression und Widerstand,'" *SHL-Info* (October 28, 1977), 52–7. In a different vein, the Maoist *Rote Fahne* and other newsletters and publications put out by K-Gruppen issued critiques of the RAF and armed revolt for the first time, in line with the public disavowals coming from Moscow, Peking, and East Berlin in the wake of Mogadishu.

[36] Petra Kelly and Roland Vogt, "Ökologie und Frieden: Der Kampf gegen Atomkraftwerke aus der Sicht von Hiroshima," *Forum E* (January/February 1977) cited in: Stephen Milder, "Thinking Globally, Acting (Trans-) Locally: Petra Kelly and the Transnational Roots of West German Green Politics," *Central European History* 43 (2010): 301–26; here, 321. Analyzing the transnational nature of Kelly's politics, Milder argues that she was able to find "new territories of democratic practice only outside the fold of the Left, 'old' or 'new.'" While he sees this as evidence of Europe's importance for the early Greens and I emphasize a shift internal to the West German left, we are both pointing at the same phenomenon: the self-enclosure of left politics before the 1980s and its opening thereafter.

[37] It should be noted that much of the initial impetus for a Green party came from conservatives such as Herbert Gruhl (CDU) and Baldur Springmann, and that many leftists – famously, Joschka Fischer – first understood Green politics as outside the socialist tradition. For the history of the West German Greens, see Andrei S. Markovits and Philip S. Gorski, *The German Left: Red, Green, and Beyond* (New York: Oxford University Press, 1993); Margit Mayer and John Ely, *German Greens: Paradox Between Movement and Party* (Philadelphia: Temple University Press, 1998).

The belief that political means could not be separated from political ends was, for the vast majority of extraparliamentary leftists, one of the indisputable lessons drawn from the experience of terrorism. Particularly evident among members of the growing peace movement was the embrace of nonviolence as the only true revolutionary path for, ironically, the very reason it had previously been dismissed as an ineffective political tool: In a world where violence was the norm, the use of violence was now understood to reproduce and thus reaffirm (and not undermine) structural violence. If revolution negated the existing system, then nonviolence was the singularly revolutionary act. "The more violence, the less revolution" – a phrase penned by Dutch anarcho-pacifist Bart de Ligt in the 1930s – now resonated such that it became a common motto among West German protesters.[38] Rather than run the risk of violent conflict, activists rejected site occupations and folk festivals as inappropriate forms of protest and sought out new or less commonly used forms of civil disobedience.[39] Popular were noncooperation campaigns such as "Account Blue," which asked West Germans to give utility companies a hangover (for which "blue" was the slang) by paying their electric bills manually rather than by automatic, monthly withdrawals.[40] If enough consumers participated, the flood of paperwork and strain on computer systems would negatively impact the companies' infrastructure and force attention onto citizens' concerns. Changing external power relations remained important, but leftists increasingly located the effectiveness of nonviolent resistance – and thus the promise of change – in the essential humanity of the individual resister. An outpouring of admiration for the Red Cells' feminist wing, the Rote Zora, prompted Sibylle Plogstedt to openly denounce political violence in 1981. She once again used *Courage* as a forum but this time in order to discuss the contradictory mixture of power and fear her own acts of counterviolence had instilled in her and what she had come to understand as the central importance of the nonviolent resister to the goal of emancipation and enlightenment.[41] "Violence is illusory power that says more about the person who uses it, than about the goal justifying the violence." Rather than embracing it – or admiring it – Plogstedt insisted that women needed to free themselves from it, particularly the "violence ... in our heads" that caused women to doubt themselves, to settle for what they need, and, in this way, to leave great things to others. Not an easy task, to be sure, but one that Plogstedt no longer doubted was essential to living a human life.

One of the clearest expressions of the new revolutionary spirit sweeping the West German left at the dawn of the 1980s was captured in a 1984 antinuclear protest announcement (Figure 6.1).[42] A full page, it recast a canonical photo

[38] E.g., Erik, "Je mehr Gewalt, desto weniger Revolution," *Stadtzeitung*, June 3, 1983.

[39] Essener-Initiative-gegen-Atomlagen, "Großdemonstration in Kalkar," *Atom-Express* 30 (1982): 7–10.

[40] "Strich durch die Rechnung," *Kölnischer Volksblatt*, October 15, 1983, 1.

[41] Sibylle Plogstedt, "Ist die Gewalt in der Frauenbewegung angekommen?" *Courage* 9 (1981): 30–5.

[42] Found in: IISG ID-Archiv.

FIGURE 6.1. This 1984 Alternative List announcement altered Vladimir Aleksandrovich Serov's 1954 oil painting of Lenin to argue for the revolutionary nature of the Greens and its leader, Petra Kelly. International Institute for Social History, ID-Archiv.

from the Russian Revolution, in which Lenin – the work's central focus – stands ready to lead a crowd of eager Russians toward a better tomorrow, by swapping Lenin's head for that of Petra Kelly. Despite the awkward fit of the superimposed image, whose distinctly feminine characteristics were set off by the traditional three-piece suit under them, the final result maintained the original's momentous excitement and was clearly intended to inspire a new group of nonviolent revolutionaries. Viewed alongside the *taz*'s self-designation as an oppositional forum and the self-description of the Greens as an "anti-party party," there can be little doubt that the possibilities for resistance had been dramatically reconceived.[43] Instead of being defined against the state and fought outside mainstream politics, resistance was, as Kelly herself described it, being waged *within* the existing institutions.[44]

[43] "Herbst 77: Es wird ZEITung," 5; Petra Kelly, "Wir müssen die Etablierten entblössen wo wir können," in *Die Grünen*, ed. Jörg Mettke (Reinbek: Rowohlt, 1982).

[44] Petra Kelly, *Nonviolence Speaks to Power*, eds. Glenn D. Paige and Sarah Gilliatt (Honolulu: Institute for Peace, University of Hawaii, 1992), 11.

That this shift relied on a simultaneous reconception of resistance's context was articulated by another prominent figure in the newly founded Greens Party, Antje Vollmer. Unlike Kelly and other long-standing advocates of nonviolence in the party, Vollmer had identified strongly as part of the extraparliamentary left. In an article explicitly addressing the question of violence, Vollmer reflected on her generation's experience of state violence, their very real belief in the state's fascist character, the violent events of the 1970s, and her own eventual rejection of violence as a legitimate form of resistance or protest.[45] While she gave no single reason for her shift, the first factor Vollmer listed was her realization that not only fascist systems but also democracies have a potential for violence that should – and can – be watched. Clearly implied was also a distinction: unlike fascism, liberal democracy had built-in mechanisms for curbing this tendency. For Vollmer and others like her, understanding that the potential for state abuse of power was normal and not, as she put it, "a cause for emergency" was crucial to allowing the past to remain in the past.[46] Put slightly differently, the necessary condition for a new understanding of resistance and oppositional politics in the FRG was the extraparliamentary left's conclusion that the West German state was, despite its many flaws, fundamentally different from its Nazi predecessor.

On the twentieth anniversary of Benno Ohnesorg's death, a former radical defended the prominence of nonviolence in the Greens' platform by describing how he had come to hold this position. Despite having described himself as a pacifist, even in the 1960s, Uli Fischer recounted how he had admired "what the armed comrades were doing." His categorical rejection of violence had been a long and difficult journey:

> From 2 June on, the student revolt and later groups that formed ... felt – and I felt, too – authorized to think about violence in practice ... we used the Tupamaros as our model.... What arose from this was, on the one hand, the K-Gruppen, who verbally defended revolutionary violence ... and, on the other hand, the armed combat groups.... We all were directly mired in [these developments] and had a very undifferentiated relationship to violence, finding it both good and just.... Back then we actually developed fantasies of violence ... and tried to put them into practice. And we self-destructed as a result.
>
> [I]t was a difficult process for me and for many other people as well, to come to such a different notion of the radical-democratic change of society ... not like simply testing the parliamentary path instead of APO, but a radical-democratic rejection of violence – completely unambiguous – and ... the development of civilian forms of resistance and of nonviolent resistance. This belongs ... to the radical-democratic project that is the Greens.[47]

The confrontation with violence – the state's, the RAF's, and their own conflicted relationship to it – was not straightforward nor did it occur uniformly across the extraparliamentary left. At the same time, a view to the concerted

45 Antje Vollmer, "Die Faszination der Gewalt und die eigene Geschichte," *links* 9 (1986): 18–20.
46 Ibid., 19.
47 Uli Fischer, "Schwerpunktthema: Gewalt," 55–7.

and constructive efforts made to translate the lessons of the 1970s into new forms of socially engaged resistance demands that we revise the image of defeat commonly associated with left politics in the aftermath of the German Autumn.

This is not to suggest that the apex of terrorist and counterterrorist violence during the German Autumn led directly to a new consensus on what form oppositional politics in West Germany should take. Nor did all members of the left denounce violence as a legitimate form of resistance. The Autonomen, who first formed, according to the movement's own autobiographers, in the "political hole" left by the German Autumn and the subsequent integration of extraparliamentary forces, are ample (if also extreme) evidence to the contrary.[48] Self-identifying leftists who have employed a wide variety of protest actions, the Autonomen are nonetheless most famous for their violent confrontations with police, skinheads, and neo-Nazis – especially each May Day – as well as their embrace of violent resistance in house occupations, antinuclear demonstrations, and protests against various urban development projects, including the expansion of Frankfurt's airport in the early 1980s. Because the Autonomen are highly diverse and extremely theory averse, it is dangerous to make generalizations about them. But even they can be seen to reflect the changes that occurred at the end of the 1970s, not least because they so consciously distanced themselves from the political ideas, actions, and debates of the '68ers. If one thing originally united the Autonomen, it was the wholesale rejection of the state – any state, in the anarchist tradition – as antithetical to the self-determined, decentralized, and fully hierarchy-free society and lifestyle they desired. Antifascist, to be sure, their resistance was not, however, grounded in an understanding of structural continuities between the Third Reich and the FRG. Having come of age amidst the citizens' initiatives and counterterrorism of the 1970s, the Autonomen fought the nightmares of nuclear war, economic insecurity, and state repression (which they strongly identified with the rise of a new right) and justified the use of violence not with theory and an optimistic vision for tomorrow but rather the sense that they had nothing – literally, "no future" – to lose.[49] Many members of the Greens responded favorably to aspects of this militancy; however, a genuine divide separated them. This was evident in the younger generation's open and repeated rejection of their elders and powerfully summed up by the target symbol often seen on the back of Autonomen jackets along with the command for police to "go ahead, shoot!"[50] Whatever else this is, it is not the sense of empowerment and need to defend

[48] Thomas Schultze and Almut Gross, *Die Autonomen: Ursprünge, Entwicklung und Profil der Autonomen Bewegung* (Hamburg: Konkret, 1997), 8, 34. In their introduction, Schultze and Gross acknowledge drawing on their own personal experiences as well as the impossibility of offering a general representation applicable to all Autonomen.

[49] Schultze and Gross describe the Autonomen's pessimism and actionism as deriving from their "No-future-Vorstellungen" and emphasize their constituency's younger age (around twenty years old in 1980/81). Ibid., 34–7.

[50] Ibid., 37.

democracy – however imagined – that mobilized an earlier generation to take action or that had called the Red Army Faction into existence.

THE CONSERVATIVE *WENDE*

"A Freeing Act: Mogadishu Proves German Democracy's Ability to Put Up a Fight."[51] Ernst Cramer, close friend and confidant of media mogul Axel Springer, summed up in a simple headline what was, for more conservative West Germans, most noteworthy about the autumn's confrontation with terrorism. The question of whether the second German republic could (and would) defend itself in the manner of a truly sovereign state had finally been answered, and answered in the affirmative. It is tempting to conclude that the easing of doubts on this score served mainly to bolster conservatives' traditional position on state power – in their own minds as well as with the general public – given that in 1983 the Christian Union received the second highest election returns of its history. In government again, they also did little to refute this conclusion, demonstrating unwavering support for further nuclear armament and pushing a new antiterrorism package through parliament in 1986. But West German conservatives underwent their own period of renegotiation and change at the end of the 1970s that, if less dramatic than that experienced on the left, also drew on the lessons – and opportunities – presented by terrorism.

On the level of concrete policy, the experience of terrorism had made converts of many who previously resisted the reorganization and centralization of power, particularly in the realm of police force. No one, not even the most ardent Social Democrats, desired the elimination of West Germany's federalist system. But the need – and the seeming continued inability – to contain terrorism had encouraged CDU/CSU leaders at the Land level to promote the integration and concentration of police intelligence and computer database systems. Just as significant, they came to accept both federal coordination of police action and a federal police force. Though it was not always clear from their rhetoric, the change was apparent in their repeated use of federal police powers. Indeed, police historian Heiner Busch notes with some irony that CDU/CSU-governed Länder used the new federal police powers far more than those governed by the SPD.[52] Where once Christian Democrats and Christian Socials both demanded police be recognized as part of local culture (and thus, like education, outside federal jurisdiction), just two weeks after Mogadishu politicians like Alfred Dregger stood before Bundestag and announced the need for a single, federal law that would regulate the duties and authority of police in each of the Länder.[53] Moreover, unlike the FDP and SPD, who revised several

[51] Ernst Cramer, "Die befreiende Handlung: Mogadischu beweist die Wehrhaftigkeit der deutschen Demokratie," *Die Welt* (October 19, 1977).

[52] Heiner Busch et al., *Die Polizei in der Bundesrepublik* (Frankfurt: Campus, 1985), 101.

[53] *Verhandlungen des deutschen Bundestages: Stenographische Berichte*, VIII. Bundestag, 53. Sitzung (October 28, 1977), 4101. Dregger listed the federal regulation as one of the Union's top priorities in its newest proposal for antiterrorism legislation.

of the legislative decisions made in their effort to contain terrorism, the CDU/CSU, having conceded the new age of information technology and international crime, embraced their changed position on federal power and did not appear to look back.

Of greatest significance, however, was the way the debate over terrorism's origins opened the doors to the right's reappropriation of solutions they had previously rejected (or been denied) because of those options' association with National Socialism. In this, terrorism and the German Autumn helped conservatives in and out of parliament make "the turn" toward an invigoration of the movement that many had been campaigning for since the early 1970s. Prominent among the latter was new right ideologue Armin Mohler, who had diagnosed Germans' putative "fear of power" in his 1965 treatise, *What Germans Fear*.[54] In 1974 he narrowed his gaze to postwar conservatism and argued that when it came to the FRG, the political right was divided into two camps: those who simply imagined it as a bulwark against communism and those fixated on practical concerns about its longevity. In short, he claimed that all conservatives did was complain and offer doom-and-gloom predictions instead of constructive alternatives; ideological vision was, needless to say, sorely lacking.[55] Whether one shares Mohler's assessment of postwar conservatism or not, terrorism certainly encouraged the tendencies he criticized. Even those who excitedly welcomed the return of a state of exception devoted themselves primarily to penning tales of catastrophe should West Germans refuse – even now – to confront the problem of state power they had deliberately side-stepped in founding the FRG.[56] In this way, the crisis of terrorism provided life support to a conservatism already outdated by the end of the 1960s. Its resolution, however, also helped pull the plug and usher in a new conservative era.

One only need look at the difference between the elections of 1976, when the CDU/CSU regained its position as the largest party in parliament with the slogan "Freedom not Socialism," and 1980, when the party had its lowest returns since 1949. The brash, hard-hitting style of Franz-Josef Strauß, the Christian Union's candidate for chancellor in 1980, and an election campaign for "Security and Freedom" against the alleged horrors of socialist mismanagement and procommunist foreign policy (i.e., *Ostpolitik*), bespoke a politics upon which the sun had set. Not only was Helmut Schmidt almost as

[54] Armin Mohler, *Was die Deutschen fürchten: Angst vor der Politik, Angst vor der Geschichte, Angst vor der Macht* (Stuttgart: Seewald, 1965).

[55] idem, "Zum deutschen Konservatismus seit 1945," in *Die Herausforderung der Konservativen: Absage an Illusion*, ed. Gerd-Klaus Kaltenbrunner (Munich: Herderbücherei, 1974), 164–89; here, 183.

[56] For a brief discussion of the euphoria – and doom and gloom mantra – of Schmittian thinkers in response to 1970s terrorism, see Jan-Werner Müller, *A Dangerous Mind: Carl Schmitt in Post-War European Thought* (New Haven: Yale University Press, 2003), 187–8. One of the clearest products of this was a 1978 conference and conference volume dedicated to the subject of emergency: Carl Friedrich von Siemens Stiftung, *Der Ernstfall* (Berlin: Propyläen, 1979).

unlikely a Marxist as Strauß himself, but geopolitical tensions had replaced political extremism as the most likely threat to the Federal Republic's existence.[57] To be sure, West Germans gathered in ever greater numbers to demand an end to nuclear armament but protest – politically diverse as it was now recognized to be – was no longer enough of a radical bogeyman to rouse the fears and loyalties of conservatives much less increasingly influential centrist voters.[58] Strauß's poor showing removed the last obstacles to the party program commissioned years before by Helmut Kohl and conceived by the likes of Richard von Weizsäcker, Kurt Biedenkopf, and Heiner Geißler.[59] Similar to Mohler, these party thinkers were convinced that the previous generation, riding on the coattails of reconstruction and economic growth, had neglected politics' cultural and ideological dimensions. Part of their attempt to solve this problem entailed imitating the Social Democrats. The CDU began to court intellectuals and to engage the public by funding paperbacks and various other sorts of propaganda publications it previously neglected.[60] In this, the push for internal party reform dovetailed nicely with a conservative renaissance taking shape outside party confines. The efforts of Gerd-Klaus Kaltenbrunner, for example, to resurrect a highbrow sphere of conservative published opinion with his Herder-Initiative book series and the founding of journals such as *Criticon* paralleled Helmut Kohl's 1973 call for the reinvigoration of a conservative "community of values and ideas."[61] Instead of "security and freedom" they were now asked to rally around "freedom, solidarity, justice."[62]

Happy as many intellectuals were to answer this call, not all of them were politically acceptable to party conservatives. The Gaullism and nationalism espoused by Mohler and his followers, for instance, did not fit the Christian Union's profile as a right-leaning people's party, of the center.[63] This, and its unwavering commitment to Western integration, instead, encouraged strong ties between the CDU/CSU and conservative liberals like Hermann Lübbe who, having drifted rightward over the course of the 1970s, decided to stay there – abandoning the SPD fold once and for all due to what they perceived as that

[57] Frank Bösch provides an account of the crisis that the loss of the SPD as a "Gegner" at the end of the 1970s caused the Union as well as the anachronistic campaign waged by Strauß in 1980. Frank Bösch, *Macht und Machtverlust: Die Geschichte der CDU* (Stuttgart: DVA, 2002), esp. 42–3 and 214–17.

[58] Many younger voters, women, and northern Protestants voted for the CDU for the first time in 1976 in reaction to the economic downturn, liberalization of abortion, and other SPD reform policies. Ibid., 214.

[59] On the Grundsatzprogramm-Kommission: ibid., 34–44.

[60] Ibid., 38. Also: Jeffrey Herf, *War By Other Means: Soviet Power, West German Resistance, and the Battle of the Euromissiles* (New York: Free Press, 1991), 98–101.

[61] For his early call to arms, see Gerd-Klaus Kaltenbrunner, "Zehn Gebote für Konservative," *Christ und Welt* (September 15, 1972), 9; idem, ed., *Rekonstruktion des Konservatismus* (Freiburg: Rombach, 1972). Kohl cited in Herf, *War By Other Means*, 100.

[62] Bösch, *Macht und Machtverlust*, 39–40.

[63] See Mohler, "Zum deutschen Konservatismus," 34–53, esp. 48–9.

party's continued drift left.[64] And it was ultimately these thinkers who proved invaluable to conservatism's renewal. With the German Autumn having confirmed that Bonn was not Weimar, liberal conservatives were ever more inclined to view their ethical-political sensibilities as a neutral, common sense position, one embodied in the FRG's existing institutions. By the 1980s, postwar liberalism was, to their minds, simply prudent political practice. And this quiet certitude they bequeathed to the CDU/CSU, outfitting conservative politicians with the rhetoric of pragmatic decisionism and sober realism that, ironically, Helmut Schmidt had done so much to popularize.[65] With liberal conservatives' help, then, Helmut Kohl was able to offer conservatives a new vision of the strong state leader, one that finally displaced the authoritarian style of Konrad Adenauer and Franz-Josef Strauß – and catapulted the CDU/CSU back into power. According to one scholar of neoconservatism, liberal conservatives helped make the Christian Union culturally palatable to a broader electorate, relieving the party of its regional, confessional, and unsavory nationalist associations so that even northern Protestants might vote for it. Part of this was their ability to articulate "what many knew in their hearts" but only nationalists had previously said, namely "that the institutions of the FRG were worth defending."[66]

This last was crucial for conservatism and the rise of the new right. In refocusing on a defense of the existing order, liberal conservatives opened up new avenues for expression of German patriotism and the normalization of the nation that had been closed off to postwar conservatives. The debate over terrorism's origins petered out after the German Autumn, having culminated in a public exchange between Jürgen Habermas and Kurt Sontheimer where each man established his case by presenting the other's perspective as the seedbed from which terrorist violence sprung.[67] But liberal conservatives' diagnosis that what ultimately ailed contemporary German society was a lack of identity and strong, shared values was taken up and pursued further by

[64] Jens Hacke, *Philosophie der Bürgerlichkeit: Die liberalkonservative Begründung der Bundesrepublik* (Göttingen: Vandenhoeck & Ruprecht, 2006), 25. See also: Müller, *A Dangerous Mind*, 188f; A. Dirk Moses, *German Intellectuals and the Nazi Past* (Cambridge: Cambridge University Press, 2007), 201–3.

[65] Their influence was direct and indirect: Kohl's speeches were clearly inspired by Lübbe, for example, and Michael Stürmer served as an adviser. With polls demonstrating that the average voter preferred Schmidt over Kohl in 1976 because the former was judged more competent and a "man of the people," one might speculate that Schmidt himself influenced party conservatives' new vision of the strong state leader. For poll and election results, see David Child and Jeffrey Johnson, *West Germany, Politics and Society* (London: Helm, 1981). Here, 31.

[66] Jerry Z. Muller, "German Neo-Conservatism, ca. 1968–1985: Hermann Lübbe and Others," in *German Ideologies Since 1945: Studies in the Political Thought and Culture of the Bonn Republic*, ed. Jan-Werner Müller (New York: Palgrave, 2003), 161–84; here, 179.

[67] The publicized letter exchange, which took place over several months, was first triggered by Habermas's response to a television interview given by Sontheimer on September 11, 1977. Jürgen Habermas, "Die Bühne des Terrors: Ein Brief an Kurt Sontheimer vom 19 September 1977," *Merkur* 31 (October 1977): 944–59.

conservative politicians in the 1980s, though notably without Sontheimer's help. The CDU's 1983 promise of a spiritual-moral turn (*geistige-moralische Wende*) included addressing social unrest by restoring pride and individual investment in what West Germans had achieved in the postwar period.[68] If terrorism and political extremism were, as members of all three parliamentary parties had argued, the result of the younger generation's disaffection and materialist values, then conservatives aimed to give West Germans a sense of attachment – not to abstract principles or visions of social transformation but to the organic collectivities of family and nation.[69] One of the ways they sought to do this was by lightening the burden of history. In his first few years as chancellor, Helmut Kohl spoke of the "grace of a late birth" that freed the postwar generation of responsibility for Nazi crimes and stood at the French battlefield of Verdun alongside President François Mitterrand to officially mourn the fallen of *both* world wars. In May 1985, Kohl used the fortieth commemoration of the Allies' victory over Nazi Germany to have U.S. president Ronald Reagan visit Bitburg military cemetery, where approximately two thousand German soldiers – including forty-nine members of the Waffen-SS – were buried. The wreath-laying ceremony at Bitburg was not only intended to exhibit the close ties that had long existed between the former enemies but, following as it did on Reagan's visit to the Bergen–Belsen concentration camp, it was also a blatant attempt to equate German victims of war and Jewish victims of genocide. Surrounded by controversy both before and after the ceremony, it was nonetheless a significant step toward normalizing the Nazi past and creating a self-confident nation.[70] In the 1970s, the question of Germany's Nazi past was wrapped up with the debate on terror and counterterror. From this perspective, one of the crucial conditions laying the groundwork for Kohl's 1985 Bitburg offensive was the outpouring of international support for the successful 1977 mission of the GSG-9 and the pride West Germans were subsequently and publicly able to claim for their "young heroes" in uniform and the nation they embodied.

A NEW GERMANY?

In 1981, Heinrich Böll wrote a letter to Chancellor Schmidt describing a recent demonstration in Bonn, in which more than two hundred thousand people gathered to protest the deployment of mid-range nuclear missiles in Western

[68] Bösch, *Macht und Machtverlust*, 45.
[69] Moses, *German Intellectuals*, 223.
[70] Geoffrey H. Hartman, ed., *Bitburg in Moral and Political Perspective* (Bloomington: Indiana University Press, 1986); Deborah E. Lipstadt, "The Bitburg Controversy," *American Jewish Yearbook* 87 (1987): 21–37. For contemporary American commentary, see, e.g., Bernard Weinraub, "Reagan Joins Kohl in Brief Memorial at Bitburg Graves," *New York Times*, May 6, 1985. Even rock musicians weighed in: punk icons the Ramones recorded "My Brain Is Hanging Upside-Down (Bonzo Goes to Bitburg)" and avant-garde eclecticist Frank Zappa offered up "Reagan at Bitburg."

Europe. What had taken the writer by surprise was, he explained, "something very rare." The demonstration had revealed

> a *peaceful mass*, political in an entirely different way than the Emergency Law demonstrators of 1968. How representative this crowd was is difficult to say, but, in any case, they did not raise fear in me – me, who otherwise shuns mass events. And by no means was there only mood [*Stimmung*] present, but also voice [*Stimme*].[71]

For one insightful observer, popular politics in the early 1980s had replaced the overwrought emotions of earlier years with an atmosphere of reasoned dialogue. If, indeed, West Germans had come to accept the possibility of a peaceful mass as Böll suspected, this did not require them to agree on exactly what constituted legitimate civil action and state intervention. In addition to the conflicts discussed previously, debates within the Greens over the course of the 1980s and 1990s – including over Germany's military role in Kosovo in 1998 and Afghanistan in 2001 – proved time and again that the question of legitimate violence was not dead.[72] More recently, the public response to a 2005 exhibition on the RAF has indicated that the history of the extraparliamentary left and its relationship to violence is still being worked through.[73] If this multiplicity of answers raises doubt over the depth of the transformation in West German political culture, then, there is perhaps no better evidence for it than the continued polemics in which the defenders of "1968" refute the relevance of violence for the 1960s and 1970s in response to those who would draw strong connections between terrorism and student protest. Both sides' positions pivot on the conviction that nonviolence is *the* fundamental condition for morally and politically acceptable protest and resistance – hence the impulse to protect student protesters from the implication that they operated within a different code. The absoluteness of this consensus is testimony to the experiences of the 1970s and the revised political landscape of the following decades, in which fascism and postwar conceptions of counterviolence and resistance no longer defined the field of action.

Böll's letter to Schmidt, however, captures more than the changes wrought to extraparliamentary politics and conceptions of resistance in the FRG. As a former supporter of the SPD who joined the Greens' electoral initiative in its infancy, Böll was also a potent (if subtle) communicator of the deep dissatisfaction within the SPD over recent transgressions of previous limits on power.

[71] Heinrich Böll to Helmut Schmidt, November 4, 1981, AdsD Helmut Schmidt Papers 6382.

[72] See, e.g., a chronology of the "violence discussion" from October 1979 to July 1983 in: Alternative Liste Berlin, "Dokumentation über die Gewaltdiskussion in der Alternativen Liste Berlin" (Berlin: Geschäftsführender Ausschuß der Alternativen Liste für Demokratie und Umweltschutz, 1983), IISG ID Bro 531/25 fol.

[73] The RAF exhibit embroiled the press, politicians, and scholars in debate over the relationship between art, media, politics, and contemporary research; it outraged the family and friends of RAF victims; and it prompted angry exchanges over the relationship between the RAF and the 1960s student movement. Klaus Biesenbach, ed., *Zur Vorstellung des Terrors: Die RAF-Ausstellung* (Göttingen, Steidl, 2005).

In 1979, this came to include the support demonstrated by Helmut Schmidt – newly nicknamed the "missile chancellor" – for NATO's double-track decision, a policy of deterrence through nuclear parity that only increased the FRG's chances of becoming a venue for mutually assured destruction.[74] This latest demonstration of executive power encouraged significant numbers of Social Democrats to join the West German peace movement and brought the SPD's left wing into open opposition against the leadership. It also pushed a last, critical contingent of voters as well as deputies over to the Greens/Alternative List camp.[75] Dieter Lattmann, a key voice of dissent during the parliamentary debates on counterterrorism legislation, decided not to run in the 1980 elections; Karl-Heinz Hansen, who not only voted against the Contact Ban but also denounced party leaders for pressuring deputies to pass a bill they did not support, was finally expelled from the party for derogatory remarks about Schmidt; and Manfred Coppick resigned his party membership in 1982.[76] In one fashion or another, those members who had struggled to maintain a "critical solidarity" with the SPD-led government in its fight against terrorism finally left the party. But the SPD's fracturing over the issue of state power did far more than seal its rightward turn; considered alongside simultaneous developments within the extraparliamentary left, it spelled a dramatic realignment of left politics. This involved processes of domestication and integration, it is true, but also productive reorganization. Most obviously, the Greens succeeded where previous left-of-SPD parties failed. They obtained a national presence by crossing the five percent hurdle into Bundestag in 1983.

Moreover, those who remained committed to the SPD were by no means content with the position on state power represented by Helmut Schmidt. Almost immediately after the German Autumn, Social Democrats began debating the actions taken during the terrorist crisis in a final negotiation of democratic force. To conservatives' consternation, Social Democrats joined members of the FDP to repeal Paragraphs 88a and 130a of the Criminal Code – the amendments criminalizing support for and incitement to violence – having since determined them an illegitimate infringement on civil liberties. And the remaining SPD membership effectively drew a line on state power that placed nuclear weaponization *outside* the legitimate use of force. Though one might argue that Schmidt simply pursued a familiar course of prevention and international cooperation, prominent Social Democrats such as Egon Bahr, Erhard Eppler, and Oskar Lafontaine insisted that when the threat was nuclear annihilation on an ever-increasing scale, deterrence through strategic parity should no longer be pursued. Even Brandt and Vogel, who had firmly supported Schmidt during the terrorist crisis, openly distanced themselves from the double-track decision. The end of the 1970s thus also found

74 The so-called Euromissiles plan included the deployment of cruise and Pershing II missiles to counterbalance the Soviet SS-20s stationed in Eastern Europe.

75 Markovits and Gorski, *Red, Green, and Beyond*, 106.

76 Gerard Braunthal, *The German Social Democrats Since 1969: A Party in Power and Opposition* (Boulder: Westview, 1994), 271–3.

the parliamentary left entering a period of intense self-examination and reorientation, a fact underscored by the collapse of the SPD-FDP coalition in 1982 and the beginning of Helmut Kohl's sixteen-year reign.

Despite the fierce debate and the SPD's loss of both right-wing and left-wing members over precisely the issue of state power, the new conclusions reached by Social Democrats in their confrontation with terrorism were not pushed under the carpet but rather, with some negotiation, became part of a new party consensus on democratic governance. This was strikingly demonstrated at the turn of the new century when the SPD found itself, once again, in government – this time as part of the so-called Red-Green coalition – and faced with the threat of a different terrorism. Immediately following the September 11 attacks, the SPD government unanimously supported new antiterrorism legislation that included a number of civil rights infringements.[77] Controversial as a result, the "anti-terror packages" were, somewhat ironically, authored by former RAF attorney Otto Schily, who started his political career in the Greens but eventually left it for the SPD in 1989 and served as Germany's interior minister from 1998 to 2005. Even more striking, in late 2001, former Juso president and Schmidt critic Gerhard Schröder became the first chancellor of a newly unified Germany to mobilize ground forces for a combat (rather than peacekeeping) mission abroad. Like the antiterrorism legislation, Schröder's decision to send German troops into Afghanistan – and the domestic and international acceptance of his decision – is difficult to imagine without the series of changes initiated during the German Autumn of 1977.

***

This book has emphasized the normalization of democracy's defense that accompanied West Germans' confrontation with terrorism at the end of the 1970s – a process whereby militant democracy and resistance were reconceived as part of ordinary rather than exceptional politics. This is not to propose a monocausal answer to the political reorientations and relative stability of the 1980s. The study of West German terrorism reveals how often the debates generated were about democracy, but they were also about the economy, technology, and even the simultaneous sense of loss and empowerment that both state and civilian actors experienced with the dissolution of traditional nation-state territoriality. The containment of terrorism thus entailed far more than the negotiation of past and present terror.

And did all this amount to a working through of the Nazi past as it revised Germans' long-standing insecurity regarding democracy? The German "*jein*" – "*ja und nein*," yes and no – seems appropriate here. The experience of terrorism did not seem to inspire West Germans to reflect productively on their relationship to National Socialism or the crimes perpetrated in its name. Indeed, the eagerness with which actors on all sides of the debate invoked vague and

[77] For a detailed examination of the new antiterrorism legislation, see Oliver Lepsius, "Liberty, Security, and Terrorism: The Legal Position in Germany," *German Law Journal* 5 (2004): 435–60.

unspecific notions of fascism and "Auschwitz" to use as weapons against their opponents would suggest that little progress was made in this arena. But the new conclusions drawn about the existing liberal order undoubtedly de-escalated West Germans' antifascist vigilance and in this way changed the tenor of conflict. Freeing West Germans as it did from the particular logics embedded in their postwar, postfascist relationships to the state, this process strengthened democratic legitimacy at the same time that it integrated a previously disaffected (and genuinely disruptive) population. In this respect, the successful containment of both terrorism and counterterrorism – and the blow this dealt to a vitally important political-cultural framework – contributed to the eventual demise of the postwar political order.

The process of normalization also highlights the vital importance of the international stage to recent changes in the FRG. Over the course of the 1970s, West Germans were leaders in counterterrorism at least in part because solutions from technological modernization to political multilateralism offered safety from their past as well as from new and unforeseen threats. International and transnational cooperation – between governments as well as among citizens – was critical for assuaging fears of state abuse and legitimating German leaders' actions. Once informal norms were gradually supplemented by European antiterrorist legislation, a recognized standard emerged by which to prove the democratic legitimacy of West German – and all European countries' – counterterrorism efforts. Meanwhile organizations such as Amnesty International and the Russell Tribunal offered citizens a high-visibility legal forum through which to contest state abuses of power and the increasingly broad definition of national security interests. In short, West Germans were able to revise previous assumptions regarding democracy and gain some distance from their troubled past in part because, by the beginning of the 1980s, the "German factor" was well on its way to being eclipsed by Europe in questions of security.

It would be easy to leave the story of West Germans' confrontation with terrorism here, as a narrative of liberal democracy's triumph – when Germans finally got it right and entered into the fold of securely democratic nations. This is not an uncommon take on postwar German history for, although it was far from an inevitable outcome, it seems clear that liberalism has emerged the big winner. To end on a self-satisfied note would be unfortunate, however, because it would miss what the example of the FRG can teach us about the general problem of terrorism and democracy. One of the more common assessments of 1970s West Germany is that, though it was certainly not fascist, it proved democratically insecure, with a notable "liberal deficit."[78] This seems a reasonable conclusion. But a comparative view shows that the corresponding assumption, namely that a presumably secure democracy like Great Britain or the United States will prove an unfailing guarantor of civil liberties and freedoms – and thus set the ideal for which others should strive – is flawed. For all its democratic insecurity, the Federal Republic was far less prone to illiberal overreaches

[78] I take this particular formulation from Müller, *A Dangerous Mind*, 184.

by the state than its Western counterparts, whose long histories of democratic governance seem to encourage certain kinds of complacency among citizens and political leaders alike. Given that this is just as dangerous to democracy in the long run as are immediate attacks on the state, we should perhaps be leery of interpreting passivity and silence as signs of a population's democratic maturity. It might, in fact, be worth considering how to regain that which is lost when a democratic society feels itself *overly* secure. For if they revealed themselves combative, at turns undemocratic, and intensely emotional about their politics, West Germans also proved to be critically engaged. If the trust and dialogue associated with civility was initially beyond them, they nonetheless came to talk with one another and to do so productively. For in the end, it is true: One should not believe either the critical or rapturous media hype about the German Autumn. Terrorism was not only defeated in Mogadishu by a crack counterterrorism squad but, just as importantly, in the public debate that raged in the institutions, streets, and multitudinous publications of the FRG.

Over thirty years after the German Autumn and a decade after September 11, terrorism is seen exclusively as a threat to democratic systems, both in its sheer capacity for destruction and in the potentially repressive character of measures taken to combat it. The result is an overwhelming tendency on the part of citizens and governments to fear and forestall public discussion on dissent, authority, and violence. If the example of 1970s West Germany has any insight to offer, however, it is that open dialogue between political decision makers and the public on the very issues of security and freedom can actually build consensus around democratic institutions and empower a critical civil society. In fact, it suggests that a society's ability to successfully cope with crises – "emergency situations" and "states of exception" – relies on this very debate. How, then, to remain securely insecure so as to see not merely theoretical merit but a very real practical need for open communication on that which scares us most? That is a question that remains to be debated.

Select Bibliography

ARCHIVES

Archiv für Christlich-Demokratische Politik. Konrad-Adenauer-Stiftung, Sankt-Augustin.
Archiv Grünes Gedächtnis. Heinrich-Böll-Stiftung, Berlin.
Archiv der sozialen Demokratie. Friedrich Ebert Stiftung, Bad Godesberg.
  Helmut Schmidt Papers
  Hans-Jochen Vogel Papers
Außerparlamentarische Opposition Archiv. Freie Universität, Berlin.
Bundesarchiv Koblenz.
  Federal Chancellor's Office
  Federal Ministry of Interior
  Federal Ministry of Justice
  Carl Karstens Papers
Dokumentationsstelle für unkonventionelle Literatur, Stuttgart.
Hamburger Institut für Sozialforschung.
International Institute for Social History (IISG), Amsterdam.
  ID-Archiv
  Projekt Arthur

NEWSPAPERS AND JOURNALS

Arbeiterkampf
Das Argument
Autonomie: Materialien gegen die Fabrikgesellschaft
Courage
Frankfurter Allgemeine Zeitung
Frankfurter Hefte
Frankfurter Rundschau
konkret
Kursbuch
Der Lange Marsch – Zeitung für eine Neue Linke
links
Pflasterstrand

radikal
RC-Bulletin
Der Spiegel
Süddeutsche Zeitung
tageszeitung
Vorwärts
Die Welt
Die Zeit

PUBLISHED PRIMARY SOURCES

Adorno, Theodor W. "Education after Auschwitz." In *Can One Live after Auschwitz?: A Philosophical Reader*. Edited by Rolf Tiedemann. Stanford: Stanford University Press, 2003.

Adorno, Theodor W., Elise Frenkel-Brunswik, Daniel J. Levinson, and R. Nevitt Sanford. *The Authoritarian Personality*. New York: Harper, 1950.

Anders, Ann, ed. *Autonome Frauen: Schlüsseltexte der neuen Frauenbewegung seit 1968*. Frankfurt: Athenäum, 1988.

Arato, Andrew, and Eike Gebhardt, eds. *The Essential Frankfurt School Reader*. New York: Continuum, 1982.

Autorenkollektiv. *Die Linke antwortet Jürgen Habermas*. Frankfurt: Europäische Verlagsanstalt, 1968.

Bakker Schut, Pieter H., ed. *Das Info – Briefe der Gefangenen aus der RAF, 1973–1977*. Kiel: Neuer Malik, 1987.

Baumann, Bommi. *How It All Began: The Personal Account of a West German Urban Guerrilla*. Translated by Helen Ellenbogen. Vancouver: Arsenal, 2002.

Benda, Ernst. *Die Notstandsverfassung*. Munich: Olzog, 1966.

Benz, Wolfgang, ed. *"Bewegt von der Hoffnung aller Deutschen": Zur Geschichte des Grundgesetzes: Entwürfe und Diskussion, 1941–1949*. Munich: Deutscher Verlag, 1979.

Bergmann, Uwe, ed. *Bedingungen und Organisation des Widerstandes: Der Kongreß in Hannover*. Berlin: Voltaire, 1967.

Bewaffneter Kampf: Texte der RAF: Auseinandersetzung und Kritik. Graz: Rote Sonne, 1973.

Billstein, H., and K. Naumann, eds. *Für eine bessere Republik: Alternative der demokratischen Bewegung*. Cologne: Pahl-Rugenstein, 1981.

Böckenförde, Ernst-Wolfgang. *Recht, Staat, Freiheit: Studien zur Rechtsphilosophie, Staatstheorie, und Verfassungsgeschichte*. Frankfurt: Suhrkamp, 1991.

Staat, Gesellschaft, Freiheit: Studien zur Staatstheorie und zum Verfassungsrecht. Frankfurt: Suhrkamp, 1976.

"Der verdrängte Ausnahmezustand: Zum Handeln der Staatsgewalt in außergewöhnlichen Lagen." *Neue Juristische Wochenschrift* 38 (1978): 1881–90.

Böll, Heinrich. *Die verlorene Ehre der Katharina Blum oder: Wie Gewalt entstehen und wohin sie führen kann*. Cologne: Kiepenheuer & Witsch, 1974.

Braun, Otto. *Von Weimar zu Hitler*. New York: Europa, 1940.

Brückner, Peter. *Die Mescalero-Affäre: Ein Lehrstück für Aufklärung und politische Kultur*. Hannover: Internationalismus, 1978.

Brückner, Peter, and Barbara Sichtermann. *Gewalt und Solidarität: Zur Ermordung Ulrich Schmückers durch Genossen: Dokumente und Analysen*. Berlin: Wagenbach, 1974.

Butterwegge, Christoph, and Heinz-Gerd Hofschen. *Sozialdemokratie, Krieg und Frieden: Die Stellung der SPD zur Friedensfrage von den Anfängen bis zur Gegenwart: Eine kommentierte Dokumentation*. Heilbronn: Distel, 1984.

Carl Friedrich von Siemens Stiftung. *Der Ernstfall*. Berlin: Propyläen, 1979.

Christlich Demokratische Union Deutschlands. *Terrorismus in der Bundesrepublik Deutschland – Eine Auswahl von Zitaten*. Bonn: CDU-Bundesgeschäftsstelle, September 1977.

Dirks, Walter. "Sozialisten ausserhalb der Parteien," *Das Sozialistische Jahrhundert* 3 (1949): 5–12.

Dutschke, Rudi. *Geschichte ist machbar: Texte über das herrschende Falsche und die Radikalität des Friedens*. Edited by J. Miermeister. Berlin: Wagenbuch, 1980.

Dutschke, Rudi, Wolfgang Lefevre, and Bernd Rabehl. *Rebellion der Studenten*. Reinbek: Rowohlt, 1968.

Duve, Freimut, Heinrich Böll, and Klaus Staeck, eds. *Briefe zur Verteidigung der Republik*. Reinbek: Rowohlt, 1977.

Ehmke, Horst, ed. *Perspektiven sozialdemokratischer Politik im Übergang zu den siebziger Jahren*. Reinbek: Rowohlt, 1969.

Erler, Fritz. *Soll Deutschland rüsten? Die SPD zum Wehrbeitrag*. Bonn: SPD-Vorstand, 1952.

Eyck, Erich. *A History of the Weimar Republic*. Translated by Harlan P. Hanson and Roberg G. L. Waite. Cambridge: Harvard University Press, 1963.

Forsthoff, Ernst. *Rechtsstaat im Wandel: Verfassungsrechtliche Abhandlungen, 1954–1973*. 2nd ed. Munich: Beck, 1976.

Der Staat der Industriegesellschaft: Dargestellt am Beispiel der Bundesrepublik Deutschlands. Munich: Beck, 1971.

Verfassungsprobleme des Sozialstaates. Münster: Aschendorff, 1954.

Germany, West. *Der Baader-Meinhof-Report: Dokumente, Analysen, Zusammenhänge aus den Akten des Bundeskriminalamtes, der "Sonderkomission Bonn" und dem Bundesamt für Verfassungsschutz*. Mainz: Hase & Koehler, 1972.

Bundesgesetzblatt. Bonn: Bundesministerium der Justiz.

Dokumentation der Bundesregierung zur Entführung von Hanns Martin Schleyer. Augsburg: Goldman Sachbuch, 1977.

Verhandlungen des Deutschen Bundestages: Drucksachen. Bonn: Deutscher Bundestag.

Verhandlungen des Deutschen Bundestages: Stenographische Berichte. Bonn: Deutscher Bundestag.

Gladitz, Nina, ed. *Lieber heute aktiv als morgen Radioaktiv*. Berlin: Wagenbach, 1976.

Glotz, Peter. "Systemüberwindende Reformen?" In *Beiträge zur Theoriediskussion*, edited by Georg Lührs, 205–44. Berlin: Dietz, 1973.

Glum, Friedrich. "Bemerkungen zum organisatorischen Teil einer künftigen deutschen Verfassung." *Süddeutsche Juristen Zeitung* 3 (March 1948): 113–18.

Die Grünen. *Der Deutsche Herbst 1977: Pressestimmen zur Fraktionssitzung der Grünen am 13. 10. 87*. Bonn: Grünen-Fraktion, 1987.

Hennis, Wilhelm, Peter Graf Kielmansegg, and Ulrich Matz, eds. *Regierbarkeit: Studien zu ihrer Problematisierung*. Stuttgart: Klett-Cotta, 1977.

Herold, Horst. "Demokratisierung und Internationalisierung – Zwei Schritte in die Zukunft der Polizei." *Die Neue Polizei* (1967): 145–6.

"Gesellschaftlicher Wandel – Chance der Polizei?" *Die Polizei* 63 (1972): 133–7.

"Kybernetik und Polizeiorganization." *Die Polizei* 2 (1970): 33–7.

Hoffmann-Axthelm, Dieter, Otto Kallscheuer, Eberhard Knödler-Bunte, and Brigitte Wartmann, eds. *Zwei Kulturen? Tunix, Mescalero und die Folgen*. Berlin: Ästhetik & Kommunikation, 1978.

Hollstein, Walter, and Boris Penth. *Alternativprojekte: Beispiel gegen der Resignation*. Reinbek: Rowohlt, 1980.

Holz, Hans Heinz. "Notstand der Demokratie – Ergebnisse und Perspektiven des Frankfurter Kongresses." *Blätter* 2 (1966): 976–82.

Horkheimer, Max, and Theodor W. Adorno. *Dialectic of Enlightenment: Philosophical Fragments*. Translated by Edmund Jephcott. Stanford: Stanford University Press, 2002.

ID-Archiv, ed. *Die Früchte des Zorns: Texte und Materialien zur Geschichte der Revolutionären Zellen und Roten Zora*. Berlin: ID-Archiv, 1993.

Jacobson, Arthur J., and Bernhard Schlink, eds. *Weimar: Jurisprudence of Crisis*. Berkeley: University of California Press, 2000.

Jaspers, Karl. *Wohin treibt die Bundesrepublik? Tatsachen, Gefahren, Chance*. Munich: Piper, 1966.

Kaltenbrunner, Gerd-Klaus. *Rekonstruktion des Konservatismus*. Freiburg: Rombach, 1972.

ed. *Die Herausforderung der Konservativen: Absage an Illusion*. Munich: Herderbücherei, 1974.

Kelsen, Hans. "Verteidigung der Demokratie." In *Demokratie und Sozialismus: Ausgewählte Aufsätze*, edited by Norbert Leser, 60–8. Vienna: Wiener Volksbuchhandlung, 1967.

Küster, Otto. "Föderative Probleme einer deutschen Verfassung." *Süddeutsche Juristen Zeitung* 3 (March 1948): 118–31.

Larsson, Bernard, ed. *Demonstrationen: Ein Berliner Modell*. Berlin: Voltaire, n.d.

Lenz, Ilse, ed. *Die Neue Frauenbewegung in Deutschland: Abschied vom kleinen Unterschied. Eine Quellensammlung*. Wiesbaden: VS-Verlag, 2008.

Loewenstein, Karl. "Autocracy versus Democracy." *American Political Science Review* 29 (1935): 571–93, 755–84.

"Militant Democracy and Fundamental Rights, I and II." *American Political Science Review* 31 (June 1937): 417–32 and 638–58.

Political Reconstruction. New York: Macmillan, 1946.

Loewenstein, Karl, and Lawrence Packard. *America's Eleventh Hour*. Easthampton, MA: Easthampton News, 1940.

Mannheim, Karl. *Diagnosis of Our Time: Wartime Essays of a Sociologist*. London: Paul, Trench, Trubner, 1943.

Marcuse, Herbert. *Das Ende der Utopie: Vorträge und Diskussionen in Berlin 1967*. Frankfurt: neue kritik, 1980.

Five Lectures: Psychoanalysis, Politics, and Utopia. Translated by Jeremy J. Shapiro and Shierry M. Weber. Boston: Beacon, 1970.

"Repressive Toleranz." In *Kritik der reinen Toleranz*, edited by Robert Paul Wolff, B. Moore, and Herbert Marcuse, 91–128. Frankfurt: Suhrkamp, 1968.

Martini, Winfried. *Freiheit auf Abruf: Die Lebenserwartung der Bundesrepublik*. Cologne: Kiepenheuer & Witsch, 1960.

Meinhof, Ulrike Marie. *Everybody Talks About the Weather...We Don't: The Writings of Ulrike Meinhof*. Edited by Karin Bauer. New York: Seven Stories, 2008.

Mescalero [pseud.]. "Buback-Ein Nachruf." *Göttinger Nachrichten*, April 27, 1977.

Mohler, Armin. *Was die Deutschen fürchten: Angst vor der Politik, Angst vor der Geschichte, Angst vor der Macht*. Stuttgart: Seewald, 1965.

Narr, Wolf-Dieter, ed. *Wir Bürger als Sicherheitsrisiko: Berufsverbot und Lauschangriff: Beiträge zur Verfassung unserer Republik*. Reinbek: Rowohlt, 1977.

neue kritik, ed. *Demokratie vor dem Notstand: Protokoll des Bonner Kongresses gegen die Notstandsgesetze am 30. Mai 1965*. Frankfurt: neue kritik, 1965.

Paczensky, Susanne von, ed. *Frauen und Terror: Versuche, die Beteilung von Frauen an Gewalttaten zu erklären*. Reinbek: Rowohlt, 1978.

Plogstedt, Sibylle, ed. *Der Kampf des vietnamischen Volkes und die Globalstrategie des Imperialismus: Internationaler Vietnam-Kongress-Westberlin*. Berlin: INFI, 1968.

Rote Armee Fraktion. *Texte und Materialien zur Geschichte der RAF*. Berlin: ID-Verlag, 1997.

"Die Rote Armee aufbauen," *Agit 883* 62 (June 5, 1970), 6.

Salzmann, Rainer, ed. *Die CDU/CSU im Parlamentarischen Rat: Sitzungsprotokolle der Unionsfraktion*. Stuttgart: Klett-Cotta, 1981.

Schäfer, Friedrich. *Die Notstandsgesetz: Vorsorge für den Menschen und den demokratischen Rechtsstaat*. Cologne: Westdeutscher, 1966.

Schmid, Carlo. "Gliederung und Einheit: Die verfassungspolitischen Richtlinien der SPD." *Die Gegenwart* 3, no. 16 (August 20, 1948): 15–17.

"Rückblick auf die Verhandlungen." *Die Wandlung* 4 (July 1949): 652–69.

Schmitt, Carl. *Political Theology: Four Chapters on the Theory of Sovereignty*. Translated by George Schwab. Cambridge: MIT, 1986.

The Concept of the Political. Translated by George Schwab. University of Chicago: Chicago, 1996.

The Crisis of Parliamentary Democracy. Translated by Ellen Kennedy. Cambridge: MIT, 1994.

Dictatorship. Cambridge: Polity, 2012.

Der Hüter der Verfassung. Berlin: Duncker & Humblot, 1996.

Schneider, Peter. *....schon bist du ein Verfassungsfeind: Das unerwartete Anschwellen der Personalakte des Lehrers Kleff*. Berlin: Rotbuch, 1975.

"Wir haben Fehler gemacht." In *Demonstrationen: Ein Berliner Modell*, edited by Bernard Larsson, 158–63. Berlin: Voltaire, n.d.

Schubert, Alex. *Stadtguerilla: Tupamaros in Uruguay – Rote Armee Fraktion in der Bundesrepublik*. Berlin: Wagenbach, 1971.

Schwarzer, Alice. *Der "kleine Unterschied" und seine großen Folgen*. Frankfurt: Fischer, 1975.

ed. *So fing es an! 10 Jahre Frauenbewegung*. Cologne: Emma-Verlag, 1981.

Severing, Carl. *Mein Lebensweg*. Vol. 2, *Im auf und ab der Republik*. Cologne: Greven, 1950.

Sontheimer, Kurt. *Das Elend unserer Intellektuellen: Linke Theorie in der Bundesrepublik*. Hamburg, 1976.

Sozialdemokratische Partei Deutschlands. *Jahrbuch der Sozialdemokratischen Partei Deutschlands 1954/55*. Bonn: SPD-Vorstand, 1956.

Protokoll über die Verhandlungen des Parteitages der Sozialdemokratischen Partei Deutschlands. Bonn: SPD-Vorstand.

Sternberger, Dolf. "Demokratie der Furcht oder Demokratie der Courage?" *Wandlung* 4 (1949): 5–13.

Vereinigung der Deutschen Staatsrechtslehrer. *Kabinettsfrage und Gesetzgebungsnotstand nach dem Grundgesetz; Tragweite der Generalklausel im Art. 19 Abs. 4. des Bonner Grundgesetzes: Berichte*. Berlin: DeGruyter, 1950.

Vester, Michael. "Die Strategie der direkten Aktion." *neue kritik* 6 (1965): 12–20.

Weber, Werner. *Weimarer Verfassung und Bonner Grundgesetz*. Göttingen: Fleischer, 1949.

Werner, Wolfram, ed. *Der Parlamentarische Rat 1948–1949: Akten und Protokolle*, Vols. 1–13. Boppard am Rhein/Munich: Harald Boldt Verlag, 1975–2002.

SECONDARY ARTICLES AND ESSAYS

Apter, David E. "Notes on the Underground: Left Violence and the National State." *Daedalus* 108 (Fall 1979): 155–72.

Barak, Aharon. "Forward: A Judge on Judging: The Role of a Supreme Court in a Democracy." *Harvard Law Review* 116, no. 16 (2002): 19–162.

Benz, Wolfgang. "Konzeptionen für die Nachkriegsdemokratie: Pläne und Überlegungen im Widerstand, im Exil und in der Besatzungszeit." In *Deutschland nach Hitler: Zukunftspläne im Exil und aus der Besatzungszeit, 1939–49*, edited by Thomas Koebner, Gert Sautermeister, and Sigrid Schneider-Grube, 201–13. Opladen: Westdeutscher, 1987.

Bessel, Richard. "The Nazi Capture of Power." *Journal of Contemporary History* 39 (April 2004): 169–88.

Blankenburg, Erhard. "Politik der Inneren Sicherheit: Eine Einleitung." In *Politik der Inneren Sicherheit*, edited by Erhard Blankenburg, 7–15. Frankfurt: Suhrkamp, 1980.

Böckenförde, Christopher. "Die Kodifizierung des Widerstandsrecht im Grundgesetz." *Juristenzeitung* 25 (1970): 168–72.

Braunthal, Gerard. "The Free Democratic Party in West German Politics." *The Western Political Quarterly* 13 (June 1960): 332–48.

"Emergency Legislation in the Federal Republic of Germany." In *Festschrift für Karl Loewenstein*, edited by Henry Steele Commager, 71–86. Tübingen: Mohr, 1971.

Bude, Heinz. "The German Kriegskinder: Origins and Impact of the Generation of 1968." In *Generations in Conflict: Youth Revolt and Generation Formation in Germany, 1770–1968*, edited by Mark Roseman. Cambridge: Cambridge University Press, 1995.

Caldwell, Peter. "Ernst Forsthoff and the Legacy of Racial Conservative State Theory in the Federal Republic of Germany." *History of Political Thought* 15 (Winter 1994): 615–41.

Davis, Belinda. "Activism from Starbuck to Starbucks, or Terror: What's in a Name?" *Radical History Review* 85 (Winter 2003): 37–57.

"What's Left? Popular Political Participation in Postwar Europe." *American Historical Review* 113 (April 2008): 363–90.

"'Women's Strength Against Crazy Male Power': Gendered Language in the West German Peace Movement of the 1980s." In *Frieden, Gewalt, Geschlecht: Friedens- und Konfliktforschung als Geschlechterforschung*, edited by Jennifer A. Davy, 244–65. Essen: Klartext, 2005.

Dyzenhaus, David. "Legal Theory in the Collapse of Weimar: Contemporary Lessons?" *American Political Science Review* 91 (March 1997): 121–34.

"The Permanence of the Temporary: Can Emergency Powers be Normalized?" In *The Security of Freedom. Essays on Canada's Anti-Terrorism Bill*, edited by Patrick Macklem, Kent Roach, and Ronald J. Daniels, 21–37. Toronto: University of Toronto Press, 2001.

Faulenbach, Bernd. "Die Siebzigerjahre – ein sozialdemokratisches Jahrzehnt?" *Archiv für Sozialgeschichte* 44 (2004): 1–38.

Ferejohn, John and Pasquale Pasquino. "The Law of the Exception: A Typology of Emergency Powers." *I.CON* 2 (2004): 210–39.

Forner, Sean A. "Für eine demokratische Erneuerung Deutschlands: Kommunikationsprozesse und Deutungsmuster engagierter Demokraten nach 1945." *Geschichte und Gesellschaft* 33, no. 2 (2007): 228–57.

Geppert, Dominik. "Von der Staatsskepsis zum parteipolitischen Engagement." In *Streit um Staat: Intellektuelle Debatten in der Bundesrepublik, 1960–1980*, edited by, idem and Jens Hacke, 46–68. Göttingen: Vandenhoeck & Ruprecht, 2008.

Gómez, Alan Eladio. "Resisting Living Death at Marion Federal Penitentiary, 1972." *Radical History Review* 96 (Fall 2006): 58–86.

Jacobs, James B. "The Prisoners' Rights Movement and Its Impacts, 1960–80." *Crime and Justice* 2 (1980): 429–70.

Klug, Ulrich. "Das Widerstandsrecht als allgemeines Menschenrecht." In *Widerstand und Staatsgewalt: Recht im Streit mit dem Gesetz*, edited by Werner Hill. Gütersloh: Gütersloher Verlagshaus Mohn, 1984.

Large, David Clay. "Normifying the Unnormifiable: The Right to Resistance in West German Constitutional History." In *Cornerstone of Democracy: The West German Grundgesetz, 1949–1989*, edited by Detlef Junker, Manfred F. Boemeke, and Janine Micunek, 83–95. Washington, DC: German Historical Institute, 1995.

Mazower, Mark. "Violence and the State in the Twentieth Century." *American Historical Review* 107, no. 4 (2002): 1158–78.

Melzer, Patricia. "'Death in the Shape of a Young Girl': Feminist Responses to Media Representations of Women Terrorists During the 'German Autumn' of 1977." *International Feminist Journal of Politics* 11 (March 2009): 35–62.

Metzler, Gabriele. "'Wir schaffen das moderne Deutschland': Sozialer Wandel in den sechziger Jahren zwischen Gesellschaftspolitik und Emanzipation." In *Bilanz: 50 Jahre Bundesrepublik Deutschland*, edited by Marie-Luise Recker, Burkhard Jellonnek, and Bernd Rauls, 279–94. St. Ingebort: Röhrig, 2001.

Milder, Stephen. "Thinking Globally, Acting (Trans-)Locally: Petra Kelly and the Transnational Roots of West German Green Politics." *Central European History* 43 (2010): 301–26.

Mommsen, Hans. "The Origins of Chancellor Democracy and the Transformation of the German Democratic Paradigm." *German Politics and Society* 25 (2007): 7–18.

Muller, Jerry Z. "German Neo-Conservatism, ca. 1968–1985: Hermann Lübbe and Others." In *German Ideologies Since 1945: Studies in the Political Thought and Culture of the Bonn Republic*, edited by Jan-Werner Müller, 161–84 (New York: Palgrave, 2003).

Münkler, Daniela. "Intellektuelle für die SPD." In *Kritik und Mandat: Intellektuelle in der deutschen Politik*, edited by Gangolf Hübinger and Thomas Hertfelder, 222–38. Stuttgart: DVA, 2000.

Notz, Gisela. "Die autonomen Frauenbewegungen der Siebzigerjahre: Entstehungsgeschichte – Organisationsformen – politische Konzepte." *Archiv für Sozialgeschichte* 44 (2004): 123–48.

Offe, Claus. "Vier Hypothesen über historische Folgen der Studentenbewegung." *Leviathan* 26, no. 4 (1998): 550–6.

Passmore, Leith. "The Art of Hunger: Self-Starvation in the Red Army Faction." *German History* 27, no. 1 (2009): 32–59.

Reichardt, Sven. "Civility, Violence and Civil Society." In *Civil Society: Berlin Perspectives*, edited by John Keane, 139–67. Providence: Berghahn, 2006.

Ryan, Mike. "Solitude as Counter-Insurgency: The U.S. Isolation Model of Political Incarcerations." In *Cages of Steel: The Politics of Imprisonment in the United States*, edited by Ward Churchill and J. J. Vander Wall, 83–109. Washington, DC: Maisonneuve, 1992.

Sewell, William H. "Historical Events as Transformations of Structures: Inventing Revolution at the Bastille." *Theory and Society* 25 (1996): 841–81.

Steitz, Jörg, and Gisbert Lepper. "'Wehrhafte Demokratie' oder Staatssicherheit in Westdeutschland." In *Notizbuch 4: Faschismus, Literatur und bürgerlicher Staat*, edited by Ilse Bindseil and Ulrich Enderwitz. Berlin: Medusa, 1981.

Terhoeven, Petra Terhoeven. "Opferbilder – Täterbilder: Die Fotographie als Medium linksterroristischer Selbstermächtigung in Deutschland und Italien während der 70er Jahre." *Geschichte in Wissenschaft und Unterricht* 58, no.7/8 (2007): 380–99.

Weisker, Albrecht. "Expertenvertrauen gegen Zukunftsangst: Zur Risikowahrnehmung der Kernenergie." In *Vertrauen: Historische Annährungen*, edited by Ute Frevert, 394–421. Göttingen: Vandenhoeck & Ruprecht, 2003.

Wunschik, Tobias. "Abwehr und Unterstützung des internationalen Terrorismus – Die Hauptabteilung XXII." In *Westarbeit des MfS: Das Zusammenspiel von "Aufklärung" und "Abwehr,"* edited by Hubertus Knabe, 263–73. Berlin: Ch. Links, 1999.

MONOGRAPHS AND EDITED WORKS

Agamben, Giorgio. *The State of Exception*. Translated by Kevin Attell. Chicago: University of Chicago Press, 2005.

Albrecht, Clemens, ed. *Die intellektuelle Gründung der Bundesrepublik: Eine Wirkungsgeschichte der Frankfurter Schule*. Frankfurt: Campus, 1999.

Albrecht, Willy. *Der Sozialistische Deutsche Studentenbund (SDS): Vom parteikonformen Studentenverband zum Repräsentanten der Neuen Linken*. Bonn: Dietz, 1994.

Aust, Stefan. *Brokdorf: Symbol einer politischen Wende*. Hamburg: Hoffman & Campe, 1982.

Der Baader-Meinhof Komplex. Hamburg: Hoffman & Campe, 1986.

Backes, Uwe. *Bleierne Jahre: Baader-Meinhof und danach*. Erlangen: Straube, 1991.

Schutz des Staates: Von der Autokratie zur Streitbaren Demokratie. Opladen: Leske & Budrich, 1998.

Backes, Uwe, and Eckhard Jesse. *Politischer Extremismus in der Bundesrepublik Deutschland*. 4th ed. Bonn: Bundeszentrale für politische Bildung, 1996.

Basten, Thomas. *Von der Reform des politischen Strafrechts bis zu den Anti-Terror-Gesetzen: Die Entwicklung des Strafrechts zur Bekämpfung politisch motivierter Kriminalität in der Sozialliberalen Ära*. Cologne: Pahl-Rugenstein, 1983.

Bauss, Gerhard. *Die Studentenbewegung der sechziger Jahre*. 2nd ed. Cologne: Pahl-Rugenstein, 1983.

Berendse, Gerrit-Jan, and Ingo Cornils, eds. *Baader-Meinhof Returns: History and Cultural Memory of German Left-Wing Terrorism*. Amsterdam: Rodopi, 2008.

Bessel, Richard. *Political Violence and the Rise of Nazism: The Storm Troopers in Eastern Germany, 1925–1934*. New Haven: Yale University Press, 1984.

Blanke, Bernhard and Helmut Wollmann, eds. *Die alte Bundesrepublik: Kontinuität und Wandel*. Opladen: Westdeutscher, 1991.

Blasius, Dirk. *Weimars Ende: Bürgerkrieg und Politik, 1930–1933*. Göttingen: Vandenhoeck & Ruprecht, 2005.

Bösch, Frank. *Macht und Machtverlust: Die Geschichte der CDU*. Stuttgart: DVA, 2002.

Bourg, Julian. *From Revolution to Ethics: May 1968 and Contemporary French Thought*. London: McGill-Queen's University Press, 2007.

Brand, Enno. *Staatsgewalt: Politische Unterdrückung und Innere Sicherheit in der Bundesrepublik*. Göttingen: Werkstaat, 1988.

Brand, Karl-Werner, Detlef Büsser, and Dieter Rucht. *Aufbruch in eine andere Gesellschaft: Neue soziale Bewegungen in der Bundesrepublik*. Frankfurt: Campus, 1983.

Braunthal, Gerard. *The German Social Democrats since 1969: A Party in Power and Opposition*. 2nd ed. Boulder: Westview, 1994.

Political Loyalty and Public Service in West Germany: The 1972 Decree against Radicals and Its Consequences. Amherst: University of Massachusetts Press, 1990.

Breloer, Heinrich. *Todesspiel: Von der Schleyer-Entfuhrung bis Mogadischu. Eine dokumentarische Erzählung*. Cologne: Kiepenheuer & Witsch, 1997.

Bundesamt für Verfassungsschutz, ed. *Verfassungsschutz in der Demokratie: Beiträge aus Wissenschaft und Praxis*. Bonn: Heymann, 1990.

Burns, Rob, and Wilfried van der Will. *Protest and Democracy in West Germany: Extra-Parliamentary Opposition and the Democratic Agenda*. New York: St. Martin's, 1988.

Busch, Heiner, Albrecht Funk, Udo Kauss, Wolf-Dieter Narr, and Falco Werkentin. *Die Polizei in der Bundesrepublik*. Franfurt: Campus, 1985.

Caldwell, Peter C. *Popular Sovereignty and the Crisis of German Constitutional Law: The Theory and Practice of Weimar Constitutionalism*. Durham: Duke University Press, 1997.

Chalk, Peter. *Western European Terrorism and Counter-Terrorism: The Evolving Dynamic*. New York: St. Martin's, 1996.

Cioc, Mark. *Pax Atomica: The Nuclear Defense Debate in West Germany during the Adenauer Era*. New York: Columbia University Press, 1988.

Cobler, Sebastian. *Law, Order and Politics in West Germany*, translated by Francis McDonagh. New York: Penguin, 1978.

Colin, Nicole, Beatrice de Graaf, Jacco Pekelder, and Joachim Umlauf, eds. *Der "Deutsche Herbst" und die RAF in Politik, Medien, und Kunst: Nationale und Internationale Perspektive*. Bielefeld: Transcript, 2008.

Colvin, Sarah. *Ulrike Meinhof and West German Terrorism: Language, Violence, and Identity*. Rochester, NY: Camden House, 2009.

Cooper, Alice Holmes. *Paradoxes of Peace: German Peace Movements since 1945*. Ann Arbor: University of Michigan, 1995.

Davis, Belinda, Wilfried Mausbach, Martin Klimke, and Carla MacDougall, eds. *Changing the World, Changing Oneself: Political Protest and Collective Identities in West Germany and the U.S. in the 1960s and 1970s*. New York: Berghahn, 2010.

Ein deutscher Herbst: Zustände 1977. Frankfurt: neue kritik, 1997.

Dirke, Sabine von. *"All Power to the Imagination!" The West German Counterculture from the Student Movement to the Greens*. Lincoln: University of Nebraska Press, 1997.

Dyzenhaus, David, ed. *Law as Politics: Carl Schmitt's Critique of Liberalism*. Durham: Duke University Press, 1998.

Legality and Legitimacy: Carl Schmitt, Hans Kelsen, and Hermann Heller in Weimar. Oxford: Oxford University Press, 1997.

Eley, Geoff. *Forging Democracy: The History of the Left in Europe, 1850–2000*. New York: Oxford University Press, 2002.

Elter, Andreas. *Propaganda der Tat: Die RAF und die Medien*. Frankfurt: Suhrkamp, 2008.

Faber, Richard, and Erhard Stölting, eds. *Die Phantasie an die Macht? 1968 – Versuch einer Bilanz*. Berlin: Philo, 2002.

Feldkamp, Michael F. *Der Parlamentarische Rat, 1948–1949: Die Entstehung des Grundgesetzes*. Göttingen: Vandenhoeck & Ruprecht, 1998.

Fels, Gerhard. *Der Aufruhr der 68er: Zu den geistigen Grundlagen der Studentenbewegung und der RAF*. Bonn: Bouvier, 1998.

Fink, Carole, Philipp Gassert, and Detlef Junker, eds. *1968: The World Transformed*. Cambridge: Cambridge University Press, 1998.

Finn, John E. *Constitutions in Crisis: Political Violence and the Rule of Law*. New York: Oxford University Press, 1991.

Flaherty, David H. *Protecting Privacy in Surveillance Societies*. Chapel Hill: University of North Carolina Press, 1989.

Frankel, Richard Evan. *Bismarck's Shadow: The Cult of Leadership and the Transformation of the German Right, 1898–1945*. New York: Berg, 2005.

Gätje, Olaf. *Der Gruppenstil der RAF im "Info"-System: Eine soziostilistische Untersuchung aus systemtheoretischer Perspektive*. Berlin: Gruyter, 2008.

Geyer, Michael, and John W. Boyer, eds. *Resistance against the Third Reich, 1933–1990*. Chicago: University of Chicago Press, 1992.

Gilcher-Holtey, Ingrid, ed. *1968: Vom Ereignis zum Gegenstand der Geschichtswissenschaft*. Göttingen: Vandenhoeck & Ruprecht, 1998.

ed. *1968 – Vom Ereignis zum Mythos*. Frankfurt: Suhrkamp, 2008.

Glaessner, Gert-Joachim. *Sicherheit in Freiheit: Die Schutzfunktion des demokratischen Staates und die Freiheit der Bürger*. Opladen: Leske & Budrich, 2003.

Glaser, Hermann. *The Rubble Years: The Cultural Roots of Postwar Germany*. New York: Paragon, 1986.

Gossner, Rolf. *Das Anti-Terror-System: Politische Justiz im präventiven Sicherheitsstaat*. Hamburg: VSA-Verlag, 1991.

Hacke, Jens. *Philosophie der Bürgerlichkeit: Die liberalkonservative Begründung der Bundesrepublik*. Göttingen: Vandenhoeck & Ruprecht, 2006.

Hartung, Klaus, ed. *Der Blinde Fleck: Die Linke, Die RAF und der Staat*. Frankfurt: neue kritik, 1987.

Held, David. *Introduction to Critical Theory: Horkheimer to Habermas*. Berkeley: University of California Press, 1980.

Models of Democracy. Stanford: Stanford University Press, 1996.

Hess, Henner. *Angriff auf das Herz des Staates*. Vol. 1, *Soziale Entwicklung und Terrorismus*. Frankfurt: Suhrkamp, 1988.

Hipt, Manfred Opp de. *Denkbilder in der Politik: Der Staat in der Sprache von CDU und SPD*. Opladen: Westdeustcher Verlag, 1987.

Hirsch, Joachim. *Der Sicherheitsstaat: Das "Modell Deutschland," seine Krise und die neue sozialen Bewegungen*. Frankfurt: Athenäum, 1986.

Hoffmann, Bruce. *Inside Terrorism*. New York: Columbia University Press, 1998.

Horchem, Hans Josef. *Die verlorene Revolution: Terrorismus in Deutschland*. Herford: Busse Seewald, 1988.

Horn, Gerd-Rainer. *The Spirit of '68: Rebellion in Western Europe and North America, 1956–1976*. Oxford: Oxford University Press, 2007.

Janssen, Helmut, and Michael Schubert, eds. *Staatssicherheit: Die Bekämpfung des politischen Feindes im Inneren*. Bielefeld: AJZ Verlag, 1990.

Jaschke, Hans-Gerd. *Streitbare Demokratie und Innere Sicherheit: Grundlagen, Praxis und Kritik*. Opladen: Westdeutscher Verlag, 1991.

Jay, Martin. *The Dialectical Imagination: A History of the Frankfurt School and the Institute of Social Research, 1923–1950*. Boston: Little, Brown, 1973.

Jesse, Eckhard. *Streitbare Demokratie: Theorie, Praxis und Herausforderungen in der Bundesrepublik Deutschland*. Edited by Peter Haungs and Eckhard Jesse. Berlin: Colloquium-Verlag, 1980.

Joppke, Christian. *Mobilizing Against Nuclear Energy: A Comparison of Germany and the United States*. Berkeley: University of California Press, 1993.

Juchler, Ingo. *Die Studentbewegungen in den Vereinigten Staaten und der Bundesrepublik Deutschland der sechziger Jahre: Eine Untersuchung hinsichtlich ihrer Beeinflussung durch Befreiungsbewegungen und -Theorien aus der Dritten Welt*. Berlin: Duncker & Humblot, 1996.

Karapin, Roger. *Protest Politics in Germany: Movements on the Left and Right Since the 1960s*. University Park: Pennsylvania State University Press, 2007.

Katzenstein, Peter J. *West Germany's Internal Security Policy: State and Violence in the 1970s and 1980s*. Ithaca, NY: Cornell University, 1990.

Keane, John. *Civil Society: Old Images, New Visions*. Stanford: Stanford University Press, 1998.

Violence and Democracy. Cambridge: Cambridge University Press, 2004.

Kleinmann, Hans-Otto. *Geschichte der CDU, 1945–1982*. Stuttgart: DVA, 1993.

Klimke, Martin. *The Other Alliance: Student Protest in West Germany and the United States in the Global Sixties*. Princeton: Princeton University Press, 2009.

Koenen, Gerd. *Das Rote Jahrzehnt: Unsere kleine deutsche Kulturrevolution, 1967–1977*. Cologne: Kiepenheuer & Witsch, 2001.

Vesper, Ensslin und Baader: Urszenen des deutschen Terrorismus. Cologne: Kiepenheuer & Witsch, 2003.

Koopmans, Ruud. *Democracy from Below: New Social Movements and the Political System in West Germany*. Boulder: Westview, 1995.

Kraushaar, Wolfgang, *1968 als Mythos, Chiffre und Zäsur*. Hamburg: Hamburger Edition, 2000.

Die Bombe im Jüdischen Gemeindehaus. Hamburg: Hamburger Edition, 2005.

ed. *Frankfurter Schule und Studentenbewegung: Von der Flaschenpost zum Molotovcocktail, 1946 bis 1995*. 3 vols. Hamburg: Roger & Bernhard, 1998.

ed. *Die Protestchronik der Bundesrepublik*. 3 vols. Hamburg: Hamburger Edition, 1996.

ed. *Die RAF und der linke Terrorismus*. 2 vols. Hamburg: Hamburger Edition, 2006.

Kraushaar, Wolfgang, Jan Philipp Reemtsma, and Karin Wieland. *Rudi Dutschke, Andreas Baader und die RAF*. Hamburg: Hamburger Edition, 2005.

Krohn, Maren. *Die gesellschaftlichen Auseinandersetzungen um die Notstandesgesetze*. Cologne: Pahl-Rugenstein, 1981.

Kutscha, Martin, and Norman Paech, eds. *Im Staat der "Inneren Sicherheit": Polizei, Verfassungsschutz, Geheimdienste, Datenkontrolle im Betrieb. Beiträge und Dokumente*. Frankfurt: Röderberg, 1981.

Laak, Dirk van. *Gespräche in der Sicherheit des Schweigens: Carl Schmitt in der Geistesgeschichte der frühen Bundesrepublik*. Berlin: Akademie, 1993.

Lang, Markus. *Karl Loewenstein: Transatlantischer Denker der Politik*. Stuttgart: Steiner, 2007.

Lange, Erhard H. M. *Die Würde des Menschen ist unantastbar: Der Parlamentarische Rat und das Grundgesetz*. Heidelberg: Decker & Müller, 1993.

Lange, Hans-Jürgen. *Innere Sicherheit im politischen System der Bundesrepublik Deutschland*. Opladen: Leske & Budrich, 1999.

Die Polizei der Gesellschaft: Zur Soziologie der inneren Sicherheit. Opladen: Leske & Budrich, 2003.

Staat, Demokratie und Innere Sicherheit in Deutschland. Opladen: Leske & Budrich, 2000.

Langguth, Gerd. *Mythos '68: Die Gewaltphilosophie von Rudi Dutschke. Ursachen und Folgen der Studentenbewegung*. Munich: Olzog, 2001.

Large, David Clay. *Germans to the Front: West German Rearmament in the Adenauer Era*. Chapel Hill: University of North Carolina Press, 1996.

Livingston, Steven. *The Terrorism Spectacle*. Boulder: Westview, 1993.

Loader, Colin. *The Intellectual Development of Karl Mannheim: Culture, Politics, and Planning*. Cambridge: Cambridge University Press, 1985.

Lönnendonker, Siegward and Tilman Fichter, eds. *Freie Universität Berlin, 1948–1973: Hochschule im Umbruch*. 4 vols. Berlin: Freie Universität, 1975.

Lönnendonker, Siegward, Bernd Rabehl, and Jochen Staadt. *Die Antiautoritäre Revolte: Der Sozialistische Deutsche Studentenbund nach der Trennung von der SPD*. Wiesbaden: Westdeutscher, 2002.

Löw, Konrad, ed. *Terror und Extremismus*. Berlin: Duncker & Humblot, 1994.

Markovits, Andrei S., and Philip S. Gorski. *The German Left: Red, Green and Beyond*. New York: Oxford University Press, 1993.

Matz, Ulrich, and Gerhard Schmidtchen. *Analysen Zum Terrorismus: Gewalt und Legitimität*. Edited by Bundesministerium des Innern. Opladen: Westdeutscher, 1983.

Merkl, Peter H., ed. *Political Violence and Terror*. Berkeley: University of California Press, 1986.

Mettke, Jörg, ed. *Die Grünen*. Reinbek: Rowohlt, 1982.

Metzler, Gabrielle. *Konzeptionen politischen Handelns von Adenauer bis Brandt: Politische Plannung in der pluralistischen Gesellschaft*. Paderborn: Schöningh, 2005.

Michalka, Wolfgang, ed. *Extremismus und Streitbare Demokratie: Mit Beiträgen von Uwe Backes und Eckhard Jesse*. Wiesbaden: Franz Steiner, 1987.

Mies, Maria. *Patriarchy and Accumulation on a World Scale: Women in the International Division of Labour*. 2nd ed. London: Zed Books, 1998.

Mohr, Reinhard. *Zaungäste: Die Generation, die nach der Revolte kam*. Frankfurt: Fischer, 1992.

Mommsen, Wolfgang J., and Gerhard Hirschfeld. *Sozialprotest, Gewalt, Terror: Gewaltanwendung durch politische und gesellschaftliche Randgruppen im 19. und 20. Jahrhundert*. Stuttgart: Klett-Cotta, 1982.

Moses, A. Dirk. *German Intellectuals and the Nazi Past*. Cambridge: Cambridge University Press, 2007.

Müller, Jan-Werner. *Dangerous Mind: Carl Schmitt in Post-War European Thought*. New Haven: Yale University Press, 2003.

Nacos, Brigette L. *Mass-Mediated Terrorism: The Central Role of the Media in Terrorism and Counter-Terrorism*. New York: Rowman & Littlefield, 2002.

Niven, Bill. *Facing the Nazi Past: United Germany and the Legacy of the Third Reich*. London: Routledge, 2002.

Olick, Jeffrey K. *In the House of the Hangman: The Agonies of German Defeat, 1943–1949*. Chicago: University of Chicago Press, 2005.

Otto, Karl A. *Vom Ostermarsch zur APO: Geschichte der Außerparlamentarischen Opposition in der Bundesrepublik, 1960–1970*. Frankfurt: Campus, 1977.

Peters, Butz. *Tödlicher Irrtum: Die Geschichte der RAF*. Berlin: Argon, 2004.

Porta, Donatella Della. *Social Movements, Political Violence, and the State: A Comparative Analysis of Germany and Italy*. Cambridge: Cambridge University Press, 1995.

Potthoff, Heinrich, and Susanne Miller. *Kleine Geschichte der SPD: Darstellungen und Dokumentation 1848–1990*. Bonn: Dietz, 1991.

Pridham, Geoffrey. *Christian Democracy in Western Germany: The CDU/CSU in Government and Opposition, 1945–1976*. London: Helm, 1977.

Rabert, Bernhard. *Links- und Rechtsterrorismus in der BRD von 1970 bis heute*. Bonn: Bernard & Graefe, 1995.

Reinhard, Wolfgang. *Geschichte der Staatsgewalt:. Eine vergleichende Verfassungsgeschichte Europas von den Anfängen bis zur Gegenwart*. Munich: Beck, 2000.

Richter, Michaela. *The Verfassungsschutz*. Washington, DC: American Institute for Contemporary German Studies, 1998.

Rossiter, Clinton. *Constitutional Dictatorship: Crisis Government in the Modern Democracies*. New Brunswick: Transaction, 2002.

Rotberg, Joachim. *Zwischen Linkskatholizismus und bürgerlicher Sammlung: Die Anfänge der CDU in Frankfurt am Main 1945–1946*. Frankfurt: Knecht, 1999.

Roth, Roland, and Dieter Rucht, eds. *Neue soziale Bewegungen in der Bundesrepublik Deutschland*. Frankfurt: Campus, 1987.

Rucht, Dieter. *Von Wyhl nach Gorleben: Bürger gegen Atomprogramm und nukleare Entsorgung*. Munich: Beck, 1980.

Rupp, Hans Karl. *Außerparlamentarische Opposition in der Ära Adenauer: Der Kampf gegen der Atombewaffnung in den fünfziger Jahren*. Cologne: Paul-Rugenstein, 1970.

Sack, Fritz, Heinz Steinert, and Uwe Berlit. *Analysen zum Terrorismus: Protest und Reaktion*. Edited by Bundesministerium des Innern. Opladen: Westdeutscher, 1984.

Schenk, Dieter. *Der Chef: Horst Herold und das BKA*. Hamburg: Hoffmann & Campe, 1998.

Schissler, Hannah, ed. *The Miracle Years: A Cultural History of West Germany, 1949–1968*. Princeton: Princeton University Press, 2001.

Schmidtke, Michael. *Der Aufbruch der jungen Intelligenz: Die 68er Jahre in der Bundesrepublik und den USA*. Frankfurt: Campus, 2003.

Schneider, Michael. *Demokratie in Gefahr? Der Konflikt um die Notstandsgesetze*. Bonn: Neue Gesellschaft, 1986.

Schoreit, Armin. *Innere Sicherheit in der Bundesrepublik Deutschland:. Organe, Behörden, Dienste*. Heidelberg: Kriminalistik Verlag, 1979.

Schultze, Thomas and Almut Gross. *Die Autonomen: Ursprünge, Entwicklung und Profil der Autonomen Bewegung*. Hamburg: Konkret, 1997.

Siegfried, Detlef. *Time Is On My Side: Konsum und Politik in der westdeutschen Jugendkultur der 60er Jahre*. Göttingen: Wallstein, 2006.

Simms, Brendan. *The Impact of Napoleon: Prussian High Politics, Foreign Policy and the Crisis of the Executive, 1797–1806*. Cambridge: Cambridge University Press, 1997.

Sontheimer, Michael, and Otto Kallscheuer, eds. *Einschüsse: Besichtigung eines Frontverlaufs: Zehn Jahre nach dem Deutschen Herbst*. Berlin: Rotbuch, 1987.

Spernol, Boris. *Notstand der Demokratie: Der Protest gegen die Notstandsgesetze und die Frage der NS-Vergangenheit*. Essen: Klartext, 2008.

Spevack, Edmund. *Allied Control and German Freedom*. Piscataway, NJ: Transaction, 2001.

Spicka, Mark E. *Selling the Economic Miracle: Economic Reconstruction and Politics in West Germany, 1949–1957*. New York: Berghahn, 2007.

Steinweg, Reiner. *Die Neue Friedensbewegung: Analysen aus der Friedensforschung*. Frankfurt: Suhrkamp, 1982.

Thomas, Nick. *Protest Movements in 1960s West Germany: A Social History of Dissent and Democracy*. Oxford: Berg, 2003.

Tolmein, Oliver, and Detlef Zumwinkel. *Nix Gerafft: 10 Jahre Deutscher Herbst und der Konservatismus der Linken*. Hamburg: Konkret, 1987.

Ullrich, Sebastion. *Der Weimar-Komplex: Das Scheitern der ersten deutschen Demokratie und die politische Kultur der frühen Bundesrepublik, 1945–1959*. Göttingen: Wallstein, 2009.

Varon, Jeremy. *Bringing the War Home: The Weather Underground, the Red Army Faction, and Revolutionary Violence in the Sixties and Seventies*. Berkeley: University of California Press, 2004.

Vowinckel, Annette. *Flugzeugentführungen: Eine Kulturgeschichte*. Göttingen: Wallstein, 2011.

Waldmann, Peter. *Terrorismus: Provokation der Macht*. Munich: Gerling, 1998..

Weber, Petra. *Carlo Schmid: 1896–1979. Eine Biographie*. Munich: Beck, 1996.

Weinberger, Marie-Luise. *Aufbruch zu neuen Ufern? Grün-Alternative zwischen Anspruch und Wirklichkeit*. Bonn: Neue Gesellschaft, 1984.

Weinhauer, Klaus. *Schutzpolizei in der Bundesrepublik: Zwischen Bürgerkrieg und Innerer Sicherheit: Die turbulenten sechziger Jahre*. Paderborn: Ferdinand Schöningh, 2003.

Weinhauer, Klaus, Jörg Requate, and Heinz-Gerhard Haupt, eds. *Terrorismus in der Bundesrepublik: Medien, Staat und Subkulturen in den 70er Jahren*. Frankfurt: Campus, 2006.

Wheatland, Thomas. *The Frankfurt School in Exile*. Minneapolis: University of Minnesota Press, 2009.

Wiggershaus, Rolf. *The Frankfurt School: Its History, Theories, and Political Significance*. Translated by Michael Robertson. Cambridge: MIT Press, 1995.

Wirth, Hans-Jürgen, ed. *Hitlers Enkel – oder Kinder der Demokratie? Die 68er-Generation, die RAF und die Fischer-Debatte*. Giessen: Psychosozial-Verlag, 2001.

Wright, Joanne. *Terrorist Propaganda: The Red Army Faction and the Provisional IRA, 1968–86*. New York: St. Martin's, 1991.

Wunschik, Tobias. *Baader-Meinhofs Kinder: Die zweite Generation der RAF*. Opladen: Westdeutscher, 1997.

Index

Abendroth, Wolfgang, 97, 98
Adenauer, Konrad, 36, 52, 57–8, 62, 71, 78, 79, 82, 88, 111, 115, 126, 142, 194, 255
Adorno, Theodor W., 75–7, 100
Algerian war, 83–4
Anschütz, Gerhard, 20
anticommunism, 4, 33, 39, 57, 71, 73, 81, 96, 103, 110, 146, 149, 164, 253
antifascism, 2, 7, 15, 16, 70, 71–2, 73, 74, 78–9, 81, 82, 83, 90, 95–6, 98, 101, 106, 107, 153, 156, 157, 172, 181, 240, 244, 251, 259–60, *See also* National Socialism; resistance
anti-imperialism, 2, 82, 83–8, 92, 100, 108, 112, 155, 160, 181, 204
antinuclear movement, 154, 169–80, 181, 186, 204, 206, 248, 256
antiterrorism legislation, 143–5, 252
  amended criminal code and procedure, 116, 143, 148–9, 164, 221, 223, 258
  Contact Ban, 220–4, 231, 232, 234
  Decree against Radicals, 132–3, 145–7, 201
  international, 216, 260
  under Weimar, 21–2
APO (Extraparliamentary Opposition), 69, 82, 99–100, 101, 107, 179, 250, 257
  strategy debate, 104–7
attorneys, RAF, 156–7, 195
  and state security, 142–3, 221–2
Auschwitz, 76, 155, 157, 158, 224, 260
Autonomen, 251–2

Baader, Andreas, 3, 102, 108, 112, 131, 141, 143, 157, 187, 192, 196, 210, 215, 222, 231, 241
Basic Law, 16, 36, 38, 52–3, 55–6, 60, 61, 145
  drafting of, 37–52
  duty to human dignity, 47, 135, 139–40, 216, 227
Baumann, Michael
  How It All Began, 164
Biedenkopf, Kurt, 137, 254
Böckenförde, Ernst-Wolfgang, 56–7
Böll, Heinrich, 164–6, 237, 256–7
  The Lost Honor of Katharina Blum, 165, 166
Bölling, Klaus, 217, 227, 228
Bracher, Karl Dietrich, 64, 207–8
Brandt, Willy, 64, 110–11, 132, 133, 134, 136, 148, 149, 151, 192, 196, 211, 225, 258
Brokdorf, 172–3, 180
  debate on violence, 175–80
Brückner, Peter, 201, 244
Brüning, Heinrich, 133
Buback, Siegfried, 3, 195, 222, *See also* Mescalero affair
  murder of, 196–7, 204, 208, 217, 224
Bundeswehr. *See* rearmament

Callaghan, James, 226, 229
capital punishment. *See* death penalty
CDU (Christian Democratic Union), 4, 5, 36, 37, 42, 45, 46, 57–8, 63, 64, 66–7, 71, 78, 96, 107, 110, 111, 114, 121, 127, 133, 135–6, 192, 208, 235, 237, 241, 254, *See also* Dregger, Alfred; Kohl, Helmut; Süsterhenn, Adolf
  on armed force, 57, 58, 60, 144
  and counterterrorism, 133, 137–8, 141–2, 143–4, 145, 147, 198, 200, 211–12, 221, 222, 223, 252–3
  on federalism, 38, 39–40, 252

CDU (*cont.*)
  state, concept of, 45, 137–8
  on states of emergency, 45, 46, 48–9, 50–1, 52, 64, 66, 135–6, 141
  citizens' initiatives, 16, 167–9, *See also* Brokdorf; Federal Association of Citizens' Initiatives for Environmental Protection (BBU); Wyhl
civil rights movement, American, 88, 89–90, 92, 101
Claussen, Detlev, 202
Communist League, West German (KBW), 171, 205
conservatives, 14, 15, 37, 53–4, 126, 192, 237, 241, 252
  liberal, 194–5, 208, 211, 254–6
  and state authority, 61, 141
  Tendenzwende, 17, 137, 253–6
Constitutional Convention, 37, 38, 43, 47–8
Constitutional Court, 44, 49, 54, 56, 65, 81, 222
  on state's duty to life, 227
Contact Ban Law. *See* antiterrorism legislation
Coppick, Manfred, 149, 223, 258
counterterrorism, 10–11, 13, 15, 16, 113–14, 117, 120–1, 124–5, 153, 154, 190, 193, 208, 243, 260, *See also* antiterrorism legislation; Federal Center for Political Education (BPB); Federal Criminal Office (BKA); GSG-9; police, West German:modernization of
  after 9/11, 259
  hostage negotiations, 139–40, 141, 209, 215–17, 225, 227
  hunt for sympathizers, 120, 132–3, 145–6, 163–7, 174, 193–5, 197–8, 200–2, 209, 214, 234, 237–8
  international opinion, 123, 147–8, 193, 215–16, 226–7, 229–30, 231, 239, 256
  media controls, 164, 198, 217–19, 228
  wiretapping, 12, 166, 195, 221
crisis staff, 139–40, 142, 216
  antecedents, 46, 65
  concept of, 214, 232
  German Autumn, 214, 215, 217, 218, 225, 228
Croissant, Claus, 143, 157, 222
CSU (Christian Social Union), 39, 43, 129, 142, 208, 212, 252, *See also* CDU (Christian Democratic Union); Strauß, Franz-Josef

Davis, Angela, 159
death penalty, 144, 212
Dirks, Walter, 52, 75, 77
Dregger, Alfred, 144, 212, 252
Drenkmann, Günter von, 134, 135, 143, 166
Dutschke, Rudi, 68, 86, 96, 98, 101, 102, 148, 157, 203, 239, 244
  organizational report, 100–1, 104

Easter riots, 102–3, 104
economic miracle, 57, 78, 254
Ehrler, Solveig, 105
emergency legislation, 6, 11–13, 29, 36, 43, 55–7, 58, 60, 62–5, 79, *See also* Loewenstein, Karl
  Article 22, 23–4, 26, 44, 48, 50, 54
  constitutional debate over, 44–52
  Emergency Laws (1968), 13, 16, 44, 53, 58, 62–7, 72, 88, 97, 99, 101, 121, 223
Ensslin, Gudrun, 3, 102, 108, 112, 131, 141, 143, 157, 160, 187, 192, 196, 210, 215, 231, 241
Enzensberger, Hans Magnus, 84–5, 87, 93, 103
Erhard, Ludwig, 57, 78, 86
executive power, 11–12, 18, 24, 25–6, 35, 36, 44, 45–6, 50–1, 53, 57, 61, 64
extraparliamentary left. *See* negative alliance
Eyck, Erich, 22

Fanon, Frantz, 84, 85, 87
Fassbinder, Rainer Werner, 241–2, 247
FDP (Liberal Democratic Party), 21, 45, 46, 58, 59, 63, 64, 65, 110, 117, 133, 143, 144, 145, 176, 208, 221, 222, 241, 258, *See also* Genscher, Hans-Dietrich; Maihofer, Werner
  on states of emergency, 45, 46, 48, 51, 52
Federal Association of Citizens' Initiatives for Environmental Protection (BBU), 180, 247
Federal Border Guard (BGS), 65, 121–3, 173, 178, 230
Federal Center for Political Education (BPB), 125–7, 213, *See also* political education
  program for the positive protection of the constitution, 127–32, 163, 193–4
Federal Criminal Office (BKA), 117–18, 119, 120–1, 128, 134, 213, 217, *See also* Herold, Horst
Federal Intelligence Agency (BND), 166, 219
Federal Office for the Protection of the Constitution (BfV), 117, 128, 145, 166, 187

Federal Republic (FRG), 2, 52
  Allied occupation of, 6, 35, 36–7, 62, 78
  compared to Nazism, 94, 114, 145, 147, 154, 155–6, 157, 212, 232
  compared to Weimar, 2, 98, 114, 126, 133, 196, 198, 207, 212
  legitimacy of, 8, 9, 13–14, 15, 17, 53, 61, 72, 78, 82, 97, 98, 124, 135, 147–8, 150, 153, 229–31, 232, 237, 240–1, 250, 255, 260–1
federalism, 117, 118, 120, 121
feminism. *See* women's movement
Filbinger, Hans, 198
Fischer, Joschka, 190–1, 203
Fischer, Uli, 236, 250
Forsthoff, Ernst, 61, 137
Foucault, Michel, 158
Frankfurt arson, 102, 108
Frankfurt School, 75–7, *See also* Adorno, Theodor W.; Horkheimer, Max; Marcuse, Herbert
  immanent critique, 77, 91
Fried, Erich, 199

Genscher, Hans-Dietrich, 65, 124, 228
German Autumn, 7–8, 13–14, 15, 16, 192–3, 207, 236–7, 241–3, 252, 261
German Democratic Republic (GDR), 57, 62, 67, 73, 86, 94, 110, 111, 149, *See also* anticommunism
  and the RAF, 111
Germany in Autumn, 241–3
Giscard d'Estaing, Valéry, 226–7
Glotz, Peter, 150, 200
Godesberg Program. *See under* SPD (Social Democratic Party)
Gollwitzer, Helmut, 105, 202, 203, 237
Grand Coalition, 63, 65, 72, 89, 97
Greens, West German, 30, 247, 250–1, 257, 258
Gremliza, Hermann L., 197, 199
Groenewold, Kurt, 143, 157
GSG-9, 121, 123, 124, 193, 224, 228, 230, 231, 233, 234, 256
  creation of, 122–3
  German Autumn, 209
  Mogadishu, 225, 228–9

Haag, Siegfried, 221–2
Habermas, Jürgen, 64, 98–9, 106, 195, 236, 255
Hanover Congress, 97–9, 100, 240
Hansen, Karl-Heinz, 223, 258
Hausner, Siegfried, 215, 222
Herold, Horst, 122, 124, 126, 130, 140, 209, 217
  as modernizer, 118–21
Herrenchiemsee. *See* Constitutional Convention
Horkheimer, Max, 75, 76–7, 100
Humanist Union, 239

Institute for Social Research. *See* Frankfurt School
internal security, 16, 114, 121, 127, 130, 134, 145, 154, 167, 173–4, 176, 193, 195, 208, 231–4, *See also* counterterrorism; Federal Center for Political Education (BPB); Federal Criminal Office (BKA); modernization; police, West German
  international cooperation in, 122–4, 260

June 2 Movement, 2, 3, 109, 134, 138–9, 140, 164, *See also* Lorenz, Peter
Jusos, 146, 150, 239

Kaltenbrunner, Gerd-Klaus, 254
Kampf dem Atomtod (KdA), 80, 81
Kelly, Petra, 180, 247, 249
Kelsen, Hans, 20, 25, 26–7
K-Gruppen, 107, 171, 175, 178, 181, 250
Klein, Hans-Jochen, 166, 204–5, 206, 222
Kogon, Eugon, 40, 75, 77
Kohl, Helmut, 137, 141, 211, 214, 254, 255, 256, 259
KPD (German Communist Party), 20, 37, 81
Krisenstab. *See* crisis staff

Landshut hijacking, 193, 224–9
  Mogadishu, 227–9, 234, 256
  rescue deliberations, 226–7
Lattmann, Dieter, 149, 152, 223, 258
Letters in Defense of the Republic, 240–1
Loewenstein, Karl, 27–30, 33, 34, 35, 48
Lorenz, Peter, 138–40, 141, 142, 166, 215, 217
Lower Elbe Environmental Protection Citizens' Initiative (BUU). *See* Brokdorf
Lübbe, Hermann, 194, 195, 254
Luxembourg, Rosa, 190, 199, 242

Mahler, Horst, 98, 104, 108, 138, 187, 240
Maihofer, Werner, 64, 139, 166–7, 208, 209, 221, 228
Mann, Golo, 194, 211, 213

Mannheim, Karl, 27–8, 31–3, 35, 48, 55, 59, 80
Marcuse, Herbert, 75, 77, 92–4, 95, 177, 237, 239, 244
  Repressive Tolerance, 92–3
media, 96, 131, 138, 174, 187–8, 198, 237, *See also* Spiegel affair; Springer press; Zimmermann, Eduard
  restrictions on, 217–19, 228
  coverage of the German Autumn, 2, 212, 220, 229–31, 233, 261
  government campaign. *See* Federal Center for Political Education
  and terrorism, 7, 10, 138, 165–6, 236–7
Meinhof, Ulrike, 3, 108, 111, 131, 141, 143, 155, 157, 185, 187, 189–90, 192, 196, 201, 203, 242
  From Protest to Resistance, 103
Meins, Holger, 134, 135, 157, 196, 222
Menzel, Walter, 41, 44
Mescalero affair, 197–202
  Buback Obituary, 193, 195, 197–9, 202, 205, 207, 246
militant democracy, 6, 7, 8, 14, 15, 16, 27–33, 38–52, 57–8, 60, 64, 72, 79, 88, 111, 114, 124, 129, 133, 192, 195, 257, 259, *See also* internal security
  critique of, 52–5, 56–7
  FRG as, 35–6
modernization, 10, 70, 115–16, 119, 134, 260, *See also* Federal Criminal Office (BKA); internal security; police, West German
Mogadishu. *See under Landshut* hijacking
Mohler, Armin, 253, 254
Moßmann, Walter, 180–2, 207
Munich Olympics (1972), 122, 134

Narr, Wolf-Dieter, 202–3
National Socialism, 5, 6, 13, 19, 20, 21–2, 27, 33, 34, 38, 39, 42, 47, 69–70, 73, 76, 79, 82, 83, 84, 90, 98, 101, 102, 126, 155, 165, 172, 243, 253, 256, 259, *See also* antifascism; Auschwitz; violence, state
  postwar continuities, 13, 38, 50, 78–9, 89, 97–8, 100, 101, 118, 153, 242, 250
negative alliance, 16, 72, 81–2, 84, 97, 101, 107, 154, 179, 181, 192–3, 237, 240, *See also* solidarity, left
  and the RAF, 153–4, 160–3, 189–91, 243, 244
  self-critique, 202–7, 242, 243, 246–7, 250
Negt, Oskar, 161–2, 190
North Atlantic Treaty Organization (NATO), 58, 79, 80, 258

occupational ban. *See* Decree against Radicals under antiterrorism legislation
Ohnesorg, Benno, 97, 109, 113, 135, 197, 240, 250
OPEC attack, Vienna, 166, 217, 222

pacifism, 58, 80, 92–3, 107, 154, 175, 177, 180, 189, *See also* resistance, nonviolent
Papen, Franz von, 21, 22–3
parliamentarism, 12, 18–19, 24–5, 26–7, 34, 39, 44, 45, 46, 50, 54, 55, 128–9, 136, 234, *See also* Mannheim, Karl; SPD on states of exception; Weimar Republic
Parliamentary Council, 37–8, 47–8, 52, 53, 54, 55, 64, *See also* Basic Law, drafting of
Pflasterstrand, 203, 204–5, 206
Plogstedt, Sibylle, 185, 186, 248
police, West German, 178, 219, 234, *See also* Federal Criminal Office (BKA); Federal Border Guard (BGS); GSG-9
  federal, 42–3, 252–3
  modernization of, 116–20, 121, 219–20
  and protesters, 94–5, 103, 122, 173, 190
political education, 31, 32–3, 42, 51, 74–7, 125, 195, *See also* Federal Center for Political Education (BPB); Mannheim, Karl
  active democrats, 49–50, 66, 74–5, 127, 132, 176
  versus propaganda, 129, 130–2
Ponto, Jürgen, 3, 187, 188, 208, 224
Popular Front for the Liberation of Palestine (PFLP), 9, 166, 224–5, *See also Landshut* hijacking
Potempa murder, 21, 207
Preuß, Hugo, 18, 20
prisoners' rights movement, 147, 158–60
  committees against torture, 156, 222
prisons, West German
  forced feedings, 135, 155, 156
  torture in, 3, 130, 155, 156, 157–60, 163

Radicals Decree. *See* Decree against Radicals under antiterrorism legislation
RAF (Red Army Faction), 1, 2–3, 8, 9, 10, 14, 101, 107–8, 111–13, 117, 121, 129, 130, 153–4, 163, 174, 181, 186–7, 189, 196, 231, 252, 257, *See also* attorneys, RAF; Buback, Siegfried; negative alliance; Ponto, Jürgen; Schleyer, Hanns-Martin; Stockholm embassy
  formation, 107–8
  in prison, 134, 155–60
  info-network, 143, 155, 156, 222

left criticisms of, 112, 161–2, 190–1, 203, 238, 239
May Offensive, 3, 113, 121, 134, 181
Stammheim deaths, 231
trial, 130, 160, 195–6
Raspe, Jan Carl, 3, 143, 157, 192, 196, 210, 215, 231, 241
rearmament, 36, 58–60, 62, 72, 79, 80, 111
Bundeswehr, 59–60, 79
Red Cells (RZ), 2, 3, 109, 204, 206, 248
Republican Club (RC), 97, 100, 105–7
resistance, 6, 7, 8, 14, 15, 16, 35, 49, 69–70, 71–2, 79, 80, 81–2, 83, 88, 91, 92, 93–4, 97, 98, 101, 105, 107, 132, 160, 174, 178, 179, 186, 192, 206, 243–4, 257, 259, *See also* APO; direct action under student movement; political education
anti-Nazi, 20, 22, 70–1, 72–4, 83, 84, 201, 203
as counterviolence, 3, 72, 82, 83, 84, 85, 86, 87–8, 93, 95, 96, 99, 100, 104, 106, 108–9, 113, 135, 153, 154, 171–2, 175, 178, 179, 180, 183, 185, 189, 203
nonviolent, 17, 89, 91, 105, 170–1, 177, 180–2, 189, 238–9, 240, 245–6, 248–51, 256–7
Röhl, Klaus Rainer, 112, 190
Roth, Karl-Heinz, 243
Russell Tribunal, International, 147–8, 239, 260

Scheel, Walter, 223
Schily, Otto, 160, 244, 259
Schleyer, Hanns-Martin, 3, 16, 208–10, 215, 217–20, 224, 227, 238, 241, 242
murder of, 231, 242, 243
Schmid, Carlo, 41, 47–8, 63–4, 214
Schmidt, Helmut, 1, 64, 83, 134, 139, 140, 173, 174, 208, 210, 211, 213, 214, 218, 225, 226, 228, 234, 253, 256, 258
as crisis manager, 134, 214, 230, 255
Schmitt, Carl, 24–6, 27, 29, 30, 46, 53
Schneider, Hans, 56
Schneider, Peter, 103
and the German Autumn, 241, 243–4
on limited rule-breaking, 95
...schon bist du ein Verfassungsfeind, 146
Schumacher, Kurt, 71
Schwarzer, Alice, 182, 185, 244
SDS (German Socialist Student League), 69, 81, 82, 83, 86, 88, 90, 100, 101, 105, 107, *See also* student movement
Seifert, Jürgen, 64, 163
Socialist Bureau, 107, 202–3, 205, 207
solidarity, left, 16, 72, 82, 83, 84, 87–8, 105, 157, 161, 162–3, 177, 178, 190–1, 199–200, 205–6, 238, 244–5
Sontheimer, Kurt, 194, 195, 208, 255
SPD (Social Democratic Party), 4, 14, 16, 20, 22–3, 36, 37, 58, 59, 63–5, 71, 83–4, 107, 110–11, 115–16, 117–18, 123, 125, 128, 133–4, 152, 154, 156, 167–8, 174, 176, 212, 230, 237, 241, 242, 252, 254, 259, *See also* Brandt, Willy; Coppick, Manfred; internal security; Lattmann, Dieter; Menzel, Walter; political education; Schmid, Carlo; Schmidt, Helmut; Vogel, Hans-Jochen
on armed force, 59–60, 65, 80, 124, 144, 224, 233, 258
on federalism, 38, 41–3, 120, 252
Godesberg Program, 79–81, 150
inability to govern, 136, 148, 151, 225, 234
internal divisions, 5, 64, 81, 114, 146–7, 148–51, 223–4, 234–5, 257–9
and SDS, 81
state, concept of, 43, 45, 79, 111, 150–1, 231
on states of emergency, 41, 43, 45–6, 47–8, 49–50, 51, 56, 65–6, 139
and terrorism, 113–14, 121, 126–7, 128, 133, 135, 143, 144–5, 194, 200, 208, 212–15, 220, 221, 222, 223, 224, 225, 231–4
Spiegel affair, 62, 88
Spontis, 107, 171, 175, 177–8, 181, 190, 203–4, 206, *See also Pflasterstrand*
Springer press, 3, 96, 103, 113, 165
Stammheim prison, 157, 210, *See also* prisons, West German; prisoners' rights movement
state of exception, 19, 25, 35, 53, 54, 56–7, 60, 61, 136, 166, 211, 253, 261, *See also* Schmitt, Carl
Sternberger, Dolf, 54–5, 194
Stockholm embassy, seizure of, 3, 140–1, 142, 166, 216, 222
Strauß, Franz-Josef, 88, 134, 141, 144, 212, 214, 255
as chancellor candidate, 253–4
student movement, 2, 4, 8, 64, 68–9, 85–8, 89–90, 93, 97, 110, 113, 152, 179, 182, 194, 242, 257, *See also* APO; negative alliance; SDS
direct action, 89–92, 94, 95–6, 98–9, 100, 180
Plakataktion, 85–6
Süsterhenn, Adolf, 39, 40

tageszeitung, 245–6, 249
Tegeler Weg, Battle of, 104–6
terrorism, 4–5, 7–8, 15, 107, 135, 152–3, 192–3, 236–7, 248, 257, 260–1, *See also* German Autumn; June 2 Movement; RAF (Red Army Faction)
  as criminal offense, 117, 126, 145
  German compared to Italian, 196–7
  international, 9–11, 188
  related to antinuclear movement, 173–5
  related to feminism, 186–9
  roots of, 125–6, 207–8, 255–6
  Club of Rome, 168
Thüsing, Klaus, 223
Traube affair, 166–7, 221
Tunix, 246

Vester, Michael, 90–2, 99
Vietnam war, 10, 69, 85–6, 87–8, 89, 94, 95, 96, 101, 147, 160, 162, 180, *See also* Frankfurt arson
violence, civil, 8, 14, 72, 85, 86, 92–3, 95–6, 103–4, 154, 174, 175, 198, 241, 242, 243, 247, 251–2, *See also* Brokdorf; Easter riots; Frankfurt arson; resistance; Tegeler Weg, Battle of; terrorism
  critique of, 98–9, 103, 154, 179–80, 181–6, 190–1, 198–9, 238, 239–40, 248
  under Weimar, 20–3, 48, 196
violence, state, 4, 8, 14, 16, 35, 39, 49, 55, 79, 82, 83, 87, 89, 91, 93, 97, 100, 106, 160, 172, 173, 178, 242, 243, 250, *See also* counterterrorism; militant democracy; prisons, West German; police, West German; Vietnam war; rearmament
Vogel, Hans-Jochen, 114, 139, 144, 151, 196, 207, 208, 209, 213, 221, 223, 234, 258
Vollmer, Antje, 250

Weber, Werner, 53–4, 61
Wegener, Ulrich, 123, 228
Wehner, Herbert, 64, 132
Weimar Republic, 5, 6, 18, 19–27, 28, 35, 38, 43, 44, 47, 50, 54, 78, 151, *See also* antiterrorism legislation; Article 48 under emergency legislation; violence, civil
  Prussian coup, 22–6
Weizsäcker, Richard von, 254
Widerstandsrecht, 13, 66–7, 98, 174, 176, 179
Wischnewski, Hans-Jürgen, 209, 217, 225, 227, 228, 229
women's movement, 16, 154, 179, 182–9
Wyhl, 169–72, 179, 180, 181

Zimmermann, Eduard, 131–2